Beyond C. L. R. James

SPORT,
CULTURE
& SOCIETY

DAVID K. WIGGINS, SERIES EDITOR

Beyond C. L. R. James

*Shifting Boundaries
of Race and Ethnicity in Sport*

EDITED BY
JOHN NAURIGHT,
ALAN G. COBLEY,
AND DAVID K. WIGGINS

The University of Arkansas Press
Fayetteville
2014

CONTENTS

Series Editor's Preface   ix

Preface   xi

I. Studying Race and Ethnicity in Sport

Introduction   3
John Nauright

1 / Beyond C. L. R. James's *Beyond a Boundary*:
From Liberation and Nationalism to Globalization
and Commodification in the West Indies   7
Sir Hilary McD. Beckles

2 / Ambiguity within the Boundary:
Rereading C. L. R. James's *Beyond a Boundary*   17
Malcolm MacLean

3 / Embodied Identities: Sport and Race in South Africa   41
Douglas Booth and John Nauright

4 / Indigenous Australians and Sport: Critical Reflections   63
Daryl Adair

5 / Beyond Black and White:
A Study of the Luis Suarez–Patrice Evra Controversy   77
Verner Møller

II. Race and Ethnicity in Historical Context

Introduction   95
David K. Wiggins

6 / On Display: Cricket and Minstrel Shows
in Australia's Colonial Far North, 1869–1911   99
Matthew Stephen

7 / Competitive Combat, Warrior Bodies, and Zulu Sport:
The Gender Relations of Stick Fighting
in South Africa, 1800–1930   125
Benedict Carton and Robert Morrell

8 / Ethnicity in Black and White: Immigration, Sport,
and the Italian Quest for Identity in the United States   145
Gerald R. Gems

9 / "The Tuskegee Flash" and "the Slender Harlem Stroker":
Black Women Athletes on the Margins   159
Jennifer H. Lansbury

III. Ethnicity, Migration, Bodies, and Sport

Introduction   181
John Nauright

10 / Tamales, Tapetes, and Basketball:
Signs of Oaxacan Ethnicity in the United States   183
Charles Fruehling Springwood

11 / Sport in Migrant Communities:
Transnational Spaces and Gender Relations   195
Gertrud Pfister

12 / Masculinities beyond Otherness:
Cricket, Gender, and Ethnicity in Oslo, Norway   211
Thomas Michael Walle

13 / Ethnicity, National Identity, and Cricket
in Contemporary Trinidad and Tobago   239
Anand Rampersad

IV. Crossing Boundaries/Maintaining Boundaries

Introduction   255
Alan G. Cobley

14 / Into the Great White Yonder: Stabilizing
and Transcending Whiteness in Alternative Sports   259
Michael Atkinson and Kevin Young

15 / A Unique Social Tapestry:
Football, Sectarianism, and Racism in Northern Ireland   279
David Hassan and Ken McHue

16 / "Who Do 'They' Cheer For?" Cricket, Diaspora,
Hybridity, and Divided Loyalties among British Asians   293
Thomas Fletcher

17 / Usain Bolt, Celebration at Ninety: A Spatial Analysis
of the Beijing 2008 Men's 100-Meter Final   313
James A. McBean Jr., Michael Friedman, and Callie Batts

Notes   331
List of Contributors   387
Index   395

SERIES EDITOR'S PREFACE

Sport is an extraordinarily important phenomenon that pervades the lives of many people and has enormous impact on society in an assortment of different ways. At its most fundamental level, sport has the power to bring people great joy and satisfy their competitive urges while at once allowing them to form bonds and a sense of community with others from diverse backgrounds and interests and various walks of life. Sport also makes clear, especially at the highest levels of competition, the lengths that people will go to achieve victory as well as how closely connected it is to business, education, politics, economics, religion, law, family, law, family, and other societal institutions. Sport is, moreover, partly about identity development and how individuals and groups, irrespective of race, gender, ethnicity or socioeconomic class, have sought to elevate their status and realize material success and social mobility.

Sport, Culture, and Society seeks to promote a greater understanding of the aforementioned issues and many others. Recognizing sport's powerful influence and ability to change people's lives in significant and important ways, the series focuses on topics ranging from urbanization and community development to biography and intercollegiate athletics. It includes both monographs and anthologies that are characterized by excellent scholarship, accessible to a wide audience, and interesting and thoughtful in design and interpretations. Singular features of the series are authors and editors representing a variety of disciplinary areas and who adopt different methodological approaches. The series also includes works by individuals at various stages of their careers, both sport studies scholars of outstanding talent just beginning to make their mark on the field and more experienced scholars of sport with established reputations.

It is the latter group that is most represented in *Beyond C. L. R. James*. Edited by myself and John Nauright and Alan G. Cobley, the book includes essays written by academicians with international reputations. The essays—emanating largely from presentations given at the Third International Conference on Race and Ethnicity in Sport at the University of the West Indies, Cave Hill in Barbados—focus on the interconnection among sport, race, and ethnicity from a global perspective. The essays, which are all based on solid primary research and clear writing and analysis, are far ranging in that they cover such diverse topics as African American women's involvement in sport, cricket and minstrel shows in Australia, sport in South Africa, and basketball among the Oaxacan in the United States. Taken as a whole, the book provides information that will be of interest to scholars, both undergraduate and graduate level students from a variety of academic fields, and a more popular audience with an interest in how race and ethnicity impacts sports from around the world.

DAVID K. WIGGINS

PREFACE

In 1963 C. L. R. James published *Beyond a Boundary,* which has become one of the classic books ever written dealing with sport in general and race and sport in particular. We present this volume in memory of James and his pathbreaking work, in the hope of continuing the robust debate about the ways in which race and ethnicity are "seen" in and through sport, and the ways that race and ethnicity have been both barriers to participation and safe havens where sport can prosper.

The idea for this book began at the "Beyond Boundaries" Conference, which was the Third International Conference on Race and Ethnicity in Sport. The conference was held at the University of the West Indies, Cave Hill, in Barbados, and was cosponsored by the Academy of International Sport at George Mason University. It was fitting that a conference exploring the question of boundaries, race, and ethnicity in sport was held at Cave Hill, where the original manuscript of *Beyond a Boundary*—some of which remains unpublished—is housed. Not only is there a cricket oval in the middle of the campus; but also Sir Frank Worrell, the first black captain of the West Indies cricket team, is buried at Cave Hill. The conference occurred on the fiftieth anniversary of Worrell's appointment as captain, and it was also the fiftieth anniversary of Muhammed Ali's (then Cassius Clay) gold medal in boxing at the Rome Olympics. We touched on a wide range of themes at the conference, which featured keynote presentations by Daryl Adair, Sir Hilary McD. Beckles, Ben Carrington, and Charles Fruehling Springwood. Some of the best material presented at that conference has been revised, updated, and presented here alongside other cutting-edge work on race and ethnicity in sport. We seek to explore beyond the boundaries set by C. L. R. James while staying true to the core principles that guided his work. These include ideas about social justice, colonial and postcolonial struggles, the role of culture and sport in society, and an understanding of the ways in which political economy, driven by capital and the state, impacts the shaping of identities and the subjugation of peoples.

We would like to thank both the University of the West Indies and the principal of the Cave Hill campus, Sir Hilary McD. Beckles, and

George Mason University and Peter N. Stearns for their support of the conference. We would also like to thank the contributors to this volume whose patience with us and with one another has sustained us in ensuring that this research sees publication. Thanks to the team at the University of Arkansas Press for their support of this project as well.

We hope students, colleagues, and the wider public will learn more about how race and ethnicity have both shaped sports participation and led to barriers being constructed to limit participation. We offer this volume as a tribute to C. L. R. James and to all the men and women who have struggled for a place on the field and to shift the boundaries to allow all to participate in sport and in other social activities on equal terms.

I.

Studying Race and Ethnicity in Sport

INTRODUCTION

John Nauright

The work of Cyril Lionel Robert James, known to everyone as CLR James, is the starting point for an in-depth understanding of the role of sport in society. His majestic book, *Beyond a Boundary*, which he completed in the early 1960s, is a masterpiece of social analysis, history, and autobiography. The year 2013 marked the fiftieth anniversary of the first edition of the book, which is still revered as one of the must-read books in sports studies. The book largely discusses James's upbringing in Trinidad and his engagement with cricket, including an examination of the role of cricket in Caribbean society. James concludes with the campaign to have Frank Worrell appointed as the first black captain of the West Indies cricket team. That James, a well-known and respected Marxist thinker of the twentieth century, should be so well known in sporting circles for his writing on the elitist English-invented sport of cricket seems ironic. Yet, James succeeds in evoking a time and place where skin color mattered in terms of which club you played for and whether you had the opportunity to play for, or ultimately lead, the national cricket team.

The chapters in the first section of this book engage with James on explicit levels at first and then move beyond James to analyze the complexities of ethnicity and race in contemporary sport around the world. The first chapter is by Sir Hilary McD. Beckles, noted historian of West Indian cricket and successor to many of James's insights into the game that the islanders made their own in the mid- to late twentieth century. As Beckles has observed, James wrote in the "Age of Nationalism" as former colonies in the West Indies and in South Asia rose to challenge the former dominance of the English and Australians in cricket. Beckles's own work has gone beyond James in also engaging with the "Global Age" of cricket since about 1990. In the lead chapter, Beckles explores how James might have dealt with the recent history of cricket and the changes to the game and discusses how the sport has altered within the West Indies as the fight for legitimacy has waned. Malcolm MacLean then engages further with James in the second chapter, bringing in additional theories and concepts to move our thinking *beyond* C. L. R. James.

In chapter 3, Douglas Booth and John Nauright take what is always, at the least, implicit in James's work, the racialized sporting body, and places it at the center of their analysis. Focusing on South Africa, they explore the ways in which bodies have been racialized in and through sport during the eras of segregation and apartheid and into the post-apartheid era. Through engaging with Goffmann, Bourdieu, Foucault, and others, they add to concepts of embodied identity that James so evocatively explored in his essay on Sir Garfield Sobers as the embodiment of the history of West Indian struggle through his cricketing style and performativity.

Daryl Adair shifts our focus slightly in chapter 4 to explore the issue of aboriginality in sport through a discussion of race and the Aborigine issue in Australian sport. Unlike black West Indians but more akin to black South Africans, Aboriginal Australians have lived in the geographical space of Australia for somewhere between 40,000 and 70,000 years while European-descended Australians only began to arrive in 1788 with the majority arriving after 1850. Aborigines were treated as subhuman for much of Australia's history and have only recently begun to emerge as a respected people with historic traditions that can be incorporated into the history of Australia and Australian culture.

In the final chapter in this section, Verner Møller explores the complexities of "race" through a case study of the handling of the Louis Suarez–Patrice Evra racial vilification issue in English Premier League soccer. Møller guides us through the actual events and the official investigation to the ultimate match ban imposed on Suarez. He also demonstrates the complex issue of determining what is and is not actual racism in practice and that race is culturally determined in different ways in different societies around the world. What is viewed as racist in England is not viewed similarly in Suarez's home country of Uruguay, for example. Møller further demonstrates that the policing of language does not solve problems of actual intended racist behavior and that it creates more problems than it solves. Thus, he argues that we must determine what the actual intent of establishing certain rules and regulations are before coming to a determination of whether any player is or is not an actual racist or intending to practice racist behavior. Indeed, all of these chapters suggest that embodied athletes and spectators shape and reshape sporting cultures in ways that would both be recognizable to James but that also move beyond the limitations created by the political agendas of anticolonialism and overt racism.

As we move further into the twenty-first century, it is important to understand the changes to our treatment of race and ethnicity issues in sport that the globalized era of the postcolonial and post–Cold War world have delivered. We can no longer analyze race and racism from within national borders or in simplistic black-white or native-born versus immigrant ways. How we have come to understand and embed racial and ethnic identities remains significant to unpacking our interpretations, however, and the second section examines case studies of racism, assimilation, and gender in historical context before we return to case studies that present fruitful analyses that move our understanding of race and ethnicity in sport "beyond C. L. R. James."

Beyond C. L. R. James's *Beyond a Boundary:* From Liberation and Nationalism to Globalization and Commodification in the West Indies

Sir Hilary McD. Beckles

I have had the honor of discussing the rise of West Indies cricket to global excellence with C. L. R. James in England a few years before his passing in 1981. Nearly twenty years had passed since the publication of his seminal work *Beyond a Boundary.*[1] He was keenly aware that the journey of West Indies performance supremacy would be sustained long after his time. He encouraged me to make a literary contribution to the game, being as he said, "a historian from the West Indies, a cricketer, and specifically, a Bajan."

I did not take on this challenge for many years. Being a fanatical fan was a full-time occupation and I wished for no other. The years rolled by and my reflection deepened. It was Michael Manley, former Jamaican prime minister, while writing his *History of West Indies Cricket,* who got me started.[2] I told him of my discussion with C. L. R. It was at the University of Hull, my alma mater, where he was receiving an honorary degree, that the discussion had taken place. Manley merely mentioned that it would take a brave soul to deny C. L. R. He was right. I had been haunted by the conversation. Since then my efforts have been an attempt to support the excellence of their magisterial work of these two giants of West Indies cricket writing.[3]

Editors' Note: This chapter developed out of the opening keynote address of Sir Hilary McD. Beckles to the Beyond Boundaries Conference in Barbados in July 2010. It provides unique personal reflection and discussion of the post–James West Indian cricket team.

There has been no sustained challenge to C. L. R. James's argument in the 1960s that in the Caribbean, more so than in any other part of the cricketing world, the game has had a direct, determining, and reflective relationship to the social changes and institutional transformations associated with modernity. The project of nation-building, particularly its accompanying notions of national identity, he asserted, found precise expressions in the formation and evolution of the sociopolitical construct called "The West Indies Cricket Team."

For James it was a phenomenal political achievement that a small cluster of economically un-competitive colonies, collectively marginalized within the British Empire, could be organized as a single, internationally competitive sporting nation. That this arrangement survived the constitutional independence of each colony during the mid-twentieth century signified the existence of something surreal. The burden of social expectation placed on the shoulders of cricketers remains unique; so too has been the game's metaphoric status as the mirror within which the turbulent West Indian self could see its clearest image.

At the core of James's argument is the idea that in no other sphere of Caribbean life was the movement from dying colonialism to enlightened national independence more precisely articulated than in the cultural practice of cricket. Indeed, books written by cricketers about the game, together with scholarly texts on its social role and importance, provide more compelling insights into West Indian political and social process, and economic arrangements, than any other body of literature. The seminal anticolonial treatise by Learie Constantine, first West Indies superstar, written in 1933, C. L. R. James's 1963 manifesto statement on the nationalist movement, and Viv Richards's defiant, postnationalist political critique, to mention but a few, constitute a body of literary expression that depict in striking terms the extent to which cricket has remained a central discursive arena within Caribbean modernity. [4]

But what of the representation of cricket culture in the postnationalist era in West Indian society? It has been over forty years since the "Big Four"—Guyana, Jamaica, Trinidad and Tobago, and Barbados—gained political sovereignty. [5] How has the growing political and social disillusionment with the nation-building agenda by the majority working-class communities affected their commitment and communion with cricket?

And how relevant is James's work to a comprehension of the current issues facing "Windies" cricket in the age of globalization? How would he have analyzed the changing image and performance decline of West Indies cricket within and beyond the boundary? I believe he would have engaged the postnationalist era with equal intellectual veracity and treated us to a sequel of superior quality.

By historicizing the political relationship between cricket and society in the West Indies, it is possible to discern the flexible parameters of James's analysis. From the colonial to nationalist era, and into this global time, West Indians have made their largest single political and economic investment in cricket. Both elite and grassroots communities continue to expect high returns. They expect, in addition to performance excellence, a cultural engagement that enhances the social popularity of the game as well as its iconic status within popular culture. This was the vision of the founding fathers' campaign for test status during the first quarter of the twentieth century.[6]

When test status was achieved in 1927, West Indies proceeded to prepare unwritten rules and guidelines that framed the game as a frontline activity within the anticolonial movement. By the last quarter of the century, the team, constituted as the world's first multiracial sporting outfit, had secured for itself considerable global respect as an ambassador for progressive causes with an enviable record of sustained excellence. [7]

This magnificent edifice of performance and personification in the decade after James's death came crashing down as the doors to the twenty-first century opened. The West Indian test team is now ranked as the weakest traditional team in the international arena with no recognizable relationship to any political movement.[8] It is ridiculed by old and new opponents, and its members heckled around the world as pathetic amateurs not able to attract a commercially viable gate and without a social agenda beyond the market.

For media experts and academics alike this descent from awesomeness to awfulness is considered one of the most dramatic dislocations in the modern history of sports. Brian Lara had been captain of the team for three terms between 1998 and 2006. Critics and supporters alike were quick in drawing the compelling conclusion that his leadership and legacy impacted negatively on the fortunes of West Indies cricket and laid the volcanic foundations for the invention of Christopher Gayle as his inevitable ideological successor.[9]

The transition from Lara to Gayle was far from smooth. With a few sacrifices in between, it took place against a backdrop of the decay of West Indian economies and the diminished energy of civil society movements. Lara left of his own accord, but swords were drawn. Gayle was not the first choice, but he seemed the one most in tune with the rudderless youth wearing maroon. In a short time the evidence of reconnection to the Lara language was evident, and a regional dialogue ensued in which postnationalist sociopolitical tensions are seen aggressively ventilated as a crisis of cricket culture.

No previous generation of West Indian cricket stars has had as divisive an impact on loyalty and imagination within the development discourse as Lara and Gayle. The failure of their teams to compensate for the spreading sense of despair in socioeconomic development led to an intensely critical perception of both as politically unfit for the role of captain. The public feels, furthermore, that despite its insistence that the team has an important political role "beyond the boundary," the game has been hijacked by an uncaring cohort of professionals, players without social concerns, who have stripped the legacy brand of its high cultural meaning.[10] Fans and fraternity are not prepared to renegotiate cricket's role along the rocky road the nation-building project has to travel. Like the Lara of the late 1990s, Gayle today is believed to be the titular leader of the reconceptualization process.[11]

The general fear at the level of regional political leadership is that at the end of the discussion West Indian cricket will have unhinged itself from nationalist sentiments, be alienated from the process of grassroots community enfranchisement, and be thrown headlong into foreign-controlled, globalized market forces. Lara was keenly aware of the public vexation associated with the discourse. He often spoke candidly about the challenges of integrating the West Indian team into a coherent nationalist operation, while opposing the historically social construction of the cricket hero as political ambassador.

No one, it appeared, was more hypersensitive to the contradictions of the category into which he was framed and hung than Lara himself. The box built around him was riddled with paradoxes. He was not prepared to be imprisoned. If the future was thick with thorns, the past was no bed of roses. Behind him was a stream of financial compromises and socially abandoned superheroes. The vast majority of his cricket mentors, from Sir Gary Sobers to Sir Vivian Richards, were never compensated in capital at a level commensurate with the degree of hero-worship they attracted. Disenfranchised, cash-starved stars were casually cast aside as new ones emerged. Lara was determined not to join the trail of broken and abandoned heroes. He was global, not local; this was the context of his safety from the political machinery and source of his social salvation.[12]

Similarly, Gayle's recent challenges with the West Indies Cricket Board (WICB), and general contest with public opinion, which called for cricket stars to play for country not cash, is indicative of the general youth revolt that characterizes postnational Caribbean society. Relationships between "star" and state are sour, unhealthy, and not likely to be mutually supportive. The images and allegories of dejected has-been players that shaped the social landscape from which Gayle hails, constitutes an energy source that drives the aggression of players who are determined to defeat the WICB by all means necessary.[13]

What is happening in the post-Lara era is that the anticolonial dream of building an integrated, sovereign West Indian nation as a real home for the West Indies team has become a nightmare. The social consequences of the postnationalist reality of a string of impoverished microstates that cannot after thirty years of independence legitimize their existence in serious, sound, and rational ways, and are insecure or pessimistic about the future, should not be placed around the neck of Gayle as villain. "West Indianness," as a lived and imagined social experience, now seems buried under the rubble of insular acrimony within a region. To be West Indian has been restructured away from the political idealism of an age of idealism by hegemonic bureaucrats and technocrats tinkering with financial instruments and institutions of trade. The Caribbean is not an open community space, but a free-trade area.[14]

Caribbean islands are not failed states. Given their meager resources they have done moderately well with respect to democratic governance and quality of social life. It is possible that too much is being read into the performance decline of the team, and it should not be expected that excellence could be sustained at a constant level over the long term.

Furthermore, it is fair to suggest that the performance history of the team reflects the norm with most sporting units; that results over time indicate highs and lows suggesting a specific logic and general pattern. The concept of "rise and fall" therefore provides a useful context within which to understand the loss of international leadership. It does not, however, explain the uniquely prolonged nature of the West Indian sojourn in the "south."

Lara is considered the "father" of the postnationalist approach to leadership, which is in galloping globalization and expressed in the Michael Jackson–style street culture of youth in revolt and glitter in the "thriller." If Lara was hailed the circus master, Gayle in this tale represents the logical consequence and ultimate fulfillment of "Prince" Lara's leadership style. Gayle commanded discipline from his boys, and set for them a standard of mental application consistent with the image of the "supercool" dude who feels no pain and sheds no tears for the test game his predecessors had mastered and improved upon for the glory of the sporting world.

The ability of Gayle to command the loyalty of players from across the region attests to the proliferation and regional acceptance of Jamaican-style street culture, its music, dance, macho mentality, and gender-relationship structure.[15] While there are still positive values for youth development in aspects of this popular culture, its inability to promote the learning systems necessary for international competitive standards suggests also its inadequacy as a pillar on which West Indies cricket can rise.

Related to cricketers' rejection of traditional political idealism is their overt, aggressive embrace of the global market economy of cricket. "Show me the green" became the mantra of the team. Stars consider the concept of the cricket hero as a moral and political standard bearer outdated and quite frankly, inimical to their interests. The idea of playing for one's country as an ultimate status that drives player motivation became obsolete in the mass mentality that sees the nation as an obstacle rather than a saviour.

Players drawn from poor families and communities that know no better experience but full employment, police brutality, drug trading, and endemic violence have asked the question "What has my country done for me?" In so doing, they speak to the political concept of "failed nations" that dominates social science discourse on postcolonial developing countries. For them, the benefits of nationhood did not pour into, nor trickle down, to their households, which fiscal and monetary policies have left them exposed to the ravages of unfettered market forces. Corporate elites defined as "unemployable" and middle class led political parties to consider them a social problem.

Two examples can be offered to reflect the seismic shift in political values of leadership within the West Indies team. The first relates to the postapartheid moment when Brian Lara and Carl Hooper, captain and vice captain, respectively, led a players' strike against the WICB on the eve of the West Indies first official tour to South Africa in 1998. Nelson Mandela waited eagerly to welcome the team he had hero-worshiped while in prison. For him it was a global monument to black achievement in a democratic ethos. He publicly stated his wish to greet and entertain the team. Meanwhile, players sequestered themselves in a London hotel, snubbing the "Great Liberator."[16]

Fifteen years earlier, following the political lead of the imprisoned Mandela, leaders and the stars of West Indies cricket, Clive Lloyd, Viv Richards, Michael Holding, and others, refused millions of dollars to play unofficial cricket in South Africa. The so-called Rebel Tours were boycotted by front-line players, though many from the reserves and a few retirees did participate. Holding had stated that he could not sell his African ancestral birthright for a mess of pottage, and Viv Richards referred to the million dollars offered him as "blood money."[17]

With the winning of more cash, the Lara team set off to South Africa. Mandela refused to meet with them subsequently. The team lost all eleven matches played—five test and six 1-day internationals. The 11–0 drubbing of the team, on arrival rejected by the agitated black South African community as villains, signaled the turning point in the political sensibility of the West Indies team that no longer related politically to movements of black resistance against colonialism and racial injustice.

The second example relates to the statement made in 2009 by Dwayne Bravo, former vice captain and leading team all-rounder, in the aftermath of the teams' refusal to play tests against Bangladesh in the Caribbean, that if offered contracts to play for the West Indies, and another sporting body such as the Indian Professional League, he would have to determine which was in his best financial interests before making a decision.[18]

This expression of financial individualism above and beyond national representation sent shivers down the spine of a weakened Caribbean nationalism in an age of globalization. Communities continued to hope that cricketers would play "nation-first cricket" and pursue other income streams between their national assignments. The inversion of this preference, said the WICB, strikes at the core of the concept as the principal representative of the West Indian nation.

The growing devaluation of cricket in West Indian society, expressed in the popular denigration of the test team, has been a consequence of an apparent failure to commit to excellence while the team is not winning. The public demands evidence of effort, and too often is outraged by a seemingly casual approach to defeat. It staunchly refuses to lower its standards in order to accommodate a generation of overpaid, mediocre players.

Against the background of shifts in player attitude and beliefs systems, and expression in an aggressive industrial relations practice, is the poor quality management that underpins the WICB. The institution with overall oversight and development responsibility for West Indies cricket, the WICB has not been able to dedicate sufficient resources to quality management in order to chart and guide the modernization of the game. Critically, it has been unable to avoid the pitfalls placed in its paths by the new player culture that sees it as its enemy rather than ally.

This environmental circumstance ensures that young West Indian cricketers are the most professionally and financially marginalized international cricketers. There is no significant sponsorship structure to support first-class cricketers; and there are few meaningful opportunities for retired players to make a respectable living.

Feeling financially insecure, and socially criticized, young cricketers seek to become cricket globetrotters while pressing for more cash from the WICB. Cricket officials categorized their legitimate demands as a protest movement that serves to further erode the possibility of joint corrective action. Mismanagement of the "Windies" brand has contributed to the spawning of disgruntlement within the cricketer fraternity, and the potential for performance enhancement is compromised by the disabling industrial relations environment.

How, then, would James have seen these developments? Remember how he described the relations between the anticolonial events of the 1950s and the rise of West Indian cricket as a democratizing force. He wrote in *Beyond a Boundary*: "once in a blue moon, that is, once in a lifetime, a writer is handed on a plate a gift from heaven. I was handed mine in 1958."[19] It was his defining moment as a scribe of Caribbean civilization.

The issue to which James referred was the relations between West Indies cricket and the rise of the West Indies Federation. "The intimate connections between cricket and West Indian social and political life," he added, "was established so that all except the willfully perverse could see."[20] For him, the campaign for Frank Worrell as captain was a metaphor for the rise of democracy in a dying colonialism. *Beyond a Boundary* was the manifesto of an ascendant nationalism that would launch West Indians on the world stage as equal citizens.

The issues before the West Indian world today are crying out once again for a great articulator. Systemic cricket decline and long-term socioeconomic recession are obviously linked in an umbilical fashion. The region continues to experience the externally driven and designed structural adjustment of economies, widespread youth disillusionment, weakening of functional regionalism, and growing political insularity. Citizens with reduced economic gains, and a cricket team reeling in pain, would have presented James with a second gift from heaven. *Beyond a Boundary: The Sequel* would be a new compass for West Indian society in these very turbulent times.

CHAPTER 2

Ambiguity within the Boundary: Rereading C. L. R. James's *Beyond a Boundary*

Malcolm MacLean

Games have long been recognized as a vital part of the cultural politics and legitimizing of power in the British Empire. Adoption of English (often seen as British) games was, in many settings, seen as proof of the beneficial and civilizing impact of Empire and Britishness on the "natives."[1] As the geographer John Bale and others have shown, there are also repeated attempts to read indigenous body movement and culture in imperial and sportified terms.[2] Reading against this imperial and sportified grain shows a British imperial historiography that suggests that sporting cultures look in two directions, as exemplified by the phenomenon of "colonial nationalism," in which "the patrimony of 'one's own' began in the colony as new society, and drew in a sense of identity with empire as world state."[3] Following such an approach, we may identify a sense of Britishness (rugby union, cricket, and netball are concentrated almost exclusively in Britain's former and residual empire) and also a sense of nationalism (styles of rugby play in New Zealand, Australia, and South Africa are seen as making the game distinctively different from that played in Britain—although Wales is an exception—and marked as iconically national; West Indies cricket has become indisputably a marker of West Indian difference and nationalism).

Yet in each place the games are the same: the formal, written laws or rules of each sport are identical. Despite this legal consistency, sport takes on different meanings in various imperial and colonial contexts. Increasing awareness of colonialism as a cultural practice and attention to the histories of colonialism's cultures has directed historians' attention to the cultural activities of colonizer and colonized. This attention to cultures of colonialism combines with these multiple meanings to pose serious questions about how to understand these seeming paradoxes: the sport may take on characteristics meaning that it is seen as British but not-British; specific matches may take on local significance justified by indigenous epistemological and ontological codes, for instance, to replay historical rivalry. Such a localized reinscription of the received and understood (but not necessarily written) cultural codes of a formally regulated game is distinct from adaptations of the sport form.

The seeming paradoxes of indigenous involvements in colonial cultures, the tension between imitation and difference, and the opposition of self and other in the same bodily or cultural practice may be explored fruitfully through postcolonial study as shown, for instance, in cultural analyst Grant Farred's view of soccer in South Africa's Cape Flats Township.[4] Anthropologist Michael Taussig's argument that a feature of the colonizer is an egocentric fascination with what is taken to be the colonizer's fascination with the colonial reveals an essential dynamic in the cultures of colonialism: the colonizers presume, first, that the colonized are in awe of their power, authority, and cultural forms and practices, and, second, that the colonized as a result of this awe both recognize and accept the colonizers' superiority, and therefore simply seek to adopt their ways.[5] The dialectical analysis developed by Farred in which Cape Flats's soccer players modify British football symbols to their own ends critiques the colonial culture outlined by Taussig and is not consistent with the dominant diffusionist approaches to understanding colonial sport: this is not adoption, but adaptation.[6] Neither is the tension between imitation and difference easily incorporated into the notion that the sport of the colonized is primarily about beating the colonizers at their own game because this presumes that the colonized are playing the game with all or most of the cultural associations and meanings intended by the colonizers, rather than adapting the game to "native" ends, only one of which might be demonstrating their physical superiority over the newcomers. A more fruitful view of colonial relations sees them as characterized by constant exchange between, and modification of, both the "natives" and the "newcomers." This constant and mutual modification is produced by "fleeting intercultural relations" that may be seen as the standard form of relations between native and newcomer in colonies of settlement. [7] This form of contact may lead to what photographer David Tomas sees as transcultural beings in transcultural space, where "natives" and "newcomers" adapt to and adopt each others' ways in a shared social, cultural, and physical space that is neither native nor newcomer: they are not just *meeting* each other but *changing* each other. The transformation of both indigenous and colonizer groups as a result of their continual if "fleeting intercultural relations," in which it becomes increasingly difficult to identify what is a mimetic "copy of the real," lends itself to postcolonial interpretation. [8]

Among sports historians, as elsewhere in the discipline, there have been some useful forays into postcolonial analyses—the collections of papers presented by Bale and Mike Cronin, for instance, and work by Paul Dimeo on soccer in colonial and postcolonial India. [9] Despite the theoretical richness of these approaches, there are sound methodological reasons for a reluctance to adopt them, not least that historians tend to see themselves as dealing with real people and events rather than abstracted texts and phenomena. One of these reasons may be that a major strand of these postcolonial developments has tended to take place within a broader post-structuralist theoretical tendency. This resistance may be exacerbated by the obfuscatory and obscurantist character of many analyses that draw on these perspectives, leading one critic to explore the discursive style of much post-structural writing as persuasive, distortive, paralyzing, performative, and controlling, and to relate it to Soviet-era "newspeak." [10] These wider methodological and conceptual debates have not eluded sports historians, some of whom have begun to challenge the notion of the archive as repository and the presumption that sports history and social history are necessarily linked or mutually theoretically informed. Douglas Booth has identified a number of writers who can be seen as part of sports history's literary turn, with others such as Jeff Hill and Bale pointing to the usefulness of literary approaches to texts and/as sources. [11]

The literary turn, which includes many of the dominant forms of postcolonial analysis, has given social and cultural analysis—including history—a new and extensive suite of tools and approaches that are good to think with, even if some of them are remarkably difficult to do. To unravel some of the potential of the postcolonial literary turn, this paper explores how one of these literary turn approaches might provide concepts for more subtle ways of thinking about sport in colonial settings. It draws on perhaps the central text of postcolonial sport, C. L. R. James's *Beyond a Boundary* (1963), and an influential theoretical approach in postcolonial literary analyses, Homi K. Bhabha's *Location of Culture* (1994/2004).[12]

One of the reasons why many people seem to find Bhabha difficult is that his work deals with issues and texts that are ambivalent, indeterminate, and flexible, in which analysis varies depending upon who is doing the interpretation. As an analyst of colonial cultures, he explores situations and events in which power relations are uneven and where the dominant group(s) tend to be outsiders or interlopers and have a zealous civilizing mission. In the case of British colonies, the normal shape of relations is that, even in settings where the colonized were literate and had a sophisticated state structure, colonized and colonizer would "talk past each other."[13]

History and/as Ironic Text

This question of indeterminacy and, more especially, ambivalence points to a further aspect of Bhabha's approach that might cause problems for historians. His analyses are grounded in post-structural theory, and as such presume that any text or event can be understood as ironic or at least as open to ironic interpretation. In this case, irony is understood as contradiction between a statement and its meaning, or "saying what is contrary to what is meant."[14] For historians, irony takes shape and meaning because we read across texts and sources, compare and contrast, explore and critique authorial intent, and contextualize the evidence provided through those sources in other contemporary and subsequent events and sources in order to develop an analysis informed by, but in many cases at odds with, that intended by the author(s) of the original source material. Despite the disciplinary imperative to develop meaning at odds with, and often unrecognizable to, the actors with whom we deal, for the most part historians are not comfortable with irony. The discipline is reliant on an assumption that the sources mean what they say. It offends the sensibilities of those trained within the discipline to suggest that this may not be so, if only because the sources are all that historians have to go on. The sense that through research historians can get to the past as it really was, or even as it essentially was, is unsettled by the notion that the archival texts may not be literally or obviously true.

Historians admit that the sources are open to interpretation. For the most part this interpretation is a question of how the events extracted from the sources are built into a narrative and recognizes the problem that the sources provide only a partial story. In practice, historians' emphasis on good history writing being the construction of a rigorous and *plausible* argument means that the gaps can often be filled or papered over—we can get away with not being definitive—thus obscuring both partiality and indeterminacy.

This problem that historians have with irony is itself ironic. As cultural historian Hayden White has noted, the very notion of modern history is ironic: to analyze the past, a historian must assume that the past means more that it actually says.[15] That is, historians read the past as if there is a meaning in and of the past that was not obvious to participants in the past itself, meaning that our histories may not mean much to the participants in the events we are discussing (the complexity of that sentence points to another of history's problems with irony—it is a slippery beast). White also noted that one of the tropes of historical writing is irony, and there is a temptation to put this to one side as only tangentially related to the relevance of Bhabha to colonial history. This desire is misplaced: the paradox of (the discipline) history's irony points to an issue at the center of the problem explored in this chapter. The problem is two fold: firstly, history's ironic character points to ways in which the past is not what it seems. In doing history, historians and readers look at the past and make sense of events in ways that participants in those events could not. This is part of David Lowenthal's observation that history is more than the past (because we know what comes next) and less than the past (because we can never know everything that happened).[16]

The second aspect of the problem of history-as-irony is more germane to the question of colonial and imperial histories, and to histories of colonial and imperial nationalisms. Again, as Lowenthal noted (reflecting the novelist L. P. Hartley), "the past is foreign country, they do things differently there."[17] In the case of colonial and imperial relations they do things differently because very often they operate according to different cultural rules, or according to a different sociocultural order.

For many historians of colonial and imperial relations there are, there-fore, multiple border crossings. First, there is the traversing of cultural difference to account for change within their own sociocultural tradition. Second, there is the need to build an insider's or at least a sympathetic view of other sociocultural traditions, requiring two further border crossings into another order's past as well as the transcultural spaces of native and newcomer. Third, there is the problem of an exploration of change: only some of that change is the product of the interaction of two sociocultural orders, often based in two very different worldviews. These three sets of border crossing begin to expose the very real diffi-culty of doing cultural history in colonial settings: they are quite possibly the norm in all cultural history, made more obvious by the heightened epistemological differences of colonial and postcolonial practice.

To work effectively in these settings historians have to be able to translate across time, across languages, and across often very different worldviews. This requires three different translations that are often concurrent. For instance, Clem Seecharan's analyses of the debates about the composition of the 1900 West Indies cricket team that visited England.[18] These bitter debates resulted in the withdrawal of Jamaica from participation, in large part because the cricket elite there felt slighted and underrepresented in the team as a whole. To make sense of the issue, Seecharan had to explore the relations between the various inchoate cricket bodies across the various British West Indies colonies— that is, the cultural politics of cricket and the relations among its elites. This set of questions centers mainly on social and formal institutional histories of the kind common in sports history. The second explores the various significances of cricket within the racialized cultural politics of the various colonies, the various colonial discourses of nation-building, and the racialized imaginary of the outlooks of those colonies' elites. These sets of questions, including the cross-cultural aspects, are stan-dard fare for sports historians, but there is another much more difficult layer: what did cricket offer to the West Indies' subaltern groups that other sports did not? This is in part an exploration of something that did not happen: the adoption of sports other than cricket. It is best under-stood as comparative: what did cricket offer that gave it cultural power and value in subaltern contexts that other sports did not? To answer this question the researcher would need to shift approach from those usually associated with history to think and act more like an anthropologist with skills in the exploration of both ethos and worldview. These anthropological skills are also part of the approach required to explore the dynamics of regional team selections and the impact of colonial, club, and other subaltern rivalries in the context of intercolonial rivalry. Seecharan's analysis is a compelling attempt to incorporate all those strands but, as the analysis that follows shows, interpreting the motivations of the subaltern is a challenge for historians. This example illustrates part of the problem of irony for historians: not only is the past not what it appears but, when working in cross-cultural and colonial/ imperial settings, epistemological differences between historical actors mean that even the events of the past are likely to have been very, perhaps even essentially or radically, different for different groups of participants. Sometimes the past is a particularly distant foreign country.

Despite the perception of difficulty, Bhabha's work offers us a useful set of tools to begin to think about how meanings differ for various groups in colonial relationships. The first problem to explore, however, is this sense of sport meaning different things: after all, the game is the same wherever it is played. The laws of rugby and the rules of soccer or of netball do not change simply because the players are Georgian, Chinese, or Jamaican. In this strictly formal sense, of course, the game is always the same—but to use James's phrase, we need to look beyond a boundary.

Sport and the History of Empire

The dominant themes in English language sports history in imperial and colonial settings are that sport was a tool that was useful in the expansion of empire, in the promulgation of Britishness abroad, in the civilization of the "native"—both indigenous and native-born colonial, and in the training of the future administrators of empire. These tropes are so widespread as to be nearly taken for granted in English language sports history and in many settings are accurate analyses of events, processes, and sociocultural relations and functions. They are also partial in that the predominant failure to consider the meanings attached to sports practice by the colonized means that they imply that indigenous and other subaltern colonized peoples reacted to, or understood, sport and other of the colonizers' cultural practices in the way that coloniz-ers understood and made use of these cultural artifacts. Clifford Geertz and other anthropologists have long called for an understanding of the cultures of complex societies "from the 'natives' point of view."[19]

Despite some significant developments toward this end in some area and regional histories, history-the-discipline retains major blind spots in relation to the perspectives of the colonized. History's reliance upon ahistorical ethnographic analysis of "traditional" society tends to make passive the colonized, freezes and immobilizes their cultural life and outlook, and condemns them, in the often-cited words of E. P. Thompson, to the "enormous condescension of posterity."[20] Among the most common of these condescensions is the failure to recognize the power and continuation of indigenous cultural practices in favor of some degree of a fatal impact outlook that presents the postcontact period as one of continual decline for the colonized.

One sustained attempt to explore the experiences of indigenous and other colonized peoples may be found in the South Asian Subaltern Studies School, where the principal approach was shaped by an attempt to explore Gramsci's analyses of the state and hegemony in colonial contexts, and to "revise the 'elitism' of colonialists and bourgeois-nationalists in the historiography of Indian nationalism."[21] Many his-torians and others are put off by the Subaltern Studies School because its members, if they can be called that, are seen as overly theoretical, too firmly rooted in Marxist analyses, and as practitioners of a writing style that in some cases may be generously described as dense. Their approach and analyses, however, can be extremely helpful in exploring colonial cultural relations. One significant line of interpretation emerg-ing from the Subaltern Studies approach is particularly useful: Ranajit Guha's argument that the colonial state in India can be characterized as exercising dominance without hegemony.[22] A necessarily crude and trun-cated summary of his case is that the parallels that the British colonial state sought to construct between British cultural structures and Indian worldviews were unable to bridge the gaps between British and Indian epistemologies and ontologies to the extent that colonized Indians did not accept the legitimacy of the colonial state. In short, Guha's case is that a number of fundamental aspects of Indian and British world-views were so seriously misunderstood by the British that the colonized peoples saw through their claims to legitimate government.

There are significant parallels between aspects of Guha's and Bhabha's work. Bhabha's case is that, in a number of crucial respects, colonized peoples engage with the cultures of the colonizers through positions and processes he calls ironic mimicry and sly civility. Bhabha is not the only analyst to explore these issues: a number of other cultural analysts have adopted similar approaches. Michele Wallace, for instance, describes Afro-American Modernism in art as "both the same and different, as imitative [of Euro-American Modernism] as it is original," while Henry Louis Gates Jr. argues that Afro-American literary cultures and literacy operate in a dialogue with Euro-American culture to the extent that the dominant culture's characteristics are both imitated and reversed.[23] Bhabha, Wallace, and Gates identify in each case both mimesis and alterity.

Gates points to the problems and limitations of these literary approaches for historians, allowing a useful illustration of the case that these post-structural avenues are good-to-think. In one of his more important essays, Gates draws on a 1964 debate between the novelist Ralph Ellison and the critic Irving Howe. Gates opens his point by citing Ellison's refutation of Howe's critique of, especially, *Invisible Man* (1952): "I agree with Howe that protest is an element of all art, though it does not necessarily take the form of speaking for a political or social program. It might appear in a novel as a *technical assault against the styles* which have gone before." Gates then explores this stylistic critique as critical parody, as repetition, and as inversion to label it "critical signification."[24] This use of the word *signification* indicates an orientation toward a semiotic or semiological approach that historians might find useful in trying to deploy these kinds of ideas in social and cultural analyses of practice rather than the literary texts to which they have been primarily applied.

A serious problem for historians in looking to these kinds of approaches, especially that of Gates, is the focus on parody. For the most part, historians find this a very difficult notion to deal with because, like irony, it is a complex literary trope and the sense that texts and sources are not literally correct or true makes for epistemological and evidential discomfort. Part of the issue here is grounded in a tendency to understand parody in fairly basic terms, usually as exaggerated, often humorous, imitation. However, Gates also notes a more subtle form of parody in which "an original . . . is distorted, with a minimum of . . .

change, to convey a new sense, often incongruous with the form."[25] This meaning of parody can be more useful to historians exploring sport in colonial and imperial settings. This sort of parody may often be seen in discussions of cricket—where it is held by some to be an Indian game invented by the English, or where the responses to the English "bodyline" tour of Australia in 1932–1933 shifted from a dispute within cricket circles to involve the diplomatic services and political leaders of the two countries. In the latter case it was the English who were acting in a parodic manner, in that they were held by Australian critics to have distorted the culture of cricket as an imperial cultural unifier to such an extent that they placed severe political pressure on the formal relations of empire. As Manning Clark notes, the "English governing classes had their motto: never apologize, never explain. . . . But a form of bowling which was obviously an attack by the bowler on the batsman was . . . an offence against the spirit of the game."[26] That is, the parody of cricket and distortion of the conventions was so extreme as to be no longer cricket: sometimes parody oversteps the mark.

In Bhabha's approach, this issue of parody and the related question of translation— that is, of colonizers' understandings of what the colonized were doing—is a central issue and is complicated by the colonizers' fascination with what they saw as the colonized's fascination with them. As noted earlier, at the core of his work are the problems of ambivalence and indeterminacy, with ambivalence as the more important. His case stems from one central premise: that the relation(s) of colonialism seek to incorporate two (or more) cultural groups. As Peter Childs and Patrick Williams note, "[C]olonial discourse seeks, rather than manages, to produce knowledges of two distinct and antithetical colonial subjects."[27] By implication, postcolonial social, cultural, and political relations can only begin when the dominant colonial cultural group starts to recognize its domination and to consider the transformative nature of colonial cultural relations for both native and newcomer. As with all problems of translation, the ways in which the colonizers conceptualize the colonized shape the cross-cultural meanings derived. There is a tendency for the colonizer to see the colonized as fixed and unchanging: that is, to see them as having a static culture (which explains the power of fatal impact ideologies). For the most part the perceived cultural challenges of cultural contact meant that the colonized were seen as licentious, as anarchic, and as disordered. Like all stereotypes, this outlook was not consistent—for instance, in both British and French imperial relations, the black African was both, and contradictorily, innocent and barbarous.

In the case being made here, however, the ambivalence of these stereotypes is less significant than the tendency to see the colonized as culturally static. The effect of this outlook is that these culturally static colonized are incapable of agency, although the innocence of the black means that they may acquire agency (the contradiction is never far away). This lack of agency means that when the colonizer sees the colonized "playing the colonial game" they can only ever see mimesis —imitation and an aspiration to be or be like the British, or French, or German, or Chinese, or Muscovite/of Rus, or whatever group the dominant may be. There is a relevant power relation here: the mimetic are seen as "good natives," and opposed in the colonizers' outlook to the nonmimetic "bad natives." But even the mimetic good natives remain natives: as Bhabha notes, they are "almost the same, but not quite," more important, they are "almost the same but not white," for, as he says, "to be Anglicised is *emphatically* not to be English."[28] In Bhabha's approach, the colonizers always see the mimetic "natives" in ironic terms as a "partial presence" (the term recurs throughout "Of Mimicry and Man"), as "not quite," as "not white," as "not . . . English."[29] That is, the colonizers recognize the natives' imitation as a deformed version of the original colonizers' practice, and deformed because the "natives" are not English (or French or German or Chinese or of Rus): the mimesis is similar, but not the same.

Bhabha suggests that this is not the way the "natives" see the situation and argues that they may act in a way he labels "sly civility." This sly civility is similar to Gates's critical signification as a more subtle form of parody, where "an original . . . is distorted, with a minimum of . . . change, to convey a new sense, often incongruous with the form." Sly civility is not just mimicry or imitation, it is the intentional modification or distortion of the colonizers' rules and practices in a form of parody to subvert and destabilize the power/knowledge relations of colonialism. It is alterity under the guise of mimesis. (The Bollywood cricket-centered film *Lagaan* (2001) is a very good example of sly civility.[30]) Some elements of mimicry are inevitably but not intentionally ironic because of the "almost the same but not quite" aspect: they may be seen by the colonizers as ironic. The challenging thing for historians here is that very often the subversive and disruptive components of sly civility are intentional but not seen by the colonizers, because the view that the colonized are incapable of agency means that they cannot intend cultural subversion. To uncover the intentionality of the subaltern, historians need to look at their sources anew.

The Problem of Sources

The difficulty and complexity of these ideas is the product not of theoretical density or of any post-structuralist or literary quirk but of the failure of colonialism to consider as legitimate any outlooks, worldviews, or epistemologies that are not metropolitan—that is, that are not of the colonizer. The colonized are cast in the mold of the "primitive," the "savage," the "innocent," the "barbarous," the "idle," the "licentious," and as such are held to be incapable of advanced thought. It is, as a consequence of the casting of the colonized as incapable, exceptionally difficult to find any record of their intent. It is this gap in the sources rather than any theoretical or conceptual problem *per se* that makes "using" rather than "thinking" Bhabha's approach difficult for historians.

Unlike historians, Bhabha is relatively lucky in his work (as is Gates) in that they are dealing with analyses of for the most part (written) literary texts, and that these are mainly single authored. Under these circumstances questions such as the intention of the author/actor/agent are relatively easy to discern. For social historians, sly civility is much more difficult to identify because so much of the issue being explored and investigated is banal, is humdrum, is everyday, and for the most part the historian's sources are at one remove (if not more) from those activities. This is even more so if the groups being investigated are relatively powerless and disenfranchised—working people, women, minority ethnic or sociocultural groups, or the indigenous peoples of the colonies. As the Indian literary critic Gayatri Chakravorty Spivak has noted, as soon as the subaltern speak they stop being subaltern, in part because their speaking is recognized as speech, as valid, and as authoritative. If the power/knowledge relations of colonialism grant authority to the subaltern, these people can by definition no longer be subaltern because they now have authority in the form of recognizable voices, discourses, and authorship.[31] The problem of sources is even more pronounced for sports historians because sport and its related body or movement cultures are so mundane as to be underreported/underrecorded and, for the second British Empire at least, sport was such a significant part of imperial ideology and practice that sly civility would be unlikely to be recognized and thoroughly inconceivable in the colonizers' mindset. This is where James becomes important. *Beyond a Boundary* constructs and represents an insider's history and politics of West Indies/Trinidadian cricket (although noting Spivak's analysis, it is not a "pure" subaltern account), and is told with vision through a sufficiently ethnographic eye to allow investigation of sly civility, if it exists at all.

James's *Beyond a Boundary*

Effective consideration of James requires attention to the circumstances in the West Indies. Unlike many other British colonies of settlement, colonial and ethnic cultural politics in the West Indies are characterized by a near absence of indigeneity. In the case of most of the island colonies in the British West Indies (and for the most part the Dutch, French, and Spanish colonies), the subaltern place often occupied by indigenous peoples is filled by forcibly displaced peoples of color: slaves, ex-slaves, and their descendants. This relatively unusual set of circumstances where the subaltern were not indigenous mean that the various emerging nationalisms in the British West Indies had to invent a sense or discourse of West Indian-ness. The particular and specific cultural problem was that there was no indigenous culture of sufficient profile that could be invoked to signify national distinctiveness: this problem applied to both colonial nationalism and national independence. Unlike nineteenth-century colonies, such as Australia, where indigenous peoples suffered massive population decrease, the myth of the extermination of the Arawak, Taino, Carib, and other peoples indigenous to the Caribbean islands had been accompanied by their near deletion from the collective cultural memory.

The absence of indigenous markers of distinctiveness and the coercive colonial relations centered on slave economies, residual languages of chattel slavery, and colonists' continuing sense of black social, cultural, and intellectual inferiority therefore presented a cultural and political problem for nationalism in the British West Indies. Given the ethnic composition there, the two most likely options for source material to mark cultural nationalism in the early twentieth century were the emerging transnational discourses of Pan-Africanism and of Britishness: both tropes were present and their deployment commonplace. That neither of the sources of British West Indies cultural nationalism is unproblematically *of* the British West Indies suggests that their relationship to West Indian nationalisms is likely to be ambivalent, indeterminate, and flexible. That the focus of both sources is elsewhere and their richness derived from other lived experiences suggests that the approaches deployed by Bhabha are worth considering.

The suggestion of irony is particularly relevant to any reading of James's work, and especially *Beyond a Boundary*. Classical literary criticism recognizes two forms of irony (the onset of the Romantic era made things much more complicated). In the first, ironic speech, what is said may not be what it appears to be: this is closely associated with the Roman orator Quintillus. In the second, the ironic personality, the aberrant or complex meanings of what is said are based in the person who says them: this is often associated with Socrates as presented in the Platonic dialogues.[32] James, the black, colonial, Marxist, classicist, and classically educated self-defined Briton (a polymath pilgrim "emblematic of modern existence itself") may be productively read through the Socratic lens as an ironic personality.[33] James's biographer Paul Buhle recognizes this (although not explicitly—irony does not sit comfortably with Buhle's fairly conventional Marxism) when he notes that James learned about himself as an artist through the great products of Western civilization, the Bible, Shakespeare, and the classic nineteenth-century novel. But he also intuitively grasped, from his Caribbean surroundings, the incapacity of the accompanying "master race" narcissism to encompass the many sidedness of humanity.[34]

That is, James's aesthetic outlook and aspect was rooted in a cultural tradition that revealed to James the weaknesses and inadequacies of those who claimed superiority in part by virtue of being the holders, possessors, inheritors, and apogee of that cultural tradition. It was on the basis of this recognized inadequacy that James, as a subaltern denigrated by "'master race' narcissism," was able to challenge the presumed superiority of colonial Britishness and to deploy cricket as a tool in his struggle against that presumed superiority. An essential aspect of this ironic James that Buhle correctly identifies was the powerfully British James, who says of himself on going to England in 1932: "The British intellectual was going to Britain."[35] More emphatically, he notes:

> I had been brought up in the public school code. . . . The striking thing was that inside the classroom the code had little success. Sneaking was taboo, but we lied and cheated without any sense of shame. . . . But as soon as we stepped on to the cricket or football field, more particularly the cricket field, all was changed. . . . [W]e learned to obey the umpire's decision without question, however irrational it was. We learned to play with the team, which meant subordinating your personal inclinations, and even interests, to the good of the whole. We kept a stiff upper lip in that we did not complain about ill-fortune. We did not denounce failures, but "Well tried" or "Hard luck" came easily to our lips. We were generous to opponents and congratulated them on victories, even when we knew they did not deserve it.[36]

It is this powerfully British James with his strict adherence to the public school code that makes the ironic James depicted by Buhle possible, but this remains for the most part a Socratic ironic personality rather than Bhabhaesque ironic mimicry. It is also the powerfully British James who, at twenty-two, "continued to view with apostolic disfavour any departure from the most vigorous ethics of the game."[37]

The intention here is not to present again an interpretation of how James's political campaigns did or did not deploy cricket as an anticolonial weapon, or to explore the explicit use of the master's tools against the master, but rather to explore whether we can use Bhabha's notions of sly civility and ironic mimicry to uncover anticolonial, ironic, or subversive moments in *Beyond a Boundary*. The principal point is to explore the usefulness of Bhabha's approach in granting increased theoretical rigor to analyses of texts such as James's and in doing so unpacking more subtle interpretations. The case is made by drawing on three players James discusses in varying degrees of detail, only one of whom (Telemarque) James presents in a way that could be seen as slyly civil, while two (Piggott and Bondman) he presents in a manner suggesting, but not achieving, ironic mimicry.

The approach foregrounds the playing of West Indies cricket as depicted by James rather than exploring the role of cricket in making James the man;[38] the ways that cricket may reveal elements of James's epistemology;[39] the ways that cricket may be used in reading James to make sense of and explain elements of West Indies national cultures;[40] cricket as a textual instance of James's literary, aesthetic, or activist politics;[41] or James's deployment of cricket as a macro-level indicator of colonial and postcolonial practice and culture.[42] Mark Kingwell's discussion of what he labels postcolonial civility is close to the analysis here, although his focus is on a broader point than James's textual use of the sport.[43] The first and most overwhelming thing to note about *Beyond a Boundary* is its explicit contextualization of cricket. The very brief preface (105 words only) poses, for the first of several times, the question: "What do they know of cricket who only cricket know?" as a pastiche of Kipling.[44] The powerful assertion of cricket's social and cultural context may be seen in the argument that the three great names of late 1950s and early 1960s West Indies cricket, Weekes, Walcott, and Worrell—the three Ws—played the way they did because of the zeitgeist.[45] James is not arguing that the spirit of the age made them exceptional players or produced superior playing skills but that it produced their style of play. Productive evidence to explore mimesis and sly civility emerges from consideration of three much less well-known players: in two of those cases, players whom James refers to by surname only.

The first case, though, is often cited in discussions of *Beyond a Boundary*. In the first chapter, James considers childhood experiences and influences and writes:

> [W]atching from [my bedroom] window shaped one of my strongest early impressions of personality in society. His name was Matthew Bondman and he lived next door to us. He was a young man already when I first remember him, medium height and size, and an awful character. He was generally dirty. He would not work. His eyes were fierce, his language was violent and his voice was loud. His lips curled back naturally and he intensified it by an almost perpetual snarl. My grandmother and my aunts detested him. . . . But that is not why I remember Matthew. For ne'er-do-well, in fact vicious, character, as he was, Matthew had one saving grace—Matthew could bat. More than that, Matthew, so crude and vulgar in every aspect of his life, with a bat in hand was all grace and style. When he practised on an afternoon with the local club

people stayed to watch and walked away when he was finished. He had one particular stroke that he played by going down low on one knee. It may have been a slash through the covers or a sweep to leg. But, whatever it was, whenever Matthew sank down and made it, a long, low "Ah!" came from many a spectator, and my own little soul thrilled with recognition and delight. Matthew's career did not last long. He would not practise regularly, he would not pay his subscription to the club. They persevered with him, helping out with flannels and white shoes for matches. I remember Razac, the Indian, watching him practise one day and shaking his head with deep regret: how could a man who could bat like that so waste his talent. . . . The contrast between Matthew's pitiable existence as an individual and the attitude people had towards him filled my growing mind and has occupied me to this day. . . . My aunts were uncompromising in their judgements of him and yet my grandmother's oft-repeated verdict: "Good for nothing except to play cricket," did not seem right. How could an ability to play cricket atone in any sense of Matthew's abominable way of life?[46]

Matthew Bondman is regularly invoked by those who use James to explore West Indies cricket and who often emphasize the sentence immediately following the last cited about cricket as atonement.[47] James writes: "Particularly as my grandmother and aunts were not in any way supporters or followers of the game."[48] In this approach cricket's role as valued cultural practice is stressed.

Matthew can be seen in a different way—not as a sign of cricket's credibility among the Puritan and literate respectable black lower middle class such as the James family women but as a marker of a newly inclusive West Indies-ness (or perhaps in this case Trinidad-ness). It is difficult, when looking at Matthew, not to think "lumpen-proletariat": disreputable lower than the lowest working class. James evokes this image by calling Matthew a "ne'er-do-well." Even Matthew's name "Bondman" suggests low origins in indenture to, if not ownership by, someone else. In James's depiction the entire Bondman family except the father is licentious, is anarchic, and is disordered. They fulfill the stereotypical colonialist image of blacks, and it would be reasonable to expect that they and families like them would be cited in justification of continuing colonial rule. Yet at the same time we see in Matthew mimicry of one of the markers of English cultural superiority, what James calls *"genus*

Britannicus: a fine batsman."[49] In fact, so fine a batsman that spectators stay specifically to watch him practice: not to play, but to practice! So fine a batsman that when he plays his down-on-one-knee stroke spectators breathe a long, low, perhaps even awestruck, "Ah!" Yet no English person watching could see anything other than irony in this mimesis: certainly the Anglicized James women saw that the appearance and the substance of Matthew were contradictory. In this Bhabha-inspired interpretation it is not the unifying cultural status of cricket that is accentuated, but the willingness of observers to set aside the recognizably ironic character of Matthew's cricket to allow the enactment of a mimetic but insubstantial performance of Englishness (or Britishness) by someone so not English that even his name marks him as outside "society." This irony and mimesis is, however, not the ironic mimicry of Bhabha. Matthew's mimesis is of the colonial performing the colonizer's body culture and in the eyes of the Anglicized colonial subaltern—James does not indicate that the colonizers watched Matthew—observing a seeming shift from the "bad native" to the "good native," even if only while temporarily, and only because of being, at the crease.

Whereas it seems that Matthew was tolerated, was made "good," because of or by his cricket abilities, and that his case was relatively straightforward, the other two cases are less so. The first reveals parody and probable violation of the code; the second, dignity. In both cases, the men involved played for Stingo—the club of the black plebeian cricketer. In the early years of the twentieth century, Trinidad's principal cricket clubs were marked and in a hierarchy determined by race, by class, and by skin color. James's discussion of the Stingo wicketkeeper Piggott centers on his skill and his exclusion from the 1923 West Indies team to tour England. James argues that the principal reason for his exclusion was that if had Piggott been chosen all five Trinidadian members of the West Indies team would have been black (rather than the lighter-skinned browns or whites), and that the powers-that-be could not tolerate the exclusion of white players or countenance a team that did not include at least one member of the Queen's Park Club (QPC)— the club of the colonial elite. As a result, the QPC wicketkeeper was selected instead.

In building his case, James paints a rich and complex picture of Piggott. He was an aggressive wicketkeeper who would stand in close even to very fast bowlers. No doubt, as James notes, many batsmen would feel themselves hemmed in and under attack from both front and rear. Furthermore, Piggott was prepared to use his legs in some cases to deflect the ball on to the wickets and get batsmen out. Such a move is legal but to attempt purposely to do so is not in keeping with the spirit of the game. What is more, Piggott was reputed to be able to flick a bail and therefore get the batter out if a fast ball went close to but missed the wicket. This is not allowed: it is "cheating," but nearly impossible to detect. James's depiction of Piggott's play is therefore of a player who violates both the rules and the spirit of the game. James also notes that "Piggott was one of the few comic characters" in West Indies cricket.[50] He was expressive, he muttered to himself, he gesticulated: all characteristics beyond the conventions of the code of cricket conduct. It tells us much about James and about cricket's code that he describes Piggott as "a man of some idiosyncrasy."[51] It is the evidence cited for idiosyncrasy that is relevant here: he "never or rarely wore a white shirt, but played usually in a shirt with colored stripes without any collar attached. He did it purposely, for all his colleagues wore white shirts."[52] In refusing to wear whites, Piggot may be seen as purposely marking himself as outside the moral universe of—and violating the Victorian codes of—cricket.

Piggott may be read as a parody of the quintessential English cricketer. He is not involved in an exaggerated imitation of the code, but in Gates's sense as "distort[ion], with a minimum of . . . change . . . often incongruous with the form."[53] Piggott refused the dress code, he was expressive to the extent of being comic, he was aggressive, and credited—this is James's word, and it is telling in its sense of admiration—with the ability to cheat by flicking a bail. Yet despite these parodic characteristics, he "was one of the world's great wicketkeepers between the wars."[54] In itself, each trait may be parodic, but when they come together in Piggott—the plebeian, black, aggressive wicketkeeper—they intensify each other so that this becomes parody as Gates-like "critical signification" verging on violation.

There is a sense of irony in James's depiction that lies not just in the parody, however, but in James's view of Piggott as one of "the world's great wicketkeepers" and that he played for the dark-skinned black plebeian club of Stingo. As a potentially world-class cricketer he should be able to manifest convincingly the attributes of Englishness, but his parody shows that he does not to the extent that he both violates and denies the efficacy of cricket's code.

Whereas Matthew Bondman and Piggott may be seen to embody and perform elements of irony in the manner of Quintillus, they cannot be said to be cases of Bhabha's lens of ironic mimicry, although Piggot comes close. Bhabha's approach and distinction helps explain the final instance—Telemarque—whose case demonstrates sly civility, possibly his own and certainly James's.[55] Telemarque also played for Stingo. As James notes:

> Telemarque was not a plebeian. He was a genuine proletarian, a shipwright or a waterfront worker of some kind. He made good money, and was a member of a very independent workers' organization, one of the few on the island at the time. In 1919 the waterfront workers had upset the island for days with a strike which they tried hard to turn into a general strike, and Telemarque may well have been one of them. That he was a different type of man from Piggott was apparent in every line of his body and every tone of his voice.[56]

James did not know Telemarque well and conjectures as to his involvement in the 1919 waterfront strike. What is not in doubt, however, is Telemarque's left-of-center politics. Not all of a leftist political stance is inconsistent with the public school code, which as James notes meant "to play with the team, which meant subordinating your personal inclinations, and even intentions, to the good of the whole."[57] Throughout *Beyond a Boundary* James stresses how this part of the code related to party discipline in his Marxist politics. But there is a part of the code that James describes as "obey[ing] the umpire's decision, however irrational it was": there is little in leftist politics, notwithstanding the irrationality of some Leninism, in both its Trotskyist and Stalinist forms, that is consistent with this requirement.[58] James reports an event concerning Telemarque that, in the context of his left-wing views, lends itself to an interpretation of sly civility. One year his form was so good that it seemed to most observers that he could not be left out of the Trinidad team—James describes him as "not a great player, but . . . good."[59] Despite his good form he was not selected for the island team. Not only were cricket supporters upset and angry about this decision, but

James reports public anger and tears in Telemarque's neighborhood. He had strong support from waterfront workers who had organized to travel to watch him play and to "fraternise and rejoice with their fellow stevedores in Barbados at this great honour which one of their number had conferred upon the whole."[60] In the racial-, epidermal-, and class-stratified world of Trinidad a dark-skinned proletarian representative cricketer who did not act with absolute humility or in an excessively parodic manner (*a la* Piggott) was a not-so-subtle challenge to the ideological underpinning of the social order. This challenge is, for this analysis, less significant than Telemarque's response to his exclusion. James reports that:

> When I saw him some days later I said to him, "Those _____ left you out." He gave one of his rare smiles, fleeting, and for that reason, in his reserved face, of a singular charm. He had a very deep voice. "These things—you know—well . . ." he said, and threw it into space with a brief upward motion of his hand. He was about thirty-five and his last chance had gone. The moral pretensions of our rulers looked very small beside the unruffled calm of this dignified man. His lip was not stiff. It was merely firm, as it always was.[61]

Sly civility is much harder to detect or interpret than ironic mimicry because so much rests on intentionality, and we cannot know Telemarque's intentions. Furthermore, given that there is no indication of the colonizer's gaze in this exchange, the degree of Telemarque's "slyness" may be questioned. That said, James's poetic final comment —"His lip was not stiff. It was merely firm"—lends itself to an interpretation of Telemarque as slyly civil in his compliance with the code. It is as if he were saying, "I'll accept your poor judgment in cricket," but through his leftist politics working to change the social order that made necessary that compliance. More importantly, and with less conjecture, his "firm upper lip" destabilizes the power/knowledge relations of colonialism that expect disorder, licentiousness, and anarchy from its subaltern peoples.

Although Telemarque's "slyness" may be questioned in this exchange —there is no indication of a colonizer present who needs to be deceived, and the tension between his apparent acceptance of the selector's decision and his leftist politics is conjecture—there is an aspect of the extract that suggests James's "slyness." That Telemarque's lip is described as "firm," not "stiff," puts James's depiction in the "almost the same, but not quite" category.[62] In being not British, not stiff, James ascribes to Telemarque his own dignity, in contrast to a "stiff upper lip" as one of British cricket's quintessential characteristics.[63]

James's ambivalent acceptance of the "stiff upper lip" is illustrated by his introduction to the section of *Beyond a Boundary* about being "brought up" in the public school code. In these few paragraphs there is James's respect for, but distancing from, a 1956 speech by Aneurin Bevan, a leading figure in the (British) Labour Party, "ripping holes" in class terms "in concepts such as 'not playing with the team' . . . 'keeping a stiff upper lip,' . . . 'playing with a straight bat' and the rest of them."[64] James's segue to the public school code begins with the statement: "I too had had my fun with [these concepts] on the public platform often enough, but . . . I was engaged in a more respectful re-examination."[65] James's depiction of Telemarque's lip as "firm" in this context may be seen in two ways: through James's own sly civility in presenting West Indies cricket to a British audience, and also through his ongoing political project to recognize and assert the agency of the colonized.

A key trope through James's work is the question of the agency of the colonized amid assertions of colonial power. *Beyond a Boundary* is subversive because it challenges the limitations of colonialist vision by granting blacks the power to act. James asks what do they know of cricket who only cricket know? Sports historians have responded to the challenge and looked to social contexts, but in the case of James we need to look to the rest of his body of work. *Black Jacobins* (1938) deals with a successful black republican revolution in the 1790s against the French Empire in Santo Domingo eventually creating Haiti; *The Case for West Indian Self Government* (1933) makes a similar case about black agency in the twentieth-century British West Indies; and the explicitly Marxist *A History of Negro Revolt* (1938) explores the widespread incidence of black anticolonial resistance.[66] There is a strong theme running through his work that challenges colonialist views of blacks as licentious, as anarchic, as disordered, and as incapable of governing themselves or even of having any independent thought or taking any independent action. In psychoanalytic terms, James's work grants to blacks subjectivity where the colonial gaze sees them only as objects.

Analysts who only look at explicit and direct challenges miss much of the artistry of the challenges to colonialism.[67] Bhabha's notions of ironic mimicry and sly civility do not provide all the answers, and the nature of historical and historians' evidence means that these tropes are nearly impossible to isolate with any certainty. As the cases of Matthew Bondman, Piggott, and Telemarque show, ironic mimicry and sly civility can be good to think, but even with careful and subtle reading of texts and sources they remain extremely difficult to identify. They can enrich our understanding of sport in colonial settings where the colonizers use it to assert their cultural superiority, and the colonized use it as part of a suite of political strategies to undermine that superiority and to seek to ensure that whatever dominance exists does so without hegemony. This is not to say that Bhabha's analytical tools are required to grapple with colonial histories, but that in deploying them we can more effectively see sport as a tool of colonialist efforts to secure both hegemony and dominance, and as a tool in the efforts of the colonized to resist, to subvert, and to deny colonialist hegemony. As such we can see more clearly the Janus face of sport and other cultural practices in colonial and imperial settings, where one face looks to metropolitan-centered inclusiveness, and the other looks to colonial distinctiveness based in subalterneity (indigenous or otherwise). Such an analysis also reminds us that sport is not unique or even distinctive in this sense—it is similar to many other forms of colonialist culture, even if the class connotations are more obvious.

CHAPTER 3

Embodied Identities:
Sport and Race in South Africa

Douglas Booth and John Nauright

*The truth of the self is manifested in the authenticity of the
body. More precisely still, it is the surface of the body which
is the mirror of the self.*

—BRYAN TURNER

In this chapter we move beyond political and historiographical perspectives of race and sport to focus on racialized and sporting bodies.
Though this case focuses on South Africa where racialized bodies have
been central elements in defining difference, there are many international parallels and a multitude of case-study examples that could be
added to our analysis.

Social historians and sociologists have collectively written thousands of volumes about sport over the last three decades. While much
of their work has been critical, exploring social relations of power,
inequality, and oppression, they have said little by comparison about
bodies. This omission contains a double paradox. First, by definition
sport is a corporeal practice, and second, power, inequality, and oppression are embodied.[1] In the case of the latter, consider the following
encounter at the height of apartheid between a black middle-class
woman and a crowd of intoxicated white rugby enthusiasts outside Ellis
Park (Johannesburg)—a citadel of white South African masculinity:

Editors' Note: An earlier version of this paper was published in the now defunct
Contours: Journal of African and Diaspora Cultures 1 (2003): 16–36.

... crowds of white men were queuing to gain standing room. Under the influence of liquor, they started pelting black passersby with *naartjies* [mandarin oranges]. To the great merriment of the crowds, most blacks dropped whatever they had with them and quickly retreated in the opposite direction—all of them that is, except a solitary black woman. She was fashionably attired with make-up, high-heeled shoes and a wig. She summed up the situation, gripped her handbag and strutted past the men. Incensed by such defiance, the men grabbed baskets full of *naartjies* and bombarded her. One *naartjie* dislodged her wig to reveal a cleanly shaven head. The men fell about in paroxysms of laughter. But without any outward show of emotion, the woman picked up the wig, dusted it, reached for her handbag to find a vanity mirror, and calmly and coolly replaced and adjusted the wig. Proudly and apparently unperturbed, she went on her way.[2]

This incident not only graphically illustrates the embodiment of class, race, and gender antagonisms in a sporting environment, it raises obvious questions about how societies shape, constrain, and even invent bodies and how societies reproduce appropriate or acceptable bodies, and, indeed, how historians historicize bodies.[3]

These questions move us well beyond traditional approaches to sport in South Africa. In their seminal study published in the early 1980s, Robert Archer and Antoine Bouillon concluded that apartheid sport was "the object of civic struggle in the name of social justice, involving not just players, but the whole population" and "the full weight of state institutions."[4] Subsequent research largely followed Archer and Bouillon, emphasizing the structural, or institutional, politics of racist sport in South Africa.[5] Bryan Turner, however, locates the body at the heart of political struggle.[6]

What is a body? Bodies are obvious and ready features of everyday life: bodies speak, listen, gesture, eat, work, and play. Bodies are affective and emotional. And bodies are vehicles of communication: people groom, dress, embellish, and adorn their bodies in a myriad of different ways to signal, or hide, their feelings and identities. Yet, despite their conspicuous presence, bodies remain notoriously "difficult to define, identify and isolate."[7] In large part this is because appearances and performances are conveyed by body idiom, or conventional forms of nonverbal language, such as the firm shake of the (right) hand, regular eye contact and square shoulders of the focused business encounter. Underpinned by tacit forms of knowledge, body idiom tends to reify the body as a natural phenomenon and a natural source of identity and inequalities. But closer analysis of the way in which individuals and groups manage their bodies, either as sets of social practices or system of signs, or the ways in which states coerce bodies and insert them into relations of power, leaves little doubt about the powerful social and cultural forces that construct the body.

Race is a classic example. On the one hand, a race is a biological group. Different physical characteristics—skin color and texture; body shape and size; nasal, eye, and hair forms—mark the human gene pool and we can group these characteristics. But grouping biological categories is a purely descriptive and essentially futile exercise. On the other hand, racial groups are also socially constructed in ways that bear precious little relationship to physical features. The apartheid state assigned social characteristics—custom, morality, and intelligence—to racial groups. Thus, dark skin pigment supposedly explained religious, economic, scientific, and moral defects: Africans were phlegmatic, indulgent, lazy, devious, concupiscent, unable to govern themselves, immature, and uncivilized. Light-skinned people by contrast, were creative, civilized and, above all, superior.

Notwithstanding sports traditional association with merit and the sports field as free from arbitrary social division, the apartheid state, and indeed its predecessor, applied racial formulas to the sporting realm and segregated blacks. Later, in propaganda, the apartheid state justified discrimination on the grounds that modern sport was alien to black culture. For example, in 1974, the *Official Year Book of South Africa* noted that

> from time in memorial the Whites, the Coloureds, the Indian community and the various Bantu peoples have administered and practised their sports separately at all levels of competition. Moreover, it is only comparatively recently that the Bantu peoples have shown a marked interest in what may be called modern sporting activities. For centuries they have found their recreation in tribal activities, such as hunting, tribal dances—even faction fights.[8]

As this quote implies, bodies have histories. We thus explore the history of embodied racial identities and relations in the production and reproduction of social power in South Africa with a specific focus on the black sporting body.[9]

Embodied Practices and Embodied Signs

"Domination," writes Hildi Hendrikson, is always "grounded in . . . face-to-face relations" in which the "visual language" of the body assumes an especially critical dimension.[10] The works of Erving Goffman, Pierre Bourdieu, and Michel Foucault and their discussions of embodied practices and embodied signs as means of body management provide valuable insights into this language.[11] Their contributions are especially pertinent in understanding noncoercive relationships typical of the pre- and late-apartheid eras.

Goffman conceptualizes the body as a vehicle for social interaction, where identity is the outcome of a process of negotiation between demeanor (public presentation) and deference (how others respond to that presentation), or the absence thereof. In Goffman's words:

> demeanor, . . . behavior typically conveyed through deportment, dress, and bearing, . . . serves to express to those in [their] immediate presence that [they are people] of certain desirable or undesirable qualities. . . . the "well" or "properly" demeaned individual displays such attributes as: discretion and sincerity; modesty in claims regarding self; sportsmanship; command of speech and physical movements; self-control over [their] emotions, [their] appetites, and [their] desires; poise under pressure; . . . Rightly or wrongly, others tend to use such qualities diagnostically, as evidence of what the actor is generally like at other times and as a performer of other activities.[12]

Correct demeanor was a critical aspect of body management and identity among the black middle classes and intelligentsia in the Cape Colony in the late nineteenth century. Educated on Christian mission stations in the Eastern Cape, they subscribed to cultural assimilation and the British civilizing mission that placed heavy emphasis on the correct presentation of the body. Indeed, sportsmanship, which Goffman explicitly refers to as a system of bodily presence and deportment, symbolized British ethics and morality, and defined civilized behavior. Nowhere was this truer than in the game of cricket, which, according to British tradition, could only be mastered by civilized gentlemen. Members of the African middle classes adopted cricket as a means of embodying respectability and status, or in Goffmanian terms, as a tool to demonstrate that they could manage their bodies and stage appropriate performances. "By enthusiastically playing the most gentlemanly and Victorian of games," writes Andre Odendaal, Africans showed that they could "assimilate European culture and behave like gentlemen—and by extension to show their fitness to be accepted as full citizens in Cape society."[13]

The black middle classes identified the cricket club as a form of finishing school for the body, a place to learn correct posture, dress, deportment, and speech, and how to position one's body in both space (respect the private space of social betters) and time (adopt a measured, self-assured tempo). Brian Willan argues that it was as joint-secretary of the Eccentrics Cricket Club in Kimberley that Sol Plaatje (a founder of the South African Native National Congress, later the African National Congress [ANC]) embodied middle-class qualities and values.[14] Similarly, the following comments by John Tengo Jabavu (leading figure in African political and social life, editor of the first African political newspaper, *Imvo Zabantsundu* [*Native Opinion*], and chairman of cricket and lawn tennis clubs in King William's Town), capture well the determination of the black middle classes to monitor their bodies and "internalize a finely demarcated set of rules about what constitutes appropriate behavior in various situations."[15] When an inexperienced King William's Town African cricket team defeated the champion local white side in 1885, Jabavu declared "it is enough to say that the contest shows that the Native is a rough diamond that needs to be polished to exhibit the same qualities that are to be found in the civilized being, and that he is not to be dismissed as a mere *schepsel* [creature] as it has been the habit of the pioneers to do so hereto."[16]

Building on the premise that sport requires "management of the body" and that such management is "central to the acquisition of status and distinction," Bourdieu shows how different classes and class factions use their sporting bodies to display and distinguish themselves and thus maintain status.[17] In the nineteenth century, the African middle classes trained their bodies to convey prestige and power, and to distinguish themselves from those they considered socially inferior. Jabavu endorsed legislation introduced by the Cape parliament in 1891 to ban "obscene" tribal amusements. Heathen boys submitting to the "barbarous rite" of traditional initiation dances and appearing in public places, Jabavu warned, will set a "bad example to young men endeavouring to cultivate good morals."[18]

In the twentieth century, the black urban middle classes continued to emulate "civilized" European culture as a way to distinguish themselves from the working classes and portray themselves as "civilized" and worthy of the political and material opportunities that they believed accompanied the cultural appellation "civilized." They preserved British manners and airs, and played tennis and cricket at clubs with classical English team names such as Daffodils, Morning Stars, Primroses, Winter Roses, Eccentrics, and Dukes of Wellington. Ordinary township dwellers referred to them as the "scuse-me-please" class. By contrast, working-class Africans and coloreds played soccer and rugby, respectively, to demonstrate a robust, physical, and aggressive masculinity consistent with their rougher, less-refined, more hedonistic habitus.[19] Tough masculinity was a critical aspect of colored rugby. One former player recounts stopping an opposing player from demolishing his team:

> I said to our captain, you must make a change man . . . we gonna lose. So he ask me what can we do? So I say the only thing you can do is change me from my position. . . . I was a loose forward and I went to go and play in his position. The first time he come past, the second time he's gone off the field, so there are no more tries coming from their side . . . It shows you the tactics you must use—you must use your brains.[20]

In colored rugby, "brains" translated into physical intimidation. While soccer is less a combative sport than rugby, African soccer teams called themselves Wild Savages, Wild Zebras, Canons, Lions, Vultures, and Assegais to evoke images of "viciousness, fury and savagery."[21]

The language adopted by African sportsmen was not a simple form of cultural mimicry. (Nor was it solely a means by which officials and players communicated technical information about the rules of the game or the organization of forthcoming matches). "Proper" accent, vocabulary, and syntax were as much prerequisites for social acceptance and status as bodily deportment. Not surprisingly then, aspirants to the black establishment sought office in leading sports clubs where

they could "perform" and display their language as well as their corporeal skills. Moreover, language, an essential component of Foucault's
concept of discourse (sets of principles that underscore, generate, and
establish relationships), is critical in the production, monitoring, and
controlling of bodies. According to Foucault, discourses impose society
on malleable bodies, linking the practices of day-to-day life with the
organization of power at the societal level.[22]

A new set of discourses progressively emerged in South Africa after
Union in 1910. These imposed new, demeaning, meanings on black
bodies. By casting them as "children," "natives," and "bare-footed non-
Europeans," white sports officials justified the exclusion of Africans from
gentlemanly British playing fields. The black presence in white sport was
increasingly confined to ancillary labor. Thus reports of sporting fixtures
referred to "small armies of bare-footed non-Europeans periodically sally-
ing forth, armed with brooms, to sweep away the water from the wicket
covers," or to Indian servants delivering "trays of cool drinks."[23] One
account described "Sixpence," a member of the ground staff, "methodi-
cally rolling up the mat" in the center of the oval. Reinforcing the black
laborer's "primitive" demeanor the author describes him "wheel[ing] away
the pitch [and] chant[ing] a tune of his kraal-land, a low-toned drawling
song that his proud ancestors were wont to sing as night fell over the rolling hills of Zululand." Another commentator referred to "Jim Fish," the
African laborer, "pulling up the last strip of matting."[24] Any notion of corporeal equality in this climate was out of the question. In 1926, the press
criticized G. H. Dodd for competing against Africans at the Bantu Men's
Social Centre; the former national tennis champion, however, played
down the occasion as "merely an exhibition" and without any "interracial
significance."[25] As the twentieth century advanced, these new demeaning
discourses were complemented by force as a means of organizing race
relations. In short, the black body was increasingly subjected to coercion.

Coerced Bodies

While the South African state never shied from using physical force to
discipline black populations, its efforts became more draconian. In 1933,
for example, a magistrate in the town of East London sentenced an
African youth, with no previous convictions, to six weeks imprisonment

with hard labor, solitary confinement, and "spare diet" for two days per week. The charge read, "insufficiently clothed" at the beach! In another case, police arrested 148 Africans for attending an "unauthorized" wedding festival. They were locked up overnight in a small, poorly ventilated shed, and the next day forced to march, on empty stomachs, to court—sixteen miles away.[26] Force and terror also prevailed in civil society. In one 2-week period in 1933, the *Star* carried the following headlines: "Piccanin dies as a result of thrashing," "Similar death at Pietersburg following striking with a stick," "Native tied up and lashed by farmer for being insolent," "Blacksmith strikes native with a red hot bar," "Digger shoots native girl," "Three cases of whites killing natives to come before sessions," and "Farmer makes native run 22 miles in front of his horse at a trot, thrashing him when tired."[27]

In the realm of sport and leisure, the state simply banned black people from facilities, although this process began in the late nineteenth century as the assimilation process and the civilizing project began to wane. The King William's Town Council prohibited Africans from the pavilion at the town's sports ground in 1885.[28] In 1894, selectors omitted Krom Hendricks, a colored cricketer, from the first South African squad to tour England after "pressure by those in high authority in the Cape Colony."[29] The state censor stopped theaters from showing British film of a boxing match in 1912 because the winner was black.[30] A group of coloreds requested the Wanderers Cricket Club (Johannesburg) to set aside a small number of seats for them in 1913. The club's reply was curt: "there is not sufficient accommodation to enable us to throw open part of the ground to Coloured people. We must point out that there is not even enough accommodation for White people."[31] By the Great War, cinemas had been segregated: whites found it offensive to sit beside blacks. As one newspaper correspondent wrote, "it is not pleasant seeing a white girl exhibiting her figure for the amusement, the applause, and the pleasure of Indians, Kaffirs and Half-castes."[32]

Yet, neither physical repression nor demeaning discourses totally subjugated the black body. On the contrary, the black intelligentsia debated different conceptions of the body. Left-leaning intellectuals in the ANC and the Communist Party disembodied the body, conceiving it instead as "mindful"; that is, "defined through its possession of consciousness, intentions and language."[33] They gave little credence to sporting culture or bodily dispositions. Rather, they warned that sport threatened black worker consciousness. *Abantu-Batho*, a newspaper partly sponsored by the ANC, argued that employers, notably the mining industry, used sport as a "weapon" to silence the African:

> When our intelligent young men are given sports they forget everything which is dear to them and their country. It is harmless to give him sports, it keeps him contented [the government and employers] say, while they exploit the poor native to the fullest extent.[34]

Similarly, the Communist Party's newspaper *Umsebenzi* explained the detrimental effects of a new sportsground in a black township in Potchefstroom:

> . . . like all other locations where the native people undergo unbearable conditions eviction cases are being carried out by the notorious Vicks, superintendent of the location. A sports ground has been made for the native people in order to keep them away from the Communist Party meetings, where the rotteness of the present system and its agents is being exposed. To enter the gates people are being made to pay 2d. failing which they are refused entrance . . . The management of this sport is under prominent idiots, the good boys, at the head of them a prominent minister of religion. Fellow Africans, kick out the good boys from your own ranks and elect your own managers from the members of your club! Down with the minister of religion! Mass refusal to pay dues of notorious Vicks for sports grounds! Organize and fight against eviction cases![35]

Black liberals, however, appeared to recognize that in its attempt to control sport, the state sought to regulate the black population as a whole. They argued that sporting facilities were integral to black well-being. Theo Twala, a member of the liberal Bantu Men's Social Centre, supported sporting facilities in black urban areas as part of the broader campaign by Africans to gain permanent urban residence:

> In a contented community all sorts of social services, recreation parks, swimming baths, picture theatres, etc, are required. But in the management of these Africans should have a voice. Choral and dramatic groups, literary and debating societies, sports clubs

and associations. The African needs these, he yearns for them. The present life dulls his ambition, discourages and reduces him to a state of mind where he curses his colour and birth and finds dissatisfaction in everything. The African has come to the city to stay, and he should, therefore, be thoroughly and adequately provided for in all those things that go to make life worthwhile.[36]

During apartheid, the state increasingly applied brute force and physical repression to control black bodies, and it also made black bodies increasingly invisible to white eyes. For most whites their sole contact with blacks was to bark orders at their servants; few experienced direct cultural links. Both the psychology and geography of apartheid meant that whites tucked blacks out of sight and most whites lost all "feeling for human fellowship with blacks."[37] Recalling his first meeting at the Bloemfontein Joint Council of Europeans and Natives,[38] lawyer and political activist Bram Fischer illustrates the inordinately negative effects segregation and propaganda had on interracial relationships:

> I arrived . . . with other newcomers. I found myself being introduced to leading members of the African community. I found I had to shake hands with them. This, I found, required an enormous effort of will on my part. Could I really, as a White adult, touch the hand of a black man in friendship?[39]

White municipal authorities literally caged black spectators at international sporting events; Johannesburg corralled them in a wire netting compound, while Cape Town confined them to space under the trees at Newlands. Such was the degree of black "invisibility" from sport in the 1950s and 1960s that even after the National Party began retreating from apartheid scripture, many whites still believed that modern sport was alien to black culture. Official propaganda reinforced this myth. Echoing the *South African Year Book*, Dawid de Villiers, South Africa's ambassador to Britain and a former Springbok rugby captain, said in 1980: "blacks have really known Western sports only for the past ten years."[40]

When asked about the absence of black players in South African representative teams, officials and administrators resorted to discourses of biological and psychological inferiority. Frank Braun, president of the South African National Olympic Committee, coined an original physiological explanation for the absence of qualified black swimmers in the Republic. It is, he said, because "the African is not suited to swimming: in swimming, the water closes their pores so they cannot get rid of carbon dioxide and they tire quickly."[41] Explaining the dearth of black archers, the secretary of an archery club in Durban insisted that there were none "anywhere in the world" because "they have deep rooted psychological fears of bows and arrows."[42] (Interestingly, Ali Mazrui suggests that the continent's tradition of archery makes it one sport in which "Africans could excel!"[43]) Officials also attributed the underrepresentation of blacks in sport to "deficiencies in temperament." Joe Pamensky, president of the South African Cricket Union, told Afrikaner university students in 1983 that blacks did not have either "the ability or the aptitude to become good cricketers."[44] Perceived biological differences provided convenient explanations for poor performances. When champion African sprinter Humphrey Khosi ran a slow race, a white athletics official announced that Africans have a peculiar physiology that functions efficiently only within a narrow temperature range: "Africans cannot perform well on a chilly day, because of their black skin. They are black because their skin must absorb heat so they do their best in warm weather."[45]

Although apartheid legislation did not stop blacks organizing or playing sport, lack of facilities was a major impediment. What passed (and continues to pass) as a "field," a "court," or a "course" in black areas is more often than not an unfenced, uneven, stone-strewn patch of ground—dusty in summer and muddy in winter—without toilets, changing facilities, or shelter for spectators. Black golfers tell the story of white golfer Harold Henning's coaching experience in Soweto. As he prepared to demonstrate his swing, Henning told his students that he would hit the ball to "the sand trap over there." "Which sand trap?" asked a black golfer. "That one over there, right ahead of us," Henning said. The students laughed. "That 'sand trap' is the green," a golfer informed the coach. Henning retorted, "Perhaps that's why you guys always land in the bunkers in the organized tournaments!"[46]

Mono Badela recently painted a graphic contrast of the different conditions under which white and black play rugby in South Africa:

> Talk South African rugby, and the images which spring to mind
> are fairly obvious. Sweaty white men in green jerseys. Springbok
> badges on their chests. Titanic battles on the plush green grass of
> Ellis Park, Loftus Versfeldt or Newlands. Currie Cup fever, tours
> to Australia, France and England . . . the pictures are vivid and

clear. As distinctive as the Afrikaans rugby war cry: *"Vat hom!"* (Take him!) But there is another side to South African rugby— the game played in the dusty Eastern Cape townships of New Brighton, Mdantsane, Kwazakhele en Zwidi. There, the images are of dilapidated stadiums which look more like cross country courses than playing fields. Scenes of African and Coloured working class people, scrumming down on a dusty stony surface, car headlights illuminating a cold winter's night.[47]

Poor black health, clearly a product of the apartheid system of social engineering as distinct from biology, also conspired against participation. Indeed, in the struggle for health it is not a question of what sport black children play, rather it is a wonder that they play at all. In 1983, the World Health Organization reported that between 30 and 40 percent of South African black children suffered from malnutrition, a statistic especially relevant to physical preparedness and sporting performance. Kwashiorkor, marasmus, pellagra, rickets, and scurvy are specific symptoms of malnutrition and are widespread in the African population, while in the early 1980s more than 30 percent of African preschool children and almost 60 percent of African school-age children were underweight for their age.[48]

Geographic and social isolation, combined with abominable facilities —when they existed at all—had marked affects on black styles of play. In cricket, for example, most black matches lasted less than one day—the maximum amount of free time available each week for leisure among the working classes. Such time constraints meant that stroke play and shot making took precedence over defensive batting. Arguably, this very disrupted way of playing became embodied in the black township cricketer as a form of muscular memory. Akin to the memory that never forgets how to ride a bike, it would later pose a particular problem for black cricketers at the end of apartheid. After spending their lives playing idiosyncratic township cricket, many would struggle to adapt to the manicured consistent conditions under which white South Africans learned the game.

Similarly, in the cramped colored working-class areas of Cape Town's Bo-Kaap and District Six, material conditions had a profound impact on sporting style and behavior in rugby, which some residents located at the center of life in the colored community. According to

Gassan Emeran, a former school principal, "whenever you meet people it was just rugby, there was nothing else it was just rugby, rugby, rugby. That was their life—rugby."[49] During the apartheid era, gangsters and protection rackets infiltrated colored working-class areas and developed close associations with rugby clubs. In the 1950s, the Globe Gang supported Roslyns, the strongest and oldest club in the largely Muslim Western Province Coloured Rugby Union. At this time, members of rugby clubs typically congregated on different street corners in District Six and the Bo-Kaap. There they held team meetings, announced team selections, analyzed previous performances, and planned forthcoming tactics. Roslyns met, along with the Globe Gang, in front of the Globe Furnishing Company. Sons of shopkeepers formed the Globe Gang in the 1940s to prevent thefts by skollies—young male petty criminals—who flooded the area from outside in search of easy pickings. As one gang member explains: "The Globe hated the skollie element in town, like the people who robbed crowds . . . Mikey and the boys would really bomb out the skollie element when they robbed the people . . . They tore them to ribbons."[50] Over time, a prison element penetrated the Globe Gang that built up its own protection racket and became more prone to violence.

Gang violence flowed into rugby through the actions of spectators as well as players. Roslyns' fans, who included Globe members, had a reputation for intimidating referees and opposing players. A former player recalls difficulties finding referees for matches against Roslyns: "The referees were frightened because Roslyns must win, if Roslyns doesn't win, it's a fight because they got their stones and their chains ready and their big swords ready, that means they're going to attack."[51]

Violence among colored rugby players did not escape the attention of whites who viewed it as a racial deficiency. Bob Watson, a peer of the legendary Springbok player and later rugby administrator Danie Craven, recalls the latter's racial paranoia and behavior at coaching clinics for coloreds. Craven shared a room with Watson and when the former arrived "he unpacked his bags and took this revolver out of his brief case. [He] stuck it underneath his pillow and said, 'You can't trust these people you know, you don't know what's going to happen at night.' [H]e believed it and believed it each time he came back . . . , to about three camps."[52] In the early 1990s, after the different rugby administrations, previously divided along racial lines, had united under the umbrella of the South African Rugby Football Union (SARFU), different approaches to the game kindled alarm among white players and fans. Violence, in particular, played on the minds of many whites such as Marius de Klerk, rugby supporter and chief of police in the small eastern Cape town of Patensie: "We know rugby is a hard game but I've never seen any players biting each other on the field. But unfortunately that is one of the things that happens when you play against black players, they actually bite you in the scrums."[53]

But more than on-field violence concerned whites. As the following comments by Hilda Ferreira, a lifelong supporter of the Patensie Rugby Football Club, reveal, spectator culture was also embodied. "We're not used to all this," Ferreira said, gesticulating to a stand packed with colored fans busily stomping their feet, cheering and clapping wildly: "We're not used to a lot of noise on the stand. Because in the past it was a pleasant experience to come here on a Saturday afternoon. Everything is new to us. Whether they [blacks] just want to get to us or whether it's just their way, I don't know."[54]

The geographic and social isolation of apartheid also prevented black sportsmen from displaying and converting what Bourdieu calls corporeal capital, or the symbolic value of the body as bearer of power and status.[55] But the real value of corporeal, or physical, capital rests on the ability of an owner to convert it to other forms. While in the contemporary realm of professional sport this typically means converting physical capital into economic capital via sporting careers, in the amateur era sportsmen invariably looked to convert their physical capital into social and cultural capital by, for example, playing for national, or representative, teams. Apartheid, of course, denied black sportsmen the opportunity to convert their physical prowess and skills into social and cultural capital: in South Africa, only white sportspeople could be national heroes and wear the famed Springbok emblem. Happily, however, that would prove to be only a historical phase and by the early 1980s black sportspeople were representing South Africa; a decade later they were even winning fame as national heroes.

Embodying the (Multiracial) Nation

Foucault identifies a historical shift in the disciplining of bodies away from coercion and force to self-discipline and meticulous work by individuals on their own bodies. In South Africa, the shift accompanied new discourses of race and, more specifically, direct political action. In the case of sport, blacks demanded equal access to the symbols of corporeal capital, notably national representation and Springbok honors.

Precisely as the South African state tightened its apartheid system in the late 1950s and early 1960s, Western powers began dismantling their racial policies and practices. A whole series of new discourses accompanied this international contraction of racism: white racial guilt in the aftermath of the Second World War, discrediting of "scientific" racism —in which the United Nations' Economic, Scientific and Cultural Organization played a major role—and its association with unpopular fascist ideas, and new white sensitivity in the era of decolonization. In this new environment, pressure mounted on South Africa to abandon apartheid and democratize as a multiracial nation.

Initially ignoring these calls, the governing National Party attracted the ire of the growing antiapartheid movement that urged the international community to isolate white South Africa. In sport, the movement campaigned to expel South Africa from the world's sporting arenas. The National Party, however, remained unperturbed and simply rationalized South Africa's exclusion from the Olympic games in 1964 and 1968 as part of a Moscow-orchestrated communist onslaught. Of particular interest here is the manner in which the government and its supporters defined protesters by their corporeality. Compared with the cream of South African manhood and manliness, the protesters were described as "long-haired, unwashed, drug-taking, communist agitators."[56] Charles Fortune, the doyen of South African sports broadcasting, condescendingly described one gathering as "a tattered and bleak little congregation of chilly-looking adolescents."[57] Another journalist referred to the protesters' uncouth habits of "spitting" and "cursing,"[58] while Danie Craven spoke contemptuously of British protesters' "childish and banal conduct" during the 1970 tour of England.[59]

The unanticipated cancelation of a proposed rugby tour by New Zealand in 1967 prompted the National Party to reevaluate its position. International rugby tests (especially those against New Zealand), and to a lesser degree cricket tests, were an integral part of white South Africa's historical and cultural ties to white, European "civilization." Thus in 1968, Prime Minister John Vorster amended traditional apartheid policy and approved the New Zealand Rugby Football Union's selection of Maori players on forthcoming tours. Consequently, three Maori and one Samoan toured South Africa with the New Zealand All Blacks in 1970.

Although a seemingly trivial concession, Vorster's move raised the hackles of right-wing Afrikaners who correctly recognized that the new policy weakened traditional ideas about race and racial difference. Albert Hertzog, the influential National Party MP, spoke strongly against tours by racially mixed teams from abroad. The inclusion of Maori, he warned, would lead to social integration: "they will sit at the table with our young men and girls, and dance with our girls."[60]

Vorster's concessions did not stem growing international isolation, and the apartheid regime continued to modify its sports policy. In 1971, in keeping with its new policy of multinationalism (a grand political scheme that divided South Africa into ten black "nations," each with its own territory), the government permitted blacks to compete against white South Africans in so-called *open* international events. Four years later it allowed sports to select multiracial *invitation* teams, although the minister for sport, Piet Koornhof, stressed that invitation sides would not represent the Republic. The French national rugby team toured South Africa that year and played an Invitation XV that included two Africans and two coloreds.[61] Also in 1975, the Comrades Marathon, an 88-kilometer race between Durban and Pietermaritzburg, accepted black entrants for the first time, although the Department of Sport, in the words of Durban's *Daily News*, "sprinkled its magic formula on the event" and restricted the number of black entrants to six from each "nation"—an infinitesimally small quota in a field of fifteen hundred! Organizers decided to use tribal armbands to embody the national identity of African runners, but their plan fell into disarray when they ran out of the correct tags and Zulus had to wear Xhosa identification.[62] Later, when asked in parliament whether he would run with a tag that identified him was an Englishman, Koornhof replied, "if I was an Englishman I suppose I wouldn't mind."[63]

In 1976, Koornhof approved "intergroup competition" at club level: sports associations and municipal councils could, "in consultation with the Minister, arrange leagues or matches enabling teams from different racial groups to compete [against each other]."[64] Shortly after, the government approved multiracial representative teams—chosen by way of racially mixed trials. Despite the convoluted selection process, blacks in mixed representative teams could at last wear the sacred emblem of white supremacy—the Springbok. The following year, seven blacks wore national colors in an international soccer match against Rhodesia (Zimbabwe) and in 1978 long-distance runner Mathews Batswadi became the first black man to receive a green and gold Springbok blazer.[65] Twenty-five blacks participated in the first mixed trials for the Springbok rugby team in 1977, although none gained selection.[66] It was another three years before selectors chose Errol Tobias as the first black rugby Springbok.[67]

Logically, integrated national teams embodied black people as full-fledged South Africans. But in reality, legally prescribed biological classifications and social judgments pertaining to race remained firmly in place as the experiences of black tennis player Mark Mathabane testify. When he applied to the Wanderers Club for membership, the president acknowledged his "qualifications": "you are a fine tennis player, well-mannered and able to speak English . . . I personally would like to see you become a member." However, "there are several serious obstacles," the president added, referring to the legal requirement of the club to provide separate showers, locker rooms, restaurants, and bathrooms for each racial group. Nonetheless, as a gesture of his "sincerity," the president invited Mathabane to play in the club's tournaments: "I don't think there'll be any problems" providing "you . . . use the servants' bathrooms and eat where they eat."[68] Similarly, despite embodying the nation, the white media and rugby officials continued to ostracize Errol Tobias. When Tobias suggested that the team's selectors were playing him out of position and he requested them to move him from center to his normal position on the wing, the team manager, Johan Claassen, resorted to traditional discourse, referring to "people without proper education" being unable to "stand up to pressure."[69]

Combined with the problem of embodied muscle memory, that is, of tuning the body to play under completely different conditions, these experiences and incidents cast doubts on the ability of multiracial sport to erase the stigma of race and color. Nonetheless, some evidence supports the view that it opened important new space in which blacks could display their corporeal capital. Samoan-born Bryan Williams, for example, was the star of the watershed All Black tour of South Africa in

1970. "He played," said one of his teammates, "the best rugby I've seen anyone play on a rugby field. He was magnificent, and he was just God to the coloreds and blacks."[70] However, opportunities to black South African sportsmen to convert their corporeal capital remained limited.

In 1991, the antiapartheid sports movement listed several prerequisites for lifting the boycott and readmitting South African sport to international competition: a single controlling association for each code; implementation of development programs to redress material inequalities caused by apartheid; affirmative action in team selection; and new flags, anthems, colors, and emblems. Not surprisingly, given its historical role in the embodiment of their identity, many whites greeted with hostility and outrage suggestions that the Springbok emblem faced extinction. According to a spokesperson from the right-wing Conservative Party, "black communists and white liberals want to remove the Springbok because it represents Christian values."[71] The antiapartheid sports movement was equally adamant: it symbolizes "too many hurtful associations" and "must go," said Sam Ramsamy, chairman of the newly formed National Olympic Committee of South Africa.[72]

White South Africans refused to passively relinquish what had become part of them, and an intense struggle developed around the Springbok. During the rugby test against New Zealand at Ellis Park in August 1992—the first official test match for eleven years between the world's two rugby powerhouses—several whites offered apartheid flags to Steve Tshwete in gestures intended to taunt the ANC's spokesperson on sport and a key figure in negotiating unity between the antiapartheid movement and "establishment" sport. Just prior to kickoff, Louis Luyt, president of the Transvaal Rugby Union and chairman of (the stock exchange listed) Ellis Park Pty. Ltd., instructed the announcer to play the national anthem—*"Die Stem van Suid Afrika"* ("The Voice of South Africa"). It was a deliberate breach of a pledge not to promote apartheid symbols. The crowd sang as one. In the ensuing controversy, the Afrikaans newspaper *Rapport* waxed lyrical about "softer tears of pride" and of the Afrikaner's defiant will, which declared, "here is my song, here is my flag. Here I stand and I will sing it today."[73]

Rugby remained firmly entrenched in the white cultural *laager* even after the first universal suffrage election in 1994. Journalist Sharon Chetty's description of the crowd's behavior during a 1995 test between

South Africa and Western Samoa reaffirmed white attachment to traditional cultural symbols and their embodied forms:

> holding aloft the old South African flag, the rugby die-hards
> sought momentary refuge in the confines of Ellis Park. [When]
> *Nkosi Sikelel' iAfrika* started up you could count the numbers who
> bothered to even keep still. But when *Die Stem* was played they
> stood to attention and sang with gusto—their voices in unison.
> Barring the good natured vendors . . . the number of darkies at
> Ellis Park could be counted on one hand. [One] young fascist . . .
> commanded a vendor to "go stand under the spotlight. Maybe
> then you will become white." His friends laughed. Rugby it seems
> is the last white outpost.[74]

President Nelson Mandela and his minister for sport, Steve Tshwete, regarded international sport as an important vehicle for building a post-apartheid rainbow nation. They went to considerable lengths to pacify white concerns about symbols, memories, and traditions, approving the retention of *Die Stem*, as one of two official anthems, and the Springbok emblem for the national rugby team. A reforming SARFU also contributed. A major factor here was the appointment to chief executive in early 1995 of former *Business Day* and *Sunday Times* sports reporter and staunch critic of establishment rugby, Edward Griffiths. Under his tutelage the Springboks embodied political correctness: they played under the slogan "one team, one country," they supported the government's *masakhane* ("let's build together") campaign, they were polite, accessible, offered themselves for photo opportunities, and attended regular press conferences.[75]

According to Turner, all professional athletes must carefully manage their public presentation to convey acceptable images—especially to potential corporate sponsors—of the body. In particular, they must demonstrate that they are self-disciplined, hard working, conscientious, and determined.[76] In the new postapartheid South Africa, while national sports representatives had to convey a completely difference set of images to those that would have engendered public appeal just a few years earlier. Their new constituency was much broader, more politically aware, critical, and demanding.

But it was Mandela's support for Springbok rugby that helped recast race relations in South Africa, albeit temporarily. The day before the 1995 Rugby World Cup began, Mandela embraced the team: "I have never been so proud of our boys. I hope we will all be cheering them on to victory. They will be playing for the entire South Africa."[77] It was an unanticipated gesture and one now available to global audiences in a stylized Hollywood rendering through the film *Invictus*. Mandela was the official host and protocol required his participation, but he could have maintained a stiff and indifferent formality. In fact, he admitted several times to supporting the Springboks' opponents during apartheid. Instead, Mandela showed a genuine and infectious enthusiasm, even describing the players as "our own children."[78] Several times during the tournament Mandela cleverly deployed his body to prove his support. On 16 June, the National Youth Day commemorating the Soweto uprising and massacre of the same date in 1976, Mandela addressed a youth rally in KwaZulu-Natal wearing a green rugby cap complete with Springbok emblem. "You see this cap that I am wearing," he told his audience, "it does honour to *our boys* who are playing France tomorrow afternoon."[79] Nine days later, in an unprecedented act by a head of state, Mandela strode on to the turf before the final against New Zealand wearing a South African team jersey. The predominantly white spectators roared their delight, rising to their feet chanting, "Nel-son, Nel-son, Nel-son."

By wrapping his body in the most potent symbols of the old white South Africa, Mandela became, for a moment, an "honorary" white and hero among those who had long dismissed him as a "terrorist" and a "communist." Eighty minutes plus extra-time later, South Africa was world rugby champion. Black and white South Africans joined in celebration. Nelson Mandela hugged team captain Francois Pienaar, who told the world that "we were inspired by the President";[80] black and white South Africans embraced in celebration and black supporters toyi-toyied through downtown Johannesburg's Carlton Centre singing the theme song *Shosholoza* and shouting "Amabokoboko."

Shosholoza, the Springbok anthem during the 1995 Rugby World Cup, has a long history and offers an excellent example of the embodiment of cultural adaption and appropriation. Originally a Ndebele song, it highlighted the plight of migrant workers who traveled from Rhodesia (Zimbabwe) to labor in the mines of South Africa. Zulu workers later took up the song to generate rhythm during group tasks and to alleviate boredom and stress. Lutheran students sang the song as an anthem in the 1960s and 1970s before it reemerged as an immensely popular sporting anthem in the mid-1990s.

Of course, it would be grossly misleading to suggest that South Africa is now an embodied multiracial nation. The "Other" retains a presence in the forms of coloreds and Indians (not black enough[81]), whites (privileged[82]), and the underprivileged (poor blacks[83]). These distinctions still persist in sport: white South Africans continue to cheer their nation to victory in rugby and cricket; notwithstanding intense political and media efforts surrounding the 2010 FIFA World Cup the most fanatical support for the national soccer team—*Bafana Bafana*—came from blacks.[84] This is not to deny progress; such denial is both obtuse and naïve. Officials and advertisers, for example, are more conscious about marketing their sporting products to a multiracial audience. They pay special attention to white rugby and cricket stars with connections to black communities. *SA Sports Illustrated*, for example, published an article in 1997 entitled "Zulu Warrior" that began with a description of Natal and national team fast bowler Lance Klusener's ability to speak Zulu and his attachments to rural Natal.[85] The fact that Kluesener is tied to an embodied concept of Zulu men as "warrior" in fact embodies him in a way that intersects with white fantasies as much as black identification.[86]

This stylized and repackaged racial marketing is a far cry from a century earlier when black intellectuals spurred tribal identities in favor of the demeanor of British colonizers. Moreover, there is some evidence that sheer athletic ability is slowly assuming a colorless hue in South Africa. Aggrey Klaaste, the editor of the *Sowetan*, South Africa's largest black newspaper, concedes that "strange things are happening to my sporting ways." He attributes these changes to the fact that his young sons "worship the ground [that white cricketer] Jonty Rhodes throws himself at with such seeming abandon" and the fact that they could cheer "pale-faced" South African cricketers against the West Indies (though Beckles's chapter above suggests that there were additional factors of perceived West Indies player greed that fed into this as well).[87] Marc Maharaj, the minister for transport, similarly recounted his children screaming support for the "Boks" and their refusal to discuss the historical meaning of the word and its embodied meanings.[88] Of course, problems still remain. Dominant South African identities still rely on masculine violence and the exclusion of women. A new black elite readily endorses masculine sporting culture. A former sports minister, the late Steve Tshwete, for example, preferred rugby to soccer and called players of the latter sissies.

Conclusion

As an embodied practice, sport offers a perfect example of the social construction of race and the sophistry of racial classifications in South Africa. During the apartheid era, a handful of light-skinned colored sportsmen won national sporting honors by passing as whites. For example, Ronnie van der Walt won the South African welterweight boxing title, and Glen Popham captained the Springbok karate team. How did the state know that van der Walt and Popham were not white? Both men had been "marked" at birth by virtue of their parents' classifications. However, later in life they, like thousands of lesser-known cases, simply crossed the color divide and lived and played as whites. Their problems arose only after they applied to the Race Classification Board for an official reclassification; in so doing they drew attention to the minutia of their corporeality. How did they walk? Did they have freckled skin or halfmoons at the base of their fingernails? Did the hair on their hands "twist?" Could the hair on their head "hold" a pencil? How did they stand? Was the skin at the base of their spine dark or light?[89] The notion that such physical characteristics might reveal profound biological truths is pure chicanery. Indeed, it was the state's attempt to apply biology to social judgments, and its determination to stop blacks from converting their physical capital into economic, social, and cultural capital that made apartheid so obnoxious.

The experiences of black sports people in the United States and Britain suggest that the end of apartheid will not mean the end of corporeal stereotyping in South Africa. If not so long ago whites considered black bodies morally and physically inferior and "therefore unfit to compete with whites," today, overrepresentation in contact sports "seems to confirm . . . [new] stereotypes of the black as bestial brute, the 'all brawn and no brains' kind of athlete." Similarly, the black sports star is an "exemplar of masculine toughness."[90] While all bodies are socially constructed, the black sportsperson illustrates the political significance of that process in the reproduction of the social relations of power and inequality.

CHAPTER 4

Indigenous Australians and Sport: Critical Reflections

Daryl Adair

This chapter has been conceived with the purpose of reaching an international audience that is largely unfamiliar with Australian society and sport, and particularly the integral role of indigenous people in both of these contexts. Such a synopsis cannot do justice to the complexity of Aboriginal experiences past and present, but the aim is to provide readers with an overview of major themes and issues. The chapter begins with a very brief analysis of the impact upon Aboriginal people of British colonial rule, then considers their circumstances when the Commonwealth of Australia was proclaimed in 1901. After this background the focus then moves abruptly to the last third of the twentieth century; this was a time when Aboriginal and Torres Strait Islander (ATSI) peoples became widely recognized contributors to Australian sport. Finally, the chapter then dwells on Australian sport in the early twenty-first century; this is a time in which indigenous people have assumed unprecedented significance in the national sporting landscape. As will be shown, such heightened ATSI involvement in high-performance sport has been lauded and applauded. However, the contemporary success of indigenous athletes on sporting fields appears to have broader ramifications. First, in terms of the complexity of "race" relations in Australia, has sport revealed or concealed these nuances? Second, in terms of ATSI aspirations to achievement, what do we know about indigenous self-perceptions in and around sport? These critical reflections are not intended to be the last word on ATSI Australians in sport. They are expected, instead, to be catalysts for further discussion.

Aborigines and Torres Strait Islanders, the indigenous peoples of

Australia, have cultures that extend over 40,000 years. In 1788, when Europeans began to annex what explorers called *Terra Australis*, there were perhaps five hundred distinct language dialects and a vast array of clan groups.[1] Aboriginal people hunted, fished, and traded with one another. Sometimes they fought. All of them lived in harmony with the land and were exemplary custodians.[2] From the late eighteenth century, however, the traditional way of Aboriginal life was eroded by colonial annexation of land, frontier violence, and the spread of foreign diseases. The oppression of Aborigines was accelerated during the nineteenth century by the imposition of laws and practices that subjugated and ostracized the original inhabitants, who attempted to resist these incursions.[3] The British Colonial Office called for "protection" of Aborigines, but many of the settlers had genocidal intentions. By the mid-nineteenth century the colonies had been granted self-government; they deemed Aborigines to be a "problem" and swiftly developed policies to enforce separation. The vast majority of Aboriginal people were institutionalized on government reserves or Christian missions—almost always in rural and remote parts of the country out of the sight and mind of Europeans.[4] In these remote places indigenous people were under surveillance; their movements were constrained and so was their cohabitation. So-called mixed-race relationships were of particular concern to colonial authorities; colored offspring provided a further complication to efforts to keep the races apart.[5]

By the turn of the twentieth century, it was wrongly presumed, at least among urban whites, that Aborigines were a "dying race." This view didn't stem from an inane interpretation of divine providence or Social Darwinism; rather the demise of Aboriginal people was in the interest of governments. State-sanctioned policies allowed the removal of Aboriginal children from their parents and permanent relocation with white families.[6] As Phillip Knightley describes it: "White welfare officers, often supported by police, would descend on Aboriginal camps, round up all the children . . . bundle them into trucks and take them away. If their parents protested they were held at bay by police."[7] These were deliberate efforts, under the guise of welfare, to try to eliminate new generations of Aboriginal families.

The prospect of denying Aboriginality suited the politicians who, in 1901, proclaimed an Australian nation. The constitution failed to mention indigenous people, and one of the first pieces of legislation to pass the Federal Parliament was the White Australia Policy.[8] This act was intended to prevent nonwhite migrants coming to Australia, but Aboriginal people were under no illusions that they lived in a society where they were largely unwanted. In 1938, when New South Wales officials ostentatiously commemorated 150 years of British settlement in Sydney, Aboriginal activists declared a "day of mourning." For them there was nothing to celebrate and much to commiserate.[9]

By the 1960s the American civil rights movement had helped to inform and radicalize Aboriginal activists and their supporters. The legendary Aboriginal leader Charlie Perkins led what was termed the "freedom ride" into rural towns in New South Wales, where he and student activists reported on racism. At the outback town of Moree, for example, Aboriginal people were excluded from many public services, including the local school and the swimming baths.[10] Segregation was rife: the local cinema partitioned Aborigines at the front of the theater, while at Moree Hospital there was a separate space for Aboriginal patients out the back of the facility. Even in death there was segregation. The town cemetery had an area where Aborigines were buried away from whites.[11] This Australia looked very much like apartheid South Africa.

The late 1960s did, however, involve change. A national referendum in 1967 allowed the federal government to make laws in respect of Aboriginal people, a role that the states had assumed previously. The rise to power of the Whitlam Labor government in 1972 facilitated the prospect of reform in the interests of Aborigines; indeed, within a week of taking office, Whitlam had established a Royal Commission into land rights for Aborigines. However, it took a further twenty years for the High Court to rule against *terra nullius*, which was the British colonial declaration that in 1788 the Australian continent was unoccupied and belonged to no one.[12] The outcome has been the concept of native title, which recognizes the continued ownership of land by local indigenous Australians, though not to the exclusion of nonindigenous proprietary rights. In some parts of rural Australia the principle of coexistence has been negotiated, whereby traditional Aboriginal landowners and pastoralists utilize the same territory.[13] However, the wealth that stems from the land, such as through corporate mining ventures in remote regions, has too rarely made its way into the hands of local Aborigines.[14]

By the early twenty-first century, Aboriginal and Torres Strait Islander peoples, once the sole custodians of the Australian continent, constituted around 2.7 percent of the national population. The raw number of indigenous people—some 450,000—is similar to most demographic estimates of the total indigenous population before the arrival of Europeans.[15] Although typecast as living in rural and remote regions, Aborigines are just as likely to be found in towns and major cities. There are, for example, more Aboriginal people residing in Sydney than in the entire Northern Territory. Common to all, though, is indigenous disadvantage—which is evident across virtually every socioeconomic indicator. Aboriginal people have, as examples, significantly lower life expectancy than other Australians,[16] much higher levels of unemployment,[17] considerably lower levels of education and income,[18] and are vastly overrepresented in the nation's prisons.[19] Colonialism has left a pernicious legacy of inequality and disengagement in the lives of Aboriginal people.

Arguments for indigenous social justice and reconciliation have been made by non-Aboriginal Australians. For example, in 1997 the federal government commissioned the *Bringing Them Home Report*, which provided irrefutable evidence of the state-sanctioned removal of Aboriginal children for much of the twentieth century—the victims were now labeled the "stolen Generations."[20] However, the conservative federal prime minister of the day, John Howard, steadfastly refused to apologize for the indigenous policies of previous state governments, preferring to convey "sadness and regret" at what had happened. There was, nonetheless, a groundswell of public disquiet that culminated in a massive march for reconciliation in Sydney—with Aboriginal people and their supporters demanding an official apology and initiatives toward reconciliation. Howard, though, was unmoved.[21] Indeed, the conservative federal government has since opportunistically engaged in what critics labeled "coercive reconciliation,"[22] which in essence has been an extension of state control over the lives of indigenous Australians.

A turning point was 2007, at which time a Northern Territory government funded report documented the widespread sexual abuse of Aboriginal children in remote parts of that region and associated problems of alcoholism and domestic violence. The report, entitled *Little Children Are Sacred*, urged swift, coordinated local responses to child protection. Prime Minister Howard, however, saw this as an opportunity for the federal government to regulate the lives of Aboriginal people under the guise of providing protection. He declared an "emergency" intervention in the Northern Territory, allowing the state to micromanage indigenous communities it deemed chronically dysfunctional. The Australian army was operationalized to monitor Aboriginal regions in the Northern Territory, social security payments were sequestered, alcohol was banned, and pornographic materials confiscated. However, this centralized approach was out of step with the *Little Children Are Sacred* report, and the Howard government followed just two of its ninety-seven recommendations. In short, the very real socioeconomic problems of remote Aboriginal communities were politicized by the federal government, allowing a return to paternalism and greater control of Aboriginal people.[23] When the Howard regime was usurped by Kevin Rudd's Labor Party in 2007, one of the new government's most important decisions was to make a formal apology to victims of the Stolen Generations. What became known as "Sorry Day," 13 February 2008, was a landmark in Australian "race" relations.[24] Concurrently, though, the Labor government did not curtail the NT emergency intervention; it was continued and remained operational through 2012.

As can be ascertained by this all-too-brief survey of Australian history and race relations, indigenous people have a multitude of reasons by which to feel disenchanted by and disengaged from Australian society, past and present. The story of Aborigines in sport has a similar tenor, particularly in the colonial era and for the bulk of the twentieth century.

The research of Colin Tatz has been instrumental to awareness of the extent of discrimination against Aboriginal people in Australian sport, past and present.[25] Too often, he argues, sport has been a vehicle through which racial prejudice has thrived. For example, in the early 1900s the Queensland Amateur Athletics Association tried to ban all Aborigines from taking part in its competitions by complaining "that they either 'lacked moral character,' 'had insufficient intelligence,' or 'couldn't resist white vice.'" Thankfully, Tatz concludes, these "appalling excuses were rejected by the national athletics body."[26] However, the Queensland Amateur Athletics Association responded defiantly by declaring that all Aboriginal runners would now be classed as professionals, and were thus made ineligible to race under the banner of an amateur organization.

Such racist opposition to Aboriginal sportsmen could also be a reaction against the ability they showed. Matthew Stephen's research is replete with examples of this. When an Aboriginal athlete won the Pine Creek Handicap in the Northern Territory in 1895, the organizers brought in a ruling that "no Aborigines or other coloured races be allowed to compete in European events."[27] Australian Rules football, played locally in Darwin from 1916, featured a similar scenario. Aborigines and nonwhite migrants, such as the Chinese, established a team for all-comers, Vesteys, which dominated the Northern Territory Football League (NTFL) in the 1920s. However, in 1926 the white-administered NTFL changed its constitution to exclude nonwhite players. A color bar was thus put into effect: only after World War II was Darwin's football league again fully integrated.[28]

For most of the twentieth century, elite-level sport competitions in Australia rarely featured Aboriginal athletes. This made exceptions all the more novel and intriguing. When Aboriginal boxer Lionel Rose claimed the world bantamweight title in Japan in 1968, he was mobbed by hundreds of thousands of well-wishers upon return to Australia. Not only was Rose the first Aborigine to win a world boxing title, he also became the first indigenous person to be awarded the prestigious title of "Australian of the Year." A year later he reached the top of the music charts with a country and western song, "I Thank You."[29] Along with tennis player Evonne Goolagong, who won seven grand-slam singles finals between 1971 and 1980, Rose presented the image of an Aborigine who had "made it" in white society. Both of these athletes appealed to nonindigenous observers who, ordinarily, had little or no contact with Aboriginal people.[30] Unlike Aboriginal dissidents who established the Aboriginal Tent Embassy outside Parliament House in Canberra, and used it to protest for land rights and a treaty with whites,[31] these Aboriginal athletes were seen as nonthreatening. The unspoken comment from some whites may have been: "Why couldn't more Aborigines be like these shining examples of assimilation?"

During the 1980s and 1990s, increased numbers of Aborigines participated at the elite level in the country's two largest football codes—Australian Rules and rugby league. By the early twenty-first century,

players from Aboriginal or Torres Strait Islander heritage now constitute around 10–13 percent of all professional players in both the AFL
and the NRL—a staggering proportion given that the indigenous population of Australia is about 3 percent of the national total.[32] However,
Aboriginal athletes have battled long and hard against verbalized racism
—both on and off the field—as a method of torment. A turning point
came in April 1993, when Aboriginal footballer Nicky Winmar raised
his St. Kilda jumper to a group of bigoted Collingwood fans, proudly
revealing to them his black skin. This was a dignified, symbolic retali-
ation.[33] However, Collingwood president Allan McAllister remarked
that so long as Aborigines "behaved themselves like white folks off
the field, they would be admired and respected" on it.[34] There is much
irony in this claim, for it seems unlikely that Winmar would want to
lower himself to behave like the Collingwood supporters who abused
him. McAllister was persuaded by the football club to apologize for his
comments and, in a transparent attempt to get himself "off the hook,"
hastily organized a match between Collingwood and a team dubbed the
Aboriginal All Stars, who promptly thrashed them.[35]

A debate had also taken place over whether on-field racial sledging was "just" a tactic or, instead, a form of serious misconduct. This
was not resolved properly until after 1995, when Essendon's Michael
Long complained that a Collingwood ruckman had racially vilified him,
and that this behavior should be treated as an offense. The Australian
Football League, while slow to respond to this type of racism, has since
become a national leader by introducing a wide-ranging antivilification
code.[36] For the league it has been something of a win-win: Aboriginal
footballers are now less likely to face on-field racism and the AFL brand
has become associated positively with cultural diversity initiatives
around the country. What is more, many Aboriginal athletes—whether
in the AFL, NRL, boxing, or athletics—are now household names and
revered by both indigenous and nonindigenous fans.

Colin Tatz, however, argues that there are "monumental contradictions" in the adulation by nonindigenous Australians for so many
Aboriginal stars of sport.[37] He believes that the affection is genuine, but
most of these fans have little knowledge about where the indigenous
players come from, or the nature of their lives before coming to prominence as boxers, runners, or footballers. It can be all too easy—indeed

convenient—for non-Aboriginal people to look to these athletes as examples of rising indigenous circumstances generally. But it is hopelessly naïve to imagine that deep-seated structural inequalities will be impacted upon in a substantive way by the individual successes of one hundred or so elite Aboriginal athletes.[38] Indeed, Tatz points to the absurdity of anyone appropriating Cathy Freeman's success at the 2000 Olympics "as though she has single-handedly transformed the whole Aboriginal experience into the opposite of what it really is."[39] Yet fantasies about such a connection exist, particularly when associated with simplistic ideas about "opportunity for all." The more that nonindigenous Australians cheer for Aboriginal athletes, the more they can lay claim to championing Aboriginal advancement and "fighting" racism.[40] Of course, some Australians do not fit this mindset at all. Toni Bruce, in a study of letters to the editor of newspapers during the Sydney 2000 Olympics, found numerous examples of correspondents vehemently opposed to the notion that Cathy Freeman, as an Aborigine, could somehow embody the Australian nation. Several of these writers raged against what they saw as the "political correctness" of having an indigenous person light the flame at the opening ceremony of the games.[41]

Chris Hallinan and Barry Judd have also examined the influence of the media on Australian sport, particularly in terms of the discursive construction of race and the impact of inferential racism.[42] They argue that media stereotypes tend to serve as an "othering" mechanism among socially constructed dominant and subordinate groups.[43] In the context of Australian sport, these descriptions sometimes insinuate that in order to be successful indigenous athletes do not need to work as hard, develop skills, or put in as much effort as nonindigenous athletes. As another researcher, Andrew Ramsey, has put it:

> There remains a school of thought that Aboriginal footballers are not the same as other players, that they process a kind of "sixth sense" that allows them a greater awareness of what's happening around them, an ability to size up pressure situations more quickly than their fair-skinned opponents and that they have an added athleticism that makes the most difficult physical tasks seem easier.[44]

Nonindigenous commentators have indeed been awestruck by some of the athletic feats of Aboriginal footballers, offering plaudits like "freak goals" and "eyes in the back of their head."[45] However, this is hardly restricted to non-Aboriginal observers. For example, when the *National Indigenous Times* reported on the inaugural rugby league match between the "Indigenous All Stars" and the "NRL All Stars," the headline read "Thurston magic clinches victory."[46] While all of this adulation may be well intended, and understandable when viewers are ensconced in the fast-moving drama of sport, an overemphasis on athletic acumen to the exclusion of other qualities may pose risks beyond the playing field. Hallinan and Judd, when interviewing AFL administrators, posed questions about the lack of Aboriginal staff in club administration, coaching and other off-field roles. They found that some respondents reverted to "racial logic" to explain this disparity: Indigenous players, it was thought, had "natural" physical prowess but were not suited to decision making or positions of responsibility outside of sport performance.[47]

However, the studies that criticize assumptions of "naturally gifted" Aboriginal athletes have a limitation in that they focus only on *non-Aboriginal* typecasting of indigenous performers. What do *Aboriginal athletes* believe? Here it is crucial to draw upon the prescient postgraduate research of two scholars: Darren Godwell and Megan Stronach.

Back in 1997 Godwell, an indigenous Australian researcher, interviewed Aboriginal professional athletes as part of his master's thesis and, in the process, gathered data about their sense of self through sport.[48] He made the argument, as John Hoberman also observed in 1997 about African Americans in the United States,[49] that sport may not be a positive force for improvements to race relations. Godwell made four telling points. First, like Hoberman, Godwell concluded that professional sport is not a realistic career path for the overwhelming majority of indigenous Australians (or, he might have added, for Australians generally). Scoring tries on the red dust of outback Queensland was the Aboriginal equivalent of "hoop dreams" basketball in urban America. It was a boyhood dream of professional sport that very few could actually realize. Second, Godwell railed against beliefs that ascribed to indigenous people innate, natural, or genetically inherited physical abilities that "predisposed" them, as a group, to be good at sport. He noted that this had been popularized by media superlatives for Aboriginal players, with descriptors like "black magic" and "wizardry." Third, Godwell noted that a belief in "genetic advantage" for Aborigines in sport was "held by both Indigenous and non-Indigenous peoples alike."[50] The inference, therefore, was that Aborigines had biologically inherited athletic giftedness, and that this natural advantage over non-Aborigines had been internalized and accepted to the point where it had become conventional wisdom. Fourth, Godwell argued that beliefs about the collective, biologically driven predisposition of indigenous people to athletic prowess "should not be accepted without critical examination."[51] He then made a contentious point: that the "natural" Aboriginal athlete was a form of "racist social myth" that ought to be critiqued by indigenous opinion leaders.[52] This is because, he insisted, racial stereotypes have the effect—intended or otherwise—of limiting the range of life and career possibilities thought "available" to Aboriginal people.[53] Godwell concluded that "Aborigines run the risk of being typecast in life as sportspeople."[54]

Stronach[55] has recently interviewed more than thirty elite indigenous athletes who have been part of the AFL, NRL, or boxing. Her focus is with career transition and retirement experiences, which has involved respondents reflecting on their sense of self both during and after sport. In almost every case, and without prompting, the interviewees indicated what they described as a shared and common belief—that in sport indigenous people are in fact naturally and genetically gifted, and as a group are therefore both "different" and athletically "superior" to their nonindigenous counterparts.

A typical example is "Jerry," a retired professional boxer: "You know yourself, you can go anywhere in Australia, any school in Australia, the best athlete is what? The best sportsman is what? Aborigines! They're gifted, high fighters, running, speed, more balance, rhythm, timing— they're gifted."[56] For another interviewee, "Billy," the Aboriginal talent for boxing was also innate: "Yeah, it's in blackfellas' blood, to fight, all blackfellas are good fighters; they just need someone to bring it out of 'em."[57] No acknowledgment here of other motivations at work, such as the incredible will and desire of indigenous fighters to excel in an ultracompetitive physical environment where, as with other minorities around the world, the boxing ring provided temporary opportunity for success. The space outside of the ring has proven to be a more formidable challenge to nonwhite boxers in Australia and other parts of the world.[58]

Yet there is evidence to suggest that hard work and practice and a learned ability to thrive under pressure are the keys to Aboriginal excellence in sport. Sean Gorman's research into the Krakouer brothers is particularly apt in this regard:[59]

> When I talked to Jimmy, I said "tell me about the magic, Jimmy" and he said, "What are you talking about, bro' [brother]?" And I said, "Well, you know, how would you be able to find one another? You would have ten blokes around you and you would get the ball out and you'd handball off and plop it in Phillip's hands and he would run off, how would that happen?" He said, "We had the ball from the time we were three years old, when we could walk, and we'd go down to the park, we'd be constantly handballing and kicking, doing all these sorts of things; it was just confidence."[60]

Similarly, Cyril Rioli, a diminutive figure in the AFL at only 177cm and 80kg, is renowned for his tackling prowess, which has led some commentators to wax lyrical about his Aboriginality.[61] However, when questioned by the media about this skill, which almost inevitably pits Rioli against a player with a larger frame, he emphasizes that tackling is something he has worked on, and that he took up martial arts over two preseasons in order to improve his tackling technique and confidence in footy.[62] No claim here from Rioli about having a natural aptitude to tackle.

Talent identification in sport is both an art and a science. In Australia there have been systematic efforts to lure Aboriginal athletic talent into the AFL, the NRL, and initiatives like the Indigenous Boxing Program at the Australian Institute of Sport. Some of this is based on folkloric assumptions rather than an evidence base. A recent initiative has been the "hunt" for Aboriginal athletic talent driven by Robert De Castella, a former Australian marathon champion. His aim is to lure indigenous people into distance running on the assumption that there is something about black skin and/or Aboriginal genes that may allow them to compete, as Kenyans and Ethiopians have, over long athletic journeys. De Castella, who is not Aboriginal, nonetheless has a dream of Aboriginal athletes taking part in the New York marathon.[63] Like so many programs to detect and lure "latent" Aboriginal athletic talent, De Castella does not intend harm. But his vision of indigenous Australians having similar genetic attributes for marathon running as East Africans is idealistic to say the least.[64]

Belief in "natural" sporting ability is cultural and psychological. After Godwell interviewed indigenous rugby league players he produced this key finding: there was "a strong link between these men believing in the existence of an innate athletic ability in Aborigines and their participation in sport."[65] Godwell concluded that this showed the importance of believing, but not that there was substance to the belief itself. The circular nature of this problem was astutely observed by one of Godwell's indigenous respondents:

> "I used to believe that all Kooris were good at sport. I don't any more. I just think that Aboriginals believe that Aboriginals are the best sportspeople . . . and believing in something makes a difference . . . I always say believing is half way to getting somewhere."[66]

Self-belief is important for any athlete; it is something that coaches try to promote and psychologists instill. Sport teams, not just their constituent players, are said to need self-belief. It is no surprise, then, that self-belief is central to Godwell's cohort. However, the nature of self-belief can be controversial. In 2008, Aboriginal football champion Adam Goodes, a dual Browlow medalist and premiership player with the Sydney Swans, contributed a chapter to the AFL's official book commemorating the 150-year history of the Australian game.[67] His topic was the indigenous contribution to footy. In this essay Goodes remarked: "I know that when Aborigines play Australian football with a clear mind and total focus, [we] were born to play it."[68] Sensationally, another contributor to *The Australian Game of Football: Since 1858*, the (non-Aboriginal) historian Gillian Hibbins, publicly attacked Goodes's viewpoint, suggesting that it was "racist." She later clarified this label by stating: "If you define racism as believing a race is superior in something, this is basically what he (Goodes) was doing."[69] Hibbins may have been feeling prickly after her own chapter had been criticized for summarily dismissing an Aboriginal connection to the origins of Australian

Rules football (the Marngrook theory) as "a seductive myth."[70] Again her choice of words seemed provocative and caused disappointment to many. The *National Indigenous Times* reported two weeks later that Hibbins felt that her "comments were taken out of context, but on reflection . . . her choice of wording may have been erroneous." She emphasized: "I certainly do not believe that Adam Goodes is a racist . . . I think he's a fantastic footballer, and I'm sure he believes what he says—that Aboriginal footballers feel a brotherhood on the field and they feel a connection with the land."[71] This was more than a clash about Aboriginal self-belief in playing footy; it went to the heart of a wider belief in who had invented the game of Australian Rules and whether indigenous people had a role in that process.[72]

Unwittingly, these various types of fascination with Aboriginal physicality reinforce the assumption that indigenous people need to focus on their bodies, rather than their minds, in order to be successful. That is, of course, a problem not unique to Australia: there has been an almost voyeuristic focus on "brilliant" black bodies (most recently in the case of Jamaican sprinter Ussain Bolt discussed later in this volume), but a correspondingly patronizing assumption that they have "fragile minds."[73] The inference is that they choose sport because that is what they can do "naturally" and that they avoid academic and intellectual pursuits because these are things they are "not suited" to in terms of "natural" ability.[74] This says nothing about the structural and cultural factors that make sport career aspirations a priority among people who, as indigenous Australians, are subjugated in other areas of life, such as in education, business, and politics.

Assumptions of "natural born" athletes are not new; nor are they peculiar to Australia and its indigenous peoples. Self-belief has advantages; being able to aspire to something worthwhile and feeling confident in being able to perform are routine components of career attainment and advancement in a range of fields. The problem that this chapter has identified, and which some Aboriginal respondents have themselves recognized, is that—in the words of Godwell—indigenous people "run the risk of being typecast in life as sportspeople."[75] There are, of course, Aboriginal achievers in a range of other fields, notably art, dance, and music, but these also accentuate the idea of indigenous people as "performers." There are, it must be said, good reasons to encourage and celebrate Aboriginal achievement in sport and other performance genres. But there are also good reasons to value, support, and promote indigenous career advancement in a range of other areas, whether business, medicine, tourism, the media, and so on.[76]

No Australian of today, black or white, is responsible for frontier conflicts in the colonial era. Yet all Australians live with the contemporary consequences of that historical experience. How people come to terms with that legacy is a vital question. Unlike issues of health, poverty, and land rights, sport appears to be a "good news" story for Aborigines. Despite a history of racism in sport, indigenous people now feature as highly respected professionals in areas like athletics, boxing, Australian Rules football, and rugby league, though considerably less so in other sports. There is, one might say, less to feel "guilty" about for whites when they gaze on professional sports as a means of engaging indigenous people.[77] Beyond the playing field, though, indigenous Australians are confronted with far greater challenges than they ever faced in sport.

CHAPTER 5

Beyond Black and White: A Study of the Luis Suarez–Patrice Evra Controversy

Verner Møller

Overview

On 15 October 2011 the world famous football clubs Liverpool FC and Manchester United played each other in the English Premier League. Subsequently, Manchester United's French player Patrice Evra complained that Liverpool's Uruguayan player Luis Suarez had racially abused him during the game. The Football Association initiated a review of the incident by an independent Regulatory Commission. The review panel found that Suarez had called Evra "negro"—a Spanish term for "black"—seven times in two minutes and concluded the investigation by handing Luis Suarez an eight-match ban and a £40,000 fine. This ruling was widely lauded in British media as a strong antiracist message. In an attempt to understand the almost univocal support of the ruling this paper begins with an analysis of the applicable rule, the Regulatory Commission's assessment of the incident, and its reasoning that led the commission to hand out a suspension twice as long as the entry point. This analysis suggests that the verdict was a result of a particularly strong condemnation of racial expressions in Britain. The paper goes on to discuss the British approach to racial issues in comparison with other cultures with a lesser degree of sensitivity to minority issues, and it finally argues that the FA's attempt to police players' language is futile as a means to eliminate racism and may even be counterproductive.

> In the midst of a major sports contest, in front of a large sta-
> dium and television audience, a confrontation occurred between
> two sportsmen [. . .]. It was alleged that a racial insult had been
> uttered, leading to an enormous outcry, and extensive discussion
> in all media across the public sphere. What was said and whether
> it was indeed racist, or simply a misunderstood epithet across cul-
> tural and linguistic divides, was the subject of intense speculation.
> Systematic attempts were made to discern what was said from the
> television footage, and the sport authorities became involved and
> initiated disciplinary proceedings.[1]

The above quote perfectly comprises the theme of this chapter.
However, it is not written with the Luis Suarez–Patrice Evra controversy in mind. That incident took place in October 2011. It is the words
by which Professor David Rowe opened his paper "The Televised Sport
'Monkey Trial': Race and the Politics of Post-colonial Cricket." The
incident Rowe refers to played out in a different sport, on the other
side of the world, during the third day of the second test at the Sydney
Cricket Ground in January 2008 when allegedly the Indian Harbhajan
Singh abused Australia's black batsman Andrew Symonds by calling him
a monkey. The disciplinary proceedings concluded with a three-match
ban to Singh.

Rowe's introduction shows that the Luis Suarez versus Patrice Evra
case is not unique. Tellingly, Rowe made the same observation in his
immediate continuation of the above quote:

> Followers of the worlds most popular game, association football
> (soccer), would be likely to conclude that the above description
> refers to the notorious conflict in the World Cup Final in Berlin
> Olympic Stadium on 9 July 2006, when the French captain of
> Algerian origin, Zinedine Zidane, was sent off from the field for
> head-butting the Italian Marco Materazzi in the chest, knocking
> him to the ground.[2]

If we find abusive language in cricket, the gentleman sport par excellence, it should be no surprise that it occurs in all high-intensity contact sports as well. The concept sportsmanship refers to an ideal ethical
attitude.[3] Accordingly, the label "unsportsmanlike conduct" adheres to
behavior that violates this conception of how, ideally, sportspersons

should behave when playing sport. But the frequency by which we experience unsporting behavior in real professional elite sport indicates that such behavior is natural—albeit regrettable—consequences of tensions invoked by participation in the sports activity itself and thus—in real terms—is very sporting indeed. In light of this it is tempting to draw the conclusion that, the Football Association's and the Regulatory Commission's handling of the Suarez-Evra case, which led to an eight-match ban and a £40,000 fine to Suarez, reflects a lack of understanding of the nature of professional football at the highest level.

Apparently the FA wants their footballers to be calm, cool headed, and sober minded, whereas the features that define the most valuable players in addition to excellent football skills are ambition, passion, determination, confidence, aggression, and a never-say-die attitude. A talented player who is easily intimidated will be bullied out of the game long before he comes even close to playing in the English Premier League. The nature of football at the elite level in general, the magnitude of the game and the intensity, rivalry, and archenemy atmosphere, always part of the Liverpool-Manchester United fixtures, was no excuse in the FA's and the Regulatory Commission's assessment of the case.

The Offense

Nobody, not even the two players in question, knows exactly what happened during the hostile exchange that Saturday afternoon on 15 October 2011 at Anfield Road in Liverpool. According to the Regulatory Commission's report, the situation was as follows. Thirteen minutes into the second half, Liverpool's Uruguayan striker Suarez fouled Manchester United's defender Patrice Evra by a kick to his knee. Five minutes later, Liverpool won a corner. It was Evra's job to mark Suarez on Liverpool's corner kicks.

Evra admitted to the commission that he moved toward Suarez in the goalmouth and opened the conversation with a sentence in Spanish, *"Concha de tu Hermana,"*[4] which directly translates as "Your sister's cunt." Evra explained that the meaning of this phrase in Spanish is more like the English "Fucking hell." The independent language experts consulted in the case admitted that as a general swear word this interpretation was correct but added that: "If directed at someone in particular, it can also be understood as '[you] son of a bitch.'"[5] Suarez registered Evra uttered something but did not get the exact wording so he asked what he said. Evra responded confrontationally: *"Porque me diste un golpe?"* (Why did you kick me?).[6] The twenty-four-year-old Suarez retaliated in Spanish by the first phrase that sprung to mind: *"Porque tu eres negro"* (Because you are black).[7]

The Frenchman Evra explained to the Regulatory Commission that he thought the Spanish word "negro" meant "nigger" since "negro" means black. So Evra got upset and warned Suarez: *"Habla otra vez asi, te voy a dar una porrada"* (Say it to me again, I'm going to punch you).[8]

Suarez probably realized that the Spanish word *negro* was winding Evra up, and rubbed salt into the wound by arrogantly replying: *"No hablo con los negros"* (I don't speak to blacks).[9] Evra, consistent with his initial misunderstanding of the Spanish word *negro,* took this to mean "Because I don't speak to niggers," and this led Evra to reiterate his threat more strongly: *"Ahora te voy a dar realmente una porrada"* (Okay now I think I am going to punch you).[10] Suarez would not relinquish so he encouragingly responded, *"Dala, negro, negro, negro"* ("Bring it on blackie, blackie, blackie") (p. 28). Suarez knew of course that if Evra snapped and slapped him, Evra would be sent off, which would give Liverpool a numerical on-field advantage.

For the sake of completeness, it should be noted that Suarez denied Evra's account. Suarez explained to the commission that he had answered Evra's initial question by saying, *"que habia sido una falta normal"* (it was just a normal foul), and that he shrugged his shoulders and put his arms out in a gesture to say that there was nothing serious about it. In response to this the Regulatory Commission observes that: "At this point on the video footage, Mr. Suarez's face is obscured but he does appear to shrug his shoulders."[11]

There is reason to believe that Suarez—in an attempt to defend himself against the accusation of racial abuse—denied Evra's correct account and told the commission what he intended to communicate to Evra in the situation. Whatever the truth is, the commission was not convinced by Suarez's explanation and states that it found Evra's account trustworthy.

What the Rule Says

Suarez's insult is obviously not acceptable. The FA Rule E3 "On general behaviour" says that:

> (1) A Participant shall at all times act in the best interests of the game and shall not act in any manner which is improper or brings the game into disrepute or use any one, or a combination of, violent conduct, serious foul play, threatening, abusive, indecent or insulting words or behaviour.[12]

Notably, the rule forbids all kinds of threat, insult, and abuse, not merely racist ones. Despite the wording of the FA Rule E3, insulting exchanges between players occur all the time. So had Suarez chosen offensive words other than "negro," he probably would have gone unpunished. In any event, Evra was neither penalized for his initial insult nor for his subsequent threat that he would punch Suarez. And Suarez's Dutch teammate, Dirk Kuyt, also went unpunished by the FA, despite admitting to the commission that he had been shouting, "stand up you prick," when he thought Evra made too much of the foul that caused the tension.

Suarez could have retaliated to Evra's: *"Porque me diste un golpe"* using the same words as Evra did when he opened the conversation: "Because you're a sister's cunt." Or he could have taken inspiration from Kuyt and replied: "Because you are a prick." Although these alternatives are prohibited, apparently the FA does not consider such epithets actionable.

In accordance with Rule E3(2), Suarez's unfortunate choice of words, "Because you are black," is deemed more offensive:

> In the event of any breach of Rule E3(1) including a reference to any one or more of a person's ethnic origin, colour, race, nationality, faith, gender, sexual orientation or disability (an "aggravating factor"), a Regulatory Commission shall consider the imposition of an increased sanction, taking into account the following entry points. For a first offence [as it was in the case of Suarez], a sanction that is double that which the Regulatory Commission would have applied had the aggravating factor not been present.[13]

Suarez's reference to Evra's skin color is aggravating. Since it was a first offense, the entry point was a sanction double that would have applied had the aggravating factor not been present. Since a red card for insulting or abusive language would automatically result in a two-match ban the reference to skin color made a four-match ban the entry point for the Regulatory Commission.

It is true that the Regulatory Commission has the discretion to impose a sanction greater or less than the entry point, according to the aggravating or mitigating factors present in each case. Insofar as a four-match ban is the entry point for racial abuse, the eight-match ban indicates that the commission found Suarez guilty of a particularly hostile form of racial abuse. Hence it is noteworthy that the commission's assessment suggests that Suarez had no intention to racially abuse Evra. The Regulatory Commission informs us (1) that it was Evra who started the confrontation; (2) that Suarez was provoked to make his unacceptable response; and (3) that there was no reason to believe Suarez meant it when he said he didn't speak to blacks or that he had kicked Evra because he was black.

Even the FA who brought the charge against Suarez concedes in its opening statement that it is unlikely that Suarez is racist. Thus the FA representative Paul Greaney emphasized:

> First, this case is not about whether Mr Suarez is in fact a racist. Indeed, the Commission will no doubt conclude that there are some indications that he is not. For example, Mr Suarez is himself of mixed heritage, it seems clear that he has experienced the diversity of life and it is plain from the materials submitted on his behalf that he has done good work in the field of community relations. Moreover, even Mr Evra says in his witness statement: "I don't think that Luis Suarez is racist."[14]

In its conclusion the Regulatory Commission sums up the mitigating and aggravating factors. Among the mitigating factors they mention are (1) Suarez had a clean record in relation to charges of this type; (2) Evra was the initiator of the confrontation; and (3) Suarez is engaged in anti-racist charity work. The commission describes this charity as follows:

> When Suarez was in South Africa for the 2010 World Cup, he became involved in a charity in conjunction with the black

Cameroon goalkeeper, Carlos Kameni, and Andres Iniesta, the Spain and Barcelona player. Each of them was filmed meeting a young South African who played football as part of a project with young black and white children to encourage solidarity and stamp out racism. The central theme of the film, which the Commission watched, is that the colour of a person's skin does not matter, they can all play together as a team. It shows Mr Suarez meeting one of the young footballers. The DVD of the film is advertised on Mr Suarez's Facebook page, via which it can be bought with all the money going to help the charity.[15]

If these mitigating factors stood alone, the commission should have considered a reduction from the four-match ban that was the entry point for racial abuse according to rule E3(2). The commission admits that the length of the ban is

> not a matter of mathematical calculation, but a matter of our discretion in the light of all the circumstances. We considered a lower suspension; we considered a greater suspension. We concluded that an eight-match suspension was appropriate and proportionate, reflecting the seriousness of the misconduct, balanced against the mitigation that was urged on us.[16]

One could be forgiven for believing that the aggravating factors that not only outweighed the above-mentioned mitigating factors but also justified the substantial penalty increase according to the Regulatory Commission was horrendously malicious. So the aggravating factors listed in the report may come as a surprise.

Controversial Aggravating Factors

The first aggravating factor is the number of times Suarez used the word "negro." The commission note that the entry point, a four-match ban, could be applied in case the offender had used insulting words referring to skin color only once, and Suarez was found to have used the word *negro* seven times. The exchange took place in the goalmouth within two minutes when the game was at a standstill in relation to a corner kick. Thus the commission could have interpreted the incident as a singular case but chose instead to count it as a series of incidents leaving the question unanswered: Would it have been less serious had

Suarez called Evra "negro" only twice and on separate occasions, once each half of the game?

The second aggravating factor was what Suarez actually said. Not only did he call Evra black, he also said that it was because Evra was black that he had kicked him and that he did not speak with blacks. It goes without saying that even though kicking one another is normal in football it is absolutely unacceptable to kick an opponent because of his skin color. Likewise, not wanting to speak with blacks is clearly racist. So taken at face value these expressions are truly aggravating. However, the commission does not believe that the expressions should be taken at face value as the further explanation reveals: "Even if Mr Suarez said these things in the heat of the moment without really meaning them, nevertheless this was more than just calling Mr Evra 'negro.'"[17] Now, if the members of the commission think Suarez acted in the heat of the moment and said things he did not mean, it could be argued that this is a mitigating rather than an aggravating factor. Consequently, if the commission is uncertain whether it was an untoward in-the-heat-of-the-moment insult or an intended racist slur, it should not have been put on any side of the aggravating-mitigating factors scale.

The third aggravating factor was that Suarez used the word in an acrimonious context where Suarez also had pinched Evra's arm and put a hand on the back of his head in a (false) friendly gesture. "Although we have found that the pinching itself was not insulting behaviour nor did [it] refer to Mr Evra's colour," the commission explains, "such physical contact as part of a confrontation in which the insulting words were used served to aggravate the misconduct."[18] Yet again, it was Evra who initiated the acrimony. Moreover, the pinching cannot have been anything serious because: "In cross-examination Mr Evra said that at the time he did not realise that Mr Suarez had pinched his arm . . . Mr Evra only realised that Mr Suarez had touched his arm in this way when he saw the video footage later."[19] And while it may be true that Suarez's hand on the back of Evra's head may have been a false friendly gesture, it remains in the dark whether it was intended to further wind up Evra or it was a (false) signal of sportsmanship aimed at the referee. In other words, the fact that Evra took offense at the gesture is no evidence that it was intended to be offensive. But Suarez was not given the benefit of the doubt.

The fourth aggravating factor mentioned by the commission is accidental. Because the FA has initiated a number of campaigns against all forms of discriminatory behavior in football related to ethnic origin, color, or race, "Mr Suarez knew or ought to have known that his behaviour was contrary to the message of those campaigns and unacceptable."[20] What the commission fails to acknowledge is that Rule E3(2) as part of the campaigning against discriminatory behavior had already doubled the penalty for insults related to a person's ethnicity, color, or race. The commission refers specifically to the FA's "Kick It Out" campaign launched in 1993. So had the FA thought discriminatory expressions were more aggravating than aggravating they had had sufficient time to adjust the entry point for such offenses to be triple or quadruple of the nondiscriminatory improper behavior. Moreover, the commission's reasoning that Suarez should have kept the FA's antiracism campaign in mind reveals lack of understanding of the notion "in the heat of the moment."

The fifth and final aggravation listed by the commission "was that the insulting words were targeted by Mr Suarez at one particular black player, Mr Evra, who Mr Suarez intended should hear the words. It was not a case of a comment or comments directed at no-one in particular."[21] Once again the commission finds what has already in the rules been defined as aggravating further aggravating. Since Rule E3(2) explicates that it refers to insult or abuse of "any one or more of *a person's* ethnic origin, colour, race" [emphasis added], it is incomprehensible why it should be extra aggravating that Suarez refers to *a* particular *person*. In any case, since addressing a person directly is considered an aggravating factor, we must understand that the mere use of the word *black* on an English football pitch—even if it is directed at no one—is a punishable offense, in the eyes of the FA's Regulatory Commission.

Cultural Differences at Play

The foregoing evaluation of the aggravating factors identified by the Regulatory Commission suggests that the commission has been overzealous and that the imposition of an eight-match (with an additional fine of £40,000) is disproportionate. As the Regulatory Commission notes, the length of the ban is "not a matter of mathematical calculation."

Still, aside from the Liverpool fan-base, and the media and pundits affiliated with the club, British opinion makers were almost univocal in their support of the verdict. A typical example was the *Guardian*'s Rodney Hinds's commentary, which opened with the following statement: "The Football Association did the sport a massive favour when it handed Liverpool's Luis Suarez an eight-match ban and a £40,000 fine after being found guilty of racially abusing Manchester United's Partrice Evra."[22] Interestingly, the commission did not find, as Hinds claims, that Suarez had racially abused Evra. The commission merely concludes that "he used insulting words which included reference to Mr Evra's colour."[23] Hinds's interpretation implies that referring to a person's skin color per se reveals a racist mind. Even if it is done in Spanish where the "direct racial slur," according to the linguistic experts consulted, "would more likely have been something like *"porque eres un negro mierda"* ("because you are a shitty black").[24] In Hinds's opinion reference to a person's physical characteristics is black and white without any shades of gray.

Presenting the same line of thinking, the famous Australian sports journalist and host of *The World Game* on SBS television network, Les Murray, wrote an interesting comment called "Why Suarez is a racist" in which he took issue with Suarez's defense that negro is not a racist term in his native Uruguay. From his marriage with a Brazilian woman whose parents were of different race Murray has personal experience in this. Soon after he had met his wife, he took her out to a Brazilian club in Australia where a guy of her kinfolk called her *"morena."* Murray wanted to know what this meant and she told him it was a reference to her skin color. "So why didn't you slap him in the face?" he asked. "Why should I have done that?" she replied. "Because, plainly, the man's a racist skunk," he said. "No he is not. What he actually said was, hey morena you're a truly beautiful woman, did you know that?" she retorted.[25] Murray later learned that South Americans habitually label people according to their skin color in a friendly, oftentimes even affectionate way. What makes all the difference for Murray in Suarez's case was that when he used the word *negro* the context was not friendly at all. He said it "during a highly charged, highly competitive football match." "I am pretty sure, in fact somewhere around 99.99 per cent certain," Murray concludes, "it could only have been a piece of blatantly racist sledging. Suarez deserves everything he gets."[26]

Another testimony to the overwhelming support of this approach was given by British newspaper the *Telegraph*'s journalist Dan Hodges, who wrote: "It doesn't matter if Suarez has a black grandfather, or done charity work to encourage solidarity amongst people with different backgrounds. We either adopt a zero tolerance approach to racism, or we don't."[27]

Hodges's eagerness to express an uncompromising antiracist attitude prevents him from realizing the paradoxical meaning of his words, which becomes clear in this paraphrase: It doesn't matter that you may not be a racist and there is no reason to believe that you are a racist, because if you were it would be partly self-hatred. Neither does it matter that you are obviously not a racist because if you were you would never have engaged in antiracism charity work. So long as you use expressions on the pitch that can be interpreted as racist you cannot be excused because you are a racist and we must show zero tolerance toward racism.

Furthermore, it is not, as Hodges suggests, a black or white issue. As rough as the FA approach may appear it is not a zero-tolerance policy. Zero tolerance means that people with authority are not allowed to exercise discretion or change a punishment to fit individual circumstances one way or the other. The punishment for a given offense must be predetermined and followed unconditionally, exactly as it is meted out, and, as we have seen, this was definitely not how the length of Suarez's ban was decided.

Tim Vickery, who covers South American football for the BBC, wrote an informative and less judgmental blog about the reception in Uruguay. The website of Uruguay's leading newspaper, *El Pais*, "was full of remarks attacking the 'hypocrisy' and 'pseudo-moralism' of the English."[28] This could comfortably be explained away by reference to sporting nationalism.[29] Vickery, however, finds more profound reasons, drawing attention to the differences in the history of the two countries. Uruguay is much more mature as a multiethnic society than England. It has "an unrivalled record of giving opportunities to afro-descendants," he explains, and reminds us that "In the face of protests from their opponents, Uruguay picked black players in the first Copa America in 1916."[30] This among other things indicates that racism in Suarez's homeland is much less of an issue and why reference to a person's skin color is not taboo. Suarez was raised in a country where the much-admired

Obdulio Varela, captain of the World Cup winning side in 1950, was nicknamed *El Jefe Negro* ("the black boss"), and in the current national side Suarez's teammate Maxi Pereira carries the nickname *El Mono* (the monkey) as a badge of honor, regardless what English and Australian people may think of it. Observing the judicial concept *"Mens rea"* (a guilty mind), the Regulatory Commission should perhaps in all fairness have recognized that Suarez was not raised in a country that—because of a profound racist past—has become hypersensitive to race issues. If Suarez did not know calling a person "black" was more offensive than calling a person "sister's cunt," how can it then be justified to penalize him way above the FA Regulations' entry point for racial abuse?

Vickery offers a compelling explanation. Prior to the case, the controversial president of the international football association (FIFA), Sepp Blatter, made headlines by suggesting that racist remarks could be settled with a handshake. This gave the FA an opportunity to parade its antiracism policy and at the same time expose FIFA's lack of integrity. But as Vickery points out:

> Some of those calling for Blatter's head on the racism issue are the very people who believed that everything was fine with Fifa while Sir Stanley Rous of England was in charge from 1961 to 1974. Rous seriously damaged the development of African football with his defence of Apartheid in South Africa—a stance which looked awful at the time and was disastrous in hindsight. In his campaign to unseat Rous in 1974, Brazilian Joao Havelange made a point of showing physical intimacy with the African delegates. An Englishman, he reasoned, would not do the same. Thankfully England is much-changed since then. English football can be proud of its anti-racism work but it should be remembered that what has happened in our country is a domestic dynamic.[31]

In light of this, it looks as if Suarez was scapegoated as a consequence of bad conscience ingrained in British culture because of its own abhorrent colonial/imperial past. It is beyond dispute that what Suarez said was against the rules, and Vickery is not apologetic. "There is a clear case for punishment as part of a process of education. But the eight-match ban would seem to go much further than that" he concludes.[32]

Vickery implies that Suarez's lengthy ban was due to Britain's racist history and unsettled multiculturalism rather than a level-headed evaluation of Suarez's offenses as such. This understanding finds support in a debate that began in the civilized welfare state of Denmark in early 2012 shortly after the center-left coalition had won the election. In the wake of the Suarez case, the new Danish minister for culture, Uffe Elbaek, who has sport within his portfolio, gave an interview and argued that "there needs to be a certain tolerance. We must understand that people under pressure can make rash comments. In all sorts of workplaces there is an understanding that one may say something stupid, which the person who has said it must apologise for. It should not be any different in sport."[33] It is noteworthy that this expression is voiced by a person who represents the most unprejudiced, immigrant-friendly, and equal-rights-minded party of all Danish parties and who by being openly gay belongs to a minority himself.

Predictably, people who take pleasure in political correctness criticized the minister for his "irresponsible" point of view but the media's attempt to put the heat on quickly faded. There was no real resonance. An expert in sports law was quoted as saying that racist remarks in a sports arena are less serious than in the wider society. "We must distinguish between the civil law and the football law. It is very common to call it racism, but verbal abuse on a football pitch is not the same as being racist." And when the journalist turned to a professor of constitutional law, he learned the same: "When you are sitting at home and write a letter to the editor or make a public speech and say derogatory things about immigrants for instance it is deliberate and more considered than if you in the heat of the moment happen to hurl abuse at an opponent. This explains why there is a bigger margin in relation to sports."[34]

Why the FA's Approach May Be Counterproductive

Despite the cultural differences presented above, there is cross-national consensus that insult, abuse, and discrimination in sport as elsewhere are unwanted. At the same time, it is also true that "casual racist remarks remain commonplace in everyday circles, in football as elsewhere."[35] So the pressing question is: Is the English Football Association's rough approach the best way to oppose it?

The answer to this question depends on what the FA wanted to achieve. If the purpose was to beat the drum once again to promote the image of English football as antiracist the answer is "yes" but if the purpose was to reduce racism in and around football the answer is "no" because it is a false assumption that the language people speak—and consequently the words people use—controls how they think. As popular as this position is within academia (where the position is known as linguistic determinism), it is hard to find much support of it in the real world.[36] Language develops by living people's creation of words whereby they can describe and talk about phenomena and ideas in a meaningful way. It is phenomena in the real world that form the conception of the phenomena in our mind.

Language cannot be the primary factor in our understanding of the world. If that were the case, it would have been impossible for humans to develop language in the first place. It is not the terms we use that form the way we perceive the things we are talking about. Unfortunately, it is not so that if we stop using negatively laden terms and replace them with neutral terms or terms with positive connotations we can change the meaning and improve the status of things and persons. For instance, it does not change the poor persons' status or material wealth that we begin calling poor people "unfortunate," "economically challenged," or even "rich." By the same token, it does not change the racist's perception of the non-Caucasian whether we identify the person in question as "negro," "person of color," "Afro-American," "black," or "African American," for example. In fact the need for consistent change of the signifier shows us that the perception of the signified is still problematic. If you want to see positive change in the world, you have to work for it in the real world. Words do not make change materialize.

The power of reality is stronger than the power of words. Policing the language only draws attention away from this. There are countless examples of terms deemed politically incorrect and replaced with a neutral term only to be replaced by another new neutral term later on because the previous neutral term did not manage to stay neutral, since it still referred to the same negatively perceived reality.

Hence, if the FA by imposing the eight-match suspension has succeeded in erasing the word *negro* form Suarez's vocabulary, they still have done nothing positive in terms of antiracism. The first serious indication that the lengthy ban was counterproductive if the purpose was to stamp out football racism came when Liverpool played

Manchester United at Anfield on 28 January 2012 in the FA Cup. This was the first game between the two sides since the eight-match ban had been imposed. Occasionally throughout the game Evra was abused from elements in the crowd. Phil Gannon, a fifty-eight-year-old father of five was even arrested and fined for having made monkey gestures while loudly taunting Evra.[37] This time the abuse was intentional and definitely not an "in-the-heat-of-the-moment" incident.

Moreover, Suarez, who was not a racist before the incident, has in people's opinion—by the media exposure and the severe punishment—been branded as a racist and thereby become a potential hero for true racists. Furthermore, exposure and severe punishment has clearly done nothing positive in terms of reconciling Evra and Suarez. The hostility between the two players was there for all to see when Suarez could not force himself to shake hands with Evra during the official fair play gesture ahead of the game at Old Trafford. And after the game, which United won, Evra ran toward Suarez and celebrated provocatively in front of him on his way out of the field. The exposition of enmity was bad for the image of the game. The FA could have taken action once again in accordance with the first sentence of rule E3: "A Participant shall at all times act in the best interests of the game and shall not act in any manner which is improper or brings the game into disrepute."[38] The fact that the FA let these improper incidents pass suggests that the organization understood that there would be no end to the sanctioning if a zero-tolerance policy was implemented because then each and every provocation and expression of hostility or disrespect should be punished according to rule E3.

What may not yet have been understood, though, is that the Regulatory Commission—by doubling of the sanction compared to the entry point—tacitly sent out the message that black people must still be regarded as a disempowered and vulnerable species that need special care and protection, and to no avail.

If Evra ever again should ask Suarez on a football pitch: "Why did you kick me?" there is no doubt he will not answer as he did. But what would happen if he answered with an arrogant smile: "Because you remind me of Michael McDonald," which could be interpreted as a racist reference to the retired black Canadian kickboxer known as "The Black Sniper," or simply "Because you are . . . ," which could mean anything but which Evra on the basis of their previous feud could easily understand as intended racial abuse in disguise? The mind always finds a way to express its thoughts and feelings. In light of this, it should be obvious that policing language is like herding cats. It is not in any way suited to force respect or to stamp out racism. All the FA achieved by its handling of the Luis Suarez–Patrice Evra controversy was to polish its image of being an antiracist organization while at the same time expose its impotence when it comes to understanding and actually remedying the real-life problem of racism in football as well as in the wider society.

This incident exposes the complexities of "race" in relation to a globalized soccer culture where players from different backgrounds and cultural upbringing establish divergent views of what does and does not constitute "racism" or other forms of differentiation— we can no longer view "race" through a British colonial apologist lens and must see it as a complex and contextual issue in the sporting world of the twenty-first century.

II.

Race and Ethnicity
in Historical Context

INTRODUCTION

David K. Wiggins

CLR James would certainly agree that an understanding of the interconnection among sport and race and ethnicity is a crucially important way to more fully comprehend power relations in most every society around the world. These interconnections, while never stable and varying in intensity over time and place, have always been especially salient during periods when sport was being transformed in different locales from an informal, unorganized activity to a more highly structured and organized phenomenon. This institutionalization process, characterized by among other things standardization over time and patterned social arrangements, make clear how individuals and groups go about contesting a place in sport and the impediments they face when attempting to do so. Unfortunately, for some individuals and groups, finding a place in sport has been particularly difficult. Skin color, nationality, citizenship, cultural differences, class, and a host of other factors have, if not resulting in categorical exclusion, segregated individuals and groups, denied them leadership positions, and influenced both their participation patterns and media portrayal realized for their athletic accomplishments.

The four chapters in this section, while varying in methodological approach and time periods and geographical locations, all address, in one way or another, the issue of different individuals and groups contesting their place in sport and the constraints they faced as minorities suffering at the hands of racialist thinking and racially discriminatory practices. Tellingly, in spite of the constraints they encountered, these individuals and groups were sometimes able, because of extraordinary physical skills and sheer force of will or social connections or pure luck, to become full participants in sport and realize local, national, and international reputations for their athletic exploits. The success of these individuals and groups was meaningful in that it served as a symbol of possibility, nurtured a sense of identity and self-worth, and both challenged and reaffirmed long-standing dominant gender ideology and social class standing.

In the first contribution in this section, Benedict Carton and Robert Morrell analyze Zulu stick fighting from 1800 to 1930. Utilizing a variety of secondary and primary source material, Carton and Morrell make clear that stick fighting among Zulu boys and young men was about reinforcing male prowess and assisting in establishing social standing. A sport that would change significantly over time, particularly following the elimination of the Zulu state in 1879, stick fighting fit squarely into the kinship-based orientation of African sport where Zulu boys and young men tested their manhood while exercising self-control and refraining from intentionally inflicting damage on their opponents. Carton and Morrell conclude their chapter by noting the increased commodification of stick fighting and that the sport is seemingly becoming a part of the fledgling hospitality industry in South Africa.

Matthew Stephen provides important insights into the socially constructed nature of race and how the concept played out between whites and people of color, especially Aborigines, in his chapter on cricket and minstrel shows in South Australia's Northern Territory between 1869 and 1911. Indicating that this period corresponded with Britain's "Age of Empire" and witnessed the development of modern sport, Stephen utilizes Benedict Anderson's concept of imagined communities and Stuart Hall's analysis of representations to illustrate via cricket and minstrel shows how whites in the isolated Northern Territory established a cohesive society in which they distanced themselves from people of color and exhibited various forms of racial discrimination and practices resembling plantations in the British Caribbean and American south. Stephen makes the important point, however, that Aborigine athletes were sometimes able to transcend white racism and participate in the higher levels of sport. Two mixed-race athletes, Willie Allen and Antonio Spain, challenged dominant racial stereotypes and their marginalized position in society by achieving success in a number of sporting activities.

The complicated and slippery nature of ethnicity and identity is the focus of Gerald R. Gems's chapter on the participation of Italians in sport in the United States. Similar to Patrick Miller's notion of muscular assimilationism—the idea that success in sport was a means for African Americans to overcome deep-seated racial stereotypes and become equal participants in all walks of American life—Gems contends that Italians realized greater respect and a degree of acceptance in the United States "through their physicality." It was not a smooth and easy process, however. As Gems notes, Italian immigrants were one of the least esteemed ethnic groups in the United States; they had to cope with ugly racial epithets and were restricted to living in segregated urban areas and working at menial jobs for low wages. Eventually, second-generation Italian boys, who had to overcome both racial discrimination in the United States and their parents' own lack of regard for sport, found a great deal of success in a variety of sports at various levels of competition. Perhaps no sport was more significant to the Italians than boxing. Like the Irish before them and later blacks, jews, and latinos, pugilism was crucial to Italians because it was perceived as a way out of the ghetto and as a means to rise up the socioeconomics ladder.

Jennifer H. Lansbury concludes this section with a chapter dealing with the careers of the great African American women athletes Alice Coachman and Althea Gibson. She provides a very nice comparative study of Coachman and Gibson, relating the press coverage given the two well-known athletes and how they were categorized along gender and racial lines. A central theme of Lansbury's chapter is that Coachman and Gibson were marginalized as athletes by both black and white newspapers and because of it have been lost to public memory. Importantly, their fading from public memory is also a result of the relatively limited scholarly attention given them and other prominent African American women athletes. While outstanding African American male athletes have had their stories told through multiple scholarly biographies, the stories of their female counterparts have generally been relegated to children's literature. Why their stories are deemed suitable for this genre rather than serious scholarly analysis is open to speculation, but there is little doubt that CLR James would have chalked it up to both racialized and gendered bodies and the complexities of a society in which power relations and social capital are of paramount importance.

On Display: Cricket and Minstrel Shows in Australia's Colonial Far North, 1869–1911

Matthew Stephen

Introduction

In 1898 A. B. Patterson, one of Australia's most popular writers, acknowledged that Palmerston, Australia's northernmost town and "capital" of South Australia's Northern Territory, had a character very different from other Australian cities.

> Palmerston is unique among Australian towns, inasmuch as it is filled with the boilings over of the great cauldron of Oriental humanity. Here comes the vagrant and shifting population of all the Eastern races. Here are gathered together Canton Coolies, Japanese pearl divers, Malays, Manilamen, Portuguese from adjacent Timor, Cingalese, Zanzibar niggers looking for billets as stokers, frail (but not fair) damsels from Kobe; all sorts and conditions of men. . . . There is an Eastern flavour to everything.[1]

When Australia's colonial masters conceived a trading entrepôt on Australia's far-north coast during Britain's Age of Empire, they hoped to create a rival to Singapore and Hong Kong. Although a failure as a trading center, because Palmerston (established in 1869, renamed Darwin, in 1911) was too far south of the rich China trade routes, it did create a British bridgehead on Australia's distant and isolated northern frontier.

The Northern Territory's development as a British outpost was forged by its social and geographical isolation on Australia's far-north coast. In early 1870, the South Australian government maneuvered to ensure that the international communications cable to Australia from Java would land at Port Darwin and continue to Adelaide via an Overland Telegraph line. The Overland Telegraph provided much-needed economic impetus to Northern Territory development during the construction from late 1870 to August 1872. The discovery of gold by construction parties also resulted in a short-lived gold rush. The telegraph line gave the settlement of the Northern Territory frontier a distinctive character. Unlike other Australian colonial settlements that grew from a coastal hub, the Overland Telegraph resulted in the frontier extending immediately along the line over the length of the Northern Territory, acting as a "safety net in the wilderness."[2]

The struggle on the frontier between the white settlers and the Aboriginal owners to possess the land was an ever-present influence on Northern Territory society. In contrast to southern colonies, where colonization overwhelmed Aboriginal nations through weight of numbers and superiority of arms, whites in the Northern Territory remained a small minority.[3] Consequently, a socio-racial hierarchy developed that gave northern Australia a distinctive character. White settlers set aside the social, economic, religious, and class differences that defined and differentiated other Australian colonial societies in favor of a unified and cohesive society that simplistically delineated and distanced a white "us" from an alien, colored "them." In the virtual absence of an educated middle-class intelligentsia, which in other Australian colonies may have ameliorated the excesses of racism toward Aborigines or other "aliens," racial attitudes were often extreme, insular, and therefore resistant to distant "outside" influences. A White hybrid imagined community evolved that combined the tropical Gothic of Britain's far-eastern empire with the plantations of the American South or the British Caribbean.

Benedict Anderson's concept of imagined communities and Stuart Hall's analysis of representations are two important related themes in considering how white settlers established and maintained a British colonial society in the Northern Territory. Anderson developed his concept in the context of evolving European nationalism and nation states in the eighteenth and nineteenth centuries.[4] He identifies "nation-ness" and nations as imagined communities, cultural artifacts with profound emotional legitimacy that distil complex historical forces into a "modular" form that can be transported and adapted to a great variety of social terrains.[5] Hall describes how representations constructed and supported white settler society:

> It sets up a symbolic frontier between the "normal" and the "deviant". . . what belongs and what does not or is "Other," between "insiders" and "outsiders," Us and Them. It facilitates the "binding" or bonding together of all of Us who are "normal" into one "imagined community"; and it sends into symbolic exile all of Them—"the Others"—who are in some way different—"beyond the pale."[6]

A cornerstone of British colonialism was a strict socio-racial hierarchy underpinned by a construction of white superiority informed by Social Darwinism that whites had an inalienable right to impose themselves as the "natural and undisputed masters"[7] of "lesser" races and occupy their lands. The small white community, anxious about its position, was close-knit and exclusive. By the turn of the twentieth century, the complicated socio-racial hierarchy was well established.[8] Although based on Broome, in northwestern Australia, Susan Sickerts's description of its social hierarchy is indicative of northern Australia generally:

> There were class distinctions within each nationality as well as racial distinctions that impacted on the whole community. At the very bottom of this hierarchy were the Aboriginal people who had become outcasts in their own land. Next were the bulk of the indentured Asian men, mixed race people and other poorly paid workers. Then came the Asian merchants, the indentured divers and tenders, and some of the mixed race population who had citizenship rights or, in the case of women, had married foreign men. At the top were the Europeans, small in number but dominant in power. There was some social interaction between Aboriginal women and indentured Asian men, but the bosses and other powerful whites did not (apart from business and clandestine nighttime visits) associate or socialise with other races.[9]

Sickert alludes to one symbolic social boundary that was often crossed, despite the social taboos and stigma: sex. As Robert Young observed in *Colonial Desire*, "sexuality was the spearhead of racial contact."[10] Nothing highlighted and threatened the maintenance of social distance and order more than the progeny that resulted from interracial relationships. Mixed-race, "hybrid," or "poly-ethnic" communities, as would develop in Palmerston and the Northern Territory, were a dangerous contradiction that threatened the imagined British community.

The white occupation of the Northern Territory from the 1869 to 1911 corresponds with Britain's "Age of Empire."[11] It was a period of unprecedented social, political, and technological convergence that included the development of modern sport and leisure. In Britain and other developed economies it was driven by "the transformation of the rural economy, industrialisation, urbanisation and the expansion of the middle class and its quest for respectability."[12] As an economic backwater on the fringe of Empire, the Northern Territory was untouched by many of these factors but it does provide a fascinating case study of the social diffusion and pervasiveness of colonialism. The later part of the nineteenth century was also a period when concepts of British Imperialism, and what it meant to be part of the Empire, became fractured. Notions of racial equality as British imperial subjects gave way to a different imagined community where identity and allegiances were shaped by "whiteness" and racism disguised as movement toward nationalism and self-governance.[13] This transcolonial[14] movement of shared "white" interests not only connected British colonies in Australia, South Africa, Rhodesia, and New Zealand but also included California and the United States. In the Northern Territory, this resulted in a society where Aboriginal rights were ignored and racist sentiment dictated that the lives of Chinese and other Southeast Asian "aliens" should be subject to restriction and control. The advent of Commonwealth control of the Northern Territory in 1911, guided by the white Australia policy, resulted in legislation that enshrined an administrative regime intent on racial segregation and the imposition of greater restrictions, surveillance, and control over the Aboriginal, Asian, and colored populations. In this chapter I explore concepts of British and transcolonial imagined communities and representations in the Northern Territory using sport, in particular cricket, and, to a lesser extent, amateur theater in the form of minstrel shows, to illustrate how social institutions were essential in constructing and supporting the social, emotional, and moral legitimacy of colonial outposts and in establishing and maintaining social "distance" and control.[15]

The modular form and transportability of British imagined communities is illustrated in the first edition of the *Moonta Herald and Northern Territory Gazette,* printed on board the *Moonta* carrying the South Australian survey part to establish Palmerston in 1869. The article "New Years Day On Board The Moonta" provides the template for a typical "British" New Year.

> On this day, so celebrated during the long ages for its sports and pastimes, fitting commencement of a New Year, our fancy carries us back to those we have left.
>
> We [illegible] a picture them to ourselves enjoying the [illegible] to their hearts' content, at Races, Picnics, and Regattas; ever and anon perhaps, casting a thought on those five hundred miles away, and probably wondering what our occupations are on this festive day.[16]

The *Moonta's* last stop for supplies before reaching the Northern Territory was Kupang, Timor, a Dutch colony approximately two hundred miles north. During an "entertainment" to mark the visit, one of the survey party delivered a "Nigger stump speech."[17] Minstrel shows were a popular form of entertainment throughout the British Empire and the United States and another component of the imagined community transported to the Northern Territory. Minstrel performances would become a common feature of amateur theater in Palmerston.[18]

Early failed attempts at British settlement in Australia's north meant Palmerston's establishment was by no means assured.[19] Although work dominated the survey camp, there was time for some recreation. The first amateur performance on 4 August was a "niger [*sic*] entertainment."[20] Cricket was observed in the surveyor's camp in August 1871[21] and an athletics carnival was held on 31 September 1871.[22] Early sports in Palmerston were organized around annual and/or holiday events. Public holidays are important elements in the construction of an imagined community because they gave a sense of normality and reinforced the social order by celebrating a shared past and present.[23] Christmas Day in 1871 was celebrated with a shooting match, and for the first time Aborigines were invited to participate in a public sporting event. "The natives were assembled in front of Government Residence, to display their ability in throwing the spear" at a target featuring the figure of a man.[24] It seems incongruous that the government resident, with the task of ensuring friendly relations with the Aborigines, would be encouraging them to target men yet he rewarded the winner, Tommy, with a blanket and a tin of flour.[25] It poses interesting questions about black and white expectations and assumptions during the early years of white settlement.

David K. Wiggins, in *Glory Bound*,[26] uses the phrase "from plantation to playing field" to describe the slow journey black Americans took to achieve recognition in American sport. Colin Tatz saw the journey of Aborigines as the reverse. "Aborigines began with an element of freedom—and became prisoners of the protection-segregation system later."[27] In most Australian colonies the 1850s to the 1870s are identified as a period of relative "freedom" for the participation of Aborigines in sports due to the lack of legislation and control over Aboriginal lives based on the prevailing belief that they were no longer a threat to Europeans and/or were a "doomed race."[28] If there was a brief window of "freedom" for Aboriginal participation in white sports, it was in Palmerston's transition period from surveyor's camp to colonial settlement from 1869 to 1873. Aborigines enjoyed relatively free movement in and around the town so their participation in public social events as spectators, if not actual participants, was commonplace. Demographics demanded that initial interactions between Aborigines and whites were more cautious and restrained. This was because white survival and security depended on it: but once their dominance was assured, race relations took on a similar aspect to other Australian colonies.

After 1873, Aboriginal involvement in Northern Territory sport became strictly controlled and restricted to segregated voyeuristic "entertainments" to bolster and protect white self-image. Direct competition between Aboriginal or nonwhite athletes and whites was very rare. There were only rare glimpses in the Northern Territory that equates to the period of freedom enjoyed by Aboriginal athletes in other colonies where they

> were very much "gladiators," objects to be bribed and bet on; but they were also free to be human beings, to socialise with competitors, to be courted by the fans, to be allowed a room in a hotel, to fraternise with the ladies, to be served in public places.[29]

Northern Territory Aboriginal sportsmen did, however, share in the experience of being treated as a "special breed" of gladiatorial entertainers.[30] Rather than being given the status of contestant, they were anonymous actors in a public spectacle for the amusement of whites.

Aboriginal motivation to participate in sports can only be speculated upon. Many were probably interested in the rations on offer as cash prizes and/or clothes, tobacco, or food.[31] While meager, they were significant at a time when there was no other support provided for Aborigines who generally lived in poverty on the fringes of society. Others may have seized upon the rare opportunity to interact with whites in a different setting beyond the constraints usually imposed on them, and take center stage when there was constant pressure to move them to the periphery of white settlement.

Although Palmerston's white society was not as rigid as those of other Australian or South East Asian colonies, it did have some enduring characteristics. At its pinnacle was the government resident ,whose office gave it a recognizable social center and leader. Although not a vice regal position, it was the Northern Territory's equivalent of governor. His social circle included senior government administrators, the British Australian Telegraph Company (BAT) staff, professionals such as barristers and doctors, and members of the small but influential white merchant community. The BAT, established in Palmerston in September 1870, developed its own niche in Palmerston "society."[32] The cable was a symbol of imperial civilization and superiority that connected the isolated white settlers to the Empire. Consequently, the cable operators gained a special social status.[33] The BAT drew its officers directly from Britain or other "oriental" cable stations, and they were well versed in the traditions and customs of the colonial middle class and exemplified the "tropical Gothic" of Britain's far-eastern empire.[34] They gave the appearance of an exclusive gentlemen's club rather than a workforce and conspicuously had a large staff of Chinese and Aborigines who filled the roles of houseboys, maids, cleaners, gardeners, punkah operators, cooks, and washerwomen. Ernestine Hill described the BAT as being "in ramshackle Darwin but not of it, top rung of that pathetic little social ladder with so many rungs missing and its props in coal tar."[35] Their colonial counterparts, the Overland Telegraph Department, were also well educated but because they were recruited from South Australia and other Australian colonies, they never attained quite the same prestige of the BAT. Nevertheless, the cable staffs were integral to Palmerston's social elite and eagerly took any opportunities to display their British credentials in the form of "manly sports," amateur theatrics, and enthusiastic participation in dances, balls, and parties.

It is no coincidence that sport became more organized and stable following the first publication of the *Northern Territory Times and Gazette* [hereafter *Northern Territory Times*] in November 1873. The advent of the *Northern Territory Times* was an indicator that Palmerston was acquiring the trappings associated with a colonial "capital" although it only catered for a middle-class white readership, which in 1873 numbered forty.[36] The *Northern Territory Times* and the later the *North Australian* continued the tradition that had long entwined sport, entertainment, and newspapers and provided a detailed chronicle of Palmerston society.[37] It was a particularly narrow view of the small white settler minority that excluded more whites than it included and almost totally excluded the nonwhite majority. Nevertheless, the newspapers meant that sporting events, sports clubs, and sportsmen were recorded in a familiar format and style recognized throughout the Empire that continually reinforced the social order, connected them to the outside world, and affirmed a sense of imperial progress and continuity.[38] A survey of the first full year of publication of the *Northern Territory Times* in 1874 indicates that sport, musical entertainments, and amateur theater were an important but not systematically organized part of Palmerston's leisure. Palmerston's sporting and social calendar would have been familiar in any British colony and was important in normalizing the social order. The most common sports in Palmerston from 1874 to 1911 were horseracing, rifle shooting, athletics, and cricket. Other less prominent sports were archery, tennis, and sailing regattas. Only rifle shooting and cricket maintained regular competitions. The most common leisure events were amateur theater, musical entertainments, picnics, dances, balls, and "at homes."[39]

Cricket was among the first sports to be organized into a regular competition with four cricket clubs playing one another in Palmerston or Southport in 1874: Palmerston, Southport, Quidnune, and the Civil Service. The white population at this time was approximately 750. As the most British of games, cricket is acknowledged by many as a cultural cement and an important agent in forging imperial bonds. Its unique language and culture is said to act as a moral, social, and physical training ground, readily transferred and adopted throughout the British

Empire.[40] During the nineteenth century, cricket was one sport where Aborigines participated in various Australian colonies. In particular, the history of Aboriginal involvement in cricket on missions and the first international Australian cricket team to tour England are well documented.[41] Although the belief among missionaries and others in most Australian colonies that cricket was a valuable "civilizing" tool would have migrated to the Northern Territory, reports of games beyond Palmerston and the Northern Goldfields are rare. Organized cricket also heralded the arrival in Palmerston of *homo ludens imperiosus*.

As an essential part of British culture, sports were imbued with a spiritual and moral dimension that deeply affected "character" and the diffusion of sport throughout British dominions.[42] Sport and the so-called games ethic were an integral part of the British imagined community, and its invented traditions and language gave a meaning, connection, and unity with "home" that transcended and counteracted physical remoteness and social isolation. It evolved from an exclusive activity—confined largely to males of the British public schools and bourgeoisie—to an increasingly expanding middle- to working-class international phenomenon that provided a means for people of differing social standings and women to bond and engage with one another and within society.[43] Mangan labeled the archetypal imperial sportsman *homo ludens imperiosus*, a "man [of] firm duty, confident ambition, moral intention and applied athletics."[44] Although only an ideal, he was an essential element in the construction of a British-imagined community and a critical social agent in Northern Territory colonial society.

Homo ludens imperiosus found familiar home in the sports committees and social clubs of Palmerston. Like all colonial outpost where "social tone triumphed most where the accompanying display mattered more than the activity itself,"[45] they were important social institutions. An almost exclusively white male preserve, committee meetings provided regular opportunities for "sportsmen" to meet with one another and constantly display their "Britishness" within the confines of the ritual and etiquette of formal meetings. In Palmerston, the "club" was more an imagined space than a physical one. Being identified a sportsman in Palmerston was an immediate "social open sesame."[46] The small white community meant that individuals could join numerous clubs and societies but essentially mix with the same group of like-minded people, constantly reinforcing their credentials as a "sport" and gentleman. The BAT and Overland Telegraph mess halls acted as clubs for their staff, while sporting and social clubs and/or committees tended to be impermanent social constructs erected and dismantled according to need, relying on the local hotels as venues. Sport and social clubs were an essential aspect of their collective identity, which required conformity and order to counter an "alien" environment. They raised morale, gave them a feeling of moral virtue, gave public expression to social relationships, and constantly reinforced their collective ideals and status while at the same time distancing "others."

The convergence of sport and social institutions is illustrated in the resurgence of interest in amateur theater and minstrelsy in 1874. The N. T. Royal Troupe of Gymnasts, which performed as the Palmerston Minstrels, was made up of well-known cricketers.[47] Such was their popularity that *Northern Territory Times* commented that "we suppose the public have seen so much of Christy minstrels, with blackened faces, at fairs, racecourses, and street corners that they are fairly tired of the thing."[48] The structure of minstrel shows, with clear roles for the performers, made it easily reproduced by amateurs while also being familiar to audiences.[49] Similarly to sport, the transportability and recognizability of amateur theater made it an important means of constructing and sustaining the Britishness of the community and demonstrates the intersection of British and American influences.

Although it is difficult to imagine a setting more removed from the archetypal English village green than a recently cleared bush block in Palmerston, cricket reports in the *Northern Territory Times* repeatedly linked the two in the imagination.[50] Although still a very small and somewhat ramshackle settlement, Palmerston's social events assumed the rituals and neo-traditions practiced throughout the empire.[51] At the 1874 Palmerston Cricket Club Dinner, G. B. Scott,[52] the government resident, commented:

> he had been a cricketer for 35 years, and should still be glad to play a game with any one in the south. But in the Northern Territory the weather was rather too hot to admit of his enjoying the game of cricket, though it did not lessen the interest which he took in all manly sports.

It was further reported that one of the umpires, Mr. Connor,[53] who,

> as an old Eton boy, spoke of the manliness of the game of cricket.
> Englishmen took it with them wherever they went; and in England
> it did more than anything else to bring the different classes of soci-
> ety into harmony with each other.

Cricket was universally admired and reports included references to its
manliness, fair play, character, and Britishness. Manliness is a trait that
was particularly imbued through British public school education and
the private schools of the colonies. Many of the Northern Territory's
early sportsmen could be characterized as "socially ambiguous,"[54] and
evidence of their educational backgrounds is scant. Indications are that
many either came from "educated" backgrounds, or purported to, and
were well versed in the language and rituals of muscular Christians and
"manly" sports.

Manliness was a multifaceted concept central to the psyche of the
British colonist, but it was not confined to sport. The "socially ambiguous" men so common in Palmerston were attracted to the outer reaches
of the colonies for many reasons but the prospect of adventure, prosperity, independence, and prestige unattainable at home were tempting inducements. Another measure of manliness was "the degree of
mastery exercised over others within or outside the home."[55] Colonial
power and status were represented by the "possession" of servants or
the authority to control and direct the labor of others.[56] In the Northern
Territory, the nature of the master-servant relationship differed mark-
edly, depending on whether it was in Palmerston, the northern goldfields or on the frontier.

Plantations, the Economy, and Black Labor

Grenfell Price famously described the Northern Territory's history
up until 1930 as "a vast iceberg of failure, unmelted by the soft warm
waters of neighbouring success."[57] It is an apt description of the South
Australian administration, which never understood the physical or social
environment. The vast tracts of land and plentiful rainfall convinced
many that the territory could mirror other British tropical colonies

in sustaining agricultural plantations. Plantations were envisaged as a catalyst to development and a means to establish basic physical and economic infrastructure. In 1872 the South Australian government passed the Sugar Act, which offered a bonus of £1,000 for the production of sugar in the Northern Territory, which was later increased to £5,000 for the first to manufacture 500 tons of sugar.[58] Agricultural plantations in colonial Northern Territory were an abject economic failure but the white community embraced the social attitudes and mores of plantation societies.

The cheap labor demanded by agricultural plantations was always in short supply in the Northern Territory. The white population was too small and many thought unsuited to tropical labor. Many believed whites in the tropics were a "doomed race" subject to "racial degeneracy and dissolution."[59] The South Australian government's response to the demand for labor was to become the first in Australia to indenture Chinese labor.[60] The first group of 186 "coolies" arrived from Singapore in 1874. Most were employed in the northern goldfields, but others established businesses in Palmerston to cater for the growing number of Chinese immigrants. Palmerston's white colonists, who often took their lead from Singapore, were quick to employ male Chinese cooks and domestic servants in an attempt duplicate its "oriental" colonial lifestyle.[61] The employment of servants and keeping "others" in their place was at the very heart of British settler societies. British eastern experience considered Chinese as the preferred household servant while it was felt Aborigines were suited to more menial outdoor tasks such as laundry, wood chopping, and carrying water.[62] The master-servant relationship was built upon its own language and culture to sustain white power and control. Embedded with multiple meanings the term *boy* was applied to all male servants regardless of their age or race. The term entrenched racial stereotypes by emasculating the servant while positioning white masters as the only "real" men. Servants were paradoxically perceived as both servile and loyal but also potentially cunning, savage, and unpredictable.[63]

In the Northern Territory the combination of thwarted economic ambitions and the ever-present threat of an Aboriginal, Chinese, and colored majority challenged white settlers to develop measures to keep "others" at a safe social distance to ensure their control. This led to differing, and at times contradictory, responses determined by race and location. "The Chinese Question" became a constant topic of heated public debate in Palmerston where a small number of influential white storekeepers and merchants vociferously employed indignant moral outrage, supposed threats to public health, and racist nationalist rhetoric to agitate for greater legislative restrictions and controls on the resident and immigrant Chinese. The rapid rise in the Chinese workforce during the construction of the transcontinental railway from Palmerston to Pine Creek between 1886 and 1888 finally prompted legislative action. White settlers argued that unless Chinese migration was stopped, "we greatly fear that without something being done very shortly to ease this pressure, we shall be unwillingly forced into collision with the Chinese."[64] Mirroring the debate preceding the Federation of Australia, South Australia gradually introduced legislation to reduce the numbers of Chinese in the Northern Territory.[65] The prohibition of Chinese from new goldfields in association with the effects of a series of South Australian immigration restriction acts and the Commonwealth *Immigration Restriction Act 1901* resulted in a gradual decline of the Chinese population.

The legislative response demanded by the perceived threat of Chinese immigration is in stark contrast to the absence of law on the frontier. On the frontier, the expansion of the pastoral industry and the usurping of Aboriginal land and labor resulted in a "bizarre pattern of savage racial conflict and frontier paternalism."[66] The strategy used to occupy the land was simple; "to kill, and after a period of ruthless extermination, the second tactic was to incorporate the survivors into the station workforce."[67] Aborigines were forced to "come in" to the relative security of white settlements where they were tolerated on the fringe until considered civilized enough to be useful to their white masters.[68] In return, Aborigines entered a life of grinding poverty and oppression under the constant threat of violence although it did provide the possibility of access to valuable resources and enabled them to stay in close proximity to their lands.[69]

The Select Committee inquiry into the *Aborigines Bill 1899*[70] provided evidence of common frontier practices where "outside the boundaries of the more settled districts, that is, pastoral settlements, a different state of relations exists between Europeans employed on stations and aborigines."[71] The evidence of government officials and police was damning.

Northern Territory police inspector Foelsche noted in his submission the practice of "running down" boys (Aborigines) and girls and forcibly taking them to stations to work.[72] Government resident Dashwood, who drafted the bill, and mounted constable R. C. Thorpe both likened the use of Aboriginal labor to slavery.[73] The issue of the "evil" of "half-castes" was also raised repeatedly throughout the hearings.[74] It was suggested that attempts to "civilize" half-caste children would be enhanced by their removal from their family.[75] Dashwood's proposed bill was unsuccessful.[76] The South Australian administration did not introduce further legislation in relation to Aborigines in the Northern Territory until 1908 when the *Northern Territory Aborigines Act 1910* was introduced to Parliament, but was not enacted until 7 December 1910. Unlike the legislative response demanded to address Chinese immigration, white settlers preferred that the frontier remain effectively lawless, in the hands of interdependent complicit police and settlers beyond the reach and control of the South Australian authorities.[77]

The influence of frontier race relations permeated all levels of white society and was reflected and reinforced in the sporting and social institutions of the town. Northern Territory white settlers routinely applied derogatory terms to Aboriginals but "nigger" was very common. A letter to the editor entitled "The Black Nuisance," written by T. Burtt, a local lawyer, cricketer, and sometimes minstrel performer, was typical of the time.

> Several of the principle streets of Palmerston are periodically infested by gangs of unkempt, jabbering niggers—loathsome in aspect, scab-stricken in body—and caricaturing the decencies of civilized citizens by an ostentatious display of semi-cinctures almost as repulsive as nudity itself. For reasons of decency and morality such exhibitions should, I think, be restricted.[78]

Despite the pervasive racism, there were occasional interracial sports. Although organized sport was infrequent for most Australian public schoolchildren in the nineteenth century, there were rare sporting events for Palmerston's students.[79] School cricket matches in 1881 marked the first nonwhite involvement in cricket. The matches included Chinese Arthur Hang Gong,[80] W. Sing, and Hi Sing. There were also three players, Johnny, Ned, and Paddy, who can be assumed to be Aboriginal because their names were not printed in full.[81] Evidence also suggests that although Aboriginal children were rarely given opportunities to participate in organized sport, they did play their own games.[82] The extent of nonwhite sport activity is "hidden" because it was not reported in the newspapers unless it involved whites. The first report of adult Aboriginal cricketers appeared in 1882. The report of the Bankers and Storekeepers versus All Comers cricket match in the *Times* illustrates why such an event was a rarity and also the extent that "Americanisms" had entered the vocabulary.

> The two coloured storekeepers whom the innocent All Comers let their enemies "ring in" on them "just to make eleven, you know," managed to put together eight before they were separated. . . . Storekeeper's assistant Charlie followed [batting], and immediately afterwards was joined by William—("A rose by any other name would smell as sweet;" so would a nigger) . . . The "cullered genelmen" had a game to themselves (in which the field reluctantly joined), until they had made eight between them, when lovely, odoriferous William skyed one.[83]

The rare involvement of Aboriginal men in the game provides a glimpse into the master and servant relationships in Palmerston. As "storekeepers" Charlie and William probably worked in a local store doing odd jobs and menial labor. It is likely that they were not paid wages but rather tobacco, clothing, and occasional rations. They were well known enough to be grudgingly invited to play yet the commentary indicates the level of racial contempt and the banal predictability of the stereotypes, language, and attitudes adopted toward nonwhites. Although it was taken for granted that cricket and manly sports "induce good feeling and fellowship between all classes,"[84] this was never applied to Aborigines and "others" who were never part of the British-imagined community.

The growth in sporting clubs and events in the 1880s is mirrored by amateur musical and theatrical performances. Minstrel shows were popular because they provided amusing variety entertainment in a familiar form that showcased the talents of local performers while being adaptable to include local themes. They defied and mocked authority, and satirized reformers intent on repressing perceived rights and freedoms while also reflecting and reinforcing racial stereotypes. On occasions Palmerston's minstrels substituted "Aboriginals" for "niggers" in their performances highlighting their shared "status."[85] Minstrel performances also served multiple purposes in reassuring and reinforcing Palmerston's white settlers that they were keeping up with the modern theatrical trends of the British Empire while also reflecting their preoccupation and esteem for America.[86] The *Times* was replete with articles on America. It often referred to California as an example of the perils of Chinese immigrants and why they should be restricted.[87] By demonizing the Chinese and branding and portraying Aboriginals as "niggers" on stage by night, white settlers not only reinforced their own feelings of superiority and but emphasized Chinese and Aboriginal "otherness" as "lesser breeds without the law"[88] that mirrored their treatment by day.

The most significant economic event in the 1880s was the construction of the Palmerston to Pine Creek Railway and wharf between 1886 and 1889. This was a major boost to the economy and greatly increased the Chinese population, who made up the majority of the labor force. Increased economic activity and population growth saw a corresponding increase in interest in sports generally, most notably pedestrian match races. Aboriginal athletes were involved in some of these wagers although it only emphasized their gladiatorial status, subservient role, and lack of opportunities in a society where many regarded them as chattels.

> A hurdle race was run on Monday afternoon between blackboys owned respectively by W. Lawrie, G.H.H. Lamond, and J. Peperill, 120 yards, for a small sweepstake. After a great race between the dusky representatives of the Palmerston Butchery, the former won by about a yard. The third nigger came to grief early in the race.[89]

The overt reference to "ownership" of Aborigines was not common, but it does reflect the perceptions and attitudes of white settlers about the place of Aborigines in society.

Increasingly through the 1880s, sport imposed itself physically on the Palmerston landscape with the development of new sporting facilities such as a cricket oval, a rifle range, and tennis courts.[90] A cricket ground was an essential component of any self-respecting British colonial town. The ground gave community sport a focus, and it was credited with improving both the quality of the sport and the town's general appearance.[91] The new facilities also had the effect of alienating parts of the landscape and extending the town boundaries, further marginalizing the Aboriginal population and pushing them to the fringes. New facilities did not, however, guarantee sporting success. Cricket was in the doldrums in the early 1890s with ad hoc games played between members of the Port Darwin Cricket Club. To overcome the isolation and absence of genuine sporting competition, the game was boosted in mid-1893, with the invention of their own "representative" fixture, the "Outcasts" versus "Electrics" series. The game, given local "test" status, quickly became the most keenly anticipated cricket games in the 1890s and 1900s. The Electrics were made up of BAT and Overland Telegraph Department workers while the Outcasts were comprised of the rest of the community, reflecting the social hierarchy of Palmerston.

The 1890s began with a rare example of Aboriginal success in Palmerston's white sports and offered a glimpse of the relative freedom enjoyed by Aborigines in other Australian colonies. C. A. Murray, "a coloured sprinter,"[92] traveled to Palmerston from Queensland where he ran professionally.[93] Murray's arrival in Palmerston went unnoticed prior to the Palmerston New Year Athletic Sports. He took local athletes and punters unawares, winning the Champion Race and the Palmerston Handicap. Murray won prize money of £12 12s, in addition to wagers. He followed up a few days later with a match race against the Kimberley champion, J. Armstrong. Murray wagered £80 against Armstrong's £100 and gave him a two-yard start. Murray won by three yards.[94] This was a unique occurrence in territory athletics. It appears that Murray made a calculated and strategic decision to attend the Palmerston Athletics knowing it was unlikely that anyone would know him as a professional runner. In comparison with Queensland, the quality of Palmerston's athletics fields was poor, and his success paid handsomely. Socially, however, Murray was shunned. Had he been white, it is likely that he would have been feted at some dinner or social event, but there is no evidence to suggest how Murray spent his time after the races in Palmerston. Later reports indicate that Murray continued on to Sydney to compete in professional events at Botany although it was noted that "he has failed to secure a heat."[95] Murray's speculative visit to Palmerston appears to have been an aberration but it was the first "symbol of possibility" that nonwhite athletes could compete on equal terms with whites and subvert their dominance of territory sport.[96] When Murray left, sports soon returned to the status quo.[97]

In the report of the Palmerston New Year Athletics of 1891, it was noted quite matter-of-factly that in the "Throwing Cricket Ball" event the winner was declared to be H. F. Holt with a "fine throw of 106 yards . . . A blackfellow . . . after the contest hurled the ball 109 yards." To acknowledge Aboriginal athletic superiority was anathema to Palmerston's respectable "manly" sports, whose rhetoric of fair play did not extend beyond their own insularity and hypocrisy. The continuing dialectical contradiction was that whites could despise, even hate blacks, yet their conditional participation in sport was essential to bolster their own sense of white superiority.

At the 1895 Pine Creek New Years Sports, an Aborigine named Bismarck won the Maiden Plate and the Pine Creek Handicap. The report acknowledged Bismarck's superior ability. "The nigger they say, is a very warm member, and if the times were accurately taken they were the fastest handicap heats ever run in the country."[98] The white response was to ensure that it could not happen again. The programs for the Pine Creek athletics events in 1896[99] and 1898[100] included the clause "No aboriginals, or other coloured races, to be allowed to compete in European events." Bismarck's brief success, like Murray's before him, demonstrates that on rare occasions Aboriginal athletes were able to prise open the barriers to their participation and they could succeed. The white response to ban Aboriginal athletes out of hand demonstrates how sensitive whites were to any challenge to their "carefully cultivated mystique of authority."[101] Aborigines, Chinese, and others were always restricted to segregated novelty events, continually reinforcing white prejudice and their notions of social order.[102]

Although conditional participation of Aborigines and Chinese in segregated races was accepted in athletics, it remained rare in other sports. In 1894, two cricket games were played between the town's merchants and the Overland Telegraph Department. In the first, the P. R. Allen & Co. team announced before the game included Aboriginal players Burber and Mimatuer, while Nim was selected for the Overland Telegraph.[103] Nim did not play the game, but Dick and Manton, recorded on the score sheet as "(ab)," were included in the team.[104] The

"Mercantiles" were soundly beaten, but Burbur took two wickets in the first innings and top scored with Mimateur in the second.[105] They were again selected to play two weeks later although they batted at ten and eleven and did not bowl.[106] Significantly, the reports, unlike the first report of Aboriginal cricketers in 1882, were free of racist comment. Aboriginal participation was again indicative of their role in Palmerston generally. The Aboriginal cricketers were probably workers employed at the store and telegraph department who had daily contact with their white employers. This was common at the time, and it suggests that there were whites in the community who displayed greater tolerance. When translated to the sports field, it shows that on a personal level, relationships between black and white were not always characterized by antagonism, prejudice, and exclusion.

A further indication that racial attitudes were changing in some quarters is found in children's sport, which was infrequent during the nineteenth century with the exception of races during the athletic carnivals. In November 1898, the *Times* reported on the first inter-school cricket games in Palmerston between the public school and the Reverend Father O'Brien's private school. The second game was significant because it included the names of Willie Allen and Antonio Spain, both of mixed-race backgrounds.[107] Although not selected in the original team, Allen excelled in the two games played.[108] Allen also competed in athletics,[109] and another series of schoolboy cricket games in 1900.[110] Allen was a Larrakia youth while the Spain family originated in the Philippines. The experiences of Allen and the Spain family typify the complex and paradoxical social relations of the Northern Territory as among the first to challenge the stereotypes that had marginalized Aborigines and "others" in sport. Their participation in sport indicates that they must have conformed to white expectations but at the same time it subverted white authority because they were part of the growing multiracial colored community that was considered such a threat to the white settler society.

Born in 1886,[111] Allen's mother, Nellie, was a Larrakia woman, and his white father was either Dr. Morris or Mr. Shepherd.[112] Illustrating the "furtive but obsessive interest"[113] British colonial governments took in tracing miscegenation, a survey was undertaken by the Northern Territory police in 1899 to identify "half-castes" in the Top End. It reveals that a thirteen-year-old Allen was employed in the household of Charles Edward Herbert, a Darwin barrister, who became government resident from 1905 to 1910. It was Allen's relationship with the Herbert family and in particularly his friendship with the sons, Lloyd and Oscar, that opened Darwin's normally exclusive sporting society.

Antonio Spain was born in Cebu, Philippines, in 1863 and migrated to Australia to work as a trepang diver, and later a tailor, on Thursday Island. In 1885, he married Elizabeth Massey, an English woman, in Cairns and they moved to Darwin in 1894.[114] Antonio worked as a barber in Darwin while Elizabeth was an enterprising businesswoman who at various times ran a boardinghouse, a catering business, and contracted on building projects. Between 1886 and 1909, Elizabeth had eleven sons and one daughter. Both Antonio and Elizabeth were highly regarded in the white community. From 1898 onward, when Antonio competed in a North Australia Cycling Club "Manilla man" race, the Spain name became well known in sporting circles, through their regular participation in athletics, cycling, rifle shooting, and boxing.[115] Their sporting participation began with children's events, and gradually they entered adult competition where they competed in the main white events.

Cricket beyond the White Boundaries

Australia's Federation 1 January 1901 was described by the *Northern Territory Times* as "the greatest event in the history of the colonies."[116] The cornerstone of Federation was its white Australia policy underpinned by the *Immigration Restriction Act 1901*. Alfred Deakin, a leader of the Federation movement and Australia's second prime member, saw the white Australia policy as a means "to draw a deep colour line of demarcation between Caucasians and all other races . . . all coloured men are stopped unless they come merely as visitors."[117] Deakin may have been somewhat surprised that Palmerston's Federation celebrations comprised of a children's sports day, a fireworks display organized by the Japanese community and a minstrel show.[118] The reality of Australia's far north and the imagined Australia encapsulated in the white Australia policy were never reconciled.

The South Australian government used federation as an opportunity to finally relinquish the debt-ridden territory to the Commonwealth although the process would take ten years to complete. Life in Palmerston was little affected by Federation although some cracks had appeared in the façade of white sporting domination and segregation beyond the boundaries of the town cricket ground and gaze of *Northern Territory Times*. Alfred Searcy, sub-collector of customs in Palmerston, noted:

> The youngsters [Aboriginal] as a rule were lively, cheerful, mischievous little devils, and great mimics. Cricket was a favourite game with them, and it always seemed to me that there was infinitely more fun in watching a crowd of these black nippers at the game—their paraphernalia simply consisting of two sticks, a couple of rusty kerosene tins, and a ball of rags, than viewing the biggest cricket match ever played.[119]

There are also occasional glimpses that in private, whites, Aborigines, and Chinese would play together. The Palmerston billiard champion was a local Chinese, "Toby" Ng King, who defeated numerous white challengers before large crowds between 1905 and 1909.[120] The *Northern Territory Times* assessed King's win in one match as "almost as damaging to white prestige as the recent Burns-Johnson combat."[121] Fred Blakely, a visitor to Palmerston, described impromptu cricket games he and his friends played in 1907 between mixed teams made up of two whites and "young Chinamen and Aboriginals to complete them."[122] The games were further evidence that whites, blacks, and Chinese were willing and able to play informally together but stereotypes and cultural taboos were difficult to overcome. The games attracted the "whole population of Chinatown . . . for they were keen cricketers, and the abo camp would there be in a body."[123] But, according to Blakely, the games ceased because his white boss disapproved.[124] Although the evidence is incomplete, these activities suggest that beyond the boundaries of public white sport there was a more diverse world of "hidden" sporting activity.

Regardless of what occurred informally, public recognition of the Aboriginal, colored, or Chinese community was rare, grudging, and veiled. White settlers staunchly supported the white Australia policy. In 1909, the *Northern Territory Times* called for the expulsion of "Asiatic and colored" children from the public school so white students were not "disadvantaged."[125] W. G. Stretton, protector of Aborigines, who had been resident in the Northern Territory since white settlement, gave a hint of what was to come in expressing his concern for the well-being of "half-caste" boys whom he considered "unfortunate beings" and that "a more complete control is most urgently required."[126] Stretton's concerns were addressed by the advent of Commonwealth control of the Northern Territory.

An Aboriginal Cricket Champion

The Commonwealth of Australia took control of the Northern Territory on 1 January 1911. Most residents felt that life could only improve after the final years of the South Australian administration, an era characterized by "bitter failure and abject resignation."[127] Like Federation, the Commonwealth takeover was marked by a sports day that encapsulated how far the Commonwealth's ideal of a white Australia was from the multiracial reality of Darwin.

> The crowd was of the usual cosmopolitan character—complexions ranging from the dark skinned native aborigine, through various shades to the white epidermis of the dominant Caucasian. . . . There were types present of many races—Japanese, Javanese, Chinese, Cingalese, Arabs, Africans, Phillipinos, and muscular islanders from South Seas with many nondescript gradations between the more sharply defined types, evolved from circumstances and propinquity. . . . the Caucasian element predominated perhaps but "colour" of varying shades was so pronounced that the ardent White Australia faddist glancing around the grounds might well be excused for feeling a trifle despairful of ever seeing his patriotic ideal realized in this tropical portion of Australia.[128]

The 1911 census figures confirm that Darwin was Australia's most racially mixed town.[129] One of the Commonwealth's first official acts was to introduce the *Aboriginals Ordinance 1911*. It provided the legal and administrative framework to control Aboriginal lives in a regime of "protection" and segregation. For the first time in the Northern Territory, legislation was instituted that formally created a racially based hierarchy built on "an oppressive paternalism that severely restricted the civil liberties of Aborigines in a way that would last for decades to come."[130] Issues of "race" and "color" within a diverse mixed population became an increasingly important part of the continuous debate on Northern Territory race relations. Willie Allen, living in Darwin's Chinatown, on Cavenagh Street, at the time was one who managed to move beyond the strictures of the *Aboriginals Ordinance*. Although there is no evidence of how he earned his living, a letter from Herbert Basedow, the Commonwealth chief protector of Aboriginals and chief medical officer, granting a request from Allen to marry indicates that he was able to support his bride.[131] Despite the growing desire to "control" and regulate the lives of Aborigines and "others," some like Allen continued to defy racial stereotypes and regulations and lived within the white community.

The influx of public servants to Darwin that accompanied the Commonwealth administration in 1911 reinvigorated sport. Civil servants had always played a significant role in sport as organizers and participants. The year 1911 was also Willie Allen's most successful sporting year, when at the age of twenty-five, he won prizes in both cricket and rifle shooting. Allen scored the first century of the cricket season that secured him the Reade trophy.[132] By mid-season Allen was top of both the batting and bowling averages, 50 and 7, respectively.[133] He also competed in two athletics carnivals during the year: the Coronation Sports in June and the North Australian Cycling and Athletics Association Sports in October where he competed in a number of events, including the "Blackboys race."[134] This is the only sporting event where Allen was identified as an Aborigine. This appears to be a curious anomaly because his Aboriginality was not reported previously. It is impossible to determine what the racial politics of this decision to enter the "Blackfellows race" may have been. It may have been as simple as wanting to secure the ten-shilling prize, but having competed with a white partner in a "siamese race" earlier in the day, it was not because he was "restricted" to Aboriginal-only races.

More sporting success followed for Allen. At the Palmerston Rifle Club closing day Allen received seven shillings six pence for his sixth place in the competition.[135] Allen's acceptance into the Rifle Club, a bastion of white society, is quite remarkable given the racial antagonism, and in particular, the fear whites had of Aborigines with guns. Greater accolades came from the Darwin Cricket Club, which acknowledged Allen as "the best all round player in the club by annexing no less than three out of six possible prizes. He is a good field, a safe bat, and at times has shown himself to be a tip-topper with the ball."[136] Despite his awards, they do not appear to have gained him an invitation to the club's end-of-year concert that featured the Darwin Nigger Minstrels, made up of his white cricket teammates.[137] Neither Allen nor the Darwin Nigger Minstrels would have known that it would be one of the last minstrel performances in Darwin. Minstrel shows had been on the wane since Federation, perhaps another indicator that racial attitudes were entering a new phase.[138] Allen's sporting year concluded in December when a number of sporting and social events were held to celebrate the visit of *HMS Prometheus*. Allen was selected to represent Darwin in both a shooting match and the first British Association football match to be held in the town.[139] Sports events against visiting British warships were considered special events because it gave the locals an opportunity to demonstrate their talents against Britain's "finest." Allen's selection in this prestigious game made Allen the first Aborigine selected to a Darwin representative team.

A "Measure of Hope"

The sporting experiences of Willie Allen and the Spain family show that change was possible. Their admission to white sport was a precursor of events to come during the Commonwealth administration of the Northern Territory and an embryonic assertiveness of the Aboriginal, colored, and Chinese communities. It demonstrates that social boundaries could shift and white perceptions of color, for those who conformed to "respectable" behavior, were selectively malleable and ambiguous. Their inclusion in white sport offered a "measure of hope"[140] that racial stereotypes, marginalization, and segregation could be overcome through talent and tenacity. Individuals could negotiate a place in sport and society demonstrating that "race" is a dynamic and changing construct that differs according to political circumstance.[141]

Although it is clear that the racial caste barriers were shifting, they were by no means broken: admission was conditional. Individuals who conformed to white expectations and cultural mores could gain entry to the white world of sport but this alone was not enough. Support from a prominent patron or from within the white community in general were also essential to gain white sanction and acceptances. Allen and the Spains had prised open the door of white sporting segregation, but for the majority of aspiring nonwhite athletes, it remained firmly closed and the struggle for greater equality and rights had not begun. Government and social affairs remained in the hands of the white elite. Their imagined ordered British middle-class community was restricted to a view of the world that rarely strayed beyond Darwin and their latticed verandas overlooking the Arafura Sea. White attitudes reflected their perception of what a "civilized" society should be. If they could continue cricket, horseracing, minstrel shows, and quadrilles in their tropical Northern outpost then surely "civilization" was assured. This cosy social world based on denial of the social reality would only change with the onset of World War I. It was only then that Darwin's sports fields transformed to become a public stage to demonstrate nonwhites' sporting talents, challenge white domination of sport, and fight for rights beyond the boundary.

CHAPTER 7

Competitive Combat, Warrior Bodies, and Zulu Sport: The Gender Relations of Stick Fighting in South Africa, 1800–1930

Benedict Carton and Robert Morrell

For at least the past two centuries, rural Zulu boys and young men, like their counterparts in neighboring Swazi, Sotho, and Xhosa communities, have reinforced their gender identity through competitive stick fighting. This contact sport tested male prowess and helped determine social rankings. Winning one-on-one bouts enhanced a Zulu boy's status in his peer pecking order.[1] While giving and taking punishment, he competed to become, in the eyes of his cohorts, a manly hero or champion (*iqhawe* or *ingqwele*), and a "bull" (*inkunzi*) in body and spirit. Thus, in the context of patriarchal hierarchies, stick fighting defined and reinforced codes of masculine success.[2] That is why losers could face scorn as effeminate rejects (*izingwadi*) and cowardly "Momma's boys" (*amagwala*).[3] To the extent that painful outcomes defined the

Editors' Note: We express our gratitude for the financial support of the National Research Foundation of South Africa; its funds helped us complete the research for this project. We thank members of the Concilium on Southern Africa at Duke University and participants in the Inaugural International Conference on Sport and the Global South at George Mason University for their timely insights. This chapter draws on some excerpts from Benedict Carton and Robert Morrell, "Zulu Masculinities, Warrior Culture and Stick Fighting: Reassessing Male Violence and Virtue in South Africa," *Journal of Southern African Studies* (March 2012); we acknowledge the editorial board of the *Journal of Southern African Studies* for granting us permission to use these excerpts. This chapter also builds on our collaborative work in Benedict Carton and Robert Morrell, "Kampfsport, stählerne Körper und Mannhaftigkeit in der südafrikanischen Zulukultur," *WerkstattGeschichte* 44 (2007), 65–78.

sport, so too did one prevailing rule, exercising self-control in the heat of confrontation. The *iqhawe* and *ingqwele* were often judged, not by the bad wounds they received or inflicted, but on victories they earned in brief clashes, which heeded the referee's plea for restraint when an opponent appeared on the verge of suffering grievous harm. Our chapter traces these dimensions of stick fighting from the beginning of the 1800s to mid-1900s. We first explore their influence in the formation of military bodies (e.g., soldiers and regiments) during the reign of Shaka kaSenzangakhona and other independent Zulu kings. We then consider the fate of stick fighters and their sport after British troops in 1879 destroyed the Zulu state and eventually brought it under the dominion of the Natal colony (see map below). Many coming-of-age practices died in this imperialist conquest but some managed to survive. In the final decade of the nineteenth century, Natal authorities restricted Zulu martial socialization while they also expanded migrant labor, opening other avenues for rural youths to engage in competitive combat. By the early 1900s, stick fighting had begun to inspire young Zulu men to meld influences of modernity and tradition into hybrid expressions of leisure such as competitive *ngoma* dancing, which maintained long-standing rituals of peer belonging and, in some cases, led to collective action that resisted the forces of white domination. It is in our discussion of twentieth-century stick fighting that we detail the rules and maneuvers of this contact sport.

Our theoretical framework draws on R. W. Connell's critique of homosocial sports that bolstered "hegemonic" masculinities.[4] Writing in this vein, scholars of gender relations have probed how macho school games promote the belligerent behavior of boys, especially in relation to girls and sexual minorities (e.g., gay males and females).[5] This mode of recreation shares much in common with the group violence that entrenches sexism and other types of oppression. Connell's ideas have inspired some South African historians, in turn, to investigate both the deleterious and constructive effects of contact sports in colonized black societies.[6] Whatever the case, it is still widely assumed that when Zulu competitors, in particular, hit each other with sticks, their actions merely symbolize injurious patriarchy. Though we accept that the bodies of these sportsmen never stopped being potential weapons of destruction, we challenge this supposition. Stick fighting adhered to conventions that militated against permanently damaging a person. Thus, the question we pose at the outset is: did stick fighting promote a particular understanding of masculinity among Zulu men that fostered aggression in some contexts and respect in others?

In addition, this chapter advances a line of argument that emerges from recent pathbreaking studies of leisure and sport in Africa.[7] A 2002 review article published in the *International Journal of African Historical Studies*, written by Emmanuel Akyeampong and Charles Ambler, surveys much of this scholarship. African leisure and sport, they argue, are collective experiences linked to the generational obligations of kinship-based societies, as opposed to a Western idea that encapsulates individual activity outside the realm of work.[8] Telling evidence in the *isiZulu* language supports their view. One of the most comprehensive Zulu-English dictionaries compiled over decades by expert linguists defines sport as *ukudlala*, meaning to play or frolic with others. Stick fighting has long been understood as *ukudlala indunku/izinduku* (stick/ sticks) and *ukudlalisa indunku*, which in English translates into the following phrase: "to cause to contend" against an opponent who belonged to a peer group (i.e., *iviyo*, adolescent company; plural, *amaviyo*; and *ibutho*, regiment of young men or adult men; plural *amabutho*).[9]

Indeed, atomized notions of play would not capture the motivations of Zulu stick fighters who learned to spar with fellow herd boys from the same district. Or, *izingqwele* who entered wage migrancy in age-sets at the turn of the twentieth century, when young African men in Natal were conscripted by colonial authorities into labor brigades to build roads between settler towns, commercial farms, and the bustling port of Durban harbor.[10]

"It Would Be a Fighting Bull, Pitch Black in Colour"

The cultural idioms associated with stick fighting (*ukudlalisa indunku*) are rooted in oral histories that are difficult to verify. While fragmentary details of stick fighting in the Zulu kingdom appear in European travelers' accounts, these sources are complicated by ethnocentric exaggerations, which require a critical appreciation of the nineteenth-century Western disdain of Africans and what they did in their "primitive" times with their "savage" bodies. Data generated by archaeologists offer less biased evidence and a good outline of the life of stick fighters in precolonial homesteads bound by marriage, birth, and allegiance to a chief.[11] Since at least the sixteenth century, the homestead (*umuzi*) served as a focal point of everyday activities, with one patriarch controlling rights to labor in a domestic hierarchy subordinating women to men and juniors to seniors. Livestock husbandry was the domain of males, while crop cultivation was the responsibility of females. In hills and valleys surrounding their familial homestead (*umuzi*), herd boys passed some of their time sparring (*ukungcweka*). The skills they honed with wood switches were employed to guard cattle, a preeminent source of bridewealth that enabled children eventually to marry and create their own families. Of course this sketch of gender divisions presents a static portrait of domestic responsibilities, which, according to Sifiso Ndlovu, were far more "interchangeable." Ndlovu's groundbreaking investigation of "women's power in the Zulu kingdom" highlights how girls took care of livestock and even participated in combat. They "'alusa[ed] or looked after cattle" for homestead patriarchs who did not have sons to perform this task, he writes. Moreover, during the early Zulu kingdom, "the presence of girls in military zones (amakhanda or barracks)" meant that "females actively participated in . . . warfare." King Shaka enlisted them in his regiments. Before entering combat, they constructed their own weapons from wood (spear handles) and hides (war shields). Such skill implies they had previous herding experiences, which invariably entailed making switches and skinning livestock.[12] Given these examples, it should come as no surprise that there is evidence to suggest Zulu girls also engaged in stick fighting, if only occasionally. However, we found few informative sources, beyond the anomalous reference in colonial-era ethnographies,[13] to flesh out this illuminating claim. We would have relished uncovering a snapshot like the one below taken in 1981 by the medical anthropologist Rachel Jewkes during her fieldwork. It depicts Xhosa women swinging into their sport in the rural Transkei, a territory three hundred miles south and west of the historic Zulu kingdom. But such visual representations of indigenous female recreation are rare finds in the primary records of South African history. We know of no similar image in photograph collections of relevant archival repositories, cultural museums, and university libraries, but we hope one day to be proven wrong.

What we do know is that leaders of the Zulu state exploited the social conventions of livestock husbandry to enhance their martial institutions. Despite Ndlovu's important qualification, it remains the case that Shaka's kingdom state was highly patriarchal; Zulu men largely exercised decision-making powers and reserved for themselves numerous privileges that attested to their superior ranking over women. At formative stages of their masculine development, men would also shoulder the principal responsibility of defending the realm. King Shaka's army derived its organization from the very structure of age-sets, which consisted of herd boys who were commanded by young men expert in stick combat (*izingqwele*). By the end of the eighteenth century, when European merchants in Delagoa Bay (Maputo, Mozambique) increased ivory trafficking, chiefs had begun sending age-sets to kill elephants for coastal traders. Hunting on this scale molded boys who tended cattle into disciplined, fleet-footed soldiers. As ambitious chiefs sought to control the profitable sale of tusks, they clashed violently. In subsequent regional conflicts that facilitated the rise of Shaka, age-sets transformed into the regiments (*amabutho*) that underpinned Zulu military might.[14] Other evidence indicates that Shaka promoted stick fighting as a training workout for his recruits. In the early twentieth century a renowned Natal official and ethnographer, R. C. Samuelson, illustrated the ways in which Zulu boys exercised loyalty to "King and country, hearth and home." Samuelson delved into the formative practices of martial culture, featuring recollections of aged oral historians who were once hardened soldiers, among them "one Mthende, a Zulu of the Zulus, . . . of the uFasimba regiment that saw military service under Kings Tshaka [*sic*], Dingana and Mpande."[15] Their transcribed accounts reveal as much about warrior manhood as they do their singular recorder. Samuelson not only spoke isiZulu fluently with his informants; he also spoke confidently about stick play, which he embraced while gamboling as a child in the bush around his father's mission station in KwaMagwaza, an area ruled by independent Zulu kings. Samuelson elaborated on this sporting life and the upbringing of his local cohort, the rural Zulu boy who "would, at the age of about seven years, when he commenced to look after the calves, . . . [receive a] name from his comrades [reflecting his combat aspirations], and yet another when he reached the age of about fifteen—the fighting age. When he . . . qualified as a soldier for the

[Zulu] King, he would be given still another name. . . . [Thus, the] male child . . . would be taken step by step in the way he should go until he became a full-fledged soldier." Samuelson believed the identity of every Zulu boy was given distinctive meaning through one form of physical competition, stick fencing, which transformed the herder into an "effective defender." The most basic "fencing was called . . . UkuQagulisana," signifying a joking relationship. Such good-natured contests required "[n]o shield . . . at first . . . but as the boy grew older, he would be given a diminutive shield, followed later by larger ones, until he eventually received the war shield." At this stage, adolescents recognized that *ukuqagulisana* had become stick fighting, which was no laughing matter, for they had to "take hard blows" and simulate "methods of warfare."[16]

Samuelson's research focused on the expansive development of Shaka's army, when *amabutho* proliferated in number and size to support campaigns that extended the territorial dominion of the royal house. But soon after the Zulu founder was assassinated in 1828 and his successor King Dingane took control, the strength and scope of the regiments were considerably diminished. By the mid- to late nineteenth century, subsequent Zulu leaders such as King Mpande and his eventual heir, Cetshwayo, faced even more limited military options. For one, their political territory was hemmed in by the British colony of Natal to the south and Boer Transvaal Republic to the west.[17] Thus, the regiments turned to internal (national) concerns such as patrolling the boundaries of the Zulu state. Occasionally, they battled one another when civil strife racked the royal house, but more often they maintained their preparedness through extraordinary ritual spectacles in which they performed martial anthems (*amahubo*) and war dances (*ukugiya*), and arranged competitive stick bouts. During the king's annual "first fruits" celebration, for example, soldiers were rewarded for their service by being allowed to consume a bull's body (*umzimba wenkunzi*) in a tradition called the *umkhosi wokweshwama*. A Zulu patriarch named Mshanyankomo, whose father was King Mpande's court praiser, recalled in 1922 that such "umkosi ceremonies in the Zulu country" entailed sending conscripted male youths to capture "a fighting bull, pitch black in colour [*inkunzemnyama*], a big one . . . that would rip out people's innards."[18] The *inkunzemnyama* was driven back to the royal enclosure and ritually handed over to the young men, who circled their quarry like stick fighters. At first, they pawed at their bovine opponent, keeping him within striking range. Then they rushed in for the clench, grabbed the bull's horns and in quick, coordinated movements wrenched his body down. On the ground, the bull's tongue was pulled out and mouth clamped shut. After the *inkunzemnyama* was strangled to death, commanders slaughtered and roasted it, shortly thereafter parceling strips of meat to the young warriors.

This grand ceremony is still performed by Shaka's royal house in contemporary South Africa. Despite the international outcry of animal rights activists, the *umkhosi wokweshwama* is conducted by the current Zulu King, Goodwill (Jabulani) Zwelithini, and attended by the democratically elected president, Jacob Zuma, a former herd boy and stick fighter from rural Nkandla, KwaZulu-Natal province.[19] Especially noteworthy are the ornamental regalia of stick fighters, visible on the arms and across the waist of young men taking on the bull.

During the time of the Zulu kingdom, *umkhosi ukweshwama* observance instilled an esprit de corps in the royal army. Although regiments no longer embarked on wide-scale operations by the mid-nineteenth century, they belonged to a drilled and motivated military with a robust defensive capacity. Within the Zulu polity, their ability to protect the king and his subjects was highly valued. Immediately beyond their borders, however, the attitude was decidedly different. To colonial power, the *amabutho* were an unmitigated menace, particularly in Natal where British bureaucrats and settlers worried endlessly about an impending attack of "savages" from Zululand. By the 1870s, imperialist policymakers in London were demonizing Zulu regiments as the gravest threat to Anglo-Saxon civilization in Africa. Some of these officials conspired to erode the sovereignty of King Cetshwayo and convert his soldiers into cheap labor for white capitalist farmers in nearby Natal and diamond mine owners profiting from the mineral revolution in distant Kimberley, a boomtown in the Cape colony. English-speaking settlers in Natal, for their part, continued to vent fears that the "man-slaying" Zulu would wipe them out; their voices joined a chorus clamoring for a British confederation over all of southern Africa.[20] In 1878 the British high commissioner Bartle Frere promised to fulfill these demands. He was fascinated by the "fine fitness" of "Kaffir tribes," but regarded King Cetshwayo's regiments as blindly driven, since they learned to play with

sticks in boyhood, to partake in "bloodthirsty" conquest. Frere's fixation on Zulu martial socialization was shared up by others in his military circle such as Carl Griesbach, an officer in the Royal Fusiliers who
would miss the Anglo-Zulu conflict but not the ensuing "small war of
Empire" in Afghanistan.[21] In January 1879 Frere was instrumental in
initiating a British invasion of the Zulu kingdom. Early in the operation, several columns under the command of Lord Chelmsford were
annihilated after Cetshwayo's regiments, racing into rifle fire, stormed
an encampment of imperial soldiers at a place called Isandlwana. In
that battle Zulu soldiers used their weapons in hand-to-hand combat—a
crucial skill acquired in stick fighting—to deliver one of the most devas-
tating defeats suffered by the British in colonized Africa. But by midyear,
Queen Victoria's troops had overrun the kingdom, killing thousands
of civilians, deposing King Cetshwayo, and pulverizing his *amabutho*.[22]

"Nobody Will Throw Dust in My Eyes!"

With the Zulu state defeated and its regiments disbanded, white Natal
authorities from the 1880s onward accelerated their appropriation of
land and imposition of taxes.[23] Yet, even with these intrusions, herding
practices that inculcated customary norms of male toughness persisted
from Zululand and Natal into Pondoland and Lesotho,[24] where livestock husbandry was a central feature of local indigenous economies.[25]
Meanwhile, an industrial boom around the First World War hastened
the flow of migrant labor to growing towns like Durban, where officials
enforced draconian measures to safeguard whites-only leisure facilities
and residential areas, thus laying a legal foundation for the apartheid
system. The tightening of racial segregation prompted some black elites
like African National Congress (ANC) founder Pixley Seme to press
for the preservation of tribal vestiges of male socialization like competitive combat. Indeed, as white rulers proscribed large-scale military
exercises associated with the training of Zulu regiments, stick fighting grew in importance as a symbol of black resistance to emasculating colonialism.[26] Rural-born Zulu workers, for their part, sought to
assert their masculine presence in urban areas by creating spectacles
animated, in part, by warrior codes of stick fighting.[27] They attracted
crowds to their municipal compounds by organizing *ngoma* (dance)

competitions, with teams of performers adorned in insignia recalling the late nineteenth-century battle Isandlwana and mimicking the routines of stick fighting. Labor migrants also formed street gangs known as *amalaita*, which marched abreast on sidewalks, armed with sticks and the confidence of champion combatants.[28]

Not surprisingly, from the end of the nineteenth century onward, settlers expressed a range of responses to the shifts in stick fighting. Some recognized the changing nature of this martial art by sponsoring public performances of choreographed practices, as the imprimatur of Durban's native welfare officer and publicity bureau on the *ngoma* program above illustrates. Most white authorities, however, continued to regard stick fighting as a frightening bellwether of violent "tribal" undercurrents.[29] Thus, they closely monitored the social turbulence attributed to the sport, noting in police files and trial transcripts what their local interpreters reported about the sexual machinations of young Zulu sportsmen. Some of this documentation contains muted references to assaults, which could be triggered when a fighter beat an opponent and saw his victory as a sign of future success in another arena of "conquest," involving girls who he presumed would accede to his "winning" advances, whether they liked to or not. Defeat in a stick bout could also bring feelings of emasculation and incitement to rape.[30] Certain primary materials offer perspectives of this phenomenon, among them "native law" cases dealing with the "seduction" of girls and young women in tribal reserves. White officials attributed this crime of "indecent assault" to disintegrating patriarchal order and mounting youth defiance. In this context, government courts accepted at face value the worst stereotypes of defendants. Young Zulu men charged with rape were arraigned as "boys rabid with bloodlust." These legal proceedings, especially the testimony elicited by prosecutors, prompted us to ask: what was at stake for competitors in stick-fighting bouts that led to sexual violence?[31] In seeking answers we branched into other fields of African studies.

Scholars researching this question in several Sub-Saharan regions have reached interesting conclusions. For example, Margrethe Silberschmidt shows that in the 1990s when young East African men, once touted by the international aid lobby as the engine of postindependence prosperity, could not secure jobs due to collapsing labor markets, they turned their backs on family and became destructive and

self-focused. Their detrimental behaviors included abusing female relations, having multiple sexual partners, and drinking excessively, just as
the AIDS pandemic arrived on the continent. In South Africa, Thokozani
Xaba found that young male activists who rose to prominence in townships during fierce antiapartheid protests in the 1980s resorted a decade
later to car hijacking and gang rape. Their criminal conduct intensified during the incipient years of postapartheid democracy, when pro-
jected educational training and enrichment opportunities (touted by
the African National Congress, the liberation movement in power from
1994 to the present) never fully materialized. In these two cases disaf-
fected young men encountered situations poles apart from what they
were promised, that is, a new dispensation that fulfilled the restorative
needs of the marginalized masses. Instead, the unpredictable location of
men made them more vulnerable, which, in turn, heightened levels of
contestation over the meaning of manhood.[32] Under these circumstances
it is possible to comprehend why gender violence could become commonplace. Without the material means of asserting their dignity *and*
control—through work with a living wage—men were moved to exert
their bodily muscle. This may be one of the reasons why stick fighting in
rural Zulu communities is still popular. The sport remains a vital conduit
for expressions of masculinity because most boys and men can participate in it, whether they have employment or not.

A hundred years ago, this fact was not lost on authorities in settler-
ruled Natal where black subjects vastly outnumbered white citizens.[33]
Although legal officials lacked the wherewithal—i.e., the will and
manpower—to abolish stick fighting, they still sought to manage what
they envisaged as the broader violence that this sport allegedly incited.
The gender sensibilities influencing this governing impulse need to be
clarified. The pioneering anthropological research of Jonathan Clegg,
the isiZulu linguist and world music impresario, reveals that such colonial concerns did not extend in meaningful ways to the safety of girls
and women. In fact, he argues, magistrates truly worried about the all-
male repercussions of stick fighting when older boys and young men
mobilized into armed bodies and targeted one another, first for competition, then for retribution.[34] Thus, by the end of the nineteenth century
and turn of the twentieth century, Natal Native Affairs officials were
implementing specific laws that expressly outlawed the enrollment of

military regiments and any chief's proclamation to gather for a "first fruits" ceremony. In tribal reserves magistrates increasingly regulated the number of sticks that could be carried in public, particularly when bands of unmarried men traveled to community celebrations like weddings, where they courted sweethearts and took part in their favorite martial art.[35] Finally, through mounting prosecutions, courts clamped down on a wider range of peer rivalries involving young men using sticks and sometimes more deadly weapons like clubs and spears.[36] Nowhere was this more the case than in Msinga district of the Thukela Basin, which according to Clegg's study of "ideologies of vengeance," was a hotbed of youth feuding over land use and territorial boundaries.[37] This compelling topic will be discussed later in the chapter.

Yet despite these government interventions, stick fighting retained remarkable continuities over the course of the twentieth century. This view emerges in many of the interviews that we conducted. Our informants represented different generations—old and young, and some in between. They came from rural chiefdoms in the Thukela Basin, a geographical and historical divide between the Zulu kingdom and the Natal colony. The questions we posed covered diverse topics, from the rules of engagement to perceptions of the sporting body. All respondents described how they confronted opponents on communal ground away from homesteads and entered combat aware they were required to heed the instructions of "coaches and umpires" (*izingqwele*). Sparring or "good-natured" fencing (*ukungcweka*) was a favorite way for boys to learn the regime of giving and taking punishment, as well as priming muscle groups for the clench and backpedal, whirling hits, and fast footwork. An aesthetic model of the tested fighter was also discussed. He was supposed to be dexterous with a bull-like torso. In rural Zulu communities, this ideal of fitness is as coveted today as it apparently was long ago.[38]

When integrated together, the archival and oral sources divulge even more about the intricate customs and various outlets of stick fighting. For example, early twentieth-century ethnographies and contemporary informants reported similar rhetorical approaches to beginning a contest. It was common, they said, for a stick fighter at the start of a bout to communicate his zeal verbally by singing regimental anthems (*amahubo*) that cautioned his competitor against winning at all costs.

When contestants ignored this warning, the consequences could be disastrous, not just to the combatants but to society at large. In 1920 a Zulu patriarch named Mangati alluded to verses of one ballad describing a tragic battle between two Zulu princes and stick fighters, Cetshwayo and Mbuyazi, both of whom claimed to be King Mpande's heir apparent. Their royal row ignited a civil war in 1856 that killed thousands in the Zulu kingdom.[39] A stick fighter could also initiate hostilities by daring an opponent with a "throw-down," an *inselelo*, such as "I challenge you to a fight." If agreed to, "the reply would be Woz'uzithathe 'Izinduku' (sticks understood), meaning 'come and take them,' i.e., 'come and see if you can master me and deprive me of my sticks.'"[40] Other challenges politely cloaked belligerence. A contestant might jab his rival in the following way: "Gee, you, I won't let you, so-and-so, throw dust in my eyes. Nobody throws dust in my eyes!" As further barbs were traded, one of the competitors might raucously praise his heroic (*iqhawe*) virtues or leap into a solo war dance (*ukugiya*) that climaxed in stomping. His pounding feet evoked bovine fury and the sheer force a young man displayed when with his bare hand he chopped the hardest bone of a slaughtered bull, its jaw (*elifuphi*). Today, older boys and young men arrive at rural weddings ready to instigate rhetorical combat using the call-and-response mode as their first weapon of choice. Their accompanying headman (*induna yezinsizwa*) might stir things up by loudly inquiring, "Where are the bulls?" To which his charges might respond lustily, "*Nanzi izinkunzi!*" Here are the bulls! This word play could lead to *ukugiya* square-offs and a stick-fighting contest in a field far from the nuptials, pitting the young men in the groom's party against their counterparts in the bride's contingent. In Clegg's recent study titled, "The Social Construction of Zulu Masculinity—Stick-fighting, the Giya and the Dance," he explains that *inkunzi* men were "not easily controlled." In fact, they had to be "constantly marshaled and cajoled" into behavior befitting the gravitas of patriarchal homestead heads.[41]

Big (multiday) marriage ceremonies invariably included a stick-fighting tournament. It was usually arranged by male youths and refereed by their designated "war captain," an *igoso* who drilled fighters from a cluster of homesteads.[42] He presided over a contest, which lasted no more than a few minutes, the standard duration of almost every organized bout. The *igoso* normally intervened after there was a decisive collision or one of the opponents crumpled to the ground. Each fighter typically carried a long blocking stick (*ubhoko*); a short stick (*umsila*) to slide through the back of the shield and grasp as a handle; and the striking weapon (*umshiza*), "the straight and smooth one, about 3½ feet long, and one inch or 1½ inch in diameter."[43] The start of action was tightly regulated "[w]hen the Umtshiza [*sic*] was used." If one competitor "was not equally armed, those [among the spectators] who were nearby would stop him until they had handed to his opponent weapons of equal quality."[44] Once two fighters faced each other, they normally tapped sticks or shields; then they launched into feints and charges, wheeling to deliver chopping blows. Onlookers such as the male guests at a wedding could observe a bout and spur on the action, but rarely did they bay for blood.[45] There was strict etiquette to follow. "When one got in a blow," a colonial ethnographer who witnessed stick fighting remarked, "he would shout to his opponent 'Yivume,'" meaning "'admit that the stick has reached you'"; and the one successfully warding off a blow would shout out Hlala, meaning, literally, 'sit down,' but actually meaning you are foiled." Many fighters valued a fair triumph, which left a beaten, if not maimed loser.[46] Still a contact sport like stick fighting led to serious and occasionally crippling injuries: a blinded eye, a punctured eardrum, a broken wrist. A crushing hit to the crown or temple could produce a brain injury. Lasting marks—dented brows and other signs of harm to joints and extremities—were seen as badges of honor, especially the head scar (*ingozi*).

Sometimes a competitor could flout rules of engagement and pummel his fallen foe, despite the umpire's cries of *"Maluju-wethu!"* and shouts from the crowd of *"Khumu!"* proclaiming "Enough!" This aggression most likely occurred when two adversaries from different districts desired to settle a grudge based on some rivalry over grazing land. Their clash could ignite an all-out "faction fight" involving the opposing members of each contestant's *iviyo*, which brought their sticks, along with knobbed clubs and short-stabbing spears.[47] In this context, tournament stick fighting could profoundly affect an entire community, especially in overpopulated "tribal reserves" around which white settlers claimed the most productive soil. In these chiefdoms, vendetta-driven conflicts over land were rife, and the threat of youths ambushing one another hung heavily over joyous events such as weddings. Consequently, as early as the turn of the twentieth century, patriarchal elders scheduled inter-district stick fights (*umgangela*) for a prearranged spot and time, thus affording a sanctioned space for young men's aggression and release valve for tensions caused by material scarcity.[48]

Whether a bout was scheduled by elders or organized by youths, it was not always the venue to express pent-up frustration, particularly if that frustration resulted from the shame experienced by timid or inept competitors, those otherwise derided as an *ingwadi*, the reject, and Momma's boy or coward, *igwala*. The name *ingwadi* carried a gendered insult; another idiomatic word for *ingwadi/umgwadi* was *umakoti*, meaning bride.[49] When a suitor courted a prospective bride, he could try to impress her by confronting another suitor with the saying, *uying-wadi* (you are the loser), before colliding with this rival in a stick fight. Another idiom recorded in a nineteenth-century ethnographic account revealed the emasculating ridicule embedded in *igwala*: "*Leli 'gwalana el'efuza unina!* (This little coward who resembles his mother)!" With few ways to escape this abuse, other than leaving home as a labor migrant, the *igwala* could face bullying throughout his childhood.[50] Although the primary sources testifying to this kind of harassment are sketchy, we have a sense of it from biographies of the Zulu king Shaka. During his childhood, Shaka's age-cohort purportedly teased and shunned him while he worked alongside other herd boys in pastures far from his protective family members. From the first hour of his life, the young Shaka was especially vulnerable to being scorned as an *ingwadi*, in this case a reject who bore one serious social disability. He was the "bastard" son of a prominent man who ruled over homestead patriarchs that acknowledged, as a matter of custom, the paternity of their children. Shaka's mother, Nandi, was not ritually recognized by his father, Senzangakhona, the chief of the Zulu people. Senzangakhona neither offered bridewealth cattle (*ilobolo*) for Nandi's hand in marriage nor, according to some oral traditions, paid the fine (*inhlawulo*, given in livestock) to the elders of this unwed woman whom he made pregnant. It is believed that Shaka's awareness of his own "illegitimacy" spurred the future king to prove his worthiness by training to be a fearsome warrior in theaters of combat, including the stick-fighting arena of his youth where he responded to verbal sniping with ferociously effective maneuvers.[51] A recent study by the medical anthropologists Yandisa

Sikweyiya and Rachel Jewkes presents another relevant, if unique, perspective on the link between illicit sex and boyhood bullying. They critically explore the contemporary dynamics of male socialization on cattle stations in Xhosa-speaking African communities of the Eastern Cape, a region just south and west of historic Zululand. In their findings Sikweyiya and Jewkes graphically describe the secret, systematic, and humiliating rapes of younger herd boys by older herd boys—and the revenge exacted by at least one victim against his perpetrator in a fight involving the use of a stick as a nonlethal weapon.[52]

The explanations for bullying in Zulu society do not allude to this pattern of intimate brutality, though we reserve judgment until comprehensive research is conducted on the possibilities of male-male rape in the Thukela Basin or elsewhere in present-day KwaZulu-Natal province. Suffice to say here, it appears from our archival and interview sources that childhood bullying took other forms because it was rooted in the uncompromising expectations of combat and the punishments that boys endured if they avoided or failed in battle. In the middle nineteenth century, a Zulu man from a lineage of "valorous" soldiers, Mpengula Mbande, explained how his father and his father's chief conveyed the connection between martial performance and manly reputation: *"A ng' azi ke mina. Ni ya 'kuba ni zihleba nina. Ubaba wa e ikqawe; a ku bonanga kwiti ku be kona igwala. . . . Uma ngi bona ni buya n' ahluliwe, ngi ya 'ku ni bulala; a ni yi 'kufumana 'ndawo lapa ekaya; ngi impi name uma n'esaba."* Our translation considers nineteenth-century definitions of *ikqawe*, hero or *iqhawe*. Mbande said his father was adamant about what was expected of a Zulu warrior: "I do not know what more I could do (or tell you). If you do not conquer, you will disgrace yourselves for this failure will be your own." Mbande noted that his father eliminated any "option to be a coward. . . . If I see you coming back conquered, I will kill you" *(ngi ya 'ku ni bulala)*. The connotation of *(uku)bulala*, to kill, could be taken literally or perhaps as a severe warning that should a boy or man become *igwala* he would deal with ostracism in his own community. To wit, the last sentence reads: "you will find no place for you here at home; I too am an enemy if you are cowards" *(a ni yi 'kufumana 'ndawo lapa ekaya, ngi impi name uma n'esaba).*[53]

Samuelson recorded similar sentiments in his ethnographic descriptions of "able-bodied men" who answered the call, "'Mayihlome!' ('to arms').'' He elaborated: "every male, from boyhood, entertained the instinct that he must be up . . . . There were no slackers in Zululand, and those that proved themselves cowards . . . [were expendable]. During the time of peace any member of a regiment found showing the white feather [the sign of idleness and surrender] was laughed to scorn by his comrades, and when the meat had been roasted for the regiment, the portion that was given to the Igwala, alias Ivaka ("coward") was first dipped in cold water and handed to him."[54]

This creed of valor—and attendant injunction against cowardice—appealed to great political figures of the twentieth century such as the African National Congress leader Pixley Seme, who in the 1920s extolled the spirit of stick fighters in the hopes of spurring indigenous opposition to white supremacy.[55] To this end, Seme spoke about the need to imbue future generations of Africans with the fortitude of Zulu boys who herded and sparred. The latter were, in his estimation, the opposite of white children enfeebled by bourgeois leisure and economics:

> He [the Zulu boy] does not need to be taken visiting all the time, like the child of a white person, which is always having balls and carts bought for it. For this came with the white people; it is their equivalent of looking after cattle. The beast of the white people is money. For money brings all the knowledge of the things which children of the white people have to learn about as they grow up. It prepares them for their kind of manhood. This kind of manhood, we see, is also ruled by money. Among black people it is ruled by cattle.[56]

While Western parents coddled their offspring, boys in Zululand traversed rugged pastures and forged solidarity: "For in the Zulu country looking after cattle was the great school for boys. Boys had their own *izinduna* [headmen] the *izingqwele* [the leaders of stick fighters and herd boys] who gave them orders, like soldiers, and who were obeyed by all the other boys." Stick bouts solidified their brotherhood: "If boys fought with one another, if they disputed over the grazing-grounds of the cattle, these matters were not interfered with by older people. For boys did not fight at their homes; they fought out in the countryside (*endhle*), where they were in charge."[57]

Seme longed for his vanguard of Zulu males to reflect proudly on their "country" values wherever they went. During his lifetime (1881–1951), this meant the urban world of capitalist production. By the middle twentieth century, the number of able-bodied Zulu patriarchs living year-round with their family was fast diminishing. The more typical male provider was a phantom figure in the reserves that spent months in town seeking employment or toiling in a menial job.[58] However, by leaving home, these migrants were not necessarily abandoning "tradition." Customary pursuits such as stick fighting were imported and adapted to the city setting, where along with other related (and evolving) cultural performances, they would leave profound marks on urban life. Labor migrants incorporated stick fighting into their town pursuits like warrior team-dancing (*ngoma*), which they rehearsed in and around labor compounds. During set routines on a Saturday or work holiday they donned precolonial combat regalia. On center stage, typically a patch of field, they brandished sticks in response to cues from their "war captain" (*igoso*) and stepped to syncophated regimental anthems (*amahubo*). More dramatic movements imitated a stick fighter's dance (*ukugiya*) before a bout.[59]

In the wake of the First World War, *ngoma* performances became one of the most popular forms of entertainment for many Africans in the mining industry around Johannesburg and for those working as domestic servants and stevedores in the Durban area. They turned their "Native Recreation Grounds" into leisure sites for weekend *ngoma* competitions. In doing so their outsized cultural interpretations of stick fighting and dance came to be a fixture of urban social life, attracting both uneducated labor migrants and "enlightened Bantu," the mission-schooled Christian (*amakholwa*) elite who could be quite critical of these displays of "raw tribalism." There was also a degree of white control over the production of *ngoma*, with police supervising teams at worker compounds and the Native Affairs Department sponsoring exhibitions.[60]

Most important, *ngoma* lured a number of audiences. In Durban white spectators such as government bureaucrats and settler families flocked to watch what was billed as "the spectacle of the full gala kit . . . [that] engender[ed] pride in the national costume" and an award ceremony by "His Worship the Mayor," who presented trophies for "Deportment and Discipline" as well as "Poise."[61] In addition *ngoma* electrified black crowds and stirred their martial feeling, which sometime triggered clashes between stick-wielding migrants and city policemen.[62] Needless to say, such acts of armed resistance, linked to warrior team dancing, alarmed municipal authorities. They associated it with other unlawful behavior, principally of gangs known as *amalaita* whose members were *ngoma* performers. The *amalaita* were said to have "specialised in theft, robbery and attacks on white residents,"[63] but this categorization of criminality overlooked their organization as hybrid regiments (i.e., urban versions of *iviyo* and *ibutho*) with the "obvious resonance [of] . . . stick-fighting of rural youth."[64] Gang membership involved obeying "captains and officers," namely, *igoso* and *ingqwele*, adopting group names like the "black bull," *Nkunzemnyama*, as well as patrolling turf "with sticks at night." These activities, even if antisocial, gave Zulu labor migrants a sense of masculine worth and channeled their frustrations, exacerbated by daily indignities like being "[d]riven violently off Durban's pavement by white males and frequently fired without notice by employers."[65] Hence, by the early to middle twentieth century, stick fighting had transformed from a form of combat preparation in defense of Zulu sovereignty to a proving ground for labor migrants confronting the forces of legalized racism.

Past as Prologue?

Today, stick fighting is no longer an explicit expression of young Zulu men resisting white supremacy in South Africa. Yet it still is part of traditional Zulu life, especially in rural communities where the martial sport reinforces male pecking orders and primes boys entering migrant labor for challenges of the urban street, hostel, factory, and shop. Yet with high unemployment (near 40 percent nationally and endemic now for a decade), stick fighting may no longer be preparing many young men in the countryside for the rigorous world of salaried work. One might ask, then, with South Africa continuing to shed thousands of jobs in industrial and manufacturing sectors, what processes are likely to transform the purposes of stick fighting? Such a question might focus on global currents buffeting the postapartheid democratic order as it seeks to lure overseas investors and tourists.

The fastest-growing segment of the South Africa's neoliberal economy is the hospitality industry, which not only receives injections of foreign capital, but also packages the country's top brands, wildlife safaris and "tribal" adventures. Besides game parks, one of the popular destinations is the cultural village resort, offering visitors from across the world a chance to participate in ethnographic dramas of the "real Africa." For example, at Simunye Zulu Lodge, a designated Natural Heritage Site and premier tourist attraction near King Cetshwayo's grave, daily entertainment includes stick fights. After watching a simulated bout, guests are invited to try combat with padded wooden weapons under the command of a Zulu-speaking lodge employee playing war captain.[66] If Simunye is any indication, a sport enjoyed by Zulu male youths might be shifting to an arena of greater commodification. Indeed, a boy growing up in the shadow of a "cultural village" who tests his prowess against peers might, if he is lucky, secure employment as a mock "warrior" in the hospitality industry.

Ethnicity in Black and White: Immigration, Sport, and the Italian Quest for Identity in the United States

Gerald R. Gems

In 1922, Jim Rollins, a black man, won acquittal in an Alabama miscegenation case when the judge decided that the Sicilian woman with whom he had been cohabiting was inconclusively white.[1] Such a ruling symbolized the liminal status of Italians within American society. Italian immigrants arrived in the United States without a national identity or any allegiance to the newly unified Italian state, which had only been liberated from centuries of foreign rule in the 1860s. Throughout the remainder of the nineteenth century, the largely illiterate southern Italians and Sicilians, who lived in squalid villages, labored the land for feudal overlords, and spoke in polyglot tongues unintelligible outside their immediate region. Their identity and their loyalty lay with their village, their clan, and their immediate family. Italians sought relief from their abysmal poverty and dire conditions, but not necessarily permanent residence, in the United States. Between 1880 and 1924 more than 4,000,000 journeyed to the United States, where they offered their bodies, in the form of physical labor, to build America. In return, they earned dismal, yet much higher wages than in Italy.[2]

America provided opportunities, but not respect. In the United States Italians were derogatively referred to as "guineas," a reference to the slaves from the west coast of Africa. In the sugarcane fields of Louisiana, Italians were called "niggers." In 1898 the Louisiana legislature moved to disenfranchise both Italians and African Americans by stating, "when we speak of white man's government, they (Italians) are as black as the blackest Negro in existence."[3] In the northern states, Italians, like African Americans, were segregated in confined urban areas, unwelcome in white neighborhoods. Like the Jews, Italians, as Catholics, carried the additional burden of an alien religion deemed to be unfit for assimilation in Protestant America.

The Americanization process proved to be a long one. Italians, largely segregated from and despised by the mainstream society, first had to recognize themselves as Italians. Italian language newspaper editors, usually northern Italian migrants, began the calls for unity and a national identity in the latter nineteenth century. Italians began celebrating Columbus Day as early as 1866. By 1893 Italian newspaper editors and mutual aid societies coalesced in a campaign to recognize Columbus Day as a national holiday during the Columbian Exposition in Chicago that served as the world's fair; but that movement floundered until federal recognition in 1934.[4]

I contend that Italians had greater success in attaining whiteness, a measure of respect, and a level of acceptance through their physicality. The Italians possessed an abundant masculine physicality that transferred well into American sports and games. That process, however, occurred with much generational strife, as southern Italians, who eschewed education as unattainable and disruptive to family power relations, sought economic gain in a full complement of family workers. When Progressive Era legislators passed child labor laws and required schooling, the Italians submitted only gradually and incompletely. For some, the process eased when Italian-born parents realized that their sons could actually make money, even substantial sums, by displaying their physical skills to public view.

As early as the late nineteenth century, a second generation of Italian boys (Lewis Pessano, aka Buttercup Dickerson, 1878) had taken up the American national pastime, baseball. Francisco Pizzola (aka Pezzolo), better known as Ping Bodie, became the most famous of the early Italian ballplayers as a colorful outfielder for the White Sox and Yankees in the World War I era (1911–1921); yet his father disowned him for Anglicizing his name.[5] By the 1920s Tony Lazzeri and Frank Crosetti of the New York Yankees gained stardom; but the pioneers paid a heavy price. Lazzeri indicated that the journey had not been an easy one. "It was always fight or get licked, and I never got licked."[6] He admitted that baseball was much easier than his previous occupation as a boilermaker, but he chafed at the frequent misspellings of his name in the media and designations as "the walloping Wop."[7] The media referred to Lazzeri and other Italian athletes in unflattering terms such as "wops" or "dagos" throughout the interwar period.[8]

Distance running presented an early and more acceptable recognition of Italian identity. Lawrence Brignoli, a Massachusetts blacksmith and the son of immigrants, was a champion oarsman, but he won greater fame as the winner of the 1899 Boston Marathon. As a member of two middle-class athletic clubs, Brignoli's triumph and acceptance symbolized the promise of America. He parlayed his early fame into a career as a sports entrepreneur, and his son followed in his athletic footsteps.[9]

In 1908 and 1909 Dorando Pietri of Olympic marathon fame traveled to the United States to compete in a series of long-distance races against numerous ethnic rivals. The media focus on ethnicity further drew the attention of Italians to their particular national identity; and Italians of various regional origins and social classes cheered their favorite in such encounters.[10] The auto-racing career of Ralph De Palma was presumably followed by more affluent Italians in America. Born in Italy, De Palma arrived in New York with his family in 1892, and his rapid rise to stardom in the upper-class sport of road racing further accentuated the perception of sport as a meritocracy and a means to social mobility. He graduated from racing bicycles to motorcycles to autos by 1909. De Palma captured the national championship in 1912 and 1914. In 1915 he won the Indianapolis 500, and set a world record in excess of 149 miles per hour in 1919.[11]

The less genteel sport of boxing seemed more suited to the physicality of the Italian peasantry. The ethnic rivalries of the city streets transferred readily to the boxing ring and helped to focus increasing attention on one's national identity. Sicilians, Neapolitans, Apulians, and Tuscans might all be drawn to an event that featured an "Italian" athlete, such as Casper Leon (Gaspare Leoni), born in Palermo in 1872, who boxed throughout the United States from 1891 to 1909 as "the Sicilian Swordfish." During the World War I era, others, such as Pete Herman (Peter Gulotta), the bantamweight champion, and featherweight titleholder Johnny Dundee (Giuseppe Carrora), known as the Scorch Wop, hid their ethnic identity in the throes of nativist resentment.

In a clear departure from the norms established in their ancestral homeland, young Italian women even challenged their prescribed gender roles. Maud Nelson (Clementine Brida) also learned and loved to play baseball. By 1897 at the age of sixteen she began pitching for the Boston Bloomer Girls. She pitched and played third base for a number of barnstorming teams for twenty-five years, playing with and against male teams from coast to coast. In 1911 she became manager and co-owner of her own Chicago-based team. The attraction of American sports had turned a young Italian girl into an athletic entrepreneur, which would have been impossible in Italy.[12]

Nelson's entrepreneurial ventures proved to be more than the efforts of an isolated iconoclast, for she spawned social change over the next generation of young women. In 1929 sports promoter Dick Jess formed a semipro team centered around Josephine Parodi, who assumed the moniker of Josie Caruso, possibly to capitalize on the fame of Enrico Caruso, the famed opera star. The team drew large crowds to its games and Parodi enjoyed some celebrity in newsreels until her marriage in 1931, when she returned to a more traditional domestic life. Other women stretched the gender boundaries thereafter. Margaret Gisolo starred at second base for an Indiana town team in the 1928 American Legion baseball tournament. Her winning hit in a championship game prompted a protest by males; but a tribunal that included Kennesaw Mountain Landis, the commissioner of baseball, supported Gisolo's team. The case drew national attention and spurred a multitude of other girls to take up the game. When the Legion banned girls from its competitions the next year, Maud Nelson hired Gisolo for her barnstorming teams during the 1930s. Gisolo used her ball-playing salary to gain a college education; she then became a lieutenant commander in the Navy WAVES during World War II and later became a college coach, inspiring women's teams through the Title IX era. Italian women had been among the pioneers of women's sport in America, challenging the hegemonic perceptions of gender roles and female physical abilities; while the Federazione Medici Sportivi (official sport medicine federation) in Italy warned in 1930 that "Italian women were first and foremost Italians and should, therefore, avoid any 'Americanization'" regarding their sport participation.[13]

Eleanor Garatti-Saville defied such proscriptions when she swam on the 1928 and 1932 US Olympic swim teams. She had been the national champion from 1925 to 1929, set a world record in the 100-meter freestyle, and won two gold medals on the relay teams. Three Italian American women competed for the United States gymnastic team at the 1936 Olympics. Consetta "Connie" Caruccio had been the national all around champion in 1933 and 1934, while Jennie Caputo won the 1936 US championship. Both joined Ada Lunardoni Cumiskey on the Olympic team. Caruccio returned in 1948 to join Helen Schifano and win a bronze medal. Such feats not only celebrated Italian American achievement, but served as an announcement of the changes taking place among Italian American youth in the United States. Garatti-Saville and Lunardoni Cumiskey had both married before their last Olympic competitions, a situation that would have relegated them to domestic duties and signaled the end of their athletic careers had they lived in Italy. Their athletic involvement indicated a departure from the norms and expectations of the first generation of Italian immigrants.[14]

Concurrently, Italian men made their most significant athletic strides in the sport of boxing.[15] The multitude of Italian boxers lived within the urban communities known as "Little Italies," fostering a greater sense of Italian identity for neighbors. The gradual acculturation of second-generation offspring born or raised in America spawned multiple and conflicted identities for Italians. Some even retarded the image of Italians in the United States. Luis Angel Firpo, an Italian heavyweight from Argentina known as the "Wild Bull of the Pampas," drew great media attention as a foreign body, but was deemed unfit by the American media. The *New York Times* reported that Firpo "is a combination of a Patagonian giant and a Genoese wild man. Like his progenitors, who were some of the most famous of the Italian vendettists . . . He is absolutely cold blooded."[16] When Firpo lost his championship bid to Jack Dempsey in a short, wild, and brutal match in 1923, the *Times* surmised that "If Luis Angel Firpo had the brain power in proportion to his tremendous strength, there is no denying that he . . . would be world's heavyweight champion this morning . . . But . . . (he) lacked that one essential—a fighting brain." Like thousands of Italian laborers, he was reduced to a physical body.[17]

That conflict became more evident in the boxing career of Primo Carnera, born in Italy and a favorite of the fascist government, the next

Italian to challenge for the heavyweight crown symbolic of racial superiority. Carnera's ill-fated saga drew even greater attention to one's Italian identity, compounding the dilemma over allegiance to one's ancestral or adopted home. That decision was exacerbated by the contention of the Italian government that its American residents remained Italian citizens, subject to Italian laws and military service. Many Italians had returned to Italy for service during World War I; and Mussolini considered the Italian communities in the United States as foreign colonies, in which he established Italian language schools and fostered support for his fascist policies. Italian American youth returned to summer camps in Italy to retain the bonds and identification with the motherland. With the onset of World War II, the loyalties of Italians in America remained so doubtful that even the parents of baseball star Joe Di Maggio faced detention as enemy aliens.[18]

While Mussolini's body culture promoted the fascist superman, Italian American bodybuilders and weightlifters countered such propaganda with displays of American might. Posed (literally) against the threatening body of Carnera, Charles Atlas, born in Italy as Angelo Siciliano, promoted his American developed body as the aesthetic masculine ideal.

Like the fascist leader, Mussolini, Italian culture required a public performance of masculinity. Many Italians living in the United States admired the bombastic Mussolini because he provided a measure of respect as he promoted an Italian national identity. Charles Atlas symbolized the Italian American body transformed, and he prospered within the democratic system in a growing celebrity culture. Atlas's own feelings of inadequacy were chronicled in his ads that told the story of a "97 pound weakling," a condition that mirrored the plight of many Italian Americans. To them and to others so afflicted, he sold the American dream of regeneration and a new form of robust masculinity, as he privately adhered to a traditional Italian lifestyle of domesticity, family life (a forty-seven-year marriage to Margaret Cassano), and frugality.[19]

Atlas served a particular symbolic function for Americans during the Depression. The public presentation of his body served as a performance of masculinity, an adherence to traditional Italian culture within a new American context. As Mussolini and Hitler presented images of their fascist supermen, Atlas served as an American counterpart, projecting strength in a period of economic depression. He appealed to Italians aspiring to acceptance and non-Italians whose physical bodies did not measure up to the required standards of whiteness.[20]

Tony Sansone, born to Sicilian immigrants in New York City in 1905, followed a similar path to recognition and success based on Atlas's model. A sickly child, he used sport as a means to develop his body before adopting the exercise programs of Atlas. In 1923 he won a physique contest sponsored by Atlas and engaged on a modeling career for sculptors and photographers, known as the American Adonis. His body was presented as a work of art, and he progressed into brief careers as a ballet dancer and an actor, before settling on an entrepreneurial venture as the owner of three gyms. For such men the body became a form of social capital, which provided access to the mainstream economic community. More importantly for Italians in general, in an era when scientific racialism emphasized the superiority of Social Darwinian bodies, Siciliano and Sansone were acknowledged as the most fit and most aesthetic of American men. They legitimated Italian bodies as ideal physical specimens, acceptable within the limited confines of whiteness.[21]

While Mussolini transformed the Italian image abroad, Italians in the United States experienced the transition from a racial to an ethnic group in their evolution toward whiteness. Anthropologists, such as Franz Boas at Columbia University, and sociologists such as Robert Park and Ernest Burgess at the University of Chicago, argued for a greater recognition of cultural differences rather than the biologically determined categorization of races. Ethnicity became more precisely recognized as a common ancestry, belief system, language, place of origin, religion, or a shared historical past. Such ideological changes, which took hold by the 1930s, had great repercussions for Italians and other groups on the margins of the mainstream culture. If they were categorized by ethnicity rather than race they might aspire to and gain whiteness; and for second-generation Italian children, born and raised in the United States under different historical, social, economic, and political circumstances than their parents, they might become Americans rather than Italians.[22]

But Italians' quest for acceptance was further complicated by the media emergence of a criminal element and a spate of gangster movies during the interwar period that stereotyped the Italian community.

The perception of disloyalty only increased when Mussolini declared his alliance with Germany in World War II. Italian American athletes countered that perspective. Some, like the DiMaggio brothers, learned to play the national game; and their many fans took pride in the prowess that earned them money, a measure of status, and most importantly, respect. Nonintellectual athletes, like the Di Maggios, posed no threat to the WASP hegemony. They operated within the Italian peasant culture that prized physicality and cherished family honor. Sport allowed for the amalgamation of disparate value systems and the merger of identities. Joe DiMaggio personified the multitude of Italian American athletes in the middle decades of the twentieth century who gradually overturned the stereotype of the Italian who was "good natured and sunny in disposition. The picture of the simple, happy-go-lucky, sentimental Italian . . . a child-like boy-man, a likable semi-simpleton . . . . Yet at the same time he is viewed as cynical, calculating, hard-bitten, vengeful and violent." The serious, even stoic, dignified, proud, humble, yet lonely Joe DiMaggio skirted two worlds. He reached the pinnacle of success in the American pastime, but maintained his ancestral culture in the family home. Uneasy in his brief celebrity marriage to Marilyn Monroe, he treasured and honored her memory as family (an Italian cultural trait) until his own death more than three decades later.[23]

While Joe DiMaggio graced American ballparks, Italian American boxers continued to claim honors in the ring. Rocky Graziano and Jake La Motta, both reclaimed from jails, were crowd favorites among the middleweights, while Willie Pep (Papaleo) started boxing at the age of fifteen in 1937. He Anglicized his name as a marketing device, which garnered a protest from his immigrant father. As an employee of the Works Progress Administration (WPA), a Depression-era government program that put the unemployed to work, the elder Papaleo earned $15 per week. The son earned $50 by fighting two bouts in one night and presented his father with $40 from his winnings. The father responded with his approval by stating, "If you fought tonight and you got forty dollars see if you can fight twice a week from now on."[24] By 1942 Willie Pep had become the featherweight champion of the world. The successes of such fighters only reinforced the perception of sport as a meritocracy and physical prowess as a means to social mobility.

The question of Italian American allegiance came to a head with the American entry into World War II. Mussolini had sided with Hitler and Italian Americans had to make a choice to support their ancestral homeland or their adopted country. An estimated 500,000 Italian Americans answered the call, including 70,000 sons of the "enemy aliens." As a measure of their achieved social status, all were assigned to white units in a still-segregated military. The Italian Hill neighborhood of St. Louis numbered 6,300 residents, and 1,100 joined the armed forces, including six sons from one family. Yogi Berra, future baseball star, left the Hill to join the navy and served with the D-Day invasion forces. Joe Garagiola, Berra's neighbor and a future major league baseball player, joined the military service and served in the Philippines. Twenty-four of their neighbors gave their life for the American cause. Pete Santoro, a Golden Gloves boxing champion in New England, told the recruiter for the Marine Corps, "I didn't want to go in the army because my father and mother came from Italy, and Italy was fighting against us, and I had relatives in Mussolini's army. I'd said I'd be fighting my own relatives and I'd feel bad shooting at them." Others did fight with the army in Italy, and some died there.[25]

Angelo Bertelli, star quarterback at Notre Dame and winner of the Heisman Trophy in 1943, was born in Italy, but joined the marines and earned a Purple Heart and the Bronze Star in the Pacific. Ten Italian Americans won the Navy Cross, while a dozen were awarded the Medal of Honor. John Basilone, an Italian American from New Jersey, had previously served three years in the army when he joined the marines in 1940. Basilone caddied at a golf course before joining the military, where he became a boxing champion in the Philippines, emulating his Italian hero, Primo Carnera. Still he endured the anti-Italian taunts of southerners upon enlisting in the marines until he beat the transgressors into submission. He won the Medal of Honor at Guadalcanal and the Navy Cross at Iwo Jima, where he was killed. He had eschewed a hero's retirement after his bravery at Guadalcanal made him a national celebrity in order to return to the fighting. He is considered one of the Marine Corps' greatest heroes; but Italian Americans of that era made sharper distinctions, which revealed their ongoing dilemma. Paul Pisicano, a New York Sicilian, stated that John Basilone "was our hero. He did the right things, but he did them in the Pacific. He was shooting gooks, so that's okay. It would be very painful to see the same act of courage demonstrated against Italians." Pisicano's opinion indicated the self-perception of his own whiteness in contrast to the Japanese, but a still-conflicted allegiance regarding the war in Italy.[26]

Other Italian American servicemen survived, but endured years of hardship as prisoners of war. Augie Donatelli played baseball or softball at the prisoners' camp in Germany and officiated games, a career that he resumed as a National League umpire after the war. Mickey Grasso also made it to the National League as a catcher with the New York Giants after two years in a POW camp. Mario "Motts" Tonelli was not so lucky. In Chicago he had been a superstar in four sports. "His Italian-immigrant parents, Celi and Lavania, didn't quite understand the big deal about sports in this country, but they understood the respect their son earned in a culture where slurs against recent arrivals were common."[27] Both the University of Southern California and the University of Notre Dame vied for his football talents; but the issue was decided when a priest intervened with his mother on behalf of a Catholic education. Tonelli starred on the 1938 Notre Dame team before joining the professional Chicago Cardinals team at a salary of $4,000. He enlisted in the US Army before the formal declaration of war and was sent to the Philippines as an artillery sergeant. When the Philippines fell to the Japanese in the aftermath of the Pearl Harbor attack Tonelli and 10,000–12,000 other Americans, as well as more than 60,000 Filipinos became prisoners of war and were subjected to the notorious Bataan Death March, in which 7,000–10,000 died brutal deaths. If a prisoner managed to escape, nine others were executed in retribution. Tonelli suffered from malaria and lost nearly one hundred pounds during his forty-two-month ordeal in Japanese prison camps.[28]

Lou Zamperini suffered a fate similar to Tonelli. The son of Italian immigrants, he could not speak English as a youth. Taunted and bullied in school, he fought back fiercely, a quality that would later save his life. He embarked on a life of petty crime until an older brother, a distinguished athlete, taught him to use his physical abilities for more positive results. His father, a former boxer, constructed weightlifting equipment for him. Zamperini set a national high school record for the mile run and made the 1936 US Olympic team. His athletic prowess earned an athletic scholarship to the University of Southern California; but World War II interrupted his quest for an Olympic medal in 1940 and he joined the Army Air Corps as a bombardier. He barely survived a 1943 plane crash, only to drift at sea on a life raft for forty-seven days, when he was captured by the Japanese. He endured two harsh years of torture and slave labor as a prisoner of war, followed by years of nightmares. Still, he eventually forgave his tormenters and displayed his American patriotism as an Olympic torchbearer in five Olympiads. Despite their ancestral ties to Italy the Italian Americans of the second generation had clearly chosen an American identity.[29]

Having paid for their American citizenship in blood, the 1950s seemingly presented a Golden Age for Italians. Rocky Marciano ruled the heavyweight boxing ranks, Frank Sinatra dominated pop culture, and Italian youth topped the rock-and-roll charts. The New York area produced Connie Francis (Franconero) as well as the Neons, the Regents, the Mystics, the Elegants, the Capris, Reparata (Mary Aiese) and the Delrons, Dion (Di Mucci) and the Belmonts, the Crests, Joey Dee (Di Nicola) and the Starliters, Frankie Valli (Castelluccio) and the Four Seasons, the Young Rascals, and Bobby Darin (Cassotto). Philadelphia turned out Bobby Rydell (Ridarelli), Fabian (Forte), and Frankie Avalon (Avallone), and Bobby Vee (Velline) hailed from South Dakota, all of whom became teen idols as singers/actors in the 1950s and 1960s.

On the athletic fields Italians garnered greater glory as Alan Ameche won the Heisman Trophy in 1954 and a host of Italian American players earned fame in professional football and baseball ranks.

Joe Bellino won the Heisman Trophy in 1960 and, over the next decade, Vince Lombardi personified the ideals of Cold War America, posed against the suspicion of and widespread media attention given to a secret society, the *Cosa Nostra* (Our Thing), that fueled ongoing perceptions of Italian difference. Some Italians joined the suburbanization movement of the era; but they still lacked the education required for true social mobility. A 1969 survey indicated that Italians over the age of thirty-five ranked lower than all other ethnic groups except Hispanics in education, earnings, and social mobility, with only 5.9 percent earning a college education, and only 27.6 percent with a high school diploma. A 1974 study in Chicago found that fewer than 2 percent of the 106 largest corporations had an Italian director, and fewer than 3 percent had Italians in executive positions. Seventy-five of the companies had no Italian officers at all. A year later a Detroit study uncovered similar egregious data.

Eighty of the top one hundred corporations had no Italian directors, and seventy-eight had no Italian officers in their companies. A New York investigation determined that "City University . . . has historically practiced de facto discrimination against the Italian-American." For those who remained behind, life continued much the same in ethnic enclaves where existence revolved around family and friends.[30]

A resurgence of ethnicity in the 1970s and 1980s generated a distinct pride in their Italian identity among the third generation. Mario Cuomo gained national notice as a politician. Robert De Niro and Al Pacino drew millions to the theaters, albeit often portraying Mafia lords. Italian boxers proliferated in the ring, often adorned in the national colors of their ancestral homeland. At the highest levels of sport, Bart Giamatti, former president of Yale University, reigned as commissioner of baseball; Paul Tagliabue ruled over the National Football League; and Jerry Colangelo owned both the Phoenix Suns of the National Basketball League and baseball's Arizona Diamonbacks.[31]

Despite rising intermarriage rates, a decline in religiosity, a transfer to the more conservative Republican Party, and a growing sense of multiculturalism in American society, prejudice remained. Gangster movies and television shows, such as HBO's *The Sopranos*, that depicted Italian Americans in a negative light remained among American favorites. The current popularity of the *Jersey Shore* cable televison series that proudly hails the raucous, hedonistic lifestyles of "guidos" and "guidettes" indicates the persistence of stereotypes as well as a reversal of the Italian inferiority complex. Louise Ciccone and Stefani Germanotta, better known as Madonna and Lady Gaga, respectively, continue to eschew Italian physicality to construct pseudo identities in their music careers. Lady Gaga's music "speaks to people who are disconnected from society."[32] It is a condition with which her Italian immigrant ancestors would have been familiar. Like the immigrants of a century ago, she still searches for recognition and acceptance but holds on to her ancestral roots. Her lyrics encompass the joy and misery of Italianita. She stated that "Something that carries through all my songwriting is this undertone of grit and darkness and melancholy." In the process of transforming their identities, both Madonna and Lady Gaga have engaged elements of their Italian ancestral culture while also distancing themselves from the European experiences of their predecessors.[33]

Despite more than a century in the United States, however, many Italians still seek refuge in their ethnic comfort zone, within the family and the ethnic enclaves that have been transplanted to suburban locations. Even an educated university professor, Joseph Tuisani, wondered, "Two languages, two lands, perhaps two souls . . . Am I a man or two halfs [*sic*] of one?" in a still ongoing conflict of national identity, masculinity, and cultural belonging. Democracy allowed for progress; but the term and degree remain relative.[34]

"The Tuskegee Flash" and "the Slender Harlem Stroker": Black Women Athletes on the Margins

Jennifer H. Lansbury

In July 1948, as track and field athlete Alice Coachman was arriving in London to represent the United States in the Olympic high-jump competition, the *Chicago Defender* ran a story in its sports section featuring Coachman and the US women's track and field team. Entitled "Rush Carver Peanut Oil to Olympic Team Gals," sportswriter Russ Cowans described how the prized peanut oil, long used by track and field powerhouse Tuskegee Institute as a rubbing liniment, had been left behind in the United States: "It was Miss Coachman who sent the coaches and trainers into a dither," wrote Cowans. "A day out of New York, Miss Coachman discovered that the peanut rubbing oil was not in the luggage, although Coach Cleve Abbott of Tuskegee had promised to have some in New York for the gals to take to London." The article continued by reporting how Olympic coach Harry Hainsworth wired Abbott to send the oil over as quickly as possible. "Miss Coachman and the girls from Tuskegee have talked so much about the benefits they've derived from the oil . . . that all the girls want to use it," commented Coach Hainsworth.[1]

Coachman went on to win the gold, the first African American woman to win the prized medal, and the *Defender* and other black weeklies celebrated her victory and achievement. However, despite what one scholar has labeled our own culture's "sports fixation."

Coachman's achievement and those of many other female African American athletes are all but forgotten today.[2] Even a historical field full of vitality and growth has not helped rescue these women from general obscurity.[3] Why are female African American athletes neglected to the point that they and their achievements have been essentially forgotten? This study suggests that sources for news in the 1940s and 1950s contributed to the loss of at least two black women athletes from the public memory: 1940s track star Alice Coachman and 1950s tennis great Althea Gibson. In short, by focusing primarily on race or gender rather than athletic talent, the white and black press constructed public identities for Coachman and Gibson that marginalized them as athletes.

It was not necessarily a lack of press coverage of black female athletes that led to their marginalization, although this was certainly a contributing factor in the case of Alice Coachman. Often more harmful was the type of coverage suggested by the aforementioned "peanut oil" article. The story suggests a certain vibrancy surrounding the coverage, but it also reveals a tendency to neglect the skills of the athletes and identify them in nonathletic terms. The lighthearted tone of the article and the reference to the athletes as "the gals" suggests that they were to be indulged but not taken too seriously. Indeed, contemporary sportswriters routinely constructed Coachman's and Gibson's identities along race or gender lines, leaving their athletic prowess to be inferred from their accomplishments.

While the white and black press differed in the ways they presented these two women, neither treatment proved beneficial in securing their athletic place in history. In the white press, gender became the essential element around which their careers were interpreted. This is not to say that race was never a factor, but it was generally secondary to gender. This construction worked to Alice Coachman's detriment. As a female track and field athlete, she received little coverage from the white press mainly because she participated in a male-gendered sport. Not usually isolated for being African American, she nonetheless existed on the margin in white news accounts for being a woman competing in a "man's sport." In contrast, Althea Gibson excelled in a sport in which women's participation had long been sanctioned. As a result, she enjoyed considerably more coverage through the construction of her by the white press as a female athlete. However, she also suffered from this emphasis on gender when the public began to *perceive* her tennis playing as too masculine.

Whereas the presentation of Coachman and Gibson in the white press revolved primarily around gender, race became the focal point for constructing their identities in the black press. This latter construction led to more press for Alice Coachman than she received in white papers as black sportswriters highlighted her achievements in terms of her status as an African American. However, the black press was aware of the unpopularity of track and field for women in the 1940s, and their efforts to introduce gender into news accounts with the purpose of feminizing Coachman often had the effect of trivializing her athletic talent. Althea Gibson suffered in more explicit ways from this racial construction of her identity and athletic career. Initially celebrated by the black press for her achievement in breaking down the color line in the elite world of tennis, black sportswriters eventually turned on her for her refusal to assume the role of a race hero in the vein of Jackie Robinson.

The choice of Alice Coachman and Althea Gibson grants important insights into not only change over time but also the gender and class distinctions associated with track and field versus tennis. During Coachman's career, the sport of track and field remained a decidedly masculine endeavor. While women first began competing in the 1920s and initially enjoyed popularity, physical education leaders soon began criticizing female participation in the sport, positing that the jarring movements required by track events put too much strain on the female anatomy. Furthermore, experts also expressed concern that the "masculinizing effects" of such activity would make women unfit for their feminine roles, particularly that of motherhood. As a result, participation by white women declined, and many talented African American female track athletes emerged to take advantage of the exodus. Some white women continued to flock to the sport in the 1930s and 1940s, such as Babe Didrickson, Helen Stephens, and Stella Walsh. However, their working-class backgrounds and "mannish" appearances upset the middle-class sensibilities of physical education instructors, pushing women's track and field even further to the margins of white society.[4]

The arena of track and field did not necessarily carry with it the same set of unattractive qualities for black women as it did for most white women. On the contrary, the elements of survival, even victory, in the face of adversity and struggle fit nicely into the African American woman's concept of ideal womanhood. Generally barred from the exclusive role of full-time mother, black women out of necessity assumed the multiple roles of wage earner, mother, homemaker, and community activist. African American femininity, therefore, was not constructed through limited attributes set in opposition to masculinity. Rather, ideal black womanhood was imbued with the positive qualities of strength, morality, and family and community commitments that had been forged through difficult circumstances as well as through the respect accorded them in the successful assumption of these different roles.[5]

The prowess of African American women in track and field during the 1930s and 1940s could be a double-edged sword, however. Most of the athletes enjoyed personal opportunities beyond what many of their race and gender would otherwise experience, such as the excitement of competition and educational and travel opportunities. Furthermore, their achievements served as a symbol of pride for their African American community. However, the success came at a price. White America often neglected them or, perhaps worse, perpetuated the negative stereotype of the black "mannish" woman, naturally suited to the role of athlete.[6]

While Coachman excelled in a sport that was considered unlady-like and inappropriate for women, Gibson's story was altogether differ-ent. Tennis, a sport more associated with feminine qualities, had long accepted women. Though more inclusive of women than track and field, it was not, however, more inclusive of race. Not until 1948 did the first African American play in a major United States Lawn Tennis Association (USLTA) tournament. Furthermore, the class issues associ-ated with tennis were perhaps even more rigid than that of track and field. Developed as a sport of the elite, tennis did not openly welcome working-class participants.[7]

The choice of Coachman and Gibson also introduces the contrast of individuals raised in different regions of the country. Coachman was born and educated in the Jim Crow society of the Deep South so that "separate but equal" was an entrenched way of life for this Albany, Georgia, native. Although Gibson was educated in North Carolina and Florida, she spent her formative years in Harlem. While New York was not immune to racism, Gibson noted the difference as she journeyed in the South at the age of nineteen. Confronting the "White in front, Colored in rear" sign on her first bus ride in downtown Wilmington, North Carolina, she remembered, "It disgusted me, and it made me feel ashamed in a way I'd never been ashamed back in New York."[8]

The sports in which they competed, the regions of the country in which they lived, and even the decades in which they forged their careers mark important differences in Coachman's and Gibson's lives. Despite these differences, the ways in which the press constructed the public identities of these athletes were remarkably similar. Choosing to emphasize either gender or race over athletic skill and hard work, both black and white sports journalists unknowingly contributed to confining these women to the historical margin.

"The Tuskegee Flash"

From 1937 to 1948, the women's track and field team of Tuskegee Institute dominated the Amateur Athletic Union (AAU) outdoor championships, winning every year but 1943, when they placed second to the Cleveland Olympic Club. While numerous talented African American women competed under their banner, Alice Coachman ranks among the top. Eventually referred to in the black press as the "Tuskegee flash" for her sprinting prowess, Coachman caught the attention of the Tuskegee Institute coaching staff during the late 1930s and first competed for them the summer before beginning high school classes there. During her nine years of competition, first at Tuskegee and later at Albany State College, she forged a career that stands unrivaled in the record books. From 1939 when she burst on the scene by winning the high jump at the AAU outdoor women's championship, she dominated her events by amassing twenty-six national championships, more than any other American woman with the exception of her Polish American rival, Stella Walsh.[9]

Yet, within the white press, Coachman was seldom portrayed as a record-breaking track star. In fact, women track athletes in general suffered from the portrayal of them in the white press, which generally emphasized gender over either race or athletic prowess. In Coachman's nine-year career, the limited coverage granted female track and field athletes by white newspapers and magazines is startling. Rarely did photographs of the athletes accompany the short articles that reported the national AAU outdoor championships, whereas male track and field events routinely received one- and two-page spreads, complete with pictures.[10]

At no time does the neglect of women's track and field stand out more than during coverage of the 1948 Summer Olympic Games in London.[11] Indeed, track and field was synonymous with masculinity, and the men's events in this sport completely dominated the white press coverage. Regardless of whether male track and field athletes were white or African American, they received not only extensive article coverage with accompanying photographs but also analysis by contemporary sports journalists. However, not even the very complete Olympic coverage by the *New York Times* included any pictures of American female track and field athletes. This is replicated by the *Times*'s counterparts in other US cities such as the *Chicago Tribune*, the *Boston Globe,* and the *Atlanta Constitution.*[12]

In part, the lack of coverage of American women's track and field during the 1948 Olympics may have resulted from their disappointing performances. Most of the American women failed to make it to the finals, and only Coachman and sprinter Audrey Patterson placed in their events.[13] Furthermore, the performance of Dutch runner Fanny Blankers-Koen tended to dominate the games. Her four gold track medals earned her the honor of being photographed by the American white press. However, in spite of Blankers-Koen's record-breaking Olympics, white sportswriters constructed her identity predominantly through gender. Journalists routinely referred to her as "the Dutch housewife" and "the blond, slender, 30-year-old mother of two," as opposed to confining their reports to her sprinting prowess. These descriptions served to feminize the Dutch athlete, necessary since she competed in a supposedly masculine sport.[14]

Although coverage of women track champions, regardless of race, paled in comparison to that of the men, the attention Coachman received was generally commensurate with her white female competitors. Indeed, one of the compelling things about Coachman's white press coverage is how remarkably like her white competitors' it is. As early in her career as 1942, when she began to take home multiple titles at the AAU Women's Outdoor Nationals, Coachman was mentioned by white papers, and the Tuskegee team even took the headline that year in the *Chicago Tribune*—"Tuskegee Wins 6th Women's AAU Title in Track." By 1945 and 1946, when Coachman was at the peak of her career, she began to make headlines when the *Boston Globe* reported

"Tuskegee Girl Eclipses Stella in Title Meet," and the *New York Times* reported her being awarded three places on the All-American Track and Field Team with a headline in the sports section. The white press routinely referred to Coachman as the "star sprinter," the "Tuskegee star," or the "Tuskegee flash" in ways not only similar to the black press but also quite similar to its own references to white female track and field athletes.[16] To subordinate race to gender was not to ignore it, however. While Coachman was often depicted in terms similar to white women track athletes, race did at times play a factor. Indeed, the coverage by the *New York Times* illustrates the role of race. The *Times* not only photographed Fanny Blankers-Koen but also gave her more article coverage than any member of the US women's track team. Incredibly, from 5 August when Coachman won her gold to 15 August when the *Times* wrapped up its reporting, it granted Alice Coachman—the only American woman to win a gold in track and field, the first African American, and a new Olympic record holder—just one sentence. Its startling lack of coverage of Coachman's athletic achievement reveals that second to gender came race. Athletic competence was of little significance.[17] Moreover, the Olympics were not the first time the white paper had slighted Coachman. When she became a triple winner at the 1945 AAU Women's Nationals, finally beating out Stella Walsh in the 100-meter dash after coming close the previous two years, the *Times* completely ignored the Tuskegee star's achievement. The short three-paragraph article entitled "Miss Walsh Wins Easily" covered Walsh's single win in the 200-meter despite the fact that Coachman took the title in the 50-meter, the 100-meter, and the high jump. And in 1946, while Coachman dominated both the AAU Women's Nationals as well as the *Times*'s coverage of it by retaining all three of her titles, the one photograph accompanying the article was of the white 80-meter hurdles champion, Nancy Cowperthwaite.[18]

Even when her home state overlooked gender in order to honor one of its own as a new Olympic record holder, Coachman's race came before her athletic achievement. "Albany Negress is Olympic Champ: Alice Coachman Wins High Jump," headlined the *Atlanta Constitution* in an article devoted entirely to the newest native Georgia champion. For a white paper in the Deep South in 1948, the article unexpectedly celebrates Coachman's achievement, reporting that there were over 70,000 on hand to watch Coachman set a new Olympic record, the "greatest [crowd] ever to witness a high jump exhibition." However, in addition to the several overt references to her race, the account also contains subtle messages of race and gender: "An all-around athlete, Alice is an outstanding forward on the basketball team at college, but her instructors say confidentially that she's 'just a fair student' in home economics."[19] The article hints at two negative stereotypes—that of the African American who excels athletically but not academically and of the woman who participates in a mannish sport because she is not "feminine" enough to do well in the female college course of home economics.

While the white press offered limited coverage of Alice Coachman's athletic prowess, the black press heralded her achievements, as well as those of other black female track stars. Constructing her identity primarily through race rather than gender, African American journalists overlooked the gender concerns of their white counterparts. Indeed, black weeklies often gave the Tuskegee team and Coachman headlines in the sports page, accompanied by team photos or individual shots of the athletes in action. As early as 1941, before she had become a dominant force in the sprints, the *Pittsburgh Courier* captured a photographic image of Coachman performing the high jump at the AAU Women's Nationals, noting how she "clears the bar with a spectacular leap." By 1942, three years before she bested Stella Walsh in the 100-meter sprint, the *Baltimore Afro-American* recognized that the Tuskegee team took their sixth straight championship title "paced by Alice Coachman, national indoor and outdoor jumping champion, who captured two titles in addition to running the anchor leg on the championship relay quartet." The spread featured several pictures, including a single of Coachman, the "Tuskegee flash," crossing the finish line in the 400-meter relay.[20] Moreover, in the prewar years African American sports journalists often discussed female track and field athletes in their regular columns. As early in Coachman's career as 1940, Charles Campbell of the *Baltimore Afro-American*, in his weekly column "Philly Points," predicted that she would eventually break the world record for the high jump.[21]

Although sports coverage in general fell off during the later war years, Coachman continued to be hailed by the black press for her dominance in women's track and field. Aided by descriptive monikers such as the "Tuskegee star," the "flying Miss Coachman," "Tuskegee's

21-year-old speed queen," and "Americas No. One woman track athlete," African American journalists continued to celebrate Coachman's
achievements as she came to the pinnacle of her career in the United
States.[22] Compared to the *New York Times*'s and *Chicago Tribune*'s lacklus-
ter coverage of women's track and field, black weeklies put Coachman
front and center in 1945 as they celebrated her spectacular performance
at the AAU Women's Nationals. "Alice Coachman Crowned National
Sprint Queen," headlined the *Baltimore Afro-American* that year, noting
how she had reached "the acme of her brilliant career" by dethroning
Stella Walsh, who was "generally recognized as one of the all-time greats
of feminine history." Indeed, recognizing Walsh's brilliance in the sport
served to enhance Coachman's overall achievement when she finally out-
ran her competitor in 1945 after having been nosed out by Walsh in the
100-meter for the two prior years. In an interview with Walsh in 1944,
the renowned *Afro-American's* sportswriter, Sam Lacy, reported how the
"Polish flyer" referred to Coachman as "the toughest opponent I have
ever met," and "the finest runner I've ever raced against."[23]

   In truth, the black press's extensive coverage of Coachman's
achievements, along with other African Americans, was often necessary to balance the fact that white dailies overlooked or downplayed
the contributions of African Americans. However, while black journalists constructed Coachman's public identity primarily in terms of race,
they were aware of the gender concerns that accompanied her sport. As
such, they sometimes used feature articles or weekly columns to "feminize" black women track and field athletes. In 1941 the *Baltimore Afro-
American* ran a feature article on the Tuskegee women track stars' plans
after graduation. Playing up the femininity of the athletes, Levi Jolley
wrote: "These young women, while mixing athletics with studies, enjoy
all the pleasures and indicated desires to become a nurse, . . . teachers,
and social workers." Alice Coachman's plans included teaching or social
work, but Jolley also reported that she believed "being a good wife when
she marries will probably be the fulfilment of her secret ambitions."[24]
Celebrating her achievements as an African American female track athlete, the black press was still quick to realize the importance of projecting femininity onto Coachman's identity.

   Efforts by the black press to feminize Coachman and other female
track athletes resulted in trivializing the athlete's abilities in their sport.

The peanut oil story, which originated years before the Olympics, best illustrates this tendency. In his 1940 article "Tigerettes Owe Success to Dr. Carver's Peanut Oil," Levi Jolley refused to accept Coach Christine Evans Petty's assertion that the team's success could be attributed to strict training and competing against male athletes during practice. Due to "the smooth velvet appearance of the girls' skin in addition to their rhythm in motion," the reporter repeatedly inquired about "what was used for rubbing the girls." Petty finally acknowledged that the exclusive use of Dr. George Washington Carver's peanut oil by the women's team, but also more broadly within the athletic department, helped prevent strained muscles and Charlie horses. This allowed coaches to concentrate more on form and speed during practice and not worry about muscle problems that developed from strenuous training. There was an added benefit for the women, noted Jolley: "The girls like to use it because of the smoothness it gives their skin."[25]

The images that the peanut oil story evokes are not only disturbing but also reveal how even the black press marginalized Coachman and her teammates. First, the story suggests that the athletic abilities of these women derived not from hard work but from a magic potion like peanut oil. The entire article, including its title, suggests a "scoop"—the sportswriter has discovered the secret to the Tuskegee women's years of dominance in track and field. The story goes beyond imbuing these women with feminine traits to creating images full of sensuality. While the writer's words discuss the oil's benefits largely in the very feminine terms of smooth skin, the whole concept of rubbing oil on women's bodies also evokes a very sexualized view of these women.

These efforts to project feminine, even sensualized, qualities on black women track athletes reflect their ambiguous identity even within their own community of African American supporters. Celebrated by the black press for their achievements because they were African Americans, they nonetheless had trouble overcoming the stigma of being females trying to excel in a masculine sport and being represented in the press by an essentially male cadre of sportswriters.[26] Certainly the fact that most sports journalists were men dictated, in part, the type of coverage women athletes, in general, and African American women athletes, more specifically, would receive. Defining what would make it to sports pages, white and African American sportswriters unknowingly contributed to the loss of these women athletes from the public memory. Even as Alice Coachman retired from track and field competition, the white and black presses were busy constructing the identity of another athlete coming on the scene. The creation of the public Althea Gibson would be as equally complicated.

"The Slender Harlem Stroker"

The same summer Alice Coachman won Olympic gold, Althea Gibson took the national American Tennis Association (ATA) championship for the second straight year. She would go on to win the ATA title, the African American tennis association that existed alongside the white United States Lawn Tennis Association, for eight more years. However, she was still two years away from entering the hallowed grounds of Forest Hills, the national USLTA championship that eventually became the US Open.[27]

While Gibson was living a tomboyish existence on the streets of Harlem, the African American elite saw in her an exceptional talent and, hoping she would be the one to break the color barrier, groomed her to enter and excel in the high-class world of tennis.[28] After ascending to the pinnacle of the African American tennis community, and with the help of former tennis greats like Alice Marble, Gibson finally broke into the USLTA in 1950, culminating in her play at Forest Hills in September of that year. In 1951, she became the first African American to play at Wimbledon.

What followed was a series of disappointing years in which Gibson continued to dominate the ATA but struggled in the USLTA. Ready to give up the sport and join the WACS, the State Department asked her, along with three other players, to represent the United States on a goodwill tour of Southeast Asia during the winter and spring of 1956. It was this tour that turned her career around. She won sixteen out of eighteen tournaments, although she faltered at Wimbledon and Forest Hills, losing both in the final round. It was the last time that would happen, however. In 1957, Gibson became the first African American—man or woman—to take the Wimbledon singles title. She entered the record books again in the late summer when she finally won at Forest Hills. From there, she seemed unstoppable. In 1958 she certainly was. She retained both the Wimbledon and Forest Hills titles, again entering the record books alongside the few other tennis greats who had enjoyed back-to-back wins of both tournaments.

As with Alice Coachman, the construction of Althea Gibson's identity by the white press rested primarily on gender. While she was at times singled out for special attention due to the racial significance of her accomplishments, generally, the amount and tenor of the coverage she received was commensurate with her white female tennis competitors. Although women were more accepted in a sport less masculinized than track and field, they had to endure negative gender labels if their play became too powerful or aggressive.[29]

While the sport of tennis was not gendered in the same way as track and field, Gibson and her contemporaries, male and female, were routinely described in quite physical, gendered terms. Contemporary news accounts routinely commented especially on Gibson's size, referring to her as "the lithe and muscular Miss Gibson," a "lanky jumping jack of a girl," and "tall and leggy."[30] Furthermore, they often used such physical attributes to explain the masculine power with which she played the game. Gibson is "lean and her long arms are muscular. . . . When she hits the ball, it travels like a bolt out of a crossbow," wrote Kenneth Love of the *New York Times*. Following her win at Forest Hills in 1957, *Life* magazine showed a picture of Gibson in action and explained, "Althea's service gains power from her height."[31]

With her big service and powerful delivery, Gibson was often noticed in the white press for the "masculine" way in which she played the game. Yet this was a fate common of any woman who chose to play aggressive tennis, and many shied away from such displays of power to avoid being labeled masculine by the press.[32] In a bio-piece that appeared in conjunction with her 1957 Wimbledon win, the *New York Times* noted that Gibson, as early as her debut at Forest Hills, had been compared to another female tennis great, Alice Marble, for her "mannish style of play." Her teaming with Maria Bueno of Brazil to capture the 1958 Wimbledon doubles championship garnered the attention of sports journalists who noticed how the Gibson-Bueno team "crushed" their opponents, "hitting the ball with manlike power." Following her win at Forest Hills in 1957, *Life* magazine compared Gibson's tennis to that of the men's singles champion Malcolm Anderson, "The two winners, as these pictures show, also played remarkably alike. Their power proved again that it takes a big serve to win in modern tennis."[33] Unlike Coachman, Gibson received more coverage from the white press, probably due in large measure to the acceptability of women's participation in the sport of tennis. However, she did have to contend with the attention given her for the "unladylike" way in which she played the game.[34]

As evidenced by treatments from the white press, race played a more important part in Coachman's identity than in Gibson's. The hometown papers of these athletes are particularly illustrative of this difference. During the peak of Coachman's career from 1943 to 1948, the *New York Times* occasionally overlooked Coachman's achievement, highlighting instead that of white female track athletes. The *Atlanta Constitution*, however, celebrated this native Georgian's Olympic achievement, albeit with both explicit and implicit racial commentary. The *Times* coverage of Gibson, however, was generally anything but racialized.[35] Certainly much of this could be attributed to the New York paper promoting an athlete from their city, which they did with gusto. There were likely two reasons for the differences in intensity of these athletes' hometown coverage. First, Gibson was a Harlem girl, whereas Coachman's home was the smaller southwest Georgia town of Albany rather than the city of Atlanta. Second, the white press of the more segregated South would be less likely to publicize the ongoing achievements of a young African American female athlete outside of some spectacular feat, such as the capturing of an Olympic gold medal and a new world record. The northern *New York Times*, however, quickly fashioned the tennis star as "our own Althea Gibson," and not only highlighted her tennis matches but also often mentioned her in their editorial section.[36]

The difference between Coachman's and Gibson's white press coverage in terms of race also reflected the changes that occurred in American society during the 1940s and 1950s. Although only a decade separated their achievements, the racial dynamics of the country had changed considerably. Even as Alice Coachman was capturing women's track titles year after year, America's participation in World War II became what is now recognized as a turning point in the African American struggle for civil rights.[37] Black soldiers returning from war began to question the inequity of defending a country that denied them full participation in white society. Toward the end of Coachman's career, advancement was already being made in the area of sports. In 1946 Jackie Robinson breached the color line in professional baseball when he made his debut with the Montreal Royals, the top farm team of the Brooklyn Dodgers. A year later, major league baseball saw its first African American player in the twentieth century when Robinson donned a Dodger uniform. Also in 1946, the Los Angeles Rams signed Kenny Washington and Woody Strode to break professional football's thirteen-year exclusion of black athletes.[38]

By the time Gibson won her first singles title at Wimbledon, the larger society reverberated with changes on race issues. In 1954, the Supreme Court handed down their verdict in *Brown v. Board of Education*, which declared unconstitutional the long-standing practice of "separate but equal" facilities for African Americans. Most of Gibson's advances in the world of tennis would be played, then, against the backdrop of the *Brown* decision working its way throughout the country as now well-known names in the civil rights struggle forged their way into history. Moreover, the postwar years and the onset of the Cold War further contributed to African American advances as external scrutiny of American race relations resulted in heightened internal sensitivity. Indeed, Althea Gibson benefited from this changing America. Around the same time Rosa Parks was refusing to give her seat over to a white patron on a Montgomery, Alabama, bus, Althea Gibson's beleaguered tennis career received a second chance, thanks not only to the forward momentum of the African American civil rights movement but also to national concern with Cold War enemies' criticism of racial problems within the United States.[39]

In December 1955, the State Department invited Gibson to join three other tennis players on a tour of Southeast Asian countries, playing exhibition matches and international tournaments along the way. By including a successful African American, they hoped to improve the image of race relations in the United States against attacks from its communist antagonists.[40] Looking back on the experience, Gibson herself recognized the racial significance of her participation:

> I've never been exactly sure why I was selected to make the tour
> in the first place . . . I know it happened soon after the killing of
> Emmett Till in Georgia, and world opinion of the racial situation
> in the United States was at a low ebb. So I suppose that was the

main reason why I, a colored girl, was invited to help represent our country in Southeast Asia. I certainly wasn't picked because I was a champion; at the time I was champion of nothing and unlikely ever to be.[41]

Certainly in light of the country's changing racial climate, Althea Gibson's significance as a race hero was important to a black press that viewed the achievement of black women athletes primarily in racial terms. Indeed, Gibson's first win at Forest Hills in 1957 was played against the backdrop of the events of the "Little Rock Nine," when the governor of Arkansas, Orval Faubus, called out the National Guard to prevent nine African American children from entering a white public school.[42] During this heightened struggle for civil rights, the black press looked to Gibson to be visible and vocal concerning race issues. Unfortunately, these expectations proved to be ones under which Gibson would eventually suffer when, at the height of her career, the black press turned on her for refusing to assume a more outspoken role as race hero.

Gibson's relationship with the black press began in the late 1940s when she was regularly featured in sports sections for her consecutive victories at the ATA nationals. In 1950, however, she took on new prominence in black weeklies when she was invited to play at Forest Hills and in 1951 at Wimbledon, breaking the color barrier at both of these bastions of the white tennis world. "Althea Gibson will become the first Negro tennis star to crash the 'lily-white' citadel of this American sport," printed the *Pittsburgh Courier* following the news that Gibson would participate in the 1950 Forest Hills tournament. Most black papers were quick to identify the young and inexperienced star as a work in progress, however. "She plays a good attacking game, but it is erratic," noted one journalist. Nonetheless, Jackie Reemes of the *New York Amsterdam News* represented the common opinion of the day among African American writers when he reported that "there is little doubt that more will be heard from Althea in future competition."[43]

During the lean years of 1952–1955 when Gibson continued to dominate the African American ATA tournaments but was struggling in the white USLTA, the black press remained respectively silent on her struggles. However, from the time Gibson participated in the State Department's goodwill tour in 1956 to her eventual win at Wimbledon, her exploits in the "lily-white" world of tennis once again became common fare in sports columns of the black press. During this period of Gibson's career, African American journalists celebrated her achievements through their positive physical descriptions of her and their tendency to come to her defense when necessary.[44]

Similar to the white press, black sportswriters often described Gibson in physical terms. However, their descriptions highlighted both her statuesque femininity and her powerful game, constructions the black press did not see as contradictory. Historians Patricia Vertinsky and Gwendolyn Captain have posited that African American leaders, coaches, and journalists worked hard to dispel the myth of the black "Amazon" woman by cultivating instead a more feminine image of female athletes.[45] "The willowy Miss Gibson," "the slender Harlem stroker," and "the lean New Yorker" were common descriptions of Gibson during this period in her career. The *Baltimore Afro-American* also reported that she was "looking fresh and sporting an attractive hair-do" when she appeared on the Dave Garroway *This Is New York* television show in 1956.[46]

At the same time, however, African American journalists did not shy away from referring to Gibson's power. Femininity and strength joined nicely in the female African American ideal, in contrast to white womanhood that shied away from physical strength as a masculine characteristic.[47] "Lithe and quick in action," reported the *Pittsburgh Courier* early in her career, Gibson "loves to slam the ball with exuberance." Describing her win at Wimbledon, Gibson's opponent Darlene Hard "was simply no match for the powerful all-court game of Miss Gibson." Later that year, *Ebony* highlighted her "extraordinary power and big service."[48]

The second characteristic of Gibson's coverage prior to her falling out with the black press was the tendency on the part of African American journalists to defend her, as necessary, against negative reports. Following news that she was somewhat aloof with other players at the 1956 Wimbledon tournament, a writer for the *Chicago Defender* commented, "She is one of the most dignified girls I've ever seen, with more poise and personality than all the rest of the tennis players put together." With all her positive attributes, he continued, it is no wonder that Gibson had "become the target for jealousy." The following week, after her loss at Wimbledon, Fay Young devoted his entire weekly column to the tennis star. Discussing how misunderstood she was and how he had attempted to mold her, Young wrote of how he had gently chided her at an ATA meet for not mixing more with other players. The sportswriter remembered how Gibson had graciously accepted his advice. He concluded with further support: "We are all with her—win or lose."[49]

The point at which the black press began to attack Gibson rather than revere and defend her came during the summer of 1957. Following her win at Wimbledon, she traveled to Chicago to play in the USLTA tournament at River Forest. On the surface, the black press was upset by Gibson's unwillingness to be more attentive to them at the Chicago tournament in July. Journalists for the *Chicago Defender* and the *Pittsburgh Courier* were particularly indignant. In a feature article, the *Defender's* Russ Cowans accused her of giving reporters "one of the best brush-offs most of them had ever had" and suggested that instead of the Wimbledon trophy, the "Queen" should have "given her a few words of advice on graciousness." Continuing the diatribe in his weekly column, Cowans again laid into Gibson for being "as ungracious as a stubborn jackass" and "the most arrogant athlete it has been my displeasure to meet." Wendell Smith of the *Courier* attacked Gibson for taking on the persona of a prima donna after her Wimbledon victory: "The lean girl from the streets of Harlem has become so obsessed with herself and her court skill that she apparently speaks with only kings and queens." Smith even resorted to attacking Gibson intellectually. Suggesting that she merely "skipped" through Florida A&M College with the help of her African American benefactors, he continued, "She clearly established the fact here last week that she is neither scholarly nor smart by her arrogant, despicable treatment of friendly sportswriters."[50]

Both papers also continued to attack Gibson in subtle ways. In 1958, rather than highlighting her repeat of the women's singles and doubles titles at Wimbledon, the *Defender's* coverage focused instead on her "failure" to also take the mixed doubles title. The *Courier*, though eventually somewhat more forgiving than the Chicago weekly, spoke of Gibson in masculinized terms, a description more common to the white press but unheard of by the black press prior to the Chicago affair. Their coverage of the now-famed River Forest tournament in Chicago reported that "there was never any doubts that *mannish*-playing Miss Gibson would emerge victorious" (emphasis by author).[51]

However, the prima donna explanation was, in reality, a smoke screen. References to Gibson's "difficult" personality had long been a source of discussion by the black press. In 1956, Fay Young of the *Chicago Defender* noted how he had tried to help her along in this area, as another *Defender* journalist complained that "the Gibson gal is being accused of giving herself airs" because of her incredible success on the Southeast Asia tour. *Baltimore APO-American* sportswriter Sam Lacy's biographical sketch of Gibson published just before the 1957 Wimbledon play identified these tendencies as part of her personality: "It is her makeup to be moody, indifferent, sometimes arrogant." Chalking this up to her "tomboy" upbringing on the streets of Harlem, Lacy observed that "she has a way of going into her hard shell and refusing to come out of it." In a prescient conclusion, he offered the observation that "more often than not, it is the press that feels the brunt of the Gibson arrogance."[52]

Her problems with the black press, then, are best understood if considered in terms of how they constructed her public identity as an African American. To black journalists, her acceptance into the white, high-class world of tennis was imbued with deep racial significance. Sam Lacy called her win at Wimbledon "the greatest triumph a colored athlete has accomplished in my time" and "the biggest sports victory ever placed in the record books for a person of my race." He carved out Gibson's achievement in such heroic proportions, in part, because she did it alone with no others who had come before her to smooth the way. Given the integral part Lacy played in the Jackie Robinson saga, his compliment to Gibson during the Robinson era was high praise indeed.[53]

Yet Gibson's position as a race hero in the black press was fraught with ambiguity. Earlier in her career, while defending her from attackers who called her "tight-lipped and moody," a journalist for the *Chicago Defender* assured his readers that "she looks upon herself as an evangelist whose skill with the tennis racquet, and her sincerity, is breaking the colour barriers." Apparently, while she was accepting of the role in some measure, the press was accepting of her "quirks." During the Chicago fiasco, however, reports circulated that, when asked if she liked being compared to Jackie Robinson, she responded, "No, I don't consider myself a representative of my people. I am thinking of me and nobody else."[54]

There were those of the black press who defended Gibson even after the Chicago incident. Lacy continued to suggest that her bad press was, in part, due to her personality: "She answers readily and honestly, with no thought of softening her opinion for the sake of sparing feelings or playing the diplomat." Calling her a "distaff Jackie Robinson," he compared the two, suggesting that reporters often became offended and were "set back on their heels when they learned that neither Althea nor Jackie could be patient with veneers." The *Pittsburgh Courier* even gave equal time to her supporters by printing a representative letter from a fan who attacked the black press for its treatment of Gibson. Reminding people that the State Department thought her a responsible and good representative of the country in 1956, the fan insisted that "she does not go on the tennis court to represent her race and any question put to her along this line can only be a subtle trap."[55]

Comments from the white press on this subject give insight into how much the issue centered around Gibson's position as a race hero. In the fall of 1957, the *Pittsburgh Courier* reprinted a series of biographical articles written by Ted Poston of the *New York Post*. Calling Gibson a community project, Poston suggested that she was a throwback to post-slavery days when African Americans came together to promote the most talented ones of the community. Here, he concluded, "a Harlem urchin discovered by Negroes, nurtured by Negroes, trained by Negroes, educated by Negroes, was now the best in the world in 'the game for ladies and gentlemen.'" Against the backdrop of her racial significance, a *Time* magazine cover story may grant the best insight into the source of the problem. The feature story reported how Gibson came up against some Jim Crow problems in Chicago, being refused a room at the Oak Park Hotel and a reservation at a swanky Chicago restaurant. "Officials and newsmen burned with rage," the journalist wrote, "but Althea hardly noticed it."[56] The African American community had much invested in Althea Gibson, and many were disappointed when she did not live up to their expectations as a race figure.

Finally, Gibson herself attributed her problems with the black press to her hesitancy to be a trailblazer for her race. "I have never set myself up as a champion of the Negro race," she wrote in her autobiography. Taking her hat off to Jackie Robinson's achievements, Gibson nonetheless chose to handle her success in her own way, which was to shy away from any role as a race hero. However, she recognized that there were those in the African American community who disagreed with her position. The real reason that quite a few members of the black press had been uncomplimentary, she contended, was that they resented her refusal "to turn my tennis achievements into a rousing crusade for racial equality."[57]

How do we come to terms with the contemporary press treatment of these two athletes and their subsequent neglect by the historical community? Black and white sportswriters alike covered Coachman's and Gibson's athletic careers at least to some extent, and in Gibson's case, expansively. However, the sports stories about these women were more about gender or race rather than their prowess on the track field or the tennis court. Instead of attributing their athletic accomplishments to dedication and hard work, even the black press sometimes searched for the answer in magic potions like peanut oil.

It is no wonder then that Alice Coachman, Althea Gibson, and others like them have been lost to the public memory. While sources are available, contemporary press accounts trivialized them as athletes to the extent that they have been essentially forgotten for the very achievements that made them newsworthy in the first place. Yet the status of these women within the African American community, as well as their contributions toward breaking down racial barriers, make them important subjects of study. However, even as black women athletes are popular subjects for children's biographies, their absence from the genre of the historical biography is striking and begs for correction.[58] Moreover, more research into the ways in which the contemporary African American community viewed these athletes' achievements and their position in the African American public memory are other areas ripe for study.

In 1956, Kenneth Love of the *New York Times* related a comment from Gibson regarding her public identity. "I am just another tennis player, not a Negro tennis player," she insisted.[59] Yet even at the height of her career, neither the white or black press cast her as such. Rather, as the press constructed Alice Coachman and Althea Gibson primarily in terms of gender or race, their identities as athletes were relegated to a distant third. Fraught with ambiguity for both these athletes during their careers, such construction has also led to their current status as black women athletes on the margin.

III.

Ethnicity, Migration,
Bodies, and Sport

INTRODUCTION

John Nauright

C. L. R. James engaged with migration in much of his writing, particularly of his own, and others' migration among the Caribbean and the United Kingdom and the United States. In *Beyond a Boundary* he examines in part the career of Learie Constantine, the great Trinidadian cricketer who went on to become the first black member of the House of Lords. James spent much of his adult life overseas as have many black West Indians, the majority of whom have ended up in the United Kingdom, the United States, or Canada. In this section we examine embodied practices in sport as they help to shape identities of migrants in new environments.

In the first chapter of the section, Charles Springwood examines Oaxacan basketball as practiced in Mexico and in a migrant setting in Los Angeles. In Mexico, the playing of basketball has long set Oaxacan sporting culture apart from those of other regions of the country where soccer and/or baseball dominate. The playing of basketball in Los Angeles further provides a sense of Oaxacan-ness read against Mexican immigrant and Hispanic designations apparent in wider American culture. Oaxacan's use basketball to both foster a sense of identity and to create communal zones of embodied practice where their identity is a lived experience. In addition, basketball tournaments in the United States generate revenue that can be sent back to communities in Mexico.

In the next chapter, Gertrud Pfister explores experiences of migrant women from Turkey living in Denmark with comparisons to the German experience. Turkish migrant women have to negotiate a culture in which sport for women is more accepted, yet come from a culture where women playing sport is discouraged. While sport allows Turkish women space to begin to integrate into wider society, Walle demonstrates that Pakistani men in Oslo, Norway, utilize cricket to maintain a sense of ethnic identity that is established both through their playing of the sport and through engagement with the Pakistani national team. The Pakistani team provides sporting heroes for migrant men.

Anand Rampersad finishes this section in his exploration of ethnicity in CLR James's home country of Trinidad and Tobago. Over the past several decades, migrants from South Asia have become significant components of the population of both Trinidad and Guyana, two countries that are major suppliers of cricketing talent to the West Indies cricket team. Rampersad examines multifaceted identities that appear with attachments to South Asia, similar to Thomas Fletcher's discussion in the next section on migrants to England. In Trinidad, however, there has emerged less of a sense of racist isolation and more of an embrace of Indian-descended players as key elements of both the national and the pan-national West Indies team.

Each of the chapters provides us with clear examples of the intersection of ethnicity, sport, and embodiment as well as how sport as a cultural form can enhance integration or perpetuate distinctiveness. Read together, they provide clear insights into issues of ethnicity and sport that permeates James's discussion of color and caste in *Beyond a Boundary*, yet present examples of the complex ways in which sport and ethnicity are linked.

Tamales, Tapetes, and Basketball: Signs of Oaxacan Ethnicity in the United States

Charles Fruehling Springwood

In 1995, having strayed a bit too far into the margins of my graduate discipline, cultural anthropology, by doing a dissertation on baseball and the Hall of Fame, I found the job market exceedingly uncooperative. And so, I traveled to southern Mexico, the state of Oaxaca, to study something more orthodox, if only a little: indigenous textile museums in local villages. Between the many hours examining tapestries made by indigenous Zapotec weavers, despite having enjoyed far too many cups of mescal, I noticed what was unmistakably a significant source of pleasure for the residents of the village of Teotitlan del Valle: basketball. To my surprise, the American sport was more popular in Teotitlan than was baseball, or even soccer. As gifts, I had carried with me mementos from the 1994 World Cup of soccer (held in the United States), and while those trinkets were appreciated, most folks repeatedly asked whether or not I had brought any Chicago Bulls items.

More recently in 2009, I was working about ninety minutes north of Mexico City, in Ixtmiqulipan, in a small Nhanhu village, where many had crossed the border to El Norte, specifically to Las Vegas, and had returned. They perform a touristic reenactment of crossing the border, in which the villagers play the parts of the US Border Patrol agents and the coyotes (hired brokers who help migrants cross into the United States). For twenty dollars visitors participate in this mock nighttime excursion (actually many, many hours south of the border, mind you), becoming the migrants themselves. A NhaNhu villager told me stories about the Oaxacan basketball leagues in Las Vegas, and his fascination with their sophistication enticed me to look more closely.

In truth, though I had not anticipated the ubiquity of basketball in Zapotec-, Mixtec-, and Mayan-speaking communities (the three most populous indigenous groups in southern Mexico), its popularity made sense in terms of all I thought I knew about the global circulation of media imagery and the commodification of the NBA. I was well aware of the more conspicuous dimensions of what has been termed "the global Jordanscape"[1] and as a race theorist, I was predisposed to read the racial stories that surely animated the practice of basketball in these Mexican villages. I wondered at once about how the fascinating and fearful spectacle of the black body and the commodification of blackness informed the identities of basketball players in Mexico. Once I began to look closely, however, I did not encounter as readily as I had been expecting signs of the appropriation and performance of blackness, effected through style, talk, and politics. To be certain, the indigenous players understand that in America, many people saw basketball as black at its surface and black to its core. And while they sported some of the commodity apparel of the NBA, missing was a more prominent embodiment of the "cool pose" caricature, neither in voice, dress, nor movement, that so often accompanies the circulation of basketball across national and ethnic space.

Within the broader spaces of a more nationalized popular culture and nonindigenous, mestizo social world, the youthful engagement of black pose, from music to dress to slang, is visible. And, indeed, reflecting the increasing global popularity of basketball, Mexicans play hoops with greater frequency than in the past. But in terms of national consciousness, basketball is nowhere close to as significant as it is in the indigenous communities where, from the hinterland villages to ethnic barrios in Mexico City to Los Angeles, it is practiced as a form of commitment, community, and ethnicity. Playing basketball is a way of thinking about the meaning of indigenousness, of relating to one's self and to other ethnic groups, and of integrating action, movement, habit, and discovery. And throughout, I argue, while playing this game with so much passion, the players are devising their own sets of racial and ethnic premises, authoring, as it were, their own theories of difference and identity.

In order to contextualize the sporting practices of these folks, I rely on the concept of "community of practice," developed in the work of Jean Lave and Etienne Wenger,[2] who explained that such groups are inscribed as a "set of relations among persons, activity, and world, over time and in relation with other tangential and overlapping communities of practice." Their central preoccupation is with theories and ways of learning and knowing based on a Vitgotskian model of learning via action and participation, and therefore, they assert the "relational interdependence" of participants in a community of practice. William W. Wood, who advances the applications of the notion of a community of practice in an ethnography of Zapotec weavers, argues that these relational communities turn on social action and performance, "in which people engage . . . the social and cultural worlds created though such practice, and the people themselves, who, to no small degree, also create themselves through their practice."[3] The learning community has been successfully applied to analyses of sport, in the work of Matthew Atencio and Cana Koca,[4] who identify the networks of young males playing soccer in Turkey as communities of learning and engaging masculine identities.

Zapotec and Mixtec peoples comprise the vast majority of the indigenous population in the state of Oaxaca,[5] and it is segments of these two communities that have pursued—in numbers greater than any other indigenous groups—a transnational, transbordered path northward to Los Angeles, bringing with them not only traditional elements of their culture, from ceremonial rituals, language, and music, but also, of course, basketball. The research for this project centered on fieldwork and interviews with athletes from the Zapotec immigrant community, which is larger than the Mixtec community. The intensity with which Zapotecs are invested in the practice of basketball suggests that this game offers a complex space for the performance of ethnic identity, for the maintenance of community, and—as the players claim—for survival in the face of globalization as well as racial and class hierarchy. Indeed, theirs is a story of and about globalization, but it does not support a simplified reading, for example, of an indigenous group courageously hanging on to one or another particular tradition in order to resist the homogenizing hegemony of global culture. Nor is it the story of hybridity,[6] in which a group adopting or co-opting one or another ritual or game, such as Trobriand cricket, onto which a host of new meaning and functions are quickly mapped. And, unlike so many sites of indigenous performativity, which are shaped by and responsive to a field of touristic consumerism and spectacle,[7] from the point of view of the outsider, Zapotec basketball games and tourneys are relatively subdued proceedings, appearing suspiciously like basketball games in any number of other rural or urban communities. While an element of these aforementioned narratives is undoubtedly present in Oaxacan basketball, their game suggests instead a globalization of everyday struggles, punctuated by uneven flows of capital and opportunity, and by a resilient agency always constrained by the forces of poverty, racism, and state surveillance.

From a paucity of documentation, it does appear that basketball was first played with any regularity in the 1920s, when the Mexican government introduced sport as a way of tempering the "rebellious peasants" and in order to civilize indigenous people. Federal money paid for the construction of basketball courts and baseball fields in outlying villages. In these regions, basketball has outpaced both soccer and baseball in popularity. The game has become so seamlessly integrated into indigenous social and ritual life that an outsider might assume that basquetbol was as traditional as maize. Anthropologist Ben Feinberg lived in Hautla, Oaxaca, in the 1990s while researching the local and global articulations of Mazatec identity. The 6'3" "gringo" was invited to join a team called Los Lobos to play in the local tournament, but he couldn't crack the starting line-up. Basketball tournaments, it turns out, are often the featured event at village fiestas, such that after the dances, speeches, rodeo, carnival, church mass, and orchestra performances that occupy the central square (often the basketball court) are finished, the game emerges to dominate the public space. Feinberg realized that these basketball tournaments, featuring teams from nearby and faraway villages, emerged as a contemporary form of a very traditional, institutionalized system of "intraregional travel and [social] integration." He notes:

> The Aztecs, Olmecs, and Mayas played a similar ball game, of
> course, but the source of the current Mesoamerican Indian fas-
> cination for the sport more likely comes from Naismith's version

and not Quetzacoatl's. It is important to note, though, that basketball is not seen in the Sierra as anything new, or as an instance of
acculturation. I asked the official in charge of the tournament in
San Antonio, said to be the oldest in the Sierra, when the tournament there began. "Years and years," he told me. I asked, "Since
when, before you were born?" "Yes," he replied, "Forever."[8]

Although it would be an overstatement to claim that the high-scale,
postmodern global marketing regime of the NBA has not influenced
the sport's stature in hinterland Mexico, the political economy of this
indigenous basketball is much older than the more recent transnational circulation of the Nike, Jordan, and the Dream Team semiotic
triumvirate.

One particular basketball tournament in Hautla started very late
in the day, and the championship game was not completed until about
3:30 A.M., by which time the mountain cold had frozen the very large
audience, still in attendance. Feinberg's Lobos team, though not the
local favorite, prevailed to win the championship prize, a "highly reluctant bull." Most of the villagers rooted for the team known as El Tri,
also the nickname of the national soccer team (indicating the three
colors of the national flag), which was comprised completely by Hautla
natives. Feinberg's unpopular team of outsiders has been started by
a young lawyer from one of the wealthiest Hautla families, who had
recruited a few "ringers" from Mexico City, who stood over six feet tall.
"The games stayed close, and [the audience] taunted the hot-headed
mestizo . . . until [he] slugged someone in the crowd and the latter was
assessed a technical foul for arguing a referee's call. They yelled and
laughed: '¡Viva el Tri' '¡Viva el Tri' 'Viva el Ejercito Zapatista.'"

In a wonderful ethnography of Oaxacan village life, Jeff Cohen ana-
lyzes the many forms of cooperation and reciprocity between households
and communities. An important feature of these community systems is
the invention of new relationships and practices in response to novel
challenges from global forces. Basketball has emerged as a centerpiece
of the village festival in southern Mexico, as a ritual encounter between
particular villages, but just as importantly, between Zapotec (or Mixtec,
or Triquis, or Mayan) villages and the outside world. Indeed, "[many]
of the economic reasons for the travel which once inscribed a regional
identity of a sort (particularly at fiestas) have vanished, but the basketball

tournaments continue to provide a form of cohesion based not on same-ness but on interaction between differentiated communities, and on the exhibition of difference through competition." These players dedicate significant amounts of time for practice as well as material resources for travel, in support of their tournament play. While they are not insulated from the desires of the global Jordanscape—occasionally revealing signs of its seduction—they seem motivated by a commitment to creating indigenous community through a cooperative, sporting embodiment.

Non-mestizo indigenous people face extreme discrimination coupled with great poverty. Middle-class Mexicans commonly view "Indios" as dirty, ignorant, and lazy at the same time as they glorify indigenous art and performance. Many Mayan-, Mixtec-, and Zapotec-speaking people, in communities spread across the hinterland of the two poorest Mexican states, Chiapas and Oaxaca, don't even view them-selves, culturally, as Mexican. Sam Quinones suggests, "That Oaxacan mountain Indians have been playing basketball for more than half a century—not soccer or baseball—is a metaphor for their separation from Mexico." During the twentieth century, the Mexican government seemingly paid little attention to indigenous communities, often victim-ized by land policies, environmental destruction resulting from various government projects, and inadequate educational and health programs. Indeed, "things" erupted in the early nineties, and on New Year's Day in 1994, the Zapatistas moved from the cover of their small villages and rainforest canopies to seize a handful of towns in the state of Chiapas.

As some indigenous communities were focusing their energies on organizing and participating in the Zapatista movement, people from other villages in Indian Mexico moved to the United States, reinforcing paths of migration many decades old. In fact, the largest Mexican ethnic group in the United States is the Zapotecos, who number in Los Angeles alone perhaps as many as 200,000. Ironically, to America they brought with them their beloved sport of basketball, and today, there is no pau-city of Zapoteco basketball tournaments. At least one such tournament hosts up to fifty teams on any given weekend, generating income, from entry fees to refreshment sales, which is sent back to Mexican villages. In fact, L.A. teams often send tournament prize money back home, used in turn for prize money and uniforms in Oaxaca.

Indeed, the complex of Los Angeles Oaxacans, their teams and

tournaments, are at once an inflection of one of the more chronicled communities of transbordered, diasporic indigenes, one that has
invented a series of interlinked networks, or to borrow Arturo Escobar's
phrase, "meshworks." In these spaces, people from Zapotec and Mixtec
villages are always and already "connected to one another through ties
of kinship, compadrazgo, and transborder forms of association such
as hometown associations or transborder public works committees,"[9]
with multiple urban and rural US, Mexican, and even Canadian nodes
of social relations, intermeshed through remittances, loans, restaurants,
labor, sometimes even coyotes, and of course, basketball teams.

Playing ball, and speaking their native idiom in public spaces,
Zapotecs nurture connections to their Mexican homes. Observers agree
that these games do not signify Mexicanness. And while some, including
myself, have argued that to play ball is to be Zapotec or Mixtec, if not
Oaxacan, perhaps that which is most at stake in these contests is one's
village identity. Carole Nagengast and Michael Kearney note the following about Mixtec as well as Zapotec peoples:

> Although linguistic differences from one village to another do not
> always render local dialects mutually unintelligible, they under-
> score separateness, as do distinctive variations in women's cos-
> tumes. Marrying within the village . . . is the rule, and reciprocal
> suspicion of those from [nearby] villages is the norm. Thus . . .
> individuals identify themselves as being from a given village [and]
> the primary opposition is between villages, and ethnicity is only
> occasionally salient.[10]

Of course, Oaxacans in the United States engage multiple constructions
of race and ethnicity, and they may assert the increasingly global sense
of an indigenous if not first nations people; other times they will need
to highlight their Mexicanness, if not occasionally their Latino-ness. Yet
even in the United States, Mexican mestizo bigotry injures them.

In Mexico, Zapotec and Mixtec, as well as other indigenous identities, are defined and experienced less as phenotypically marked (race), as
much as linguistically and cultural marked (ethnicity), but for indigenous
migrants coming to the west coast of the United States, "the racial/
ethnic hierarchy is overlaid with U.S.-based racial categories" and their
"Mexicanness" is treated as a racial identity.[11] In other words, Zapotecs

face certain forms of discrimination from Mestizo Mexicans, Mexican Americans, and other Latino groups, for their very "Indianness," while as Mexicans, and often as undocumented immigrants, also suffering the oppression of American society at large. Moreover, there are times and places when it might be advantageous to assert either Zapotec-ness —at local diversity festivals and in the ethnic barrio context—or their Mexicanness, or even Hispanic identity, for uniting with others for political purposes.

Zeus García, who is featured in a nuanced portrait of Zapotec basketball by journalist Sam Quinones,[12] moved in the early eighties to the Los Angeles suburb of Torrance, from his Oaxacan hometown, Santa Ana. He soon discovered, fifteen miles away, in West Los Angeles, Zapotecos regularly played pickup basketball games, so he immediately moved there. García had been quite a well-known player in Oaxaca, and once he realized just how many Zapotecos resided in L.A., he began to envision the possibility of a more extensive network of tournaments and opportunities for Oaxacans. He scouted players, coached teams, sought tournament sponsorships, emerging as the de facto president of Zapotec basketball in Los Angeles. After playing with African American and white players in L.A., García offered his own reading of racial difference in basketball, as quoted in Quinones: "I liked playing with [black guys] because it was really hard basketball. They're arguing all the time. But I liked playing with them because they were tall, and I liked trying to fight them for the ball. [White guys], you can't run into even a little, because they'll turn and say, 'Are you all right?' They're very worried about you. Blacks don't care about that."

While generally, the Zapotec basketball community has incorporated some of the prevailing American stereotypes regarding athleticism and race, players seem to remain focused on what is often termed a dream that eventually, with perseverance, Zapotecos will achieve success in at the collegiate level, Division I, or even in the NBA. They assert that their brand of basketball is unique, not so much for its technical qualities—although the play is focused on defense, passing, and jump shots—but for its spirit of intensity and teamwork. Nonetheless, as the following comment by a fifty-something Zapotec basketball coach in Los Angeles indicates, an awareness of the physical and cultural differences that might enhance one's basketball prowess existed, even in southern Mexico, in decades past:

Let me tell you something you might not know professor: in Oaxaca there's a small town called Xiacui; about 20 miles east of Guelatao. That small town has a neighboring town called Natividad where in the early 50's they had a Mineral Mine where people from other towns worked, and it had many workers coming from the state of Chihuahua. Well they started to get involved with women from that town and started to build a family with them, so the children that were born from those relationships started to look different, a little more whiter and much taller than normal people born there before, and those kids in the early 60's and 70's started to play basketball and dominate all over Oaxaca because of their height and because they could play.[13]

While most Oaxacan teams are comprised of players from the same village, García had a different vision. He formed a team called Raza Unida ("One Race"), the only Zapotec team with players from a variety of different villages. According to Quinones, all from lowland Oaxacan villages, the Raza Unida players approach their sport with great seriousness: they wear slick uniforms with warm-up jackets, skip work to attend tournaments, and they have a coach who brings a clipboard to practices. Owing to their largely lowland heritage, the team has upset the political landscape of Zapotec basketball in Los Angeles. In Mexico, the highland villages tend to be a bit more affluent, play on better courts, and sport fancier uniforms. Even in Los Angeles, the lowland-highland differences prevail, and as a result, in the beginning at least, the larger, more well-funded and public tournaments were run by highland Zapotecos. Zeus and Raza Unida showed up to play in one of these highland tournaments in 1997, and initially, nobody wanted them to play. For one thing, there was fear that they would dominate the tournament. Nobody wanted a lowland team to win, particularly one made up of players from different villages. Nevertheless, in a gesture of goodwill, the captains of the other teams allowed Raza Unida to play, and indeed, they won the tournament with ease. They have continued to play, and to win, effectively dominating the Zapotec basketball scene into the present. Generally hated for being so good, they are also respected for their willingness to risk crossing boundaries and are sometimes lauded as a symbol of Zapotec unity.

For Zapotecs, basketball is masculinely gendered, especially in L.A. In Oaxaca, girls and young women may take their turn on the court, but tournaments are exclusively for men. East and south of Oaxaca, however, pick-up basketball games are more likely to include female players. This is especially so in the state of Chiapas, where many Mayan-speaking communities exist and where the Zapista National Liberation Army (EZLN) movement originated and continues to flourish. In fact, a common feature of Zapatista gatherings—along with food, dance, music, and fireworks—is basketball. Both male and female ski-masked participants populate the basketball court while more senior-level Zapatista commanders (including both women and men) meet in nearby tents. EZLN's famous spokesperson, known as Subcommander Marcos, posts periodic communiqués to the Mexican newspaper *La Jornada* and online at the international EZLN website. In one of these messages, dated July 2003, Marcos playfully announces to the world a Zapatista basketball tournament, in which he jokingly invites international teams to compete, including the US, Spanish, and French national teams as well as "Euzkal Herria," or the team from Basque Country. These teams, Marcos indicates, will play against the "Dream Team" of the "January 1st 1994 Rebels Secondary School of the Autonomous Zapatistas." Of course, the final contest will be EZLN versus EZLN because, "in order to guarantee it, generous portions of sour *pozole* (corn gruel) will be served to the other teams." Marcos adds that any foreign team daring to defeat the Zapatista team will be taken prisoner and forced to listen to the program "Fox Contigo," a radio broadcast of then president Vicente Fox's weekly messages.

Some indigenous basketball-playing communities may be growing self-conscious about their passion for hoops, fearing that non-Indian Mexico might see their pastime as backward. They might be consciously turning to soccer, a more cosmopolitan, international sport. Subcommander Marcos sent a formal proposal in the spring of 2005 to the Italian soccer club, A. C. Milan, inviting them to a soccer match against an all-Zapatista team. The invitation called for a two-match series, with one game in Mexico City and a follow-up game in Italy. Although some of the A. C. Milan players were enthusiastic, wanting to assist the EZLN by participating in the tournament, the logistical difficulties proved too great. And, in Hautla, where Feinberg documented a fanaticism for basketball, the sport seems to have fallen from favor. Feinberg[14] claims that it has been replaced with "futbol rapido," a smaller, faster version of soccer played on the basketball court, with small goals. Mazatecans from Haulta are claiming that soccer is more sophisticated to the outside world while basketball is "too indigenous."

Nonetheless, indigenous basketball in Mexico matters. It matters because it is pleasurable to its participants. It matters because it demands from its participants material and emotional investments. It matters also because it reproduces social relationships and creates new ones. But mostly, it matters because it circumscribes a discursive space of difference and identity for indigenous Mexicans and their transnational ethnicities. Norman Denzin,[15] urging interactionists to embrace a performative approach to analyzing race, explains that ethnic and racial communities form images of themselves and others in the larger context of race relations "based on a constantly changing set of social constructions that classify and locate individuals within" a prevailing racial order. The racial subject emerges out of a politics of representation, transformed through the sites and practices of embodied interaction. For Zapotecos, Zapatistas, and other Mexican communities, basketball (partially) unifies these sites and practices. Through the game, the indigenous Mexican, especially the Californian immigrant, contemplates and inflects its identity in terms of race and ethnicity, but in ways very much different from black, white, or Latino youth in the United States.

Long since retired from active participation in games, García now coaches, and during a field interview, he told me that his vision for what basketball might offer the community has matured to include a more politicized and interventionist agenda. He is now president of the Instituto Oaxaca, located in L.A. but which seeks to provide social, cultural, financial, and legal services to all indigenous Oaxacan people, wherever they are located within or along the Oaxacan diaspora. This diaspora has truly crystallized as an internationally observed multisited swath of movement and dwelling whose two most prominent nodes are Oaxaca state and California. Remarkably, basketball seems to remain critical to the management of this diaspora in myriad ways. García has worked with the greater Los Angeles Public School District to establish a coed after-school basketball program for Latino, but mostly Oaxacan youth, in which students receive nourishment and tutoring prior to their basketball training sessions. They are provided with glossy uniforms and warm-up clothing. And under the umbrella of the Instituto Oaxaca, over thirty youth teams have been organized, whose players are all children of parents who have been deported to Mexico by the Immigration and Naturalization Service. Monies generated by regional basketball tournaments are directed toward paying for legal services for detained and deported immigrants, and also on occasion to transport sick Oaxacans to the United States for medical treatment.

To Zeus García and the thousands and thousands of Zapotecos living in Los Angeles, basketball is a way of animating ethnic traditions, in order to define themselves against, and indeed buffer themselves from, not only a dominant white America as well as a pervasive black and Asian America, but from a prevailing Latino and mestizo Mexican population in Los Angeles that too often scorns them. Their sporting pleasure teaches something about globalization and the mediation of the local and the global. In order to understand it, the cultural critic must account for not only "hybridity" and transnational flows of labor and capital, but also for structures of feeling and interaction. Basketball in this framework reveals a "postmodern emotional self" for the indigenous Mexican that is at once gendered, racialized, resistant and complicit, flexible, and strategic. Even though there is nothing fixed about Oaxacan identity, to play basketball is to remain Oaxacan.

If the way in which Zapotecos and Mixtecos tend to talk about Oaxacan basketball seems to turn on essentialism, we must recognize that essentializing is sometimes a subaltern social strategy. L.A. Oaxacans are negotiating many things at once, from poverty, liminality, state and federal regimes of oppression designed to control and vanquish their bodies, whiteness, mestizo bigotry, and a repressive neoliberal labor circuit. Is basketball an effective site of agency for these folks? As a white American man, asking this question is patronizing and presumptuous, but still, I am curious about what Oaxacan immigrants identify as their most urgent political projects and how they locate their own practices and pleasures within those projects. I believe "hoops" unfolds in what so far remains largely an emerging consciousness. These transbordered Oaxaqueños are leading the contested—always ambivalent—conversation about what constitutes indigenous culture, and what ethnicity might mean.

CHAPTER 11

Sport in Migrant Communities: Transnational Spaces and Gender Relations

Gertrud Pfister

Introduction

In recent decades, waves of migration have been steadily growing, increasing the complexities and dynamics of modern societies. Wherever they go, migrants[1] take with them their tastes and habits, their skills and qualifications, their wishes and dreams, and their worldviews—according to Bourdieu,[2] their "habitus." During their travels they meet and interact with people of different orientations and lifestyles. These transcultural confrontations and negotiations focus not only on ways of life, ideologies, and religions but also on discourses and practices referring to the body and to physical activities. In Western countries, migrants are confronted with healthism as a moral imperative, which also includes physical activity as a means of health promotion. Furthermore, they come to live in societies that value competition and surpassing others not only in sport but also in everyday life. Migrants may adopt perspectives, habits, and body cultures of the mainstream population; they may adapt them to their own lives; or they may refuse to integrate.

The aim of this chapter is to analyze, understand, and evaluate transnational flows and negotiations as far as they concern sport and physical activities, as well as the way they influence sporting discourses and practices in migrant communities. My main focus will be on people from a Turkish background living in Germany. In addition, data from my research in Denmark, in particular an interview study, will be used, providing in-depth insights into migrants' lives. These countries and the groups of Turkish migrants were selected because there is sufficient information available (e.g., the results of surveys), in addition to my own studies, publications of German, Danish, and Turkish colleagues. This information will be analyzed and interpreted using theoretical approaches to transnationalism, intersectionalities, gender, and socialization.

Theoretical Approaches: Gender and Body Cultures from the Perspectives of Transnationalism, Intersectionality, and Socialization

The intersecting categories of gender, ethnicity, religion, culture, social class, and place of residence (cities, rural areas, etc.) are acquired in socialization processes, integrated in identities, negotiated in interactions, and crystallized into worldviews and lifestyles that are adopted in the home countries and challenged by transnational migrations.

The term *transnational* refers to human activities as well as networks, organizations, and institutions that transcend national borders.[3] In recent decades, interest in and research on transnational movements and activities has increased in various academic disciplines such as sociology, economics, and political science, not least because the flow of people, information, ideas, and money, as well as conflicts and problems, are not (or are no longer) limited to a specific country or society. Increasing numbers of actors, processes, and institutions crisscross national boundaries, and more and more transnational spaces, communities, and cultures emerge.

In contrast to traditional notions of immigration, a transnationalist approach to migration and migrants emphasizes the diversity, complexity, and fluidity of migrants' situations, their "incorporation" into two or more cultures, and their interrelations with various peoples, groups, and societies.[4] Migrants create a fluid cross-national space of communication, engage in cross-border discourses and practices, initiate "creolization" processes, and constitute hybrid cultures.[5]

Numerous studies have shown that today's migration has many causes, aims, and purposes and often does not mean a permanent translocation of individuals or families. Moreover, migrants maintain numerous and various ties to their home countries, even though they may have settled for good elsewhere.[6] Modern means of communication and transportation, as well as, according to Giddens,[7] disembeddedness and time-space distanciation, contribute decisively to the establishment of not only transcultural habits, tastes, and practices, but also contacts and relationships. Currently migrants may have their relatives, their friends, and their work in different places simultaneously.

Several studies, among others an interview study with Turkish women in Denmark, provide excellent examples of how individuals and families with a migrant background preserve strong bonds with their relatives and friends "back home." They stay connected via phone, e-mail, skype, and so forth, and they send one another gifts and visit one another regularly. The life stories of the women interviewed revealed that their relatives in Turkey had a strong impact on their lives in Denmark, for instance, with regard to marriages and divorces. In addition, Turkish television ensures the continuous involvement of migrants with Turkish (popular) culture and enhances their identification with Turkish values, habits, and way of life.[8]

Studies—for example, in Denmark—indicate that a high percentage of migrants marry partners from their own ethnic group, which contributes to the preservation of their own culture.[9] But Turkish Danish residents also draw on the worldviews and ways of life of the mainstream "Danish" or "German" population, thus developing hyphenated identities and hybrid cultures. However, diaspora cultures are not uniform; rather, they are influenced by education and social class, as well as individual tastes and priorities.

Men and women are involved in migration processes to an almost equal degree, and gender has a decisive impact on the opportunities and challenges of men and women in transnational endeavors.[10] Studies have revealed that women not only migrate with their families, but also are often agents in transnational journeys and diaspora communities. However, gender relations are power relations, and in the home countries of many migrant groups women are still regarded and treated as the "second sex." Although women have equal rights in Turkey, most of them do not have equal access to resources and power.[11] In ethnic communities in Western countries, unequal gender arrangements are often sustained, not least because they may be regarded as an observance of religious and/or cultural values and norms.[12] However, the transfer of traditional gender roles to Western countries provides not only problems for women, but also for men.[13]

Gender is here understood as a social construction. According to Judith Lorber, societies are "gendered," meaning "work, family and other major areas . . . are organized by dividing people in two categories, 'men' and 'women'. . . . Gender is a binary system of social organization that creates inequality."[14] At the same time, gender is acquired by individuals, enacted in social situations and "embodied." But gender is not something we are or have, it is "something we do and something we think with, both a set of social practices and a system of cultural meaning."[15] The way we—natives and migrants alike—do gender—for example, wearing a bikini or a hijab—and the way we think in terms of gender—for example, identifying childcare as a mother's duty—we reproduce gender differences, and "once the differences have been constructed, they are used to reinforce the 'essentialness of gender.'"[16]

Gender always intersects with other categories such as age, social class, and ethnicity.[17] Ethnicity, too, can be understood as a social construction, which is "done" in social interactions. Ethnicity and gender are of more, or less, relevance depending on the context: they can be emphasized or downplayed, used as a demonstration of ethnic pride or femininity, or may have little relevance; for example, in interactions with one's parents.

The coalescence of the various intersecting categories and their embodiment must be explored in order to understand individuals' actions and reactions.[18] In this chapter the focus is on intersections relating to gender and ethnicity.

Bourdieu[19] describes the adoption of differing sporting practices as an instance of interplay between supply and demand, as "the result of relating two homologous spaces, a space of possible practices, the supply, and a space of dispositions to practise, the demand. On the supply side, there is a space of sports understood as a programme of sporting practices. . . . On the other hand, there is, on the demand side, a space of sporting dispositions which, as a dimension of the system of dispositions (habitus), are relationally and structurally determined."[20]

The German sociologist Klaus Heinemann[21] has developed an intri-

cate scheme for elucidating the backgrounds and processes of becoming active (or inactive) in sport, which can be used to shed light on
the gendering of sporting activities of Turkish migrants in Western
countries. He points, on the one hand, to individuals with their abilities,
skills, and knowledge; their experience, feelings, and motives; their likes
and dislikes; as well as their potentials, which are influenced by political,
social, and economic factors, and, generally, by society and culture, both
Turkish and German. Both cultures are based on a gender order that
provides different scripts for women and men and encourages gendered
attitudes to, demands for, and participation in sport. On the other hand,
Heinemann emphasizes the significance of sporting opportunities and
the appeal that sport, or a specific type of sport, has for individuals, be
they migrants or Germans, women or men. People will engage in sporting (or other) activities when the activity suits their aptitudes, tastes, and
expectations acquired during lifelong socialization processes whereby
socialization is understood as "active learning" and self-training in and
through cultural practices. Via interactions and encounters with the
socioecological environment (family, peers, physical surroundings, for
example) in national and transnational spaces, individuals react to and
"appropriate" the norms, rules, and expectations; that is, the pertinent
"scripts" of their respective communities (mainstream or migrant). In
doing so, they also develop conceptions and attitudes, and perhaps also
skills, relating to body cultures, which either encourage or hinder participation in physical activities and sport.[22]

These theoretical concepts provide an insight into, and understanding of, sport-related discourses and practices among male and female
migrants and facilitate the identification of the numerous influences
on sports participation, in particular the intersections of gender, religion and faith, ethnicity, social class, and other categories.[23] The physical
activities and sport-related experiences of migrants are closely interrelated with their current circumstances of life, as well as with the values, tastes, and habits rooted in the cultures of their home countries.
They are influenced not only by culturally situated gender ideologies,
constructions, and relations but also by religion, which has a decisive
impact on the ways in which physicality and physical activities are evalu-
ated by communities and lived by their male and female members.[24]
Although religion and faith influence the opportunities of girls and

women in particular, they do not deny them access to sport, as numerous studies on gender, sport, and Islam have revealed.[25]

Sport and Physical Activities among Individuals with a Migrant Background: Germany as an Example

Sport[26] is *per se* a transnational concept and has, during the last century, developed into the largest international community worldwide. However, sport is a Western "invention" and is not necessarily compatible with the cultural values and body concepts of countries with a majority of Muslim inhabitants such as those in Turkey.

Research—often not with but about "immigrants" and their lifestyles and sporting activities—has focused on their willingness or ability to adapt to the mainstream culture. Lack of compliance of Muslim migrants, such as wearing the *hijab* and fasting during Ramadan, as well as disinterest in sport, is often labeled (particularly by the mass media) as an act of segregation and even resistance or, in the case of women, as backwardness and/or an outcome of adherence to a repressive religion, thus concealing the diversities of migrant cultures.[27] Thus, Muslim migrants and sport appear to be contradictions. However, studies and statistics show a highly diverse situation with regard to the leisure activities of "Germans" and migrants, depending on age, gender, education, and ethnic origin. An important source here is the German DJI-Youth Survey (2003),[28] which included around 9,000 twelve- to twenty-nine-year-old individuals, among them 1,871 with a migrant background. Reliable information is also provided by the "socio-economic panel" (SOEP), a regular representative survey of more than 12,000 private households in Germany,[29] and the SPRINT study, which focused on physical education but has also provided insights into the out-of-school sporting activities of 8,000 eight- to eighteen-year-old respondents.[30] These and other surveys on smaller scales on participation in sport and physical activities in Germany have revealed even higher rates of activity among adolescents/young adults with a "migrant" than those of a German background, in particular when the focus is on *daily* physical activity.[31] Besides age, gender had a decisive impact on rates of activity. Girls with a migrant background are significantly less physically active than German girls and boys.[32] Sports clubs still seem to be a domain of ethnic Germans: according to the German Youth Survey 43 percent of twelve- to twenty-nine-year-old Germans but only 37 percent of second-generation and 21 percent of first-generation migrants of this age cohort have joined a club.[33]

The German data of the International Student Assessment (PISA) was based on 30,000 fifteen-year-old school students. The results of the study seemed to confirm the trends mentioned above, showing as they did that 47 percent of adolescents with a German background but only 43 percent of those with a migrant background were members of a sports club.[34] However, the impression that more German adolescents than their migrant classmates are sports club members has to be modified, at least for boys. Gender-differentiated data has revealed that sports clubs seem to have a special appeal for Turkish boys of this age; 57 percent of fifteen-year-old boys from migrant families and even 68 percent of boys with a Turkish background belong to a sports club. The same is true of 53 percent of German boys, 43 percent of German girls and only 28 percent of girls from ethnic minorities. Only 21 percent of girls with a Turkish background are members of a club.[35]

Boys and girls with a migrant background seem to prefer extracurricular activities at school, in which according to the SPRINT study 17 percent of girls and 24 percent of boys participate (compared with 14 percent of German girls and 18 percent of boys).[36] In particular for girls, schools provide a safe environment and are a legitimate place to spend their time. Favorite sports are football among boys (84 percent of Turkish migrants) and dancing among girls. Basketball is more popular with migrant than with German adolescents.

The differences between the two genders with regard to sporting activities decrease, in "migrant" groups, too, with an increase in the socioeconomic status of the family, although girls with a migrant background do not reach the activity level of "German" girls. The rate of participation among girls with a migrant background increases when German is the everyday language spoken in their families. However, 79 percent of Turkish families speak Turkish at home.[37]

These studies also provide information on the impact of religion and gender role orientation on sports participation. Muslim girls and girls who agree with traditional gender arrangements are active in a sports club to a much lesser degree than other girls. Religion and gender role orientation does not influence sports participation or club member-ship among boys.[38] However, in the last decade a growing number of girls with a migrant background have begun to participate in competi-tions, many of them in combat sports. Although these girls are still a tiny minority, they are visible and in some ways pioneers, and they may even be role models for other girls. As interviews have revealed, though, there is often a precarious balance between the ideas and expectations of their parents, the demands of their school or vocational training, and their own wishes for a sporting career.[39] According to interviews, the mothers of the girls are not as a rule active in sport or physical activities, and they often do not understand and support the participation of their daughters in sports competitions.

Sport-related studies conducted in several Danish cities have shown similar differences with regard to gender and ethnic origin, although activity rates seem to be higher in Denmark than in Germany. A survey of ten- to sixteen-year-old students in Århus, a Danish city, revealed, for instance, that 87 percent of the Danish boys and 82 percent of the girls surveyed were active in sports. Among migrants of the first generation, the corresponding figures were 94 percent for the boys and 50 percent for the girls, and among the descendants of migrants 89 percent for the boys and 63 percent for the girls. Agergaard's study also showed that a high percentage of boys from ethnic minorities participated in informal sporting activities, especially football games in streets or parks.[40]

Girls and women with a non-Western background are a small minority among the physically active population, although Danish girls have a higher dropout rate from sport and physical activity than boys. Among older adults, Danish women seem to be more physically active than men, whereas most women with a migrant background have adopted an inactive lifestyle. More men than women from ethnic minorities are involved in sport, but they are less active than ethnic Danes.[41]

Children of migrant families prefer different sports from their Danish peers. They are scarcely interested in activities that are popular in Denmark, such as badminton and team handball. Besides football, boys favor basketball, weight training, and combat sports, which can be explained by the ideals of masculinity in migrant cultures. Dancing, gymnastics, badminton, horse riding, and team handball are popular among Danish girls. Of these activities, only dancing attracts girls from ethnic minority families.[42] Flemming Mikkelsen, moreover, noted great differences between adult men's and women's sporting activities.[43] Men with a migrant background showed particular interest in football, weight training, jogging, and fishing, while the few active women favored swimming (often in women-only environments), gymnastics/aerobics, and jogging.

The results of all available studies indicate that football in particular provides a chance for activities and also recognition among boys and young men. The football field seems to be a transnational space of social integration and for male bonding. According to an interview study conducted in Denmark and Sweden, club managers and coaches insisted that their football teams consisted of players regardless of their ethnic origin.[44]

Turkish football clubs have existed in Germany since the 1980s,[45] but boys with migrant backgrounds are also integrated into mainstream sport teams and clubs. As in Denmark, "migrant" boys in Germany are very active at playing football in informal settings. However, it seems that sport/football is not a lifelong activity among Turkish migrants since adult men are not, as a rule, members of sport clubs and do not play football, even though they may be ardent football fans.

In contrast to boys, few Turkish girls and women play football, and this is true of both countries. Women's football is also a relatively new trend in migrant communities. One of the first teams in Germany was set up in the Türkiyemspor sports club in Berlin in 2004.[46] Many of the players had to overcome fierce resistance from their families, in particular their mothers. "You will never get a husband if you show your bare legs in public," was one of the comments of the mother of Hülya Kaya, the best player in the girls' team. She did not care; she wanted to play football and she did so. Her father, Mehmet, supports her and was very proud when she was selected to play for Turkey in the Turkish under-seventeen national team.[47]

What are the backgrounds and reasons for the widespread abstinence of girls and women with a Turkish background from sport and the disproportionally large interest of boys and young men in football? The football mania of boys does not seem to need an explanation—at least, there are no studies focusing on this topic. By contrast, the (dis) interest of girls and women in sport has always been an issue of scholarly interest and research.[48] Explanations for this phenomenon range from traditional gender arrangements to lack of resources. Gender-specific work in particular, that is, assigning women and girls to the housework, and Islamic laws (especially those pertaining to "modesty") are assumed to hinder girls' activities and opportunities—not only in the sports arena. There is no doubt that these explanations apply to the situation of many Turkish girls, but these barriers can be overcome more easily than the embodied habits, tastes and everyday theories embedded in traditional Turkish culture and confirmed in and through transnational contacts. Consequently, it is necessary to take not only the situation in Germany or Denmark into consideration but also body cultures and habits in Turkey itself, which differ significantly according to region, place of residence, and the socioeconomic status of girls and women.

Sport and Gender in Turkey

From a transnational perspective, it is imperative to approach the body cultures of migrants and their descendants by exploring their roots, meaning concepts of the body and bodily activities in their home countries, as well as the transformations of physicalities and physical activities as a consequence of migration processes.

FOOTBALL AND MALE BONDING

Turkey is "football crazy"; in particular, the large and famous clubs such as Galatasaray S.K., Fenerbahçe or Beşiktaş Istanbul, as well as the other teams of the "super league," have countless numbers of excited, devoted, and often violent supporters. "Even by the high European standard of soccer fanaticism, it's rare to find such large-scale, life-and-death investment surrounding a match . . . Although virtually every Turkish city has its own team, the majority of Turks support one of the nation's "big three" teams—Galatasaray, Fenerbahçe, and Beşiktaş, all of which are based in Istanbul."[49]

Football is a spectator or media event for men, maybe also for many women; but for young men it is both a spectacle and a social practice. Turkish boys define and display masculinity by way of athletic activities (and appearance), and sport, in particular football, is used as a symbol of male prowess. Atencio and Koca[50] have investigated how secondary school students "do gender" during "free time" in physical education, which provided "conditions where young men could create and participate in activities which reflect a traditional version of masculinity based around the exhibition of physical strength and skill." Those students who displayed these traits could most significantly participate in the young men's community of practice. Activities such as football and fighting underpinned "the shared meanings and practices of masculinity and sustained boundaries of participation and non-participation."[51] Except for two boys, all the male students in the class played football in and out of school, and all were fans of Turkish football teams. They claimed and appropriated the "physical activity" space and gained hegemony by excluding female students and "un-athletic" males.

The dominance of football in Turkish culture is confirmed by other studies, such as a survey of students of Çanakkale Onsekiz Mart University: seventy-four out of ninety-nine male students played football, fifty-five played table tennis, and fifty-four took part in swimming.[52] The high degree of sports participation among the respondents can be explained by their social class, as well as their age and their specific status as students.

Turkish migrants in Western countries have brought their football fever with them. Living in Germany or Denmark, they follow their teams on TV or the Internet. During their holidays in Turkey, their football expertise and skills provide prestige and support the integration of the "Deutschländer" in their home communities. However, German Turks mostly have multiple loyalties; often being fans of German clubs, too—not least because players with Turkish backgrounds are members of German teams, and even the national team. More than 40,000 Turks attended a game during the European championship in Berlin in 2012. "Turkey lost the game with one goal coming from Mesut Özil, the German national football player of Turkish origin. The Turkish fans did not like it a bit, but this is what you call integration in the high-speed, multiculturalist, multicentered world of ours."[53]

Being a (former) football player and fan fits into both Turkish and Western cultures. Football provides a common language and a topic of discussion; it is a means of male bonding, conveys status, and creates communities of fans. Fieldwork at two London schools with a high number of Turkish migrants revealed that "football and fighting simultaneously solidify and cut across ethnic boundaries and that many boys become deeply invested in these activities as the primary signifiers of masculinity. For these boys, being a 'real man' is established through their prowess in both activities and they gain popularity and status . . . through them."[54]

Studies showed migrants in Western countries also are accepted in competitive sports where performance is considered more important than ethnic origin.[55] Football can thus overcome social, cultural, and religious barriers; however, conflicts among ethnic groups, in particular among the fans, should not be underestimated.[56]

GIRLS AND WOMEN—OPPORTUNITIES AND CONSTRAINTS IN TURKEY

The situation of girls and women in Turkey is greatly diverse, depending on many variables such as social class, place of residence, religion, and faith. Turkey, a secular country with a large majority of Muslim inhabitants, allows both modern and traditional lifestyles. Women "officially" have the same rights as men, but despite the claim of gender equality, the majority of women's lives are decisively influenced by traditions and also traditional gender ideologies.[57] The gendered segregation of work is still embedded in Turkish society,[58] and most men and women accept and have internalized the roles assigned to them.[59] According to M. Müftüler-Bac, "it seems contradictory that despite modernization efforts and legal changes, Turkish women are still oppressed by the patriarchal system."[60] However, there are great differences between orientations and lifestyles in Turkey depending on where a person lives and to what social class he or she belongs. Middle-class women in the cities have the freedom to adopt a Western lifestyle. But even "emancipated" women seem to regard it as their greatest duty to be a good wife and a good mother.[61]

Large-scale surveys of sport and physical activities among the Turkish population or specific groups such as adolescents are not available. However, information that does exist shows that girls' and women's sport (for all) is not widely practiced in Turkey, although some sports like gymnastics and volleyball are "female domains."[62] Young women who play football form a tiny minority. As of the 2007–08 season, a total of 798 female footballers were licensed in fifty-one Turkish women's football teams.[63] However, in recent years, the interest of women in martial art has increased[64] and young women even participate in the national Turkish sport, wrestling. Women's wrestling, however, is not a "sport for all" but a professional activity, and the female participants are members of the lower classes struggling for a better life.[65] In the above-mentioned study conducted at the Çanakkale Onsekiz Mart University, none of the sixty-six female students played football, while thirty-seven named swimming, thirty-one cycling, and thirty-one dancing as their sports.[66] No information is given about the frequency and intensity of their activities, however.

A survey of four hundred Turkish Muslim female students of Mugla University revealed that it was primarily the constraints imposed by their parents (47 percent) and only to a lesser degree by religion (21 percent) and social pressure (14 percent) that influenced their leisure habits. All students adhered to Islam and the majority agreed that religion intervened with exercises, but their attitudes to the rules "dictated" by religion differed greatly. Whereas some believed that women should not exercise in the presence of men, others did not name any restrictions.[67]

In-depth interviews with Turkish migrants in Denmark showed that only one woman out of the five participants in the study had learned to cycle and to swim in Turkey. She had a middle-class background, was Muslim but not religious, and had studied engineering.[68] Various studies conducted in Turkey, nevertheless, indicate that Turkish middle- and in particular upper-class women, infected by the "slimming mania," have recently been using fitness centers in increasing numbers.

A body of literature deals with the "leisure constraints" of women in Turkey.[69] Among other factors named include lack of financial resources, facilities, and time, as well as job or family obligations. In a study with Turkish undergraduates, Cengiz Demir found that the female respondents in particular found it difficult to take part in sports because of household responsibilities, lack of money, or lack of opportunities.[70] However, a focus on these constraints diverts attention from the structural and cultural backgrounds and obscures the opportunities that women have of negotiating their leisure activities or even resisting social pressures.

A recent interview study with forty-three women in Ankara (aged twenty-seven to fifty-five) who trained either in women-only facilities provided by the government or in private fitness clubs revealed large differences between these two groups of women.[71] The women training in the government-run facilities were mostly migrants from villages, whereas the women in the fitness clubs belonged to the middle classes. With few exceptions, the women in both groups were married and had children.

Despite their different backgrounds and orientations, all women found it difficult to attend a fitness center because of their family responsibilities, and they all complained about their lack of time. A further problem was that family members did not approve of their physical activities and thought it dangerous, or at any rate, a waste of time. The lower-class women exercising in the government-run facilities also complained about financial problems and that they had to struggle to find the money for the fitness center. However, all the women had managed to negotiate with their families or relatives and find ways of attending the training sessions. They had gained a new balance between caring for others and caring for themselves and had found a certain measure of freedom to experience a world outside their homes.

The available studies demonstrate that sport, in particular football, plays an important role in the lives of Turkish boys and (young) men. By contrast, girls and women are often not supposed to and sometimes not allowed to participate in sport. Depending on social class and where they live, girls and women are more, or less, able to negotiate the necessary freedom for physical activities, often in fitness centers. Islamic laws may restrict women's participation in sport and physical activities; however, there are diverse ways of dealing with religious demands and reconciling religion with playing sports.

Transnational Perspectives on the Sports Participation of Turkish Migrants in Germany/ Denmark

Migrants from Turkey come to Western countries with gendered and embodied cultural practices, including attitudes toward sporting activities as well as sport-related abilities and skills they have adopted through various socialization processes. In encounters with body and movement cultures in Germany or Denmark, boys and young men can use football as their "sporting capital," find social networks, and gain recognition. Turkish girls and women, by contrast, do not have sport in the "luggage" they bring with them since they come from an environment that emphasize normative and hierarchical gender relations and does not encourage females to be physically active in their leisure. This means that many girls and women have not had any opportunity of developing sport-related skills, tastes, and habits in Turkey.

Girls may even face resistance in Turkey and in Germany when they wish to take up sport. Traditional gender roles and religious precepts may be further issues that perhaps do not prevent, but may hinder, sporting activities among girls and women. Not only the families and ethnic communities, but also the girls and women themselves, influenced as they have been by the ideals of femininity and gender roles in Turkey, may regard sport as "unfeminine" and inappropriate.

Living in a transnational space, migrants are still confronted with the sport discourses and practices in their home countries. Parents try to educate their children according to their own "Turkish" value system, and the larger family, the ethnic community, and not to forget their relatives in Turkey as well as the Turkish mass media also have an impact. A good example of the influence of "Turkish" perspectives on "women and sport" is the refusal of many parents to let their daughters play football, particularly when they reach puberty. When Türkiyemspor, the Turkish sports club mentioned above, founded a girls' football team, the parents, notably the mothers, had to be convinced that playing football did not endanger their daughters' health. However, there were also parents who were proud of their girls and encouraged them to play.[72] In the past few years, several German Turkish women have entered the transnational space of football, playing for the Turkish national team. In 2008, eight team members came from Germany.[73]

As numerous initiatives and projects in Germany and in Denmark clearly demonstrate, girls and women with migrant backgrounds can be motivated to be physically active. Information, encouragement, popular forms of gymnastics, dance, and sports, and also, in the case of religious women, a female-only environment are appropriate means of attracting female migrants.

Perspectives

Currently, not only in sport but also in the field of education, young women with migrant backgrounds are changing gender arrangements of their cultures. In Denmark, 41 percent of women of the second generation of migrants are at present in a continuing education program— more than girls in the mainstream population and many more than young men with a migrant background (25 percent). One of these "new women," who is studying to become a dentist, stated in an interview that her parents supported her in all her decisions and even accepted her headscarf, although they did not like it in the beginning. Many of her relatives and friends are also continuing their education because they want to be independent and have a "good life." "No matter if you wear a cross or a scarf, education is extremely important. Education is a form of power, something which can protect you."[74] These young educated women are currently developing hybrid cultures in and outside the world of sport. Running marathons with a headscarf or boxing with a t-shirt instead of a bra are signs of bridging cultures. The increasing number of female students with migrant backgrounds and their visibility in public spaces such as cafes indicates adaptations, changing aspirations, and new perspectives not only of minorities but also of Danish society as a whole.

Boys and young men do not experience any cultural conflicts when playing sport, either in Germany or during their holidays in Turkey. On the contrary, getting involved in soccer, as a player and/or as a fan, earns them acceptance and prestige wherever they are.[75] Football helps to navigate between the cultures. The question arises whether—and, if so, how—this form of transnational bonding can be transformed into integration in other areas of the society.

Little is known how the presence and adaptation of migrants affects the Western societies and in which way the transnational flows of people and ideas have an impact on the life in Turkey. This could be the topic of a transnational research project with international cooperation, which would provide new knowledge on gender, ethnicity, and sport in a cross-cultural setting.

CHAPTER 12

Masculinities beyond Otherness: Cricket, Gender, and Ethnicity in Oslo, Norway

Thomas Michael Walle

Introduction

Much research on ethnic minority men in Norway tend to address what is regarded as a social problem, seeing men as perpetrators of gang-related criminality and bearers of a patriarchal culture characterized by honor-related violence and killings.[1] Research into gender and ethnicity, if concerned at all with men, set out to find a specific cultural or social explanation for the particular style of masculinity that is believed to be dominant within certain segments of the migrant population.[2] In later years, with increasing attention directed at fundamentalist Islamic terrorism in media and public debate, the position of Muslim men as the abject "Other" in European national narratives has been further strengthened, resulting in a widespread stigmatization of male Muslims.[3]

Even if such studies may have an ambition to de-essentialize masculine practices of Muslim, ethnic minority men, Alan Petersen warns that "scholars can be seen to perpetuate stereotypes of black and ethnic men through the approaches that they bring to their work, in their selec-

Editors' Note: This chapter is based on work for the PhD in Social Anthropology, and draws on text from the dissertation, chapters 1, 3, and 5, in particular; see Thomas Michael Walle, *A Passion for Cricket: Masculinity, Ethnicity and Diasporic Spaces in Oslo* (Department of Social Anthropology, Faculty of Social Sciences, University of Oslo, 2010).

tive use of data, and in their reliance on pre-existing popular images."[4] In 1985, the seminal article "Toward a New Sociology of Masculinity" was published, drafting what was ten years later elaborated in the highly influential book *Masculinities* as a refined theory on the relations of power among men, as well as men's universal power over women.[5] In the book, the theoretical model of gender relations is structured around the alleged existence of a hegemonic masculinity that, although corresponding to the characteristics of only a few men, is supported by a larger group because they benefit from the current structures of power and the patriarchal dividend. In relation to this culturally exalted form of masculinity, the masculine identities of black men and ethnic minority men are treated as marginalized masculinities, placed in an inevitably inferior position to the culturally exalted form.

While theories on hegemonic masculinity draw attention to the dominant relations of power within which the masculine identities of ethnic minority men are shaped, they are insufficient in accounting for the relations of power that exist between men of a given ethnic minority. Raewyn W. Connell does acknowledge diversity within any group, but maintains that analyses of power relations between different masculinities must have the culturally exalted hegemonic masculinity as a point of reference.[6] The relational dimension is one of the strengths of Connell's theory on masculinity, but structuring the model around the hegemonic masculinity tends to determine which relations are of analytical relevance. Stephen Whitehead remarks how men are thus forced into an analytical relationship with hegemonic masculinity: "Even those men who would wish not to associate with hegemonic masculinity are somehow inevitably drawn into living their lives in a constant state of tension with this dominant form of masculine being."[7]

This study is based on ethnographic fieldwork conducted in Oslo, Norway, 2003–04. During fieldwork, a cricket club consisting of players of Pakistani descent were followed at practices, matches, and social gatherings, and some workers established individual relations to some of the players. Some recorded interviews were conducted, but the main part of the material is produced through participant observation. An ambition with the research project has been to expand and diversify images of ethnic minority men, contributing to representations that are alternative to those predominant in the media. Cricket was chosen as an ethnographic point of departure because it provides a social setting where relations *among* men of the Norwegian Pakistani community have prominence over the community members' relations to the majority population. In Norway cricket is a sport dominated by players of Pakistani descent, and it was established as an organized activity with the arrival of Pakistani labor migrants around 1970. Richard Cashman argues that in many countries the formation, by migrants from Pakistan or India, of a cricket club with a predominantly Asian membership: "is a significant way of maintaining culture in an alien environment."[8] Despite this postulation, popular culture in general and cricket in particular are generally overlooked when researchers investigate the cultural characteristics of the Pakistani community, the largest non-European migrant community in Norway.[9]

I suggest that processes of "othering" affects the men's self-presentation. Cricket becomes a site and a source for expressing resistance against this "othering," negating popular perceptions, playing up to stereotypes in a mockery way, and arguing for a refinement and complexity in cricket that is lacking in the dominant sports of Norwegian society. Ben Carrington proposes that the forming of the Caribbean Cricket Club in northern England constitutes a "Black space within a White environment."[10] Although it is argued that this club is used by black men as a form of resistance to white racism, when it comes to the internal relations among club members, Carrington contends, "Blackness takes on a lesser significance."[11] If we assert that ethnicity, in a similar way, takes on lesser significance within Norwegian cricket, an analysis of gender as it is formed and performed among a group of Pakistani cricket players also provides evidences of masculinities "beyond otherness." Drawing on the concept "mutedness" as developed by Edwin Ardener, it is suggested that the cricketers represent a muted group.[12] I argue, that by ascribing significance to cricket in an analysis of Pakistani masculinities, we allow the men agency and give voice to experiences that escape the white hegemonic gaze.

The Establishment of Cricket in Norway

Cricket in Norway is interrelated with the Pakistani migration to the country, which started in late 1960s when there was demand for manual workers. In this early period, the migrants were mainly young men, some of them married and with children, while the majority saw the stay in Norway as a way to prepare, financially, for a settled family life upon their return to Pakistan. Some of the migrants brought balls and bats to Norway after visits home to Pakistan, and they enjoyed *knocking* between the barracks at the industrial area where they worked and lived, during the limited leisure they had. Gradually they started to explore the possibilities of getting more suitable facilities, enabling the play of proper cricket games, and a lengthy process negotiating with the authorities was initiated. In the common narrative of the consolidating period of cricket, these hardships figure as an instructive backdrop when assessing any obstacles that cricket faces today, although they do admit that there were persons and institutions in the bureaucracy that extended a lot of help.

It is important to acknowledge how drafting the establishment of cricket in Norway contributes to a story of the Pakistani migration to Norway strikingly different from the common narrative that has developed within the community and in public perception over the years: one of hard work, neglect of the need for or benefits of integration, and only a gradual and rather late awakening to the realities that temporarily has become permanent and that life strategies may have to be altered or modified. What is missed in this story is the fact that even with the prospect of a possibly short stay in Norway, migrants have obviously tried to make the best of their situation. Despite limited means, there was still amusement to be found, between hard labor and long working hours.

Through fieldwork, it has been documented how cricket represents a significant social network within the Pakistani ethnic community, related to sense of belonging and diasporic sentiments, as well as to the development of social capital and internal hierarchies in regard to community leadership and political influence. However, cricket was not from the start seen as a particular "Pakistani space." On the contrary, cricket was initiated by the "townspeople," a minority within the Pakistani migrant population, teaming up with other South Asian migrants of similar urban background, as well as with some white players from the English-speaking world. In the initial period, cricket was a multiethnic activity, and this may have facilitated the cricketers' negotiations with the authorities, arguing from the position as sports people rather than a particular ethnic group. This reasoning has persisted over the years, despite the Pakistani domination strengthening, increasingly making cricket a tightly knit social network that the men can benefit from socially in a variety of ways. Jack Williams found a similar dual and contradictory development in Bolton in England, where South Asian cricket was established partly as a response to the exclusion of ethnic minority players from "white" clubs, and thus to campaign for a more inclusive cricket, but eventually developed into ethnically homogeneous clubs each of which mainly recruits players from the circle of its dominant group.[13]

Mutedness and Othering

A lesson learned in the early stages of fieldwork was that presenting the research project as an investigation into masculine ideals and male practice did not resonate with the men's self-understanding. The fact that they were men, and that men do gender in particular ways, was not immediately seen by them as a relevant subject matter in a homosocial context. They were, however, much more mindful of their position as an ethnic minority in Norway, and I habitually introduced this as a topic of interest. By introducing the minority-majority relation as part of the societal framework within which these masculinities should be investigated—that is, by presenting the stereotype of the "immigrant man" as the outsider's view—it was easier to have the men reflect upon their gender practices as viewed from the inside, often within the scope of opposing these stereotypic images.

Hence, although the intention in the research project was to document the varied male practices among a group of Norwegian Pakistanis, the fieldwork inevitably generated many accounts of the experience of being discriminated against and marginalized as an "immigrant man." The men could tell a lot about cricket, and they could say a lot about how misguided people's general notion of Norwegian Pakistani men was. However, there was hardly anything said on what it meant to them, as men, to play cricket. This fact proved to be an important reminder of how the relation between minority life and society's understanding of a given minority group is structured.

The "immigrant man" has emerged as an often-used term and concept in the contemporary Norwegian debate, framed within a larger picture that is often seen as contrasting with the notion of the

"Norwegian/common man." Considering the fact that the immigrant population is diverse, and consists of people from all continents and from all kinds of backgrounds, such a term is imprecise, to say the least. In general use, then, people are talking about a particular segment of the population that is thought to be different from the majority on especially crucial issues. This process of ascribing a set of different characteristics to particular groups is obviously just as much about how the majority society wishes to perceive itself. The "orientalism" of the colonial era has been transferred to the postcolonial period, and any effort to characterize the ethnic "other" must be seen in relation to the constitution of a national "self."[14] Thus the features that are typically seen to characterize the "immigrant man" are more about what the majority society does *not* wish to be associated with than about any general and widespread qualities of ethnic minority men. This is illustrated by Rebecca Ouis's historical analysis of the changing perception of male Muslim sexuality in the West.[15] While the Muslim male during the Victorian period was depicted as a man of uncontrolled sexuality, with a harem of available women, today, in the aftermath of sexual awakening and liberal moral attitudes in the West, he is regarded as puritanical to the extreme, with an almost hostile view of sexuality: "We thus have two completely opposite perceptions of Muslim sexuality, which, by closer examination, merely show how Muslims are constructed as 'the Other' in relation to the West."[16]

Although there are historical changes in what groups are at any time included within the term *immigrant men,* similar to the change from the image of sexually hyperactive sultans of the Ottoman Empire to today's fierce image of Osama bin Laden and his like loathing the immorality of the West, there tends in general to be a shared notion of what the ideas about immigrant men imply in a particular historical context. Thus, on the basis of historical patterns of migration, particular events and the national and international political climate, today's stereotypic "immigrant man" in Norway is a South Asian or African Muslim male of dark complexion. Disregarding the fact that many of the Pakistani cricketers have never migrated, or came to Norway at a very young age, the image of the Muslim immigrant man predominant in public discourse is a reality they must cope with daily.

According to Ardener, subdominant groups are muted because their

way of fighting for recognition is through "the dominant communicative system of society—expressed as it must be through the dominant
ideology."[17] In regards of analyzing Norwegian Pakistani masculinities,
I will argue that cricket can be seen to represent a muted field. Despite
the significance of cricket for the individual players, as well as crickets
central position in their perception of what constitutes Pakistani culture
and what nourishes their sense of belonging to a globally dispersed
Pakistani people, it is not included in the rather massive attention that
is given in the majority society to the problems and challenges associated with the immigrant man. It is therefore not that Pakistani men are
invisible or ignored in the public debate, and neither that they are not
offered the opportunity to participate in it, but they are seldom granted
the opportunity to talk about what matters most to them. Cricket does
not present itself as an adequate reply to queries about whether or not
one represents a threat to the values of society, because it is not recognized as a position in the moral landscape of the majority society.
Employing the concept of muted groups particularly to address a male
bias in research and the mutedness of women, Henrietta Moore elaborates on what "muted" means: "It is not that women are silent; it is
just that they cannot be heard."[18] Subdominant groups, according to
Moore, are "silenced by the structures of dominance."[19] I argue that
there exist structures of dominance that keep cricket as an essential part
of Norwegian Pakistani (male) life in the shadows.

Stigmatization and Otherness

I now present some examples of how cricket provides a site and source
for expressing resistance against stigmatization and experiences of
being "othered" by the majority society. In the context of this chapter,
it will be possible to present only a very brief analysis of these cases,
which are elaborated more fully elsewhere.[20]

"NOT THE KIND OF GANG THEY ARE THINKING OF"

During one of my first visits to the cricket venue at Ekeberg in
Oslo, I discuss the scope of my research with Shoaib, captain of the
cricket club that I base the research on and my closest associate during
fieldwork.[21] He comments in a resigned manner:

> I started a "gang" several years ago, but not the kind of gang they
> are thinking of. They're not interested in writing about other issues
> than crime and those things. But the people playing cricket don't
> get involved in such things—they don't have time for it [laughs].

Despite the humorous punch line, referring to the length of a typical
cricket match as well as time-consuming regular practice, Shoaib here
presents cricket as an activity and a social arena fundamentally different from the way Norwegian Pakistani men are usually pictured in the
media. However, as he sadly notes on frequent occasions, the media
show little interest in cricket or in the unspectacular life of most of the
Norwegian Pakistanis that he knows. Shoaib also demonstrates an understanding for the dual and contradictory meaning of the term *gjeng* (gang)
in the Norwegian language, which can refer both positively to a group
of friends and acquaintances that meet regularly and more negatively to
a group of troublemakers or criminals. He also expresses sensitivity to
the way the negative connotation of "gang" in the contemporary debate
is typically associated with groups of immigrant men, adding that his
cricket-playing gang does not fit into the general image of Norwegian
Pakistani men in the media. This prevailing image, in Shoaib's opinion, is
the reason why cricket and other similar immigrant activities are seldom
to be found in the newspapers or on TV or the radio.

Despite Shoaib's justifiable observation, which is supported by
media research, several of the men within the cricket circle acknowledge the realities behind the reports in the press, although stressing that
such stories represented only a handful of persons.[22] Yousuf remarks:

> Every group has its problematic individuals—that goes for
> Norwegians as well as Pakistanis. The difference is that if a
> Pakistani does something wrong, he is taken to represent all
> Pakistanis.

Kamran is more consciously aware of the possible dangers of city life for
his Norwegian Pakistani fellows. Although he is in the early twenties and
thus a relatively young man in terms of cricket, he informs me that he
has paid for a substantial amount of cricket equipment out of his own
pocket, in order to help the younger ones getting started with cricket:

> It's too expensive for the kids to buy the gear, they can't afford it.
> Cricket is important, because it helps to keep them away from
> the street.

Inzaman shows a similar understanding of how a male adolescent in the city is particularly vulnerable. He tells of his recent decision to move out of Oslo in order to provide a safer environment for his children to grow up, and particularly to keep his young teenaged son away from the lure of the city:

> There's so many bad things that they may encounter in the city— like drinking, roaming in the streets or going downtown. Where we live now it's much safer. There's no dangers outside—actually there's nothing much to do at all [laughs]! So they spend a lot of their time indoors or at the nearby sports field.

What we can read from the above statements from Yousuf, Kamran, and Inzaman is that the men express awareness of the possible mischief that people in Oslo (especially the young and adolescent) may be caught up in, although they tend to see it mainly as an urban phenomenon that is not related to ethnic belonging or cultural background. They also share the idea that cricket serves as a cure for, or a preventive force against, this threat. Cricket, in their opinion, is related to particular nationalities and ethnic groups, and it is arguably the fact that cricket today is regarded as intrinsic to Pakistani culture more than as a crucial part of British cultural identity.[23] These statements can thus be seen to represent the opposite of the way the majority society tends to perceive and explain the current outlook in Oslo. Men of immigrant background are overrepresented in the criminal statistics, although the numbers are low, and it has been argued these figures can be explained by social indicators rather than cultural background.[24] The view that this situation is a product of their particular "background culture" has wide popular support, however, and is used explicitly in the political debate. Kamran and Inzaman, on the contrary, regard these problems as related to a Norwegian urban culture, against which a fundamental element of their own Pakistani cultural heritage can serve as a bulwark.

Religion is not an essential part of everyday social interaction among the cricketers, and although all of the Norwegian Pakistani players consider themselves to be Muslims, cricket is a secular sphere including many men who could be labeled "Muslim light," as Shoaib called himself. Nevertheless, the way Islam figures in the current debate affects the men personally, as they identify with Islam in its broader cultural sense. Also, the fact that they are seen as Muslims by a majority society that has little knowledge of the complexities and the multitude of ways of being a Muslim results in a situation where the men fall prey to the majority society's periodic hysteria about Islamic fundamentalism (in periods following high-profile terrorist attacks, as in New York in 2001, Madrid in 2004, and London in 2005) as well as the more constant suspicion toward Muslim people. An excerpt from the documentary series *Migrapolis* on NRK (the Norwegian Broadcasting Corporation) on 14 September 2005 may serve as an example.

The program accompanies the Norwegian National Cricket Team to the European Championship (3rd Division) in Belgium in 2005. One of the players, Atta, recounts the situation when he was informed that he was chosen for the team:

> I'm a cabdriver in Oslo. I was busy explaining to an older lady that I am not related to Osama bin Laden [laughs]. Then they called, and I had to take leave from driving.

Then he explains that in his opinion representing Norway in an international tournament may improve the current situation:

> I contribute to something positive. There's been quite a bit of negative focus on foreigners lately.

This statement, in addition to those from Shoaib and Yousuf above, sheds light on how the men experience processes of "othering" by the majority both as individuals and as members of an ethnic minority group.

"WE ARE NOT TERRORISTS"

Another case is from the inaugural match of the Rafi Memorial Cricket Festival, held in June 2004 in memory of one of the founding fathers of Norwegian cricket. The tournament is arranged as a cup, and the matches are limited to 15 overs. As a consequence, there is little room for mistakes and limited time to get into the game. The performance on the field is poor at first, maybe because of the unusual arrangement of the match, which causes a lot of stress for the players.[25] The commentaries among the spectators on the sidelines point to this as well. Since the organizers have installed a PA system, a speaker service is provided—not a common feature of cricket in Norway. Inspired by the festive occasion and the less than thrilling play, the speaker gradually starts joking more than commenting on the game itself. Shifting between English, Urdu, Norwegian, and gibberish-Arabic, the speaker has the crowd laughing.[26] He reaches the peak of comedy when, sounding like a soft-spoken mullah on the Al-Jazeera television station, he reassures some imaginary outsider that they are not going to harm anyone. There is a sting to his words, however, as he repeatedly announces in English:

> We are not *terrorister*! We only want peace in the world!

The audience, obviously, are in no need of such a reassurance. Consisting almost exclusively of Muslim men of Pakistani descent, they see the commentaries as an amusing allusion to the far more bitter experience they all have of being stigmatized as a group, increasingly so in the wake of international fundamentalist terrorism and a national preoccupation with the challenges of Muslim minorities' presence.

While the particular pronunciation of the Norwegian word *terrorister* (terrorists) in an English sentence may have been accidental, the context within which the remark occurred brought together the experiences of being marginalized as an ethnic minority in Norway and of the cricketers belonging to a global Muslim population that had become the focus of the US-led "War on Terror." Cricket, to them, represents the opposite of what is perceived to constitute the values and ideas of the radical and militant Islamist movements like Al-Qaeda and the Taliban. The laughter all round indicates how absurd the cricketers regard the suspicion that their religious affiliation arouses. Being grouped together with Osama bin Laden is the ultimate expression of abjection from an imagined Norwegian collective identity.

Within postcolonial theory, the process of "othering" relates to the way the self-understanding of the colonial rulers and the imperial culture were based on notions of the systematic difference of the colonized subject.[27] These processes continue in the postcolonial period, and by extension serve to establish a dichotomous relationship between the West and the Oriental, the majority citizen and the immigrant, white and colored, Christianity and Islam, and so on: "So, by identifying what the Other is, the west identifies what *it* itself is."[28] The process of Othering merges with the majority society's tendency to see the masculinity of the Other as one dimensional and negatively framed. The otherness of the ethnic minority men is thus inextricably linked to masculine practices that the majority society disapproves of.[29] Masculine practices that fit into this discursive framework thus work to reinforce the particular image of the Other, whereas masculine practices not fitting into this framework do not work similarly to modify the image of the masculine Other. Correspondingly, an ethnic minority man who is regarded as more like "Us" is expected to display a kind of masculinity that is more akin to that of the majority.

DISCRIMINATION

Moin and Yousuf both used to play organized football (soccer), but shifted to cricket after several incidents that they perceived as discriminatory. Yousuf tells about his experience:

> I used to play football, but my impression was that it was not particularly welcome to have a Pakistani on the team. We were discriminated against on the team. So I started a football club together with some other foreigners. But then it was like the Norwegians were playing against the foreigners. After I started with cricket, I didn't have to deal with those problems.

Moin was playing for the junior team of one of the top football clubs in the region. Things changed when they engaged a new coach, however, and he was frequently excluded from the team line-up when the club was playing matches. Now he has taken a year off from football, he relates, and is spending more time on cricket. Such experiences reinforce the men's notion that they suffer as a minority group, and that Norwegian Pakistanis and Muslims are particularly targeted—and they are indeed underrepresented in football by comparison with other ethnic minorities, although the reasons for this are probably complex and one may doubt that it can be explained by discrimination only.

The everyday experience as an ethnic minority affects the way the cricketers perceive the obstacles they face in organizing and playing cricket. In their view, it is the otherness of cricket players, in the eyes of the majority society, which is the main reason why they are not treated on equal terms with other activities. The fact that cricket serves as a refuge for men that are "othered" within sports dominated by the majority population, as the stories from Yousuf and Moin indicate, only goes to strengthen this notion.

Shoaib expresses a wish that through playing cricket, the Norwegian Pakistani men who dominate cricket in Norway will contribute to a change in the image of Norwegian Pakistanis more generally, and this is also implicit in the other statements above. Any news report or article on cricket will most likely feature men of Pakistani origin and will help increase the visibility of a more diverse Norwegian Pakistani community. Cricket is thus seen by the men as a suitable way to communicate to the majority society who they are and what they take pride in doing.

THE EXCELLENCE OF CRICKET

The pride the cricketers take in cricket frequently takes the shape of stories and claims about how cricket is far superior to any other sport undertaken in Norway, and how mastery of this physically and mentally demanding sport takes a long time to learn and often requires that you are born to it.

I am standing next to Javed, who is giving advice to teammates at a batting practice. He considers himself to be a true batsman, one of the best in the country, he reveals. Javed shows me his bat, explains the importance of the various details, and informs me that he is eagerly awaiting the arrival of his new bat, ordered from Pakistan. It is the very same type of bat that the Indian star batsmen Tendulkar and Shewaq are using. Javed is clearly proud about the fact that Tendulkar has opted for a bat made in Pakistan, India's traditional foe both in sports and in politics. It speaks volumes about the first-class quality of the bat he is about to acquire, made in his country of origin:

> It caused a lot of controversy in India that Tendulkar has chosen a Pakistani manufacturer. It is difficult to make a cricket bat. It must be well-balanced. They use different types of wood to achieve the perfect combination. It's science on a high level!

He elaborates on the different types of players in cricket: bowlers, allrounders, and batsmen:

> Bowling and batting demand very different skills from the player. Everyone is able to bowl, although not all know how to give a good delivery, of course. Batting is more difficult. Cricket is a

highly technical sport, and batting is the most technically demanding. In cricket, if you make one mistake you're instantly punished.
In football, a mistake isn't that critical.

Javed's view of the difference between bowling and batting may be
disputed, and the fact is that whereas during a one-day match all eleven
players are scheduled to bat, only a few selected players will be bowling.
There may be a connection between Javed's view and the traditional
structuring of cricket in Victorian Britain, consisting of upper-class
amateur batsmen and lower-class professional bowlers (the latter being
regarded as socially inferior, and also lower in the hierarchy of cricket),
a structuring that is still an element in positions that players may hold
in English cricket today, although related less to class than to ethnicity,
"race," and nationality.[30] More interestingly for the current argument,
however, is the way Javed compares the tasks of the batsman with
those of a football player. One mistake in football may result in that
decisive goal, whereas a fatal mistake on the part of a batsman may,
in the worst case, lead to his dismissal, the dismissal of just one of
eleven batsmen. It is difficult to decide which of the two mistakes is
the more serious, but Javed's view is clearly that cricket, because of
the difference he sees, requires the full attention of the players all the
time and thus is more challenging and exciting than football, and in
all far superior.

It is obviously not just cricket that is discussed as part of the resistance against the dominant majority. Javed is also, by implication, making claims about the type of men they are when playing cricket, suggesting that this requires masculine virtues that supersede those of football.
Javed is not only countering the popular image of Norwegian Pakistani
Muslim men by claiming that they are not as the media would have
them to be, but he is also challenging what they see as the hegemonic
masculinity of the white majority.

In this respect, then, Connell's theoretical framework of relations
between differently positioned masculinities does have some explanatory power.[31] It is, however, only in certain contexts that the various
masculinity formations of Norwegian Pakistani men are best understood as a possible response to, or function of, the masculine ideals of
the dominant group in society. The antagonism that is present in Javed's
story is thus only one side of the coin with regard to cricket's role in the

construction of Norwegian Pakistani masculinities. I would even argue that it is the flipside of the coin, but this very side is the one that tends to be attainable and visible for an outsider, more so if that outsider is representing the majority society. The men's experiences of othering, present in the frequently uttered reassurances that "we are not as bad as you think / as the media would have it / as researchers tend to argue," are thus supplemented by claims that "we are better than you," expressing a sense of resistance to the dominant majority.

It is an irony of history that the means by which Javed and other cricketers express this resistance are partly inherited from the imperial rulers who once held the subcontinental subject in low esteem (a hierarchical relation that is far from neutralized even sixty years after independence). During the years before and after independence cricket was transformed into a South Asian game, more representative of Indian and Pakistani culture, to many people, than any primordial games like polo or *kabaddi*.[32]

Masculinities beyond Otherness

Whenever I asked the men whether they regarded cricket as significant for them *as men*, they denied it. When elaborating on why they played cricket, many of the men emphasized the social benefits of cricket in addition to a passionate interest in the game. The possibility to meet and socialize with male friends was a crucial aspect of how the men could legitimize for themselves and their families the large portion of their leisure time that they spent on cricket, rather than on family and domestic duties. What they did not do, however, was see their activities within this male preserve as an element constituting their male gender identity as such.

The men's perception of their own gender identity is effected by the structural relationship between the majority and minority populations. Therefore, the way the men elaborated on their experiences as ethnic minority men was as much about being labeled "the Other" by the majority society as about making explicit how they experience the gendered aspects of their life. Through long-term fieldwork, however, a set of male practices and gender ideals came to expression that goes beyond the hegemonic gaze of the majority society.

CRICKET MASCULINITIES

> These values [of the Victorian elite] [. . .] can be summarized
> as follows. Cricket was a quintessentially masculine activity and
> expressed the codes that were expected to govern all masculine
> behavior: sportsmanship, a sense of fair play, thorough control
> over the expression of strong sentiments by players on the field,
> subordination of personal sentiments and interests to those of the
> group, unquestioned loyalty to the team.[33]

As one looks through a selection of old and more recent writings
on cricket, the link between cricket and the virtues of the ideal man
seems to be self-evident. Most writers tend to take the masculinity of
cricket as a fact, and those who propose to review this critically do so
in the context of the imperial colonizers' effort to civilize their subjects
through "the manly game."[34] Cricket is thus recognized as a site for masculine performances and a source for masculine status. Furthermore,
the dual and contradictory characteristics of cricket masculinities are
not critically assessed in view of recent theories of gender, but are
expressed mostly in concern or celebration about the way cricket is
changing in the face of increasing commercialization and professional-
ization of contemporary sports.[35]

By presenting a couple of cases from a cricket match, I propose an
analytical distinction between physical excellence and mental prowess
as competing ideals of cricket masculinity. I will relate this to the situation within international cricket, and also to changes within commercial
sports more generally. While specific to cricket, the masculine ideals and
the tension that exists among them have relevance in understanding
performances and ideals outside cricket as well.

PHYSICAL EXCELLENCE AND MENTAL PROWESS

> The embodiment of masculinity in sport involves a whole pattern
> of body development and use, not just one organ. Highly specific
> skills are of course involved. For instance, bowling a googly in
> cricket—an off-break ball delivered deceptively with a leg-break
> action out of the back of the hand with the elbow held straight—
> must be among the most exotic physical performances in the entire
> human repertoire. But players who can do only one thing are

regarded as freaks. It is the integrated performance of the whole body, the capacity to do a range of things wonderfully well, that is admired in the greatest exemplars of competitive sports . . . .[36]

The excerpt above is from the book *Masculinities*, and Connell argues that sport serves as a significant means for the embodiment of hegemonic masculinity and also as a site where failure to live up to the masculine standards is deeply felt: "The constitution of masculinity through bodily performance means that gender is vulnerable when the performance cannot be sustained—for instance, as a result of physical disability."[37] From the statement of Connell, one would think that the all-rounder is the one who is most admired and is thus closest to representing the ideal of cricket masculinity. Indeed, those who master the full range of cricketing skills are highly respected. However, we should not underestimate the masculine appeal of the specialist. A cricket expert may compliment the versatility of an all-rounder, but as television broadcasts of cricket matches become ever more popular, a growing number of spectators and viewers are intrigued by the spectacular play that a designated bowler or brilliant batsman can produce. The potency of an accurate bowler may prove to be far more attractive than the steadiness of an all-rounder, and the batsman who chases fours or sixes at any ball played provides more entertainment for some than the strategically wise player who holds back for several overs. With the increasing popularity of One Day cricket, a specialist like the Pakistani fast bowler Shoaib "The Rawalpindi Express" Akhtar may rise to levels of playboy fame that on the subcontinent are only surpassed by the heroes of the Bollywood film industry. What this further suggests is that the style you employ on field is seen as indicative of the man you are off field.

WISE PLAY, SPECTACULAR CATCH

Aker Cricket Club, the club I have been following during research, is playing against Haugenstua Cricket Club at the Stovner venue. Aker is batting first and the batsmen's performances are worse than expected. Several of Aker's usually top batsmen are out early, and at twenty-five overs the team has managed only one hundred runs. Waqar enters to bat, and he knows he has a tough task ahead. As the bowler gets at him, he repeatedly flicks the ball to the side, earning no runs. He continues for a long time, defending the wicket, and going for few or no runs at each ball. Then he suddenly changes his approach, and starts striking long balls in all directions. He keeps on taking fours and sixes. Shoaib, an old hand at the game and next to bat, is impressed:

> This is great cricket! He enters the field and eases the play. If one batsman is out, it is easier for the bowler to go from wicket to wicket. "Knock, knock." It's boring for the players, but it enables Waqar to gain control of the game. He doesn't overdo it; he's simply telling the bowler who's in charge. Then the bowler becomes frustrated and starts making mistakes. And then Waqar can begin to hit!

Waqar makes a century, not out, and is later accompanied by Shoaib, who makes a half century, not out. Aker CC finishes at 281 and the spectators cheer and compliment them as they move over to the supporters and teammates. Waqar makes a phone call to brag about his own achievement, and he is visibly proud of himself. Shoaib is less wound up, jokes about his own performance, and is apparently eager to convey his own insignificance: "I got a very loose delivery."

After a short break, Haugenstua CC is batting and all of Aker's players are on field. The batsman strikes the ball hard toward the boundary, destined to score a six. Yousuf is standing mid-wicket, quite a distance from the path of the ball. Quickly he throws himself toward the ball with one arm stretched out and makes a catch. As he falls to the ground, he manages to keep the ball up in the air so that it does not touch the ground, and the batsman is out. The Aker players and the audience cheer, and they praise Yousuf's performance. On the sidelines, two younger men in their early twenties comment on the spectacular catch, and one of them says:

> It was amazing, don't you think. Considering that he's over forty years old, it's even more impressive—the oldest guy on the field. He's even a grandfather! But he does work out every day.

The other one nods in approval, and informs that he has seen Yousuf excel on other occasions as well:

> At one match, he was standing close to the boundary when a ball was struck high and long. Everyone expected it to be a six. Then

> Yousuf simply stretched out his arm—like this [stretches his arm
> far above the head]—caught it with no sign of strain, and simply
> picked it down with perfect control! I really like him!

Eventually Aker wins the match—Haugenstua CC is not even close to
equaling Aker's score. A couple of days later, I overhear Salman—who
has been playing domestic cricket in Pakistan—as he talks about the
game to a friend: "It was an amazing performance by Waqar. He really
is a big superstar!"

These two incidents illustrate the strategic and the spectacular
aspects of cricket, expressed both in the different performances and
in the comments upon them by spectators and players. They may
also point to different masculine ideals that are operational within
Norwegian as well as international cricket, a difference that according
to Gary Whannel is a more general aspect of many sports.[38] Within
cricket, as in football, different factors have led to the gradual shift from
idealization of the collective-minded team player to celebration of the
individualistic player with a character that enables him or her to stand
out from other players. This has happened, Whannel claims, as a result
of the increasing commercialization of sports and television's demand
for entertainment and star figures.[39] This development is not free from
criticism, and within the cricket world the tension that it has provoked
finds expression in the different versions of cricket that exist side by side:
the more traditional test cricket and one-day cricket, the first being seen
by many as the proper type of cricket while the second—they would
argue—is attractive mainly to those who according to Manu Madan
watch "cricket for the spectacle's sake" rather than "for cricket's sake."[40]

In light of this, the cases just mentioned can be placed within a
larger discussion of ideal cricket masculinities. First, there is the mental
victory of Waqar, who manages to insert such a level of calmness and
control into the game that a terrible inning is turned into a winning
score for Aker CC. He is a mature team player and is highly respected,
more so because he is able to deliver brilliant play as both a bowler and
a batsman. His play is in accordance with the ideals of cricket that were
moulded in Britain during the Victorian and Edwardian period, when
for a long time amateurism and collective thinking were the celebrated
values.[41] Second, there is the athletic excellence of Yousuf, who despite
his age has a well-moulded body. Few could have made that spectacular

leap, and he managed to get one of Haugenstua CC's batsmen out. However, he did not turn the match in his team's favor single-handedly, as Waqar did. And whereas Waqar is always regarded as reliable when he plays, Yousuf occasionally has a bad day on the field. Yousuf might be more akin to those who have grown up with cricket as TV entertainment, where the pace is faster and the demand for stunning play is on every ball played.[42] Such performances may fit better with the competitive individualism that is ever more present within the globalized and commoditized cricket that has emerged from World Series Cricket and in recent years Twenty20 cricket.

Also relevant here is Yousuf's attitude in other situations: he will typically prefer to exercise on his own, warming up before a match by running around the field rather than participating in the organized preparatory activities that the captain initiates. Often he opts for a smoke and a chat with the younger ones, rather than getting involved in the politics of his age-mates. Thus there is also a tension here between the individualist and the team player, something that is even evident in the different responses of Waqar and Shoaib to the spectators' compliments, Waqar obviously being immensely proud of himself, whereas Shoaib appears to be less concerned about how he himself contributed to the team's victory. Accordingly, the three men could be positioned differently within an individualistic-collective dimension, and it is also apparent from the case of Waqar that there is no absolute consistency in that position either; while he stands up for his team at a crucial point in the match, Waqar is not indifferent to the personal gain and appreciation his performance leads to. It should be noted that owing to Shoaib's role in the establishing of cricket in Norway and his record as a player, he possesses a level of authority among the cricketers that probably makes it less necessary for him to enhance his own status on the basis of individual performances on field: "Everyone within Norwegian cricket knows me," he noted on one occasion. It is noteworthy that it was Waqar who was awarded the Aker captaincy when Shoaib stepped down, despite Yousuf being older, more experienced, and arguably better liked by a wider group of people within the cricket circle.

Masculinities on and off the Field

It should come as no surprise that the masculine ideals within Norwegian cricket are influenced by what happens on the international cricket scene in general and among Pakistani-born players in particular. Whenever I asked the cricket players if they had any role models when developing their own cricket style, they would typically mention the names of legendary and now retired players like Wasim Akram and Imran Khan, both members of Pakistan's World Cup winning team of 1992.

If challenged to mention a current cricket idol, the men will differ more, each naming a player who specializes in his favorite task, or who represents the kind of cricket style that he prefers. Thus, the Pakistani fast bowler Shoaib Akhtar would be mentioned by some, because of his spectacular fast bowling, wicket-taking abilities, and film-star looks. He was, however, written off by others because of his alleged huge ego, his record-breaking (selfish) ambitions, and repeated questions about his commitment to the game and his team, as well as controversies with the national team captain. Others would emphasize players like India's Sachin Tendulkar or the West Indies' Brian Lara, who both combine commitment to the game and calculated play with blistering performances and sport star qualities that Pakistan's captain during fieldwork, Inzaman-ul-haq, lacked.

It is important to note that when a player's masculine qualities are assessed, his performance on field and his life off field are regarded as interrelated. The playing styles of Pakistan's Shahid Afridi and Shoaib Akhtar suggest a private life that is wild, unruly and of a morally dubious nature. When commenting on this, people seem to suggest that once the men mature and settle down with a family—which is again seen by many as interrelated, you must be mature to settle down with a family, and correspondingly you are expected to mature when establishing yourself as a family man—their playing styles will change accordingly.[43] This means that the impatient and overly aggressive aspects of Shahid Afridi's play are expected to be polished away once he settles down with a family, while at the same time he retains the high-quality performances for which he is renowned.[44] Likewise, the captain Inzaman-ul-haq is older, lazy when it comes to physically straining tasks, and rather chubby, but with great wisdom, ability for strategic thinking, and an understanding for the game. His maturity indicates a private life that is conservative, modest, and in accordance with social ideals of a respectable family man. However, maybe because of this supposed quiet life, he is no celebrity like Shoaib Akhtar, Sachin Tendulkar, or the legendary Imran Khan.

The case of Imran Khan is particularly illustrative in this regard. While at the peak of his career, he was widely admired in Pakistan for his play as an all-rounder, and for his stunning looks. It was no secret that he enjoyed a playboy life abroad, and his wedding to the English jet-setter Jemima Goldsmith was celebrated as a national and international event. However, as long as he was a sports idol, his performance on field seemed to overshadow those other aspects of his life in assessment of Imran's morality and masculine appeal, in contrast to Shoaib Akhtar or Shahid Afridi, who have their non-cricketing life brought in as an explanatory cause whenever they perform badly on the field.[45] Few people questioned Imran Khan's personal life, because the qualities he displayed on the cricket field indicated a mature player and thus also a mature and respectable man. Pnina Werbner argues that Imran Khan can be seen as objectifications of the "exemplary person" in South Asian and Islamic thinking, similar to the Sufi saint: "Like the sportsman, the Sufi saint is an ascetic who, it is believed, has gained total control over his body. [. . .] His embodied self-denial 'opens' him up to divine knowledge which is thus embodied knowledge."[46]

This changed, however, as Imran Khan in 1997 moved from cricket stardom to politics, particularly as his newly created party Therik-e-Insaaf (Movement for Justice) was founded on an Islamic platform, challenging political corruption and fighting for social changes. His previous life as a playboy and jet-setter was now questioned by many, as was his marriage to Jemima. Allegations also emerged about an illegitimate child with a woman in the United States, with whom Imran's previous love affair was widely known. The point, then, was that the masculinity that Imran displayed on field limited the weight that was given to his private life. His ability to balance these two contradictory aspects may explain why he was admired by such a wide and diverse group of people, but with the cricket gone Imran's private life was drawn more directly into people's judgment of him. He was, however, able to brave the storm, although his first attempts at the National Assembly proved futile. Now, more than ten years later, it is apparent that Imran

Khan was successful in transforming himself into a respectable politician, while at the same time maintaining his position within national and international cricket, and figuring as a cherished ideal for Pakistani cricket aficionados throughout the world.

The Appeal of Dual Masculinities

The interrelation that is thought to exist between how a cricketer performs on the field and how he leads his personal life should obviously not be accepted uncritically, and there are elements in the stories above that indicate the reality is far more complex. Still, there are reasons to suggest that there exist, within cricket and among cricketers and spectators, different masculine ideals with opposing and partly contradicting notions about how a man should or should not behave. The various masculine practices on and off the field are judged against these ideals, and often the men themselves may try to live up to the ideals as well.

I propose an analytic typology, making a distinction between the *collectivistic masculine ideal* and the *individualistic masculine ideal*. Although this distinction derives from the tension between mental prowess and physical excellence within cricket, I do not suggest that collective masculine ideals stress the superiority of the mind while the individualistic masculine ideal elevates the physical body. This connection is only relevant in regard to the playing of cricket, where the strategically wise and mentally strong player is believed to be characterized by collective sentiments and commitment to the team, whereas the player who chases records in the statistics for personal gain, and excels only in those isolated spectacular moments, is thought to be individualistic in orientation and committed to selfish needs.

What I wish to grasp with this analytical distinction is certain aspects of male practices that go in either direction. On the field, this relates to the distinction between idealization of the collective-minded team player and celebration of the individualistic player with a character that enables him to stand out from other players. In a conversation with me, Yonis expanded on this to include a perspective on attitudes toward cricket, resembling Madan's "cricket for cricket's sake" versus "cricket for the spectacle's sake."[47] Although they do not necessarily go together in the playing styles of the different men, to be a collective-minded team player and to be passionate about cricket as a game belong to the same side of the proposed analytical divide. Deriving from this, on the one hand, there is an off-field distinction between an expectation that one should support the fellowship of men, observe, respect, and act in accordance with existing hierarchies, and express belonging to the group through verbal and physical practices, and, on the other hand, a tendency to mock group solidarity, challenge established hierarchies, and maintain a level of social and physical distance from the men's circle.

An extension of this point can be found in the distinction between the family man who respects cultural norms on interaction between the genders, and the womanizer and playboy who pursues personal lusts. This resembles a distinction that I have previously proposed between *moral masculine values* and *immoral masculine values* in Pakistan.[48] My material on relations between men and women is too limited to make any substantial claims in this direction about the Norwegian Pakistani community, but there are cases that support this assumption.

In proposing this distinction between individualistic and collectivistic masculine ideals, it is important to keep in mind that I do not intend to present a fixed and coherent account of how different men will act in a given situation. An individualist on-field need not be a lust-seeker off-field, and one who cherishes the companionship and intimacy of the Norwegian Pakistani cricket circle in one situation may mock it in another situation. The point, then, is to show how various practices can be grouped together on either side of the individualistic-collectivistic dimension. Besides these two ideal models—which though often conflicting are both just that, idealized—there are of course practices that do not fit into this scheme and are differently positioned in relation to the dominant ideals.

Model of and Model for Ideal Masculinity

To what extent can cricket masculinities inform our understanding of masculinity ideals within the Norwegian Pakistani community more generally? Not all Pakistanis play cricket or show an interest in the game. So, to the extent that there are some shared notions of ideal masculinites within this group, they are obviously not products of cricket only. Likewise, the male practices that are idealized with regard to cricket, on and off the field, are not formulated in isolation from cricket as it is played and idolized around the world, and therefore cannot be seen to represent an essential Pakistani masculine style. We may, however, argue that the way cricket masculinities are perceived by the dominant Pakistani group takes on particular cultural meaning. That is, while the collectivistic-minded player may be idolized equally in the UK, the West Indies, and Norway, how this is seen to echo a certain character type in other social contexts will differ. When adult Pakistani men in Norway see cricket as an appropriate means to introduce their adolescent sons to proper manhood, this is because cricket is believed to teach the boys values and ideal practices that are preferred in other parts of life as well. Cricket masculinities, in this regard, may be analyzed both as a model *of* gender ideals that are more widely supported and promoted within the Norwegian Pakistani community, and as a model *for* people in exemplifying preferable conduct.

Within the Norwegian Pakistani community, members of the younger generation have distanced themselves somewhat from the style, values, and appearance typically associated with their group in the 1980s and early 1990s.[49] According to Viggo Vestel, there was a noticeable change in the style of the "Pakistanis" between his first and second fieldwork among multicultural youths in Oslo during the 1990s. During these years, they rose to high popularity and influenced the music preferences and the way of dressing among their peers.[50] Meanwhile, the values and styles of earlier days are carried on by other Norwegian Pakistani boys and men, and may be supported by men who migrated to Norway in recent years.

Thus the distinction suggested above between individualistic and collectivistic masculine ideals within cricket, while not mirroring exactly a similar division in other social relations, may find resonance in a comparable tension between ideal masculinities within the Norwegian Pakistani community. This tension, furthermore, may partly account for the wide appeal of cricket, encompassing idolized masculine styles that may suit quite different age groups, ideologies, cultural backgrounds, and personal biographies. The ambivalence that accompanies some of the fathers' hesitant desire to let their sons take part in the male circle of companionship could be ascribed to an awareness of exactly this point— cricket serving the purpose as a model for a masculine style that they wish to pass on to their sons, while also being a source of less desirable practices.[51]

This division is not strictly located within a commonly assumed tension between the Westernized, individualistic values of the majority society on the one hand and the "traditional," collectivistic values of ethnic minority groups on the other hand.[52] Rather, within the cricketing world it is Englishmen who were, and to some extent still are, bearers of the collectivistic ideal, whereas the old colonies produced and still produce the outstanding individualistic players who have pushed cricket in new directions. We thus have different masculine ideals that may equally well be placed within, and are to some extent products of, international cricketing practices. Although cricket is alien to the majority of Norwegian society, the masculinity that can be traced in Yousuf's practice resonates with other masculine ideals among the Norwegian majority, seen for instance in the celebration of sportsmen like the tough cross-country skier or the football goal getter, as well as being firmly located within the contemporary South Asian world. Nevertheless, the Victorian conduct of Waqar, in all its Englishness, is placed well within what might be labeled the collective character of the good Pakistani man, as well as evoking the ideal of the team player that is often cherished, if not idolized, even within Norwegian football.

Concluding Remarks

I have focused mainly on masculine ideals that in some ways find their expression through the actual playing of the game. Elsewhere I have discussed how cricket represents a place for the expression of physical intimacy and friendships that locates the division between manliness and unmanliness different from how this division is perceived in the majority society.[53] It is also possible to regard cricket as a vantage point from where other types of relations can be observed; for example, between father and children or, on the domestic scene, between husband and wife. What all these perspectives have in common is they offer an opportunity to analyze ethnic masculinities in a context that only to some extent relates to the masculine ideals of the majority society, and, more importantly, that extends beyond the narrow hegemonic gaze of the white majority.

The research is furnished on the hypothesis that gender is not determined by ethnic identity, but rather we should regard both gender and ethnicity as constituted, performed, and challenged through social rituals and interaction that may, but need not, intersect in a given context. Ethnic identities are manifested in relation to other groups, and maintaining a focus on the hierarchies of power that are operational between these groups may divert attention away from other social contexts where gender identities manifest themselves. A central aim has been to draw attention to such contexts, and to include them in an analysis of Norwegian Pakistani masculinities.

When ethnic markers take on a lesser significance, other aspects of personal identities and social positions gain more significance accordingly. This advises us to investigate masculinity formations as they take shape and are performed within various minority groups, without seeing them as constituted in a state of tension with the dominant form.[54] Connell's relational model of masculinity urges us to analyze black masculinities (and by association, we must assume, ethnic masculinities) first and foremost in a situation where "blackness" is a marker of marginalization in relation to the dominant groups: "In a white-supremacist context, black masculinities play symbolic roles for white gender constructions."[55] Connell does not explicitly exclude black men from positions of hegemony, complicity, or subordination, but it is the marginalization of black men "relative to the *authorization* of the hegemonic masculinity of the dominant group" that grants them a position within the theoretical framework within which specific masculinities can be analyzed.[56] There is little in this framework that encourages us to analyze the specific masculinities of black or ethnic people in contexts where "blackness" or "ethnicity" takes a peripheral position in internal relations.

Arguably, cricket is strongly related to the men's perception of what characterizes them and make them Pakistani in their own eyes; thus the game as such, and cricket as a social space, should not be dissociated from the men's identification with what is regarded as Pakistani. This identification as Pakistani may be central in constituting cricket as a particular space—as is "blackness" in the case of the Caribbean Cricket Club,[57] and cricket is correspondingly an important source of ethnic pride in the men's encounter with others and in their expressions of resistance against processes of othering; however, in internal relations within cricket, there are few people against which such ethnic markers are made relevant. Thus, while the notion of a Pakistani identity is formative of the social space as such, ethnicity should not be privileged in analyzing the various masculinities that come to expression within ethnic minority spaces and in activities like cricket.

The ethnographic material presents a compelling corrective to popular images of Pakistani men in Norway, and cricket thus has the ability to discredit stereotypes and expand the notion of Norwegian Pakistani masculinities. However, I have argued that the men's fight for recognition is carried on through "the dominant communicative system of society," and that the potential of cricket to counter popular images about Norwegian Pakistani men is hampered by the men's compulsion to contradict these stereotypes. We can conclude, then, that bringing cricket to public attention as a central element in the life of Pakistani men in Norway opens the way for acknowledgment of the middle ground between the polarized position of a national "self" and the ethnic "other."

CHAPTER 13

Ethnicity, National Identity, and Cricket in Contemporary Trinidad and Tobago

Anand Rampersad

Introduction

Cricket is in the blood of Caribbean people as it provides a transparent lens to critically assess the socioeconomic and political evolution of the region. Introduced by the British as part of its leisure and recreational activities, it soon became part of its "civilizing" strategy of the Africans and other groups to enter Caribbean society. In return, the Africans incorporated cricket within its cultural construct that produced a creolized product to symbolically avenge the wrongs of colonialism. The cricket ball and bat became symbolic social whips used to exact a sense of retribution for the animosities meted out during slavery and later on in indentureship. Additionally, it has also provided a contested space for highlighting the economic and political peripheral positions of the region as a result of colonialism and neocolonialism. Therefore, the 5–0 defeat of England in 1984 in England and the repeat score line in 1986 in the Caribbean were dubbed "blackwashes" as opposed to the traditional "whitewashes." It meant that the former colonies had dealt a severe blow with an innovation of an English cultural product. Also at the national level cricket provides a social site for the unfolding of the interplay of ethnicity, race, class, and politics in the psyche of the players and the spectators whose support is filled with enthusiasm and pride. Cricket offers symbolic wealth to the economically downtrodden; it is more than a sport, it is about redemption as well as resistance. The game was creolized against a cultural backdrop of merriment, music, dance, and anticolonial national pride in addition to innovative strategies such as the use of a four-prong fast bowling attack, batting that at times was very heterodox but yet very productive and fielding prowess and agility that had opponents in both awe and envy. Cricket for West Indians as football is for Brazilians provides a rare opportunity for people of the South to reign supreme while competing against rivals from the North.

There has been a litany of works published by various authors on the history and meaning of cricket in the Caribbean.[1] However, there is a paucity of similar works on individual islands that comprise the West Indies: Trinidad and Tobago; Jamaica, Barbados; Guyana; Leeward Islands; and the Windward Islands. Furthermore, much of the available literature has focused more on the Afro-Caribbean, which is understandable in the context of the historical structure of the region. However, within countries such as Trinidad and Guyana, whose ethnically diverse population present a dynamic tapestry of ethnicity, class, and politics in every aspect of social life, the study of cricket as a descriptive and explanatory social site has been found wanting. The most notable studies have been in Guyana and in Trinidad, which attempted to deconstruct cricket through the lens of ethnicity and national identity.[2] Even the CLR James[3] classic oeuvre *Beyond a Boundary* fails to discuss the situation of Indians in the same context as he addressed the issues facing the Africans to point that the work can be misconstrued as a discourse on the relations among the whites, mulattoes, and Africans in Trinidad.[4]

The principal aim of this chapter is to argue that the field of cricket provides a scope for critical evaluative derivatives of both ethnic and national identity issues of Indo-Trinidadians in contemporary Trinidad. Cricket is the only sporting discipline for the visible identification of the Indo-Trinidadians not only as cricketers but also as administrators, officials, and even popular spectatorship. Although over the past ten to fifteen years there is an evident increasing "Indianization" of the sport, it has also become a space for the expression of a growing cultural hybridization and creolization of identity. In other words, it provides a social space for the manifestation of both an ethnic and civic identity. From an ethnic perspective it permits the display and solidification of cultural practices that defined the essence of the Indo-Trinidadian identity base in the social evolution of the society since their arrival in 1845. From a civic identity standpoint the cricket field is an active milieu for the ongoing negotiation of a "national" identity that incorporates not only social interaction with Afro-Trinidadians and other ethnic groups but also the influence of regional and global—namely, American—popular culture through music, dance, and language.[5]

Furthermore, the cricket field is active yet ignored social space for the analysis of the social evolution of Indo-Trinidadians away from the traditional areas of education, business, and ascendancy to political power. The study demonstrates that sport as an institution is yet another social site that can present a fresh discourse on an understanding of the (re) construct and manifestation of social life especially in multiethnic societies such as Trinidad and Guyana. It is reasonable to comprehend the failure of Caribbean scholars to interrogate sport as a social site of construction because sport is generally seen as essentialized and never commanded the same attention as other social issues such the creation of employment and eradicating poverty and crime.

Theoretical Context

The sociological concepts of habitus, capital, and field as employed by Pierre Bourdieu[6] may offer a theoretical insight into how Indo-Trinidadians by taking control of a sporting field have helped to reinforce its own identity yet still at the same time allow for the continued renegotiation of a national identity to which it can relate. Bourdieu employs the concept of habitus to serve as mediator between structure and agency. Habitus regulates the social practices between institutions and actors. He notes that habitus is not only a "structuring structure but also a structured structure."[7] Therefore, there is social dynamism within the interactive process. The concept of capital refers to a form of power social groups possess to enact change and control.[8] Social practices are mediated by the degree and type of capital that an individual or group may possess. These include economic capital (income, wealth, spare time),[9] cultural capital (expression of taste), educational (qualifications), and symbolic (image and reputation). The interplay between these types of capital will inform the practices of social groups and classes. The term *field* refers to social settings where there are objectively defined positions, which may be in opposition to each other. Therefore, fields are social sites of struggle between those who want to preserve the status quo and those who want to engender change through transformation.

According to Bourdieu, lifestyle choices are influenced by the access to various forms of capital.[10] The various types of capital help to reinforce the class relations of domination and subordination.[11] Cultural, educational, and symbolic capital enhance individuals or groups ability to engage various forms of social consumption and taste. Therefore, sport participation and sport spectatorship can be affected by access to the various forms of capital. The "rules" of the game may serve as a deterrent for interest or participation for some groups such as the lower class.

Historical Context

Trinidad is multiethnic immigrant society that underscores the effects of the twin evil labor systems of slavery and indentureship and the free movement of people from both within and outside of the Caribbean region.[12] The major ethnic groups are descendants of Africans and Indians, and they account for 37 and 40 percent of the population, respectively.[13] Other ethnic groups include Chinese, Portuguese, and Syrian/Lebanese. As the society has evolved, there has been a growing mixed population comprised mainly of people of Afro-Trinidadian and Indo-Trinidadian social amalgamations. They are commonly known as "douglas," however, its legitimatization as an acceptable category has been moot as it has been couched in the ongoing polemical ethnic/political debate between the two major ethnic groups.

Indians were brought to work on the sugar plantations in the Caribbean with the abolition of slavery in 1838. The first shipload of indentured workers went to Guyana (then British Guiana) in 1838. The first shipload of Indian immigrants to Trinidad was in 1845. Between 1845 and 1917 when the indentureship system ended, 143,939 persons came to the island.[14] Initially the Indians were geographically and culturally separated from the wider population as they entered on the sugar plantations to fill the labor void created with the abolition of slavery when the ex-slaves opted away from the sugar plantations for work as well as to avoid the nefarious psychological reminder of slavery.[15] The Indians were brought to the region as transient labor, hence, the island was never initially seen as their "home." In addition to being transient laborers and geographically separated from mainstream society, the Indians were provided with a degree of cultural latitude that was not available to the ex-slaves, which allowed them the opportunity to establish their ethnic identity through their religion (Hinduism and Islam), associated practices and rituals, and kinship ties.[16] Group togetherness coupled with being ostracized by the other ethnic groups meant that their identification to the island was different to that of the Africans. They were initially native outsiders.

The end of indentureship in 1917 provided new challenges for those Indians who decided to remain on the island through persuasiveness by the planters as well as the desire not to return to their place of origin in India. The tension between the Afro-Trinidadian and the Indians continued to manifest itself not only in terms of economics and culture but also in the realm of politics. According to Kevin Yelvington, politics became ethnicized with the formation of political parties.[17]

Ethnic issues permeated every aspect of society, providing for seething volcanoes of tension and pending explosions.[18] In 1958 Eric Williams referred to them as "a hostile and recalcitrant minority." The stereotype of the Indian as being clannish and docile was manifested in an attitude that was prone toward psychological protest than active engagement. Ethnic tension manifested itself not only in Trinidad but also in Guyana with the Indian tour of the West Indies in 1976. In both countries the touring Indian team was celebrated especially in Trinidad when they won the test match at the Queen's Park Oval.[19] Many persons offered the view that the "unexpected" behavior of the Indian population highlighted their perceived oppressive position in the society in terms of economics, politics, and culture. The support of the touring Indians came despite the fact that there were Indians from Trinidad in the West Indies team. The year 1976 also coincided with the general elections in Trinidad and Tobago, and the actions at the cricket match served as a forerunner as to how the general elections would have been debated and how the outcome would have mirrored the ethnic structure of the society.[20]

Sport in Trinidad and Tobago

Sport is a secondary social institution in Trinidad and Tobago and can be characterized by amateurish principles and practices. Generally speaking, the institution is not a primary source of employment, social mobility, or status. It is usually competed away for attention by the quest for education and the search for permanent and guaranteed sources of income. As a result, most athletes pursue sport as a secondary social activity to school or work or a combination of both. However, sport provides great opportunities for recreational and leisure pursuits for the general population. The bedrock of most sporting disciplines manifest the social characteristics of kith and kinship ties, religion, social class, race, and ethnicity, all of which in some cases are tied to geographical factors.

Being a secondary social institution, it is not startling that the industry is at a nascent stage of development. Most of the sporting disciplines save a few are not professionalized in structure and organization (although this may be vehemently dismissed by those who are involved), which is reflected in the lack of proper facilities, professional coaches and trainers, lack of data, heavy reliance on the state and corporate entities for financial assistance and sponsorship, poor sport management skills, and low membership. Even in the two most popular sporting disciplines—cricket and football—the level of professional development is mostly limited to the premier divisions of the respective sports.

Cricket in Trinidad and the Caribbean

Cricket in the Caribbean is more than a sport. Cricket has provided Caribbean people with an opportunity to transform a civilizing and social controlling sport of the masses into a social and cultural mechanism of resistance manifested in the style of play and festive dispositions of live spectators.[21] Cricket allows for "proletarian camaraderie" where the masses overcome the trials and tribulations of the everyday life.[22] The cricket fields in the Caribbean unlike other venues in the cricketing world are likened to a carnival stage where various actors portray their different roles to make the overall performance a success. It is a social site where historical symbolic battles have been contested.

According to Gordon Rohler, West Indian cricket values are tied to its culture through its music and literature.[23] For him, the survival of West Indies cricket is linked to the replacement of the white elites and their cultural dispositions with a black West Indian personality and sense of community.[24] He further states that this personality reflects the creolization of West Indian cultural experiences, which translates into a "sense of 'West Indianess,' which ensures continued support for the team."[25] Similarly, like Rohler, Hilary McD. Beckles sees cricket and its survival as an important social institution for the masses and the less fortunate to overcome the elites and their cultural practices in society.[26] Cricket facilitates the expression of cultural freedom through music, dance, and literature.[27]

At the same time, the culture of Caribbean people reflects degrees of complexities and contradictions that may be problematic for both rationalist and likeminded. For instance, Caribbean people may clamor for effective management and policy implementation on one hand and yet still be critical of both the policies and the administrators on the other hand. The field of sport provides excellent examples of the cultural complexities and contradictions of Caribbean people. When the West Indies cricket team or individual players are riding high on the crescent of success, they are elevated to the statuses of princes and even demigods but when performances fail to flatter, the same "subjects" become their major critics, sometimes in the most verbally outlandish manner through insular comments.

The organization of cricket in Trinidad reflected the social, economic, and political structure of the island.[28] Cricket teams were formed on the basis of race, class, and geography. The Queen's Park Cricket Club was predominantly white and from the upper class; Shamrock was predominantly white and most of its members were Catholics; the Constabulary was the police team but had a white captain; Stingo was a totally black team with no social status; Maple represented the brown-skin middle class; and Shannon were the black lower class but included teachers and law clerks.[29]

Since Indians were outside of mainstream society, their main interest was work and attaining education, which was the primary vehicle toward achieving social mobility. Hence, their involvement in sports was shaped by social relations with the other groups in society. Their participation was linked to their work on the sugar plantations where they were responsible for preparing pitches and would not have been encouraged to engage in leisure activities.[30] Their involvement in other sports such as volleyball was a corollary of the Canadian Presbyterian Missionaries to efforts to evangelize the "coolies" as part of their conversion strategy. Sporting disciplines, such as football, were controlled in geographical spaces where they were not predominant. This was particularly true in northern and southern Trinidad where they were played predominantly by Afro-Trinidadians, mulattoes, and whites.

The first Indian to play for the West Indies was Sonny Ramadhin in 1950. His participation came after the West Indies had played nine test series since gaining test status in 1928. According to Devonish in Guyana and Yelvington in Trinidad, the Indian support of the West Indies cricket team depended upon who they were playing.[31] When the West Indies were playing against India and Pakistan, the support for the Asian teams was evident. This was especially the case in matches with India due to the large number of Hindus in the Indian community. The support for the West Indies against non-subcontinent teams such as archenemies England and Australia was greater as it demonstrated a battle against the imperial center in the case of England and racial issues against Australia.

The absence of Indo-Caribbean players in the West Indies team during their period of domination, coupled with the axing of Rangy Nanan from the team after a creditable performance on debut against Pakistan in Pakistan in 1982, further reinforced the view that the West Indian team was not representative of the make-up of the region and the situation of Indo-Caribbean community reflected their oppressive positions in their respective countries of Trinidad and Guyana. Against this background the common view held was that players such as Aneil Rajah, Prakash Moosai, and later on Ranjidra Dhanraj and Dinadanth Ramnarine (Trinidad) and Timur Mohammed and Rabindranath Seereram (Guyana) were not given a fair opportunity to display their talent and skills though they performed well enough in regional matches to earn selection for representative West Indian teams. Such claims further reinforced the ethnic tension between the Afro-Caribbean and Indo-Caribbean especially in Trinidad and Guyana. The situation was not aided by West Indian captain Vivian Richards's comment in 1990: "the West Indies cricket team is the only sporting team of African descent that has been able to win repeatedly against all international opposition, bringing joy and recognition to our people."[32] It was a comment that was met with significant protest among Indo-Caribbean communities in Trinidad and Guyana.[33]

Indian cricket teams were organized on the sugar plantations and in the villages they resided in throughout the country. One of the oldest sugar plantation teams, Wanderers Cricket Club, was established in 1951 and played out of the sugar plantation located in Brechin Castle, California, in central Trinidad. The club has continued in existence even though the sugar industry was brought to closure in 2003; however, the structure of the team has undergone a tremendous ethnic changeover as many of the current players are from outside of the community as well as Afro-Trinidadians. Even though clubs from Indo-Trinidadian communities participated with other clubs from the urban areas, there was always a perception that there was not equity within the structure of the cricket field. Queen's Park Cricket Club with its urban white elite membership controlled cricket in Trinidad and Tobago until the 1980s. Clubs from the urban areas that were predominantly Afro-Trinidadian in their base were seen as privileged over clubs from central and south Trinidad where most of the Indo-Trinidadian-dominated clubs were based. Hence, the structure and control of cricket paralleled the general view of Indo-Trinidadians. There was gross inequality in society and cricket was just another example. It is therefore quite evident that cricket reflected the social structure and social relations between the two dominant ethnic groups in Trinidad.

Contemporary Period

Since their arrival as transient laborers on the sugar plantations, Indo-Trinidadians who decided to make Trinidad their homeland have made tremendous social, economic, and political strides. Using the medium of education they have made progressive steps in many of the professions becoming doctors, lawyers, accountants, and engineers. Additionally, they have established many types of small- and medium-size businesses in agriculture, manufacturing, retail, and service industries. Furthermore, in addition to having established a historical cultural ethnic identity, they have also been able to promote and solidify this identity through the medium of radio and television program as well as the commercialization of their food, music, and festivals. This cultural growth has been negotiated into evolving popular culture of the society that is now being more openly embraced by the wider population compared to the past. The celebration of Indian Arrival Day, *Divali,* and *Eid ul Fitr* as public holidays demonstrates recognition of the existence of Indians as an ethnic community as well as their major religions— Hinduism and Islam—as significant pieces in the multiethnic and multi-cultural mosaic of the society.

Arguably their biggest accomplishment has been attainment of control of the reigns of political power. In doing so they have been able to rise from the lowest rung of the social ladder where their eth-nic identity was once viewed with a degree of suspicion and in many quarters subjected to ridicule and contempt to positions of legitimate bearers of political, economic, and cultural capital. The combination of all these forms of social mobilization in society has called for a reas-sessment of the view that they are "docile" and timid. National pride, once questioned, became visible through their social, economic, and political undertakings.

Social mobility in society is apparent in cricket where Indians have moved from the realm of being participants to seeking and controlling power beyond the cricket field. This change has been demonstrated in many telling ways. The locus of influential power in cricket has shifted from the urban north to central and south Trinidad, controlled by clubs dominated by Indo-Trinidadians. In 1982, the central executive of the Trinidad and Tobago Cricket Board (TTCB) (then Trinidad and Tobago Cricket Board of Control [TTCBC]) contained three Indo-Trinidadians. In 2009 six of the eleven executive members were Indians. In 2010, Azim Bassarath became the first Indo-Trinidadian president of the TTCB; eight of his executive members were Indians. In October 2011, Bassarath and his executive were reelected for another two-year term of office unopposed. The ascendancy of Bassarath and his executive to the corridors of power in the cricket fraternity was yet another example of social, economic, and political mobility of Indians in a social site in the society. Additionally, it has allowed rural areas, which for years were kept outside the halls of power, to exercise their claim for legitimacy.

Cricket has always been part of their habitus, however; this cul-tural capital cum economic and political capital has given the Indo-

Trinidadians an opportunity to articulate themselves as never demonstrated before without any resistance or tension being shown. The extent of Indo-Trinidadian involvement in cricket is clearly visible in every aspect and layer of the sport. In the premiership, zonal, primary, and secondary school levels, Indians are dominant in terms of players, administrators, and officials—umpires, coaches, and scorers. The spectators who attend the matches are predominantly Indo-Trinidadians; a good assessment of this is seen when the attendance figures are compared for regional matches involving Trinidad and Tobago that are played at the Queen's Park Oval located in the north of the country and matches played in central and south Trinidad. The differences in attendance are starkly contrasting, reflecting where the contemporary center of cricket exists.

Discussion

In this study, the field is the sport of cricket. Within the field there are written and unwritten "rules," which define what is valued and legitimate and what is not. Historically, as indicated by Beckles,[35] the elites in society thrust their acquired colonial values and practices over and above the values and social practices of the lower classes. These superior values and practices are manifested in every facet of life from speech, attire, and mannerism. Hence, there is a structure of power relations between the dialectical positions of what is valued as acceptable and nonacceptable behavior, which is aligned to the dynamics of class, race, ethnicity, and gender.

The cricketers, administrators, and spectators in Trinidad and Tobago and the wider Caribbean have their own habitus, which has been shaped by their daily-lived experiences. Their daily experiences are shaped by the extent of the degree of economic, cultural, educational, and symbolic capital they possess. Cricket has predominantly been a sport of the masses and for the masses, which has shaped both the type and kind of attending crowds. Therefore, cricket emits high symbolic capital to the lower classes in society not only in terms of participation but also attendance. At the same time, cricketers and spectators in the Caribbean may not necessarily display the high levels of educational capital as their counterparts in England and Australia. Therefore, although cricket may offer symbolic capital, it is not enough to serve a means of economic distinction in society.

The social mobility experienced by Indo-Trinidadians over the past fifty years coincided with an improving social psyche laying the foundation for many to enter into domains that were once under the "control" of Afro-Trinidadians, such as the traditional public-sector positions, business and cultural domains, such as carnival. Furthermore, they have used their newfound strong self-belief in their social strides to compete and or developed "open" parallel cultural domains for the promotion of their own cultural identity such as chutney music in the context of a national cultural signifier. Such assertion has paved the way for a process of "open" interculturation and hybridization as opposed to attempts in the past where assimilation into the dominant Afro-creole culture was expected of Indo-Trinidadians.

Their cultural signifiers have received legitimization from within and outside the group; however, it is an ongoing negotiated process. In so doing they have added an "Indianized" element to the cultural identity mosaic. When negotiated with creolization, regionalization, and globalization, namely, through North American popular culture, the "national" identity factor is much more fluid and dynamic as opposed to a fixed ethnic identity as articulated in the past when the society was in its early stage of construction. The younger population is willing to see ethnicity as a more fluid process as opposed to the reified constructs of the previous generations where every aspect of social life was viewed through narrow lenses. Such a reality made it easy to alter positions of "us/them."

The ascendancy of Indians to the corridors of political power has helped to solidify their achievements in other areas of social life. Control of political power has provided an opportunity for Indians to correct some of the perceived inequities experienced in the past when they were on the political periphery, such as in the distribution of resources to improve infrastructural works—such as water, roads, bridges—in areas where they resided and greater recognition of their cultural identity and religions, such as more Hindu members of government and in positions of authority.

The cricket field has become the dominant sporting locus where Hindus and Muslims have being able to display their cultural identity more so than in any other sporting discipline. This manifestation of religion is further reinforced by the importance of kith and kinship ties within the Indo-Trinidadian community. Hence, cricket provides further opportunity for the extension and strengthening cultural capital as it provides social spaces for family support, religion, and celebratory cultural products such as music and food to be displayed and reinforced.

The rise of Brian Lara to elite status from humble beginnings provided a true nexus for Indo-Trinidadians to identify with him and what he represented. Lara's elevation in the cricketing world coincided with the Indo-Trinidadian rise in the political arena and hence became an ideal signifier as to what represented a "national" identity, especially since his entry into test cricket was seen as delayed by the deliberate tactics of the West Indies selectors to keep out a merited Trinidad and Tobago player. Lara's struggle became symbolic to the experiences of the Indo-Trinidadians in ascending to political power. Therefore, Lara represented not only the Afro-Trinidadian working class but also the Indo-Trinidadian ethnic struggle. He became an embodiment of a national identity that cut across race, ethnicity, class, and politics. None of the political leaders of the country such as Eric Williams, Basdeo Panday, George Chambers, A. N. R. Robinson, Basdeo Panday, and Patrick Manning had the appeal that Lara has had across ethnic, class, and political lines. Lara manifested not the rigid definition of ethnicity but one of a fluid popular culture where room exists for a potpourri of cultures to be constantly invented and reinvented.

The Lara factor is further reinforced when he mentored Indo-Trinidadian cricketer Adrian Barath under his supervision. This was seen as yet another genuine and legitimate effort of Lara to rise above ethnicity and demonstrate a true sense of national identity. At the 2007 Cricket World Cup (CWC), staged in the Caribbean, the government of Trinidad and Tobago applied for the Brown Package—the group with three teams from the subcontinent: India, Sri-Lanka, and Bangladesh. It was believed the subcontinent teams would appeal to the Indo-Trinidadian population in large numbers. However, the population including the Indo-Trinidadians did not want to see Sachin Tendulkar or Kumar Sangakarra as much as they wanted to see the West Indian team led by Brian Lara supported by Christopher Gayle. Indo-Trinidadian spectators demonstrated that their national identity of belonging to Trinidad and Tobago was paramount.

The greater visibility of Indo-Caribbean players in West Indian teams at the senior level and across various age groups since the 1990s has also contributed to a greater sense of national and regional pride that was not always present in the past. The West Indies team that won the inaugural Crosscutter under 15 World Cup in England in 1995 included six members of the Indo-Caribbean community. Furthermore, in the last fifteen years a number of players from the Indo-Caribbean community have served as either captain and or vice captains of various West Indian teams: Shivnarine Chanderpaul, Ramnaresh Sarwan, Darren Ganga, and Denesh Ramdin.

The style of play of Indo-Trinidad players also reflects the impact of constantly evolving popular culture. The batting display of Adrian Barath at the T20 2009 Champions League in India demonstrated a degree of aggression and assertiveness that would not have been associated with any Indo-Trinidadian cricketer in the past or Indo-Trinidadians in general. The on-field antics of Dave Mohammed both at the Stanford T20 tournament in 2008 and the T20 Champions League in 2009 in India also demonstrated assertiveness and the impact of contemporary popular culture on the Caribbean interpretation of how cricket is played. Additionally, Ravi Rampaul, an Indo-Trinidadian, spearheaded fast bowling in the early 2010s demonstrating further the ascendancy that Indo-Trinidadians and Indo-Guyanese players have made in the last fifteen years in an institution that was once totally dominated by whites and or the Afro-Caribbean.

Conclusion

Cricket has become a site for Indo-Trinidadians to express themselves in a way that was previously absent. As much as cricket has become a space for Indo-Trinidadians to use their various forms of capital, solidify and display its own ethnic identity, the dynamics of the field has been fomenting its own formation of a national identity through the constant negotiation of class, ethnicity, and popular culture.

Whereas in 1976, Norman Tebbit's "cricket test" may have provided a stern examination of the Indo-Trinidadians commitment to Trinidad and Tobago, in 2011 it is quite evident through their attainment of various forms of social and cultural capital on and off the cricket field that ethnic and national identities in Trinidad and Tobago are converging.

IV.

Crossing Boundaries/
Maintaining Boundaries

INTRODUCTION

Alan Gregor Cobley

CLR James invited us in his classic work, *Beyond a Boundary*, to think about boundaries in sport as not merely demarcating physical spaces where sport is enacted, but as defining zones in which sociological, cultural, ideological, and political interactions and transformations can and do occur. Literally and figuratively, embodied identities are acted out on the sports field or arena in the course of a contest: critically, however, while the rules governing the contest are predetermined, the outcome is not. The contest itself, and its possible outcomes, therefore lend fluidity to the competing identities on display, though the ultimate result may often be an affirmation or reaffirmation of the dominance of one identity over others.

Of course a boundary does not merely serve to enclose a defined space; it is a "limit-line" notionally containing the contest to that space. Yet in his work, James showed that it was possible to challenge and even transcend this physical limit—just as a cricketer can achieve the maximum score of six runs with a single blow of the bat by dispatching the ball through the air beyond the boundary. In order to achieve this feat, however, the participants in the contest must be conscious, and understand the possibilities of, the unlimited, nondemarcated territory on the other side. Paradoxically, James suggests, it is in the unmapped territory beyond the boundary that the outcome of the contest will ultimately be determined.

The chapters in this section address, in diverse ways, the significance of boundaries in sport: the ways in which some of these boundaries are maintained, how they can be challenged, and even, on occasion, how they can be broken down. In the first contribution to this section, Michael Atkinson and Kevin Young take as their case studies two sports that are not confined within agreed boundaries to a predefined playing area—Parkour and Fell Running. Yet in the course of their analysis of these "alternative sports," they seek to show that the overwhelmingly male, middle-class, and white participants in these activities, despite their self-image as free spirits communing with nature, are in fact, through their participation, reaffirming the boundaries that define their gender roles, class affiliation, and most specifically, their racial identity. In multicultural societies in North America and Northwestern Europe where the exercise of "whiteness" no longer has formal exclusionary power, these activities function, Atkinson and Young suggest, as a means to continue "white boundary-marking in supposedly unbound social places."

David Hassan and Ken McHue's thoughtful contribution considers the consequences of social, political, and religious boundary making in the recent history of Northern Ireland, through an examination of the intersections of sectarianism, racism, and sport. He argues that there is "specificity" to racism in Ireland, and especially in Northern Ireland, where the sectarianism that has traditionally pitted "British Protestant" against "Irish Catholic" identities can be seen as a particularly virulent form of racism. However, even as Northern Ireland is struggling to recover from years of sectarian violence between these two groups, efforts to break down the boundaries between them have been greatly complicated by a recent influx of immigrants from the European community. This influx has created a number of new ethnic minorities in Northern Ireland, such as Polish Catholics, who are subjected to discrimination in their own right, but also find themselves drawn unwillingly into sectarian politics. Hassan cites examples of how the underlying tensions have spilled over into association football in Northern Ireland, both on the field of play and among rival supporters, and the inadequate responses of the relevant sporting bodies and the government in their efforts to address the issues raised, or even, on occasion, to acknowledge that a problem exists.

Ethnicity and identity are also themes in Thomas Fletcher's discussion of the sporting affiliations of British Asians. What does the support of many British Asians for cricket teams representing their ancestral homes in the subcontinent against that of their adopted homeland in England tell us about the nature of diasporic identity and of nationhood? Fletcher rejects the traditional view of diasporic identity as creating an exclusionary boundary that prevents British Asians from assimilating to Britain—although it is clear from the evidence he presents that British Asians do reject that brand of "Englishness" that has been appropriated as a badge of identity by right-wing white racist groups in England. He suggests that there is "a complex process of identity negotiation" in play, which is an expression of the hybridity inherent in the diasporic condition, rather than of a process of social closure motivated by a fixed and exclusionary notion of nationhood.

The final contribution in this section, by James A. McBean, Michael Friedman, and Callie Batts, discusses a different kind of boundary—a boundary that separates "acceptable" from "unacceptable" behaviors in sport. The "field of play" in this instance is the "Olympic ethos" as defined at the time of the foundation of the modern Olympic Games by Baron Pierre de Coubertin at the end of the nineteenth century, and maintained ever since by generations of mainly white, Western administrators dedicated to preserving what the authors argue are the hegemonic metropolitan values at the heart of Olympic sport. Thus, when the Jamaican Usain Bolt broke the world record as he sprinted to the Gold Medal in the 100-meter final in the Beijing Olympics in 2008 both the manner of his victory and the manner of his celebration afterwards were criticized as transgressing the core values of the Olympic movement. Using a Lefebvrean understanding of space, the authors suggest that the controversy evoked by Bolt's victory in the Olympic stadium on that day was a result of his refusal to conform to the norms of behavior prescribed for that space—norms designed to uphold and reproduce existing global power relations. In the process he "validated" the black body and questioned the boundaries that had been fixed by the hegemonic discourse within the Olympic movement on what was deemed "acceptable" behavior. It was a moment, in short, that dramatized the postcolonial condition and simultaneously proposed an alternative to it.

All of the contributions in this share the progressive perspective offered by James in *Beyond a Boundary*, to the extent that they agree that the boundaries they identify in the communities they discuss, and which are dramatized in their case studies by the practice of sport, are by no means permanent or immutable. It is also encouraging that all may be said to end their studies on a hopeful note. In the final analysis, each demonstrates that the human spirit always has the capacity to transgress and transcend those boundaries that have been created in society through the detritus of historical circumstance. As Gary Armstrong has suggested with reference to the role of football in war-torn Liberia, sport is not a panacea for social ills as some, particularly politicians, like to claim; rather, it holds up a mirror to society, reflecting both the good and bad that exists there.* Nevertheless, as the contributions to this section show, close study of that mirror image can suggest where progressive changes are needed and point to where positive interventions can be made.

*Gary Armstrong, "Life, Death and the Biscuit: Football and the Embodiment of Society in Liberia, West Africa," in *Football in Africa: Conflict, Conciliation and Community*, ed. Gary Armstrong and Richard Giulianotti (Basingstoke: Palgrave Macmillan, 2004).

Into the Great White Yonder: Stabilizing and Transcending Whiteness in Adventure Sports

Michael Atkinson and Kevin Young

Introduction: No More Mr. White Guy?

If one were to review the sociology of sport literature, it would appear as though the study of alternative sport subcultures has, of late, fallen out of favor. Despite a groundswell of research between the 1970s and into the early 2000s, much of it influenced by the iconic Centre for Contemporary Cultural Studies at the University of Birmingham, UK, and signaling a generation of interest in non-mainstream sport, leisure, and other physical cultures,[1] shortly after the turn of the twenty-first century, subcultural research into the playful or athletic use of the body as a source of social resistance, protest, or alternative self-exploration apparently lost its appeal. Our aim in this chapter is to rejuvenate that appeal and continue this strand of inquiry, by extending it into the analysis of how racialized forms (such as white identities) are expressed and responded to within non-mainstream sports cultures.

Whiteness is often overlooked, or perhaps uncritically taken for granted, in the study of alternative sports. While, by and large, authors concur that alternative, extreme, adventure, or lifestyle sports are the terrain of white participants, the link between the social construction of whiteness inside and outside of these groups is relatively under-explored. Further, few have either connected the social performance of whiteness in non-mainstream sports with broader social challenges to white authority and hegemony or examined how certain mythic or romanticized constructions of whiteness are extolled in "frontier" sport zones that are relatively "uncomplicated" by ethnic and cultural diversity.

In this chapter, we examine two non-mainstream physical cultures in North America and the United Kingdom—Parkour and Fell Running. We approach each as an example of alternative sports, or what R. Stebbins refers to as "serious leisure" pursuits, and analyze how white participants use their involvement as a means of managing their social constructions of race.[2] Further, we explore how the spaces of these pursuits become valued as zones of (white) self-definition and existential exploration at a time when white identities in sport (and elsewhere) are increasingly being challenged, destabilized, and disrupted. Little research has explored what an existential sociology of sport might look like or how it might be theorized in the context of whiteness studies or, in fact, has treated whiteness as a problematic cultural phenomenon in and of itself; that is, not as the backdrop for analyzing how ethnic or racial minorities' identities are subjugated in sports cultures. In this chapter, we show how activities such as Parkour and Fell Running underline a range of historically relevant and recently reemerging white subjectivities in sport. In our discussion, we examine how Parkour and Fell Running thrust their participants into "unproblematic" racial zones—or spaces where one's racial identity is not complicated by competing identities or subjectivities. In these spaces, we argue, participants feel "freed" to nostalgically explore a sense of self-determined racial identity.

Whiteness Studies and Alternative/ Post-Sports Cultures

As a subfield of critical race theory, whiteness studies are surprisingly underdeveloped within sociology, and especially in sport and exercise studies. Existing research has examined the nature of white identity and white privilege, the historical process by which a white racial identity is legitimated and normalized as dominant, the relation of culture to white identity, and possible processes of social change as they affect white identities. Keystone sources such as Allen's *The Invention of the White Race*,[3] Berger's *White Lies: Race and the Myths of Whiteness*,[4] Bonnett's *White Identities: Historical and International Perspectives*,[5] Dyer's *White*,[6]

Hill's *After Whiteness: Unmaking an American Majority,*[7] Jensen's *The Heart of Whiteness: Confronting Race, Racism and White Privilege,*[8] Lipsitz's *The Possessive Investment in Whiteness: How White People Profit from Identity Politics,*[9] Roediger's *The Wages of Whiteness: Race and the Making of the American Working Class,*[10] and Young's *White Mythologies: Writing History and the West,*[11] all published within approximately a decade, vivisect race relations in North America and show how whiteness is structurally, culturally, and ideologically embedded in dominant social practices and relationships. But, by and large, what is striking, indeed ironic, about whiteness studies is how *white subjects* themselves are rarely the center of analysis in the pursuit of understanding how whiteness impacts the lived realities of Others. Whiteness studies, as an outgrowth of the critical race theory movement of the late 1970s, is predominantly contoured by accounts of how whiteness serves to marginalize and exclude racialized Others. Remarkably, there are few exceptions.

Tim Wise is a leading whiteness studies scholar whose study *White Like Me*[12] differs radically from the majority of books or readers in the field. *White Like Me* is a penetrating and reflexive narrative of white privilege in the United States.[13] In it, Wise discusses how white Americans (especially white American *men*) must recognize the arbitrary and victim-producing power lines drawn by racial categorization and hierarchies. He highlights reactionary tendencies among white men in the United States and elsewhere, and interprets the deconstruction of racial privilege and the white mainstreaming of American culture as an overt attack on white masculinities.

By contrast, a growing body of literature on white, male masculinities examines and deconstructs the notion of a burgeoning "masculinity crisis." Not so subtly embedded in white "masculinity crisis" discourses in North America and elsewhere[14] is an implicit lament of the death of white masculine society, and associated reactions against Other men claiming victimization. Crisis advocates including Clareassail argue whiteness and blackness research is polarizing and ideologically naïve, silencing men in the white middle classes.[15] Examinations of black masculinity, for example, like bell hooks's *We Real Cool*[16] and Anthony Neal's *New Black Masculinity*[17] nevertheless point to the multilayered methods by which black masculinity is far more of a measurable crisis category for young men than whiteness. hooks claims that black men have been so dehumanized by white (male) America that they are in crisis emotionally and at risk within society (i.e., through drugs, crime, gangs, chronic unemployment, and disease). She claims further that the greatest threat to black life in America is the institutional residue of white male patriarchal thinking and practices. Once more, white men in the middle end up feeling socially attacked on the basis of their whiteness (not only from all women, critical race and whiteness theorists, and from Othered men), and are told they do not have legitimate cultural access to crisis feelings, discourses, or experiences.[18]

Whiteness, Crisis, and Alternative Sports

One does not need to excavate the terrain of sociological research on the role of sport in society long before one discovers the popular argument that the organization, institutionalization, administration, and promotion of most amateur, elite, and professional sports practices in the twentieth century reflected mainstream cultural views that sport could (should) be used to translate key social values and ideologies to white males—most of which reaffirmed established social class, gender, racial, and religious lifestyles. Indeed, an entire edition of the *Sociology of Sport Journal* in 2005 (22:3), and one of the *Journal of Sport and Social Issues* in 2007 (31:1) were devoted to the analysis of how whiteness continues to be the organizing racial norm in Western sports cultures. The panorama of widely practiced and institutionalized sports fits neatly into patriarchal and techno-capitalist styles of living and doing social order. Sociological research on the physical cultural practice of sport since the late 1980s has, however, documented a growing list of sports, activities, and leisure pursuits that have counter-hegemonically resisted the tendency to frame sports in such ways.[19]

Here, we return to our interests in theorizing identity in alternative sports, physical cultures, and sports subcultures. In the world of sports practices, physical activities on the cultural fringe have long been the domain of white participants. When considering the gamut of alternative, whiz, extreme, or edge sport, one must ask how "resistant" many of these subcultures are along race lines. LeBreton describes the full panorama of alternative, adventure, or post-sport cultures from the 1970s onward as not so resistant to dominant social constructions of whiteness inside or outside of sport at all.[20] In fact, since as far back as the mid-1800s, "wilderness" and "adventure" sports (the North American precursors to contemporary subcultural risk sports) have represented places where whiteness is the unspoken norm and where white privilege has existed largely without opposition.[21]

Ray illustrates how the very essence of most adventure, risk, or otherwise alternative sports cultures predominated by whites deeply extol long-standing white, middle-class constructions of sport, physical activity, and leisure as a time-out from work, a place of controlled adventurism, an opportunity to build social capital among others "like me," as a site of moral character development, as a context for testing one's ability to take risks (in the wilderness, on water, in the sky, and in urban spaces) in the pursuit of honing one's skills in personal, spatial, and social mastery.[22] She argues, as does Nash in his study of nineteenth- and twentieth-century American wilderness cultures, that outdoor, alternative sports cultures retain an early 1900s Progressive Era sentiment of the need to develop (white) character through risk-based athletic pursuits.[23] As such, alternative/lifestyle sports subcultures have long been associated with the need for whites to test themselves and prove social character. This has been especially true, it is argued, in the face of extant social conditions that soften or discredit white masculine hegemony (since the onset of the industrial revolution) including urbanization, technological innovation, cultural diversification, and immigration and globalization. Simply put, the pursuit of "edgework"[24] has long been a boundary for whites to evidence their ability to be social leaders. Indeed, a collective middle-class, white interest in alternative sports has generationally replicated an ethos of spatial and social colonization for well over a century.

Important to us is that the late modern boom in adventure, lifestyle, or so-called alternative sports dovetails almost precisely with the contemporary crisis of white masculinity in North America and the United States. Susan Faludi's book *Stiffed: The Betrayal of the American Man* brought the masculinity crisis to public consciousness.[25] Scholars including Goldberg warned about an impending crisis of masculinity in the 1970s and early 1980s.[26] Faludi's *Stiffed* and other noteworthy books, including *Masculinity in Crisis*,[27] *Unmasking the Masculine*,[28] *Men's Lives*,[29] and *The Scapegoat Generation*,[30] tabled serious and emotionally penetrating analyses of how many (read) men in contemporary life struggle with normative expectations about *white* masculinity, confused gender identities and roles, and feelings of guilt over being complicitly white, male, and patriarchal in modern North America. By the time Tiger[31] published his controversial *The Decline of Males,* and Farrell[32] wrote the equally provocative and inflammatory *The Myth of Male Power,* fervent masculinity crisis discourses had begun to pepper academic and popular literatures.

A *masculinity crisis,* as it is argued, is common among certain men who feel as if they have been evicted from, or forcibly prevented from accessing, white-collar jobs, higher educational streams, and other sites of social power as a form of social punishment for thousands of years of patriarchy and racial dominance over others. On an ideological level, attacks on the very social construction of white masculinity (and men's exclusive ownership over so-called masculine attributes) have created cultural chaos as men no longer know how to act in gender-appropriate ways. Whitehead contends that with the rearrangement of family, economic, political, educational, sport-leisure, technological-scientific, and media power bases in the second half of the twentieth century, dominant white masculinity identities and codes have been challenged within most social settings as Others have crossed into traditionally protected white male boundaries.[33] White men no longer possess exclusive ownership over the social roles once held as bastions for establishing and performing patriarchal masculine hegemony. In Faludi's[34] terms, men have simply "lost their compass" for navigating the social world. This is especially true in the world of organized sport, for example, where (save for the exception of league or team ownership and administration) white authority and dominance in many athletic settings is rapidly becoming a thing of the past and the overrepresentation of whiteness is (in many contexts) the exception rather than the rule.[35]

In the remainder of the chapter, we examine Parkour and Fell Running as loosely protected, valued, and uncriticized spaces of white self-exploration in an era of diffuse male crisis. The practice of each by their participants is linked to long-term historical trends regarding the use of adventurism and risk-taking through athletics as a vehicle for reproducing and confirming dominant (white) identities. Importantly, each is approached as a site where white participants engage in a historically enduring form of existential self-work as "serious leisure."[36]

Reading Parkour and Fell Running as Serious (Existential) Leisure

Postcolonial studies help us understand why growing numbers of white men in the middle class feel frustrated by contemporary identity politics and localized power vacuums created by masculinity crises. This body of research extends across a full range of academic disciplines and generally seeks to challenge modernist (white, masculinist) ways of thinking, therefore creating space for the *subaltern* (socially marginalized) to speak and produce alternative discourses and knowledge.[37] Edward Said's book *Orientalism* is heralded as the pioneering text in postcolonial studies.[38] It emphasizes the degree to which scientific knowledge of the world tends to be framed around white, Western notions of reality. For Said, the ability to "name" or objectively define social processes, identities, laws, and scientific facts through academic documentation and discourses in the world is power; that power has been held by white Westerners through modernity until quite recently. Another prominent postcolonial theorist, Gayatri Spivak contends that the public must engage a sort of "epistemic violence" against colonial ways of seeing and defining the world in order to "let the subaltern speak."[39] Spivak refers to dismantling white, hegemonically male (Said's "colonial") ways of defining the world. As a postcolonialist, Homi Bhaba argues for cultural pluralism and hybridization, where socially disintegrative boundaries such as Western/Eastern, white/Other, or male/female are smashed and mixed back together as progressive cultural politics. In short, postcolonialists struggle against historically pervasive identity boundaries and forms of essentialism that serve to maintain power imbalances between cultural groups.

The accelerating interest in postcolonial studies, and their implications on everyday structural and cultural practice, is a signifier in certain respects of what legions of men in the Canadian white middle class irrationally fear and struggle to come to terms with in everyday life. The destabilization of modernist knowledge bases involves a destabilization of persons in those bases. In the process of destabilization, the lament from male whites in the middle class about postcolonial ways of thinking in the news, at work, in school, on television, in religion, and of course in sport tends to revolve around the notion of "reverse discrimination."[40] The multicultural, postcolonial reality of most Western landscapes is reacted to emotionally by particular men in the privileged middle class as an attack on some mythological "imagined community"[41] of whites. These men feel whites are collectively victimized by racial, ethnic, and other forms of identity politics that give voice to the subaltern and grant them access to social power. Roger Hewitt's *White Backlash: The Politics of Multiculturalism* documents how a host of white male backlash movements emerged in the past half a century as responses to perceived reverse discrimination in countries like the United States, Great Britain, and Canada.[42] Here, we might consider the emerging "green sport" or adventure sport movement in North America and Europe as a silent and seemingly unpolitical backlash movement with deep historical roots.

Parkour

Over the course of three years, the first author engaged in a field study of Parkour in Ontario, Canada, and in parts of the United Kingdom. During this time, he examined how Parkour enthusiasts construct the practice as a stereotypically white adventurist way of constructing the self through athletics. The Parkour enthusiasts studied were almost all white, middle class, and well educated, and most expressed a need for personal self-exploration through their chosen physical culture.

As a physical cultural practice, the philosophical roots of Parkour date back over a century. The late modern manifestation of Parkour is a particular offshoot of a style of training called "Hébertism" that emerged in the early twentieth century through the athletic philosophies and practices of French naval officer George Hébert. Hébert believed that the pursuit of physical perfection and communion with one's local environmental surroundings is a technique for developing one's sense of place in the physical and social environment; and, as a vehicle for bringing forth the underlying essence of one's humanity.[43] He designed a series of apparatuses and exercises to teach what he dubbed as his "Natural Method" of training.

Hébert believed that individuals should train in the open environment as an unfettered animal species traversing a variety of landscapes and obstacles. Hébert's Natural Method typically placed practitioners in a wooded setting, where they would be instructed to run a course ranging from 5–10 kilometers. Practitioners were simply told to run through the woods, over bushes, through streams, climb up and down trees, and traverse fields. Students (exclusively white and middle class) were also instructed, at particular time or distance points, to lift fallen logs, carry and throw heavy stones, or even to hang from trees. Hébert believed that by challenging his students to practice basic human muscular-skeletal movements in uncontrolled settings, they would develop qualities of strength and speed toward being able to walk, run, jump, climb, balance, throw, lift, defend oneself, and swim in practically any geographic landscape. Further, he felt that Natural Method practitioners would progressively learn to encounter and control any emotions or social situations they encountered in life. The Natural Method demanded that one possesses sufficient energy, willpower, courage, coolness, and *fermeté* to conquer any physical or mental obstacle. In a moral sense, by experiencing a variety of mental and emotional states (e.g., fear, doubt, anxiety, aggression, resolve, courage, and exhaustion) during training, one cultivated a self-assurance that would lead to inner peace.

Hébert became the earliest proponent of what the French call the *parcours* (obstacle course) method of training. Modern woodland challenge courses and adventure races—comprising balance beams, ladders, rope swings, and obstacles—are often described as "Hébertisme" courses both in Europe and North America. The contemporary subcultural moniker *Parkour* (the first French term to be used in reference to urban free-running) clearly derives from the Hébert's use of the term *parcours(e)*, and the French military term *parcours du combattant*. Hébert's Natural Method of training had a special impact on French military training in the 1960s. French soldiers during the Vietnam War were inspired by Hébert's method and philosophy of physical and emotional development, and employed the Natural Method as a technique for honing their jungle-warfare skills. Among the French soldiers exposed to the Natural Method was Raymond Belle.

After his tour of duty in Vietnam, Belle taught his son David the principles of the Natural Method. The younger Belle had participated in martial arts and gymnastics as a young teen and immediately took to the method. After moving to the Parisien suburb Lisses, David Belle further explored the rigors and benefits of the Natural Method with his friend Sébastien Foucan. By the age of fifteen, Belle and Focuan developed their own suburban style of the Natural Method they termed "Parkour." In the 2003 BBC documentary *Jump London*, Foucan described his initial construction of Parkour as a physical and spiritual lifestyle of movement in which, "the whole town [Lisses] was there for us; there for Parkour. You just have to look and you just have to think like children. This is the vision of Parkour."[44]

Belle and Foucan gathered followers across Europe through the 1990s. By the end of the decade, the media in France, the UK, and the Netherlands had documented the emerging lifestyle movement. Media reports predictably framed the practice as a vacuous and style-oriented urban youth counterculture. Belle later referred to Parkour's insertion into the media as part of a generational "prostitution of the art."[45] As a result of media attention, widespread youth interest, the commercialization of Parkour images and identities, and the rise of global Parkour networks, the physical culture has grown almost exponentially over the past two decades.

The relatively bourgeois, white nature of Parkour ethics regarding self-exploration and self-transcendence through physical "perfection" are immediately obvious when one spends time with *traceurs* (those who practice Parkour) in the field. Indeed, their logics of practice are remarkably similar to those espoused by white, wilderness adventurers of the late nineteenth century. Traceurs engage predominantly existential questions about the self in late modern social life through Parkour lifestyles. In Canada, Parkour enthusiasts are almost entirely white and middle class. They ask, at a time when the ontological stability about whiteness, for instance, has been called into question, whether core truths about the nature of existence and one's essence can be learned through ascetically grounded forms of athleticism and leisure. To them, Parkour is a bio-pedagogical project designed to release what traceurs believe to be a nonracialized, universal life force, spirit, a desire underpinning all human existence—only accessible to them when the boundaries of their own socially ascribed (raced, classed, gendered) selves are destabilized and crossed. Zen Buddhist scholars, as with other Chinese Buddhists, refer to such a force as the *qi* of life. In the Upanishads, Hindu philosophers refer similarly to the *prana*, or the vital life-sustaining force of living beings and energy in natural processes of the universe. Pronger describes a similar life force as the essential *puissance* of the free, desiring body and spirit.[46]

Traceurs in Canada argued that in order to tap prana, and to explore the essential aspects of the human condition in late modernity, the social self needs to be ritually broken through innovative physical cultural practice, and an emptiness of the self created. Here, their practices curiously resemble a late modern, neoliberalesque, and secular brand of religious *self-mortification*. The painful and exhaustive ritual of Parkour reminds practitioners how physical and emotional (read "ascetic") suffering can be a vehicle for self-discovery. LeBreton,[47] like Lyng,[48] has documented how similar groups of middle-class white groups increasingly seek out symbolic death experiences in high-risk adventure sports as a means of dealing with existential anxieties about being white in late modern life. Caillois[49] might argue that traceurs' quest to experience puissance through self-mortification is a form of *ilinx*; a type of play, which through the overloading of the senses during action, produces physical and cognitive vertigo that people find exhilarating. Ilinx contexts are

> based on the pursuit of vertigo and which consist of an attempt to momentarily destroy the stability of [self-] perception and inflict a kind of voluptuous panic upon an otherwise lucid [culturally framed] mind. In all cases, it is a question of surrendering to a kind of spasm, seizure, or shock which destroys reality with sovereign brusqueness.[50]

Caillois's notions of ilinx were refined and extended through conceptualizations of the "limit experience." The limit experience, principally emerging from the writing of Georges Bataille[51] and Michel Foucault,[52] is a visceral and sensual event that dislodges the subject and decentralizes identity—at least for a brief moment in time. According to Fromm, the limit-seeker carries a deep-seated frustration with heavily circumscribed modalities of late modern life, to the extent that a desire to ritually annihilate the socially dominated and confined self (which, of course, enframes one's learned sense of the possible) stirs and is mobilized through self-sadistic activities. In *America*, Baudrillard describes the limit-experience through the metaphor of the runner who hurtles forward in agony as a means of self-escape, and as an emblem of postmodern isolation, identity doubt, and confusion.[53]

Over the course of time, we learned that for the traceurs studied, their entire alternative sport lifestyle is anchored by the pursuit of liminality; a sense of escapism from the late modern crisis of identity and its frustrations. The founding fathers of free running, Belle and Foucan, described the ultimate goal of practice as an exploration of a new way, mode, or sensibility toward living. Their Parkour "way" was one chiefly resistant to the lethargy, physical atrophy, hyperindividualism, alienation, and unfettered consumption they perceived to be rife in the French (white) middle classes. Belle and Foucan believed that the late modern capitalist orientation of French (sub)urban life instilled great suffering, distress, anxiety, and physical malaise among youth cultures; in other words, it did not encourage youth to reflexively explore the puissance of an existential self. Consequently, their Parkour method of physical training extolled the need to explore the parameters of one's mind, body, and spirit (i.e., essence) with one's immediate (and even contrived or de-naturalized) environment through spectacular and risky forms of athletic movement. Engaging the urban environment as a traceur became a method of detaching temporarily from materialist modes of living and finding inner peace through physical communion with the environment, easy to experience for those in such a materially privileged position.

In the analysis of symbolic "death sports," LeBreton[54] argues that the burgeoning white, middle-class interest in liminal experiences in "natural" and "untamed" environments (versus contained gymnasia or sports facility) is a sign of a late modern anxiety and isolation, leading young urbanites like traceurs to search for a new physical cultural "way." Once the basic Parkour techniques are habituated and flow is experienced on a quasi-regular basis, a traceur often articulates feeling as if he/she possesses a "total connection" with one's pre-discursive or socially determined self, movement, and the surrounding physical environment. Temporarily losing the desire to rationally control one's self, honing flow through free running, and developing a sense of connection with the urban landscape is articulated as something purely aesthetic. The traceurs studied believe that most people are motivated by forces beyond their control (i.e., market capitalism and neoliberal consumption), and their inabilities to move as present-minded agents manifests into personal feelings of inadequacy, fear, and alienation (i.e., suffering). By contrast, traceurs speak about feeling energetically invincible during a particular *jam*. In the words of our respondent Gerry (twenty-seven years old), "the greatest power in life comes from being in a state of no power, where you have no concern for it. Parkour [free running] means being an empty vessel ready to move, not being a ball of worry about what you don't have."

Csikszentmihalyi[55] suggests that during these "flow" experiences the rational, other-oriented, and calculating self is deconstructed. Like Hebért's woodland training method, a *parcours* session is designed to stimulate doubts, anxieties, wants, fears, and frustrations so that they may be eventually negated or removed from one's mindset. In this respect, it is a liminal ritual par excellence.

What is immediately striking to us is how Parkour enthusiasts, like adventurists of nearly one hundred and fifty years ago, articulate a freedom from the [gendered, racialized, classed) self through their physical cultures. Parkour spaces and cultures are uncomplicated by race because of the relative homogeneity of race within them. As such, being a traceur is a limited experience because it is an escapist experience—at least for a short period of time.

Fell Running

Between 2007–2009, we engaged in an extended ethnographic project involving fell runners in the United Kingdom. The British physical culture of fell running is typically undertaken in expansive, rugged, inclement highland or mountain areas by white people from the middle classes, who range in age from thirteen to (well over) sixty years old. A typical fell run traverses meadows, crosses rivers or waterfalls, shoots up and down steep hills, staggers across rocky terrain, lumbers through thickets, meanders over bogs, and occasionally dodges animal herds. Fell runs vary in format and length, but normally range from two miles to (in excess of) forty or fifty miles. They can be highly organized or extremely disorganized in a traditional sporting sense. Fell runners represent a modest collective in the burgeoning global running figuration, and as such tend to maintain rather close (sub)cultural ties within local counties.

Although the date is somewhat disputed among fell running enthusiasts, the earliest "fell race" is believed to have taken place in Braemar, Scotland, between 1040–1060 CE with the staging of the Braemar Gathering hill races. From there, not much is known about fell running history in the UK until the mid-nineteenth century. By the nineteenth century, fell races were regularly staged across the Scottish highlands during village and town festivals, and alongside other sports competitions such as wrestling, sprint races, or throwing events (e.g., caber or hammer tossing). Competitors raced for both prize money and social accolade in rural communities that recognized and prized the competitors' abilities to navigate treacherous terrain. The adventure sport developed both professional and amateur wings in Scotland, England, and Wales through the mid-nineteenth century. The amateur wing, however, developed a spirit and ethos quite similar to the codes of mountaineering upheld by the British Youth Hostel Association. As such, emphasis became increasingly placed on conducting events outside of the context of a fair or public spectacle of competition, and more as a private wilderness sojourn undertaken by a few loyalists. Amateur racecourses were lengthened, located in hard-to-reach wilderness areas, and amateur fell runners developed into a small, esoteric subculture of adventure participants. The Fell Runners Association emerged in April 1970 to help organize the amateur sport in the UK, and promote the adventurist spirit of amateur fell running. Even more relevant is that entire factions or clusters of "hard-core" fell runners assembled in Scotland and in England during the late 1970s and 1980s (especially in the Peak and Lake Districts of England), who would only participate in races infrequently. To these individuals (the group with which we interacted in an ethnography over two years), fell running is a part of a selected style of life and something not to be "cheapened" through overly competitive racing.

To many fell running enthusiasts, the practice is an intentionally designed "scapeland"[56] activity. A scapeland is a place where traditional cultural maps of meaning (such as racial identity) do not necessarily apply at first. Encountering the scapeland of fell running is intended to provide a context for what Heidegger[57] first articulated, and what later Derrida[58] championed, as *rature* or "erasure." A fell running scapeland is a place where people reject the taken-for-grantedness of modernist athletic movements and forms of cultural logics and identities underpinning those movements. As Jim, a thirty-two-year-old fell runner observed, "when you get to a summit [mountain] and look at the space around you, it forces you to realize that you are beyond the ordinary. You've stepped outside of what running means as a technique, or, like as a competitive practice. It's art, it's beauty, it's everything." According to Jim and other runners, a fell "course" is a place where the technological application of modern ideology and technology to sport is disconnected from conventional athletics; it is placed *sous rature.*

While fell experiences are physically intense and structured by a "race" format, the meaning of an excursion for many fell runners is based centrally on the idea that while the practice might look like a modernist adventure race it is not underpinned by the same ethos. Runs or loosely organized races (which have only minimalist organization and administration) are not staged against the backdrop of a city, newly constructed estate, or along a faux urban greenspace. Instead, they place people in raw contexts of culturally uncontoured terrain. They are neither sponsored heavily by corporate investors, nor do running commodities surround the running field. One does not need timing chips, hi-tech gadgetry, or an ethos of dominance over others to enjoy the activity. Runners support one another to complete a run, often running in packs rather than as individuals. Thus, by their very movement across fields, streams, hills, and valleys, fell running eschews and replaces dominant constructions of modernist sports forms.

It did not take long into fieldwork on fell runners to appreciate what the participants were teaching about the ways in which communion with nature, and connection to a (present) time and place were focal points of this physical culture. Upon first glance, the act of fell running appears as a collective effort to conquer nature, traverse its boundaries with honed athletic skill, and beat its unforgiving essence. Such an interpretation is, by and large, a lingering cultural derivative of colonialist, imperialist, and modernist thinking, and reflective of how mainstream sport cultures often value the spirit of conquering in/as the athletic process. From Heidegger's[59] perspective, it is the application of sport and athletic modes of thinking, and technological applications of training to wilderness sports contexts. Gavin, a forty-five-year-old enthusiast explained: "When you [fell] run and think to yourself, I have to get up and beat this mountain, you don't know what you are doing. Embrace the mountain and its energy, don't try to beat it." To fell runners like Gavin, the physical practice is to be relished as it places the individual in a literal scapeland that is decisively untechnological, raw, stripped, and unknown.

Akin to Gavin's comments about the use of fell running scapelands as a site of religious connection with nature, Heidegger[60] stresses that not all ontological questions or human needs may be addressed by quantitatively demarcating the boundaries of lived experience or identity expression through applied mechanical and scientific means. Heidegger[61] exposes the other side of *techne*; the bringing forth or revealing of aesthetic and poetic human realities through subjective emotional expression and reflection—what the ancient Greeks called *poiesis*.

Poiesis is an artistic, aesthetic, emotional method of revealing 'different' human truths. These truths are, according to Heidegger,[62] humanistic, moral, ethic, and spiritual realities. To fell runners, there are many artistic representations of the human condition that can be uncovered through communion with nature. Poiesis is an act, a symbol, a thought, feeling or expression that brings forth knowledge of the human condition falling outside of rationally technological ways of understanding human bodies and essences the fell runners describe. Those interested in poiesis are less concerned with measuring and accounting for something quantifiable in the world (like my running ability, time to complete a course, ability to beat it, or use of running through the wilderness to maintain an identity narrative), than the possibility of *simultaneously* experiencing the material and nonmaterial parameters of human existence. Heidegger[63] suggests that the exploration of poiesis can provide moments of catharsis and liberation for people, or moments of ecstasis where the conscious and calculating mind is "let go" and the body and mind move as one as a present *Being*. The technical/techne application of running within the scapeland allows participants to experience a momentary break from the identities, thoughts, and behaviors that shape their everyday life. A physical culture like fell running, then, seeks not to reaffirm one's cultural identities but rather provides one with a time to critically inspect and/or release them.

In *The Sacred Balance*, David Suzuki[64] writes that human ecstasy and joy can be derived from accepting and embracing the idea that we, as a species, are materially and spiritually connected with the earth, air, fire, and water that is the basis of life on the planet. The human is, according to Suzuki, literally comprised of these basic elements, and thus connected to all life on earth. An athletic cultural practice that facilitates an awareness of one's connection to the elementary nature of life can instill within the individual a marked feeling of poiesis. There is ecstasis, according to the fell runner Finn (age twenty-nine), of being a part of "all non-human life while running. I love throwing myself into the mix and receiving the surge of energy which comes from being blown by wind, soaked by water, and covered with dirt . . . in knowing I am connected." It is precisely a sense of disconnection with late modern life that so many fell enthusiasts run away from. Enthusiasts lament the technologically and occupationally enframed natures of their everyday service-sector lives, and how distant they feel from the rawness of open, unmediated, or unconstrained physical existence. These boundaries demarcate the sacred and profane, nature and the city, the rational and the spiritual, sport and existentialism.

All of the above, as in the case of Parkour enthusiasm, might very well be a luxury for people whose identities (though in crisis in some manners or another) are not terribly problematic outside of sport and leisure. The "erasure" of identity through connection with nature in fell running is like a time-out from certain privilege in many ways; or, at least a time-out from worrying about how one's own whiteness is more complicated in a diverse, changing, and fragmented world. The connection with nature (and not an expressed connection with other whites) makes sense in this context, as it is a movement toward connection with a "green" universal—at a time wherein all universals and old hierarchies and meta-narratives are in doubt. From this point of view, it is unsurprising that fell running has ascended in popularity in Britain over the recent past as the nation becomes more ethnically diverse, and neoconservative, and where highly charged debates about proper "Britishnesss" are common.

Nevertheless, akin to the ideologies shared among Parkour enthusiasts, being physically and mentally "whipped" during a session is a critical facilitator for connecting with the sacredness of the land and of the impermanent self. There is a learned ecstasy of exhaustion in the culture that is based on each individual's realization that no matter how socially powerful or important one feels, the ultimate spiritual connection with life (and therefore happiness) is made when one learns to temporarily submit one's body to the power and energy of nature. Sean (forty-three) articulated such an idea in the following terms:

I never come back feeling physically "fine" from a run. But I can come back feeling invigorated because I allowed myself to be powerless for a time, and not worry about maintaining a façade of personal control in my life . . . What do I mean by that? Well, think about it. A massive amount of my psychological energy is spent controlling something; at work, at home, with my friends, whatever. That's the ego talking. I need to be in control, or I am less of a person than you. If I start out and try to exert my ego over a Category A ten mile run, and say, "I am better than you mountain," I'm bound to fail . . . Let go of the need for power, and use fatigue as a reminder of how powerless we all are, and that we shouldn't be afraid of it.

In *Being and Time*, Heidegger[65] describes his existential ontology of self-awareness as *Dasein* ("being-there"). Dasein refers to the visceral physical and existing human being who is consciously just "there," experiencing life as part of a natural world stripped from the socially constituted "Me." Dasein is an "authentic" existential state of selfhood, in which Heidegger[66] argues, "I myself, am." A sense of "mineness" (presence) occupies the mind of an existent Dasein. Dasein is thus composed of ontological (I myself, am) and present-centered existential dimensions (this is me, right now), disclosed to the person as a feeling of simply being there, being present. Heidegger[67] further categorizes Dasein as humankind's naked "thereness" in the world, one's abandonment of the "they." Through the awareness of one's Dasein, fell runners believe that they discover how their lives consist of being thrust into (and constituted by) a social environment that contours one's everyday Being. Part of the allure of fell running for those studied is, then, its power to reveal Dasein. Such is a vital feature of the fell running scapeland. This is especially important as so many of the fell runners describe leading lives filled with social (work, family) pressure, responsibilities, and anxieties that have a tendency to veil their subjectivities.

The fell runners' collective interest in transcending the daily strictures and contours of their everyday lives is, again, stereotypical "white man's work" in adventurist sport cultures. Many men from the lower-middle-class venture out onto the dales and the rugged terrain of "peaked" districts of Great Britain as a means of escaping their daily identities, but in doing so they underline the privilege they have as racialized and classed men in the first instance. While their abilities to be hegemonic men in the UK is less taken for granted than ever before, their abilities to win "white space" on the fells masked as the pursuit of connection with nature is a residual element of their power in society.

Discussion: On the White Ties That Bind

In a world where social boundary crossing is more of the norm than the exception, those social activities where boundaries are actively maintained in silent and uncriticized manners fascinate us. Both Parkour and fell running maintain decisively white, middle-class bases, and their proponents are offered social groups that pursue freedom from existential boundaries with noteworthy boundaries marking their membership nevertheless. Such has been the relative social function of adventure or alternative sports for some time. As we have discussed in this chapter, a range of theories from subcultural, postcolonial, masculinity crisis, and existential/phenomenological literatures teach us silent forms of racial reproduction matter *sociologically*—how they are constructed in seemingly banal or unthreatening manners is rather telling.

The adventure sport practice of temporarily erasing the self, connecting with nature, or freeing oneself from the identity trappings of everyday life most likely occurs because one has a certain amount of social, cultural, and economic capital to engage such pursuits. Furthermore, the members of the groups do not seek to challenge, resist, or overturn their ascribed social identities through sport so much as they seek to restabilize them in seemingly unthreatening ways. In the anonymity of busy city streets, parklands, and wooden areas, members of the two groups engage in a relatively unspectacular or muted form of social bonding as "similar" in alternative sports. Alternative sports subcultures have taken a decisive turn, then, as noted by Wheaton[68] and others.[69] While not as flamboyant or deliberately countercultural as in previous decades, they are intentionally crafted by enthusiasts as uncomplicated sites of self and social work at a time of great identity flux (especially in the West). Their burgeoning popularity in countries including Canada, the United Kingdom, the United States, Australia, the Netherlands, France, Sweden, and elsewhere illustrates, at least to us, a need to study continued white boundary marking in supposedly unbound social places.

A Unique Social Tapestry: Football, Sectarianism, and Racism in Northern Ireland

David Hassan and Ken McHue

Introduction

This chapter examines the existence and very real consequences of racism within Irish sport, specifically within the game of association football. It highlights the unique circumstances that exist in Northern Ireland, a country recovering from some of the worst excesses of sectarian violence in the developed world. Here, a society seemingly conditioned to live apart along ethnic and religious lines has also become aware of levels of inward migration into the country. This process, which has seen minority populations settling within Northern Ireland in ever-increasing numbers, has revealed efforts on the part of new arrivals to negotiate a space for themselves against a fluctuating domestic backdrop. It has proved far from a seamless process.

In its fullest form, this chapter argues that there is specificity to racism on the island of Ireland. The factors that give rise to its existence in Northern Ireland contrast with those that permeate in the Republic of Ireland.[1] Thus, in the former case, racism is partly symptomatic of a society that has been divided in many different ways since its creation in 1922 and that requires explanation in order to make sense of racially motivated behavior in the present. In the latter instance there is evidence of an abject denial by some concerning the very existence of racism, and it appears that the inertia surrounding those who govern and manage sport is only successfully overcome by the energy of highly motivated, socially responsive grassroots bodies such as Sport Against Racism Ireland (SARI).[2]

This chapter reflects upon, and critically engages with, these issues in the context of an overarching debate around racism in football in modern Ireland. In so doing of course it says little or nothing about other sports in Ireland, notably the most popular sporting activities in the country promoted by an indigenous organization, the Gaelic Athletic Association (GAA), which has over one million members. Neither does it comment upon the affairs of the Irish Rugby Football Union (IRFU), which has struggled with its own problems when field-ing an all-Ireland team containing playing members who define them-selves, at least in part, as British and who live in the United Kingdom. The exclusion of both the GAA and the IRFU should not imply that these bodies are somehow devoid of any concerns around racism or, for that matter, sectarianism. This is certainly not the case but coverage of both these organizations demands a separate and focused appraisal of their activities, which extends beyond the immediate parameters of this chapter.

Historically the Irish themselves have also been subject to racist dis-crimination, especially in Britain, as well as in other parts of the world, including the United States.[3] In such cases, as a minority ethnic group, they have typically been interpreted as homogenous, that is including Ulster unionists, many of whom see themselves more readily as being British. Likewise there has been an inability on the part of others to dif-ferentiate between people from the Republic of Ireland and those from Northern Ireland, the former almost exclusively Catholic and national-ist while the latter remains, in large parts, Protestant and unionist. This is relevant because in Northern Ireland, elements of extreme unionist culture reveal commonality with aspects of racism found on mainland Britain, which can include a particular anti-Irish component.[4] It is a reminder that the conflict in Northern Ireland was largely about the issue of sovereignty, which in turn had its roots in ethnicity. Yet mostly the focus was on sectarianism, which is division based on religion, rather than ethnicity, as a point of differentiation between that coun-try's two communities and consequently a contributing factor toward ongoing suspicion of the "Other." It would be wrong, however, not to recognize the role of sporting clubs and organizations patronized by the

Irish émigré in alleviating the worst excesses of racial intolerance for this community abroad. Of course by the same token, by congregating together, their sporting preferences offered a focal point for concerted displays of racism on the part of others and thus sport represented something of a contradiction for the Irish overseas, that is both as a safe haven and a very clear point of demarcation from their new environments and those who typically inhabited them.

Thus in any analysis of racism within sport in Northern Ireland the question of whether to include coverage of anti-Irish racism persists. In some sports, notably association football, it is the minority nationalist community that has historically borne the brunt of such vitriol.[5] For the purposes of this chapter, however, the discussion profiles the growing number of minority ethnic groups resident in Northern Ireland, including large numbers of migrants who have moved there following the expansion of the European Union (EU), while locating this in the context of an already divided society where the historical dislocate between Irish nationalists and Ulster unionists retains real significance. What emerges in the wake of such analysis is a society divided on a number of different levels and affected by geography, religion, nationality, and mythology.

Notwithstanding the presence of macro themes concerning racism within both parts of the island, it is nonetheless legitimate to refer to "Northern Ireland racism" and "Republic of Ireland racism" as two largely separate entities.[6] This should not imply that the consequences of racism are themselves different; in fact, the results of racist abuse upon those suffering it remain remarkably consistent. Nevertheless, racism in the north continues to be structured by sectarianism in a way that racism in the south does not. Moreover racism in the north tends to be "Protestant" while racism in the south is principally seen as an issue for the Catholic community.[7] Yet, as has been outlined, there also remains a degree of commonality between racism in the north and in the south, especially if a wider definition of racism, as one including the two dominant communities in Northern Ireland, is employed. There have been instances of people from Northern Ireland being identified and verbally abused in the Republic of Ireland because of their place of residency and *vice versa*. In fact, Fulton's[8] work on the experiences of fans from Northern Ireland when supporting the Republic of Ireland team is an insightful examination of this phenomenon in the sporting realm. Moreover, it is apparent that racism in Ireland is not some localized derivative of either British or American racism; instead, Irish racism is predicated upon the strength and efficacy of community.[9]

In Northern Ireland, this relationship has been conditioned and refined through sectarian conflict and social exclusion. As increasingly homogenized communities sought comfort in their own insularity, "outsiders"—or at least a perceived threat to the integrity of these communities by minority ethnic groups, especially migrant workers— became a source of malcontent for some. In this regard, minority communities are categorized as "alien invaders" involved in "taking jobs from the indigenous people," transient and therefore uncaring, devoid of an interest in integrating (assimilating), and not sufficiently aware of local mores and values. The net result of these crude portrayals and stereotypes is that minority populations have increasingly been subject to all forms of abuse, including physical attack and even enforced repatriation.[10]

It would be remiss in any coverage of racism within Irish society, north or south, to overlook the level of racism experienced by people born and raised in Ireland yet who both self-define and are regarded by others as a people apart. The Travelling community is a well-established part of the fabric of Irish life but is often viewed with suspicion by certain people who focus instead upon incidences of alleged malpractice and deviant behavior. The Race Relations Order (Northern Ireland) (1997) recognizes Irish Travellers as a distinct racial group. They are defined as "a community of people commonly so-called and who are also identified as a people with a shared history, culture, and traditions, including historically a nomadic way of life in Ireland."[11] This is true for the most part if not entirely accurate in all cases as some members of the travelling community are now choosing to settle in provincial Irish towns wishing to put an end to their once-traditional lifestyle. However this in turn does not mean the cessation of racially motivated attacks, and it's clear that affirmative action still remains necessary to remedy the situation and bring it in line with the recent European Union (EU) Racial Equality Directive.

Despite the very real presence of these issues, there is comparatively little research into the lives of minority ethnic groups in Northern

Ireland. Instead, the community there, almost by choice, continues to been constructed in binary terms with a majority unionist population and a minority nationalist one. The principle corollary of this has been the denial, from some quarters, of the existence of racism and when commentators have been forced to engage with the issues they choose to do so in pejorative terms. This means that in Northern Ireland racism continues to be understood as a "problem" that has been created by new arrivals into the country and one, in the minds of those affected by such developments, that only emerged relatively recently.[12]

Even following a series of recent, high-profile, and racially motivated incidents in Belfast and elsewhere, many linked to sport and association football in particular, popular discourse has somehow managed to blame the victims rather than the perpetrators of such attacks. The suggestion is that by wilfully transporting themselves into these communities such "new arrivals" were threatening a well-established way of life.[13] In fact, the same is true in what limited work has been undertaken into racism within domestic football in Northern Ireland. The authors of a report detailing the Irish Football Association's (IFA) response to UEFA's 10-point plan designed to address racism within European football argued that compared to the scourge of sectarianism, "there has been less evidence of racism within Northern Irish football, but this may in large part be due to the small numbers of nonwhite and non-UK or Irish nationals involved in the game."[14] The suggestion was clear—racism wasn't an issue because there were very few members of ethnic minorities playing the game in Northern Ireland. In this case the absence of players from nonindigenous backgrounds is paralleled with an absence of racism generally. However, this conclusion is drawn in such a matter-of-fact manner as to constitute a troublesome starting point when tackling discrimination and prejudice within the Irish game. Sadly it is reflective of a report that barely highlights the real issues surrounding racism and sectarianism in Northern Ireland football (notwithstanding the established terms of reference) and arguably does a disservice to the body of work undertaken by the IFA and some of its member clubs in addressing these issues "on the ground."

Instead, it is self-evident that racism is a socially constructed phenomenon, which in this case requires consideration of what appear to be simple questions surrounding sport and society in Northern

Ireland; yet they provoke incredible paradoxes. One example of this is the coexistence of a commonsense ideological construction on the part of many and unpacked above—there is no racism in Northern Irish football because there are very few minority ethnic players in the Irish League—alongside the reality of the situation, which confirms this view as both ill informed and indeed inaccurate.

Proportionally speaking, there is a sizable minority ethnic population in Northern Ireland. This includes people of South Asian, Chinese, African, and Middle Eastern origin as well as Travellers and Jews. Consequently, there are a small, but by no means insignificant, number of foreign-born players playing in the domestic league of Northern Ireland. Ultimately, however, the situation in Northern Ireland confirms that, like elsewhere, it is not necessary for a minority ethnic group to exist in a given society (or sports league) for the worst excesses of racism to be on show. Instead, *in a society already conditioned to the nuances of division*, it is a relatively minor transposition from difference based upon religion to one cohered around "race." If anything the latter is a convenient outlet for some people in Northern Ireland seeking to come to terms with the consequences of living there throughout the recent ethno-sectarian conflict. Already suspicious of their overall standing following the end of the "Troubles" in Northern Ireland and effectively left to their own devices to construct some degree of normality, the idea that a new threat to this process may emerge, this time from beyond their own national boundaries, represents an opportunity for some to redeploy the old language of division. The Racial Equality Strategy (2005) (NI) adequately captured the mood when stating "that racism in our (NI) society is, to an extent, shaped by sectarianism and while there is much to learn from other jurisdictions in addressing racism, the context for racism here (NI) is perhaps different from that in Great Britain or the Republic of Ireland."[15]

This is an important point when examining an exponential growth in racist attacks in Northern Ireland, given the existence of a belief that the growing population of minority ethnic groups in recent years has somehow *caused* racism.[16] It leads to a clear interim conclusion, which is that when people in Northern Ireland claim that racism is not a "problem," they actually mean that it is not of concern for the dominant white population. It only becomes an issue when the minority groupings become exasperated living in a racist society, which occasionally spills over into confrontation with the dominant grouping.[17] Compounded by residential segregation and an ever-heightened territorial awareness, it becomes abundantly clear quite quickly that Northern Ireland contains the component parts of simmering racial antagonism, which it seems is only ever one high-profile incident away from a full-blown violent outpouring. While this has not happened yet in Northern Ireland, football offers some interesting indicators that such a scenario is not entirely inconceivable. When serious public disorder erupted following an international match between Northern Ireland and Poland in Belfast in March 2009, it brought to the fore many unspoken, if thinly veiled, prejudices among the indigenous community of Belfast.

Elsewhere the assumed relationship between whiteness and "Northern Irishness" is so "commonsense" that in the minds of many it rarely requires articulation.[18] Yet this is to deny that Northern Ireland has, for centuries, been home to minority ethnic groupings. The Jewish community has been present in Belfast from the mid-nineteenth century while a sizable Indian population emerged and has been resident in Northern Ireland from the turn of the twentieth century. In recognizing this, it is also true that the majority unionist and nationalist blocs are profoundly divided along religious and ethnic lines. In fact, McVeigh[19] has argued that racism in Northern Ireland should be viewed as a dual majority problem, by which he means that minority ethnic groups experience racism in a particular way precisely because the white majority ethnic bloc in Northern Ireland is deeply divided. However, this conclusion is perhaps overly simplistic and offers a slightly skewed picture of reality. For instance, it implies that both sections of the majority ethnic bloc engage with minorities in the same way, yet all available evidence does not appear to support this assertion. An *Observer* survey in October 2006 found that 97 percent of all media-reported racist attacks over the previous twelve months in Northern Ireland occurred in loyalist (that is Protestant) areas.[20] In other words, if attacks on minority ethnic groups are any indication of where racism is most problematic in Northern Ireland, it is clear that it is a much greater issue within the Protestant community than it is among their Catholic counterparts. Of course this conclusion should also be read against the fact that some ethnic minorities are not fully aware of the precise nature of Northern

Ireland's divided society and, motivated instead by a desire simply to secure affordable rental accommodation, inadvertently become tenants in parts of the country, including Belfast, where Protestants constitute a sizable majority.

Nevertheless, the domestic football scene in Northern Ireland presents evidence to support the view that racism there is a much greater problem for some Protestants than it is for the majority of the Catholic population. In common with many divided societies, football clubs in Northern Ireland are patronized and constructed as "belonging" to one side of the community or the other. That said, only one club, Cliftonville FC, could be said to enjoy the support of the minority Catholic or nationalist community while the others are representative of various shades of Protestantism, including those of a strongly loyalist bent.[21] It is reasonable to conclude therefore that because football in Northern Ireland is predominantly a Protestant and unionist affair, racism within the Irish League is largely an issue for the unionist community. Regrettably there are numerous examples to support this conclusion. In a perverse contradiction, Linfield FC, whose identity is closely linked to loyalism, have had their black players racially abused by opposing fans, including followers of Glentoran FC, the other predominantly Protestant club in Belfast. In this context it is not surprising that black players at Cliftonville, whose identity is more Catholic and nationalist, have also suffered serious verbal harassment including that directed toward the now sadly deceased English striker Keith Alexander.

Indeed, there has long been an overlap between the British far right and conservative forces in Northern Ireland. Football clubs like Linfield (the name often appearing as LiNField on graffiti posted on walls in the locale with the letters "N" and "F" highlighted to reflect support for the far-right National Front organization) and fellow Belfast club Crusaders FC have a section of supporters who periodically carry fascist and racist iconography, and have links with neo-Nazi groups including Combat 18. Similar elements were behind death threats in 2006 against two foreign footballers playing with Institute FC based in Derry. In this case, both players had received intimidating phone calls in the month prior to three men with baseball bats arriving at their apartment threatening to shoot them unless they left the city. The club is based in the predominantly loyalist Waterside area of Derry where in July 2009 the

British Peoples Party held a leaflet drop espousing extreme right-wing views and advocating the expulsion of "nonwhite" groups from the UK. Surprisingly the aforementioned IFA report, commissioned to outline the organization's response to UEFA's 10-point plan to tackle racism and division in European football, appeared largely unperturbed about the incident involving the two professional players on the books of Institute FC. Not only did it barely warrant a mention, it was also dismissed as having occurred away from the actual football club and therefore, one must assume, the players' notoriety in the local community by virtue of their status as key personnel with the local Irish League team was not considered a particularly relevant factor in their targeting by those motivated by racist intent.[22]

Elsewhere Crusaders FC had been the subject of an official complaint to the IFA in January 2005 when two players from Larne FC were in receipt of verbal abuse, principally in the form of "monkey chanting," from home supporters. Other similar incidents have been reported in games over the preceding three seasons featuring Dungannon Swifts, Lisburn Distillery, and Derry City Football Clubs, the latter who play in the domestic league of the Republic of Ireland. So, if these examples demonstrate anything it is the very real presence of racism in Northern Irish football and the need for a concerted antiracism campaign within the club game. It also reaffirms a growing belief that racism and sectarianism are closely linked, in particular that the overwhelming majority of incidents involving racism in Irish League football can be attributed to supporters displaying strongly loyalist sentiments.

On the whole then what is true is that minority ethnic people find themselves struggling for equality against a backdrop of widespread sectarian division in Northern Ireland.[23] It is also particularly difficult to negotiate a place for minority ethnic identities in a setting where there is little consensus around white identity on account of the deep ethnic and religious division. In other words, the outworking of sectarianism also affects racialized groups in Northern Ireland. McVeigh and Rolston go further and conclude that sectarianism is indeed a form of racism.[24] They argue that "acknowledging sectarianism as racism frees us to apply insight from the analysis of racism elsewhere to an understanding of the north of Ireland."[25] In their analysis the state is intricately engaged in sustaining a level of sectarianism and racism in Northern Ireland, even following the signing of the Belfast–Good Friday Agreement in 1998. They conclude: "in the case of Northern Ireland, therefore, we see a continuity in relation to sectarianism that is attributable to the nature of the state itself rather than the politics it contains."[26] While there is undoubtedly a degree of merit to this argument on the face of it, the Belfast–Good Friday Agreement did at least confirm the protection and vindication of human rights for all citizens regardless of their origin, and indeed it may prove difficult to identify a society in western Europe that is as heavily protectionist of the civil liberties of its inhabitants as present-day Northern Ireland.

Moreover, reflecting upon the role of the state in this regard is interesting and relevant when studying sport as a site for racial intolerance in Ireland. Surprisingly Sport Northern Ireland (Sport NI), formerly the Sports Council for NI, does not have an official antiracism strategy in place to tackle this growing problem. Indeed Sport NI appears to be particularly silent on high-profile cases of racial abuse in Irish sport, and instead it has been left to individual governing bodies of sport to take action. Of course, the work of Carter and colleagues[27] in tracking the impact of sporting migrants in Northern Ireland did receive the support of Sport NI, where the issue of race and racism is at least recognized.[28]

The IFA has been one such governing body that has, albeit somewhat belatedly, begun to address racial intolerance in its sport, with its Community Relations Unit (CRU) at the forefront of the organization's antiracism campaign. It was regrettable then that a lot of this good work was undermined following the events of 28 March 2009 when Polish fans engaged in street battles with supporters of Northern Ireland following a World Cup qualifying match at Windsor Park. That it was Poland that formed the opposition on this occasion was not without significance. Poles represent the largest minority ethnic group in Northern Ireland—approximately 25,000 in total—and their settlement, particularly in Belfast, has been far from straightforward.[29] As indicated already, many migrants have chosen to live in the Village area of south Belfast because accommodation there is relatively inexpensive, and it is close to the hospitals and commercial premises where most of them are employed. This is a mainly loyalist, working-class community, sections of whom view their migrant neighbors in derisory terms, focusing in particular upon their predominantly Catholic faith. Elsewhere, in May

2006, the home of a Polish migrant couple in Derry was ransacked by a loyalist gang armed with a hatchet. It transpired that their home was attacked because they were identified while wearing Glasgow Celtic jerseys (the Catholic-identified team in Scotland supported by most Catholics across Ireland), again in the mainly Protestant Waterside part of the city.[30]

In the case of the recent rioting following the international match between the two countries in Belfast, it is important to note that the Polish support was comprised of members of the Polish Diaspora in Northern Ireland alongside traveling fans. Some of the latter were clearly intent on trouble with certain individuals openly taunting the home support with Irish republican symbolism. On the field of play the Poland goalkeeper, Arthur Borac—who also plays for Glasgow Celtic—chose an unfortunate occasion to have a poor game and he quickly became the embodiment of a simmering, multilayered antagonism that sections of the home support held toward what they felt he represented. Not only a Catholic and a Celtic player, Borac had also infamously blessed himself during an Old Firm match against the (Protestant-identified and loyalist-supported) Glasgow Rangers in 2006 and held a particular fascination with the deceased Pope John Paul II. This was more than sufficient grounds for racist vitriol in the minds of some Northern Ireland supporters. Whereas previously this behavior was contained within the confines of Windsor Park, on this occasion the disturbances spilled out on to the adjoining streets in riots between rival supporters and with the police. While located within the context of a football match, some observers interpreted these clashes as symbolic of much deeper and wider inter-community tensions. As if to add weight to this assertion, following this unrest, a campaign against minority ethnic groups in south Belfast (close to the original trouble) resulted in over forty people fleeing their homes, while a further five people left Northern Ireland completely. The figures in question are likely to represent a highly conservative assessment as many similar instances went unreported.

Again, in certain cases, the reaction to this turn of events has been one of denial. For example, Ulster Unionist councilor Bobby Stoker, rather than choosing to condemn the attacks stemming from the match, instead challenged the figures by understating the number of people who had presented themselves as homeless to the housing executive. A more worrying aspect was the perceived identification of Polish migrants with the republican "enemy"—terminology still used by the Northern Ireland first minister, Peter Robinson. As McVeigh and Rolston, among others, have observed such developments also contribute toward institutional segregation of loyalist and migrant communities.[31] As most Polish migrants claim Catholic heritage, their children will be educated separately from Protestant Northern Irish children. The contribution of separation to creating an "Other," thus increasing the incidence of violence, should not be underplayed. The sectarianism allowed to emerge in some sections of segregated education has the potential to evolve into racial hatred. This conflagration also impacts upon the response of the criminal justice system to racially motivated hate crime. The most recent figures show that only a third of members of a minority group considered the Police Service of Northern Ireland (PSNI) *not* to be racist.[32] Despite changes to policing arrangements in Northern Ireland, aspects of civic society are still appropriated by one side of the community or the other, and it seems that in this binary distinction migrants have sided with nationalists and republicans in expressing their resentment toward aspects of state apparatus. This should also be worrying for those who are aware of the considerable progress made by organizations like the PSNI in embracing the legacy of the Belfast–Good Friday Agreement and have sought to transform their image in the light of the country's new political dispensation. Indeed, it may prove difficult to identify a civic institution that has responded as effectively to the challenges presented in post–Belfast–Good Friday Agreement Northern Ireland than the PSNI. Therefore if the police service is continuing to experience problems convincing ethnic minorities to fully engage with its outreach activities then this in turn implies that other institutions may have a great deal more to concern themselves with than they may have been considered the case heretofore.

Amid all of this the response of the IFA to the events of March 2009 has been interesting. Officially it has been caught between condemning the rioting involving its fans and maintaining an unspoken sympathy with its predominantly unionist following. Of course condemning incidents is one thing; actually doing something to prevent them happening is an entirely different matter. The IFA's CRU has identified the issues at the heart of the problem and has indeed sought to do something to tackle them, although the extent to which the governing body can actually lay claim to the activities of its most proactive department is a matter of some debate. From addressing language barriers to providing further information to minority groupings around their activities and attempting to respond to the training needs of its members, the IFA CRU has at least made a series of useful steps in the right direction. Among a range of agendas, its innovative World United program is a community-driven initiative that breaks down barriers to inclusion in football, proactively encouraging members of minority ethnic groups to play the game in a safe and fun environment. While it is a commendable development—the program includes players from Portugal, France, Somalia, and Ivory Coast among others—there are two obvious issues to highlight. Firstly, this initiative potentially merely succeeds in sidestepping the process of real and lasting integration by isolating the players and removing them from the mainstream. Secondly, this approach also runs the risk of constructing football involving minority ethnic groups in Northern Ireland as "fun," "non-serious," and peripheral and thus relegating its overall significance in mere sporting terms.

It is ironic that amid a very genuine and worthwhile development a latent form of racism still appears to permeate. Notwithstanding this, in 2010 the IFA went further and initiated a women's World United team, which has addressed the desire of women settling and living in Northern Ireland to play football and in so doing also recognizes that among an already low level of engagement in sport on the part of ethnic minorities that women are further discriminated against when it comes to availing of opportunities to become physically active. However, in an overall sense it would be unfair to be too critical of the CRU of the IFA simply because if its capacity to address explicit forms of sectarianism at Windsor Park is any indication of its determination to overcome issues around racism then it is likely to yield impressive results.

The existence of racism in football, and indeed Northern Irish society as a whole, is an extremely complex matter.[33] Few clubs in the country's domestic league have been unaffected by racist activity, and the response from the game's governing body and the government department with responsibility for sport in Northern Ireland, Sport NI, has been largely unconvincing, certainly until comparatively recently. It highlights one obvious correlation between the Republic of Ireland and Northern Ireland in terms of football governance, which is the incapacity, and on occasions the unwillingness, of those with responsibility for the sport to tackle racism in any convincing fashion.

Conclusion

The Irish are typically portrayed as genial, fun loving, and welcoming. For the most part this is a reasonable, if somewhat stereotypical, portrayal of this nation's people. But Ireland is not immune from racial intolerance and the ill effects of racism. This chapter has examined in detail the genesis and contributing factors that give rise to these issues in one part of the island, Northern Ireland, and highlighted the apparent inactivity on the part of those charged with governing sport there to enact concerted and meaningful responses to what is evidently a growing problem. Indeed it appears that their activity has only really emerged over the last decade and has often only been undertaken following high-profile cases of racial intolerance surrounding football matches. Thus the future is far from clear, but there does appear to be the basis of a new recognition by NGBs and others concerning the need to provide a credible and strategic response to racist behavior, which appears to be present at all levels of the sport, from youth football throughout the domestic leagues and at international level. As migration into Northern Ireland continues to grow on an annual basis, it appears the capacity of sporting authorities to properly take account of the identities and needs of the "new" Irish will be the defining feature of their activities in the time ahead.

CHAPTER 16

"Who Do 'They' Cheer For?": Cricket, Diaspora, Hybridity, and Divided Loyalties among British Asians

Thomas Fletcher

This chapter explores the relationship between "British Asian"[1] sense of nationhood, citizenship, and ethnicity, and some of its manifestations in relation to sports fandom: specifically in terms of how cricket is used as a means of articulating diasporic British Asian identities. The chapter highlights how supporting "Anyone but England," thereby rejecting ethnically exclusive notions of "Englishness" and "Britishness," continues to be a definer of British Asians' cultural identities. Rather than placing British Asians in an either/or situation, viewing British "Asianness" in hybrid terms enables them to celebrate their traditions and histories, while also being proud of their British citizenship.

On 14 June 2009 England played India at Lord's, the English "home of cricket," in the International Cricket Council (ICC) World *Twenty20* Cup. Despite England achieving a memorable victory, the contest was overshadowed by the day's earlier events off the pitch, in England's pre-match warm-up. After England's win, then captain Paul Collingwood revealed that the team had been jeered and booed by hundreds of British Asians who had come to support the Indian team.[2] As this incident happened at Lord's and the majority of the perpetrators were British Asians, familiar arguments over the sporting allegiances of British Asians; their British citizenship, and whether British Asians are welcome in sport, resurfaced.

This Is England: Which Side Do They Cheer For?

The 14 June 2009 scene was not the first time sport provided a ground for questions regarding the loyalty and citizenship of British Asians. In 1990, speaking before a test match between England and India, conservative MP Norman Tebbit asked, "which side do they cheer for?" By "they," Tebbit was referring to Britain's migrant population. Tebbit had long believed that too many migrants would fail what he had dubbed "the cricket test"—a superficial measurement of fidelity and assimilation of migrant groups in Britain. Tebbit controversially argued that, to live in Britain, migrant communities had to unequivocally assimilate into the British "way of life." For Tebbit, a fundamental aspect of assimilation was for any attachment to one's nation(s) of ancestry to be severed.

Tebbit's rhetoric about segregation and citizenship has become familiar within British cultural policy. Ratna, for instance, argues how, despite successive government policies championing multiculturalism and the celebration of ethnic difference, political commentators have continued to argue that British Asian communities tend to lead separate lives, parallel to "white" ethnic groups in England.[3] This view is exemplified by Trevor Phillips, the chair of the Equality and Human Rights Commission, who argues that, for some time, Britain has been "sleep walking" into a state of cultural segregation.[4] Phillips, like many others, was worried that advocating multiculturalist principles—including the idea that ethnic minorities should cherish and preserve their "indigenous" identities—could result in some communities leading self-contained lives in isolation from broader society. Of course, under the provisions of the cricket test, and on the basis that England frequently competes against the countries of ancestry of Britain's minority ethnic communities, it is inevitable that loyalties will be tested.[5] Tebbit was canny in his decision to choose cricket as his marker of assimilation because, for centuries, the ubiquity of cricket in English popular culture has made it synonymous with expressions of "Englishness," Empire, bourgeois English nationalism, and British elitism.[6] C. L. R. James noted how—due to its position both as, perhaps, the cultural embodiment of the values and mores of "Englishness," and its "missionary" role within British imperialism and colonialism—cricket occupied a central site in many of the anticolonial struggles between colonizer and colonized.[7]

When he made his speech, Tebbit assumed that mass immigration threatened Britain's hegemonic national culture. During the early phases of their migration, South Asian communities were seen to be introducing irreversible changes to the social composition of Britain. In particular, the main threats were believed to be they provided competition for jobs and housing, that they had excessively large families, and that they were reluctant to integrate.[8] Tebbit's feeling at the time was that retaining cultural attachments to their "homeland(s)" prevented migrants' successful integration (or assimilation), which threatened Britain's long-term cohesion.[9]

During the 1960s and 1970s, talk of Britain having an "immigration epidemic" was commonplace.[10] Many people have interpreted this rhetoric of "cohesion" to represent homogeneity. For many on the Right (which represents a number of the white respondents in this research) homogeneity is favored over inclusive multiculturalism.[11] Prioritizing homogeneity requires incomers to adopt their way of life to resemble that of their host culture.[12] This is characteristic of the "assimilationist" model of citizenship, which was popular throughout the 1960s. Within this model it is expected that the incomer—along with their culture, belief systems, and practices—will be absorbed into the dominant culture.[13] The expectation of ethnic minorities within this model is for them to be "just like us." In contrast, the "integration" model of citizenship, which became popular at the height of multicultural antidiscriminatory discourses from the 1980s, represents the utopian multicultural vision whereby incomers—their culture, belief systems, and practices—are embraced and accepted by the dominant culture, even in spite of their differences.[14] Historical debates surrounding immigration have focused almost exclusively on the dangers associated with "colored" immigration, while discussions of white immigration (those people from Eastern Europe, for instance) have, until now, been notably absent. This suggests that issues of citizenship are surrounded by white privilege and cultural racisms.[15]

Evidence from this research demonstrates that Tebbit's inferences remain relevant within cricket culture at the current time.[16] Much of his rhetoric around assimilation was supported by the white respondents from Sutherland. Graham demonstrated a disturbing modern-day conceptualization of Tebbitry:

> If you're coming into this country, you've got to be seen as an English person by everyone else . . . Regardless of how long they've [the South Asians] been living in England they haven't changed. They [the men] still wear their dresses [*sic*] and have big beards and veils and whatever else, and I just feel erm . . . I know it's their tradition and whatever, but they could make themselves a bit more English. And I think the English would appreciate that as well. There's nothing stopping them sticking on a pair of jeans and just, fitting in. But they don't want to, do they? They don't even support our teams do they?[17]

Thus, according to Graham, when ethnic minorities display acts of allegiance, which transgress the expected normalized codes of "Englishness," their way of being is heavily criticized. Arguably then, British Asians are forced to negotiate their social and national identities in order to assert their allegiance to England. Those who display allegiances to religious groupings and / or places of their ancestral origin may fail to conform to the imagined template of "Englishness" and may be rejected by English sporting culture as a result.[18] However, Kalra and colleagues criticize these views and attribute such defensive mentalities as reactionary responses to diasporic communities on the part of "an overly coercive nation-state unable to comprehend the openness of diaspora."[19]

British Asians, Fandom, and Diaspora

The fact that British Asians are choosing to support the teams of their country of ancestry, rather than their country of birth and residence, reflects the complexity of British Asian and diasporic identities in the twenty-first century and has contributed to the emergence of new theoretical discourses around the hybridity of social identities.[20] Debates about British Asian identities and sporting loyalties tend to draw on the notion of "diaspora."[21] Diaspora has conventionally referred to the transnational dispersal of a cultural community. Anthias defines diaspora as a particular type of ethnic category that exists across the boundaries of nation states rather than within them.[22] Kalra and colleagues argue similarly that diaspora means to be *from* one place, but *of* another.[23] Thus, diaspora may refer to a population category or a social condition (consciousness). At the very least, understanding diaspora necessitates we understand "migrant" communities as existentially connected to a specific place of origin or an imagined body of people, which extend beyond the current dwelling place.[24] The very notion of diaspora implies that the movement of the South Asian community was temporary and that they would eventually return "home."[25] However, many of these immigrants never made the mythical return "home" and remained as residents of this country.[26]

Anthias outlines how certain conceptualizations of diaspora can be criticized for homogenizing populations and reinforcing primordial, or absolutist notions of "origin" and "true-belonging."[27] However, a central feature of a diaspora is the internal differences (gender, class, generation, political affiliations, etc.) and struggles over how ethnic boundaries are constituted and maintained, and about how group identities are defined and contested. Members of the South Asian diaspora, for instance, come from very different backgrounds, they have migrated at different points in time and for different reasons and, therefore, how they experience belonging to the diaspora, will also vary. As Stuart Hall writes:

> The diaspora experience . . . is defined, not be essence or purity, but by the recognition of a necessary heterogeneity and diversity; by a conception of "identity" which lives with and through, not despite, difference; by hybridity. Diaspora identities are those which are constantly producing and reproducing themselves anew.[28]

Diaspora should therefore be conceptualized in terms of the *routes* by which a person has got somewhere, and the *roots* they have to a particular place.[29] Belonging, then, "is never a question of affiliation to a singular idea of ethnicity or nationalism, but rather about the *multivocality of belongings*."[30] To agree that the diaspora has no fixed origin, however, makes conceptualizing the sporting and national allegiances of British Asians communities increasingly complex. According to Parekh a multicultural society should not question the divided loyalties of people within the "home" nation, as they should have the power and right to embrace dual and even multiple identifications.[31]

Nevertheless, explanations of diaspora (in a sporting context at least) frequently draw upon a notion of ethnic bonds as primarily revolving around the centrality of "origin." In many cases, the privileging of origin is central in constructing identity and solidarity. For many members of the South Asian diaspora, there exists a continuation of ethnic solidarities and attachments to the symbols of national belonging and continuing investment, emotionally, economically, and culturally in the homeland.[32] In his examination of Indian cricket supporters in Australia, Madan argues, throughout times of uncertainty and ethnic struggle, one element of their identities galvanizes the diaspora: their identification with "home":

> In the same way the diasporic subjects move beyond national boundaries, the identity "Indian" has moved beyond national ideologies, thereby challenging the modern linear link between race, nation and culture. For diasporic Indians to keep their place in the world, across time, space, and different experiences of nationality, ethnicity, and "diasprocity," one variable remains constant . . . the use of the word Indian.[33]

This "diasporic consciousness," as expressed through cricket, may be understood as reflecting a "homing desire"—that is, an identity rooted in the history of a geographic origin, rather than a desire to return to a "homeland."[34] At the heart of this analysis is the interrelationship between the diaspora (as perceived to be the settler), their neighbors (who may consider themselves to be "indigenous") and their shared habitus.[35]

Diasporic identities do not simply revolve around either the reproduction of existing cultures within new settings or the appropriation of new ones. Instead, diasporic identities must be viewed as being fluid, syncretic, and hybrid. The lives of young British Asians are grounded through a combination of the cultures and traditions of their parents and the Indian subcontinent, and in the culture and social practices of Britain.[36] Yet, this balancing act is frequently understood in terms of being "caught between cultures." Being part of a diaspora is not necessarily about identification with a single source of cultural heritage, or about having a primordial sense of "home." Diaspora should be conceptualized as a state of consciousness rather than a sure sense of rootedness and belonging.[37] The construction of young diasporic British Asian identities emerges at the intersection of local and global dynamics. As Clifford argues, diasporas think globally, but live locally.[38] Therefore, however settled diasporas are, they must navigate through complex loyalties. Even where individuals adopt some of the cultural traits of the "new" society, they may remain marginalized and be seen as strangers.[39] For many British Asians, then, the politics of sports fandom are complex and certainly are not reducible to the common "anyone but England" mantra.

This research shows how British Asians will often use cricket, and specifically their support of the England national team, as part of a wider agenda to redefine the habitus of English cricket to be more inclusive to their needs. Brah emphasizes the possibility of diasporic communities resisting the processes of exclusion through her examination of "diaspora space."[40] She argues that discussions of diaspora must not isolate the experiences of the "migrant other"; rather diaspora should be explored at the intersections of power and positionality, which invariably involves discussion of those conceived as "indigenous." For Brah, "the concept of *diaspora space* (as opposed to diaspora) includes the . . . intertwining of the genealogies of dispersion with those 'staying put.'"[41] Brah's conceptualization recognizes that one can live in a space without totalling subscribing to the dominant national discourse of that space. In so doing, the diaspora space holds transgressive and creative potential through its role in encouraging wider "diasporic consciousness."[42] This conceptualization challenges dominant discourses about authenticity, belonging, and citizenship, while also accounting for processes of identity negotiation and the formation of "new" and "hybrid" ethnicities.[43]

Home Team Advantage

Sports fandom is about expressing loyalty to a certain player, team, region, or nation. Fans support their "home" team and invest a great deal of emotional attachment and creative labor in it. One's "home" team is also synonymous with the home venue(s). Sporting venues are imbued with a sense of place, pride, and general affection by supporters.[44] Some venues, particularly those of overarching cultural significance, such as Lord's in cricket, can often be linked to discussions of nostalgia, culture, and heritage, as they call upon national pride derived from past glories and long histories.[45] It is the responsibility of the home fans to uphold the heritage of the sport and home team by claiming the space as their own. Home fans are ultimately responsible for making the visit of away players and fans uncomfortable; the very essence of being *away from home* is supposed to evoke palpable uncertainty. The number of home fans attending a live fixture, therefore, should invariably outweigh the number of away fans. This gives rise to the notion of a "home advantage." Thus, when we begin to think about fandom and its relationship with the national team, it is natural to assume the team we support would be our "home" nation.

When England played India at Lord's on 14 June 2009 it was difficult to ascertain who indeed had home advantage. The *Indian Express* wrote that "the [contest] . . . saw a packed house at the home of cricket, the 28,000-seater a sea of blue. Unfortunately for Paul Collingwood and his troops, it was the wrong shade of blue."[46] Given the size of Britain's South Asian communities, it was inevitable India, Pakistan, Sri Lanka, and Bangladesh would receive significant levels of support during the tournament. The extent of support, however, had been unanticipated. India's captain, Mahendra Singh Dhoni, had previously downplayed the significance of the level of support India had received throughout the tournament and prior to the match Collingwood had denied claims that the fixture would feel like an away match. Nevertheless, Collingwood's surprise at the reception of his team was hard to disguise in his post-match interview: "It hurt a few people and it was strange to get booed on our home ground."[47]

It has previously been asked whether British Asians should be supporting England in contests involving teams from the Indian sub-continent. However, such a question presumes that a correct answer exists. By adopting the theoretical framework within this chapter, it is more important to ask: "if British Asians are not supporting England, why not?" Similar questions were asked in 2001 when England played Pakistan at Edgbaston. On that occasion, England players were taunted in the practice nets by young British Asian fans that later created an electrifying atmosphere in the ground as they greeted the Pakistani team.[48] Although both events appear to represent the same tacit assumptions about British citizenship and divided loyalties, the difference between cheering for your team and booing the opposition, is quite significant. This point is well articulated by Sutherland's James:

> In my experience, cricket has always been different to other sports. In cricket, who you support is largely unimportant compared to the game itself. In cricket, you appreciate it if the other team does

well . . . It's less territorial in a way. I think for them . . . I mean . . .
they were British guys weren't they? . . . For them, to boo our guys
. . . their guys too . . . is disrespectful.[49]

Within a sporting context it is not uncommon for rival supporters to
boo or heckle one another. It is particularly common in relation to
national anthems and, more unsavorily, during moments of silence.
Crabbe suggests that booing/heckling is always done within the context of a "carnivalesque" spirit and usually serves the purpose of acting
as a precursor to friendly socializing among various supporter groups.[50]
Granstrom similarly suggests that booing/heckling could be interpreted
as a *friendly* invitation to take part in a cheering competition.[51] However,
both conceptualizations fail to account for politicized supporter behaviors and the role played by the sports event in galvanizing and mobiliz-
ing frustrated ethnic groups. In this context, it is not booing/heckling or
the cricket match itself that are the decisive issues, but how the British
Asians interpreted what cricket and their activities symbolized.

The events at Edgbaston in 2001 captured headlines because the
scenes were interpreted by many as a lack of patriotism shown toward
England by British Asian communities and subsequently, were used to
challenge their level of British citizenship. Nasser Hussain, who was
England's captain at the time (and of Indian descent himself), spoke of
his disappointment that British Asians cheered for Pakistan rather than
their adopted homeland:

I cannot really understand [how] those born here, or who came
here at a very young age like me, cannot support or follow England
. . . it was disappointing to see a sea of green shirts with the names
of Pakistani players instead of ours.[52]

Hussain's expression of disappointment was similarly criticized by a
number of prominent British Asian writers. Many accused him of for-
getting where he came from and denying his mixed Asian parentage.[53]
Chaudhary, for instance, challenged Hussain to "get in touch with your
brown side" and suggested for him to put himself in the shoes of young
British Asians of the time.[54] Chaudhary was challenging Hussain's
assumption that by claiming British citizenship, young British Asians
experienced equality and unquestioned insider status. However, as
noted earlier, the long-term politics of diasporic settlement means that

second- and third-generation British Asians frequently find themselves living "in" Britain, but not being a part "of" Britain.[55] Such sentiments are typified by Kaushal in *The Observer*:

> We (British Asians) may embrace Englishness, wear the national team shirt with pride, paint the cross of St. George on our cheek but when we attend cricket or football games and hear chants such as "I'd rather be a Paki than a Turk," witness mass Nazi salutes, are spat on, and, at worst, are assaulted, it tends to make it difficult to cheer the country of our birth (England).[56]

Burdsey has since rightly observed that both Hussain and his critics have demonstrated a lack of appreciation for how cricket (and sport generally) can reproduce ethnically exclusive notions of "Englishness," which demonstrate a lack of sensitivity to the concepts of diaspora, hybridity, and multiple identities.[57] By implication, British Asians are expected to identify as *either* British *or* Asian; a point well articulated by Kathleen Hall, who suggests that for British Asians "there's a time to act English and a time to act Indian."[58] This, however, represents an essentialist interpretation of both "Asianness" and "Britishness," which should be avoided. An alternative typology of fandom is hybrid in nature and one that acknowledges dual ethnicities should be preferred instead. But, far from a move toward such an ideal, I argue that the events of 2009 represent an intensified feeling of alienation and marginalization for many British Asians.

For a lot of British Asians, to support England and to be British, is predicated on their presence being acknowledged (and approved?) by white British people. Their experience of racism and wider marginalization means they feel like outsiders within British culture, and it is this racism and marginalization that deters them from identifying with the England team. Aylesworth's Azzy attended the game and recalled:

> I understand why [white English] people have got so angry about [these events] because [white English] people don't really understand what it's like to be British Asian. You guys don't really get the whole being British, but supporting India or Pakistan thing . . . There were a lot of frustrated [British Asian] people at that game. Frustrated that they still get called names . . . Paki and terrorist . . . and frustrated by racism. A lot of Asian people don't feel respected here.[59]

Azzy's use of "you guys" is significant. Regardless of being born in this country, Azzy used the terms "you" and "us," thereby positioning me as belonging to the wider white majority that he separated himself from. Azzy assumed that, as a white person, I was unable to appreciate the politics behind his hybrid identity. As a result, and as I reflect upon elsewhere, the positionality of myself (perceived as the white researcher) and Azzy (British Asian respondent) became a highly conspicuous aspect of the research process.[60] This was no more apparent than in his references to his Muslim identity and the wider tendency within Britain at this time to conflate Islam with religious fundamentalism and terrorism.[61]

For a while now, much debate has revolved around the politics of multiculturalism, or in some cases, the "death of multiculturalism" and the incompatibility of white and British Asian cultures.[62] Though it is clear from Azzy's testimony that ethnic relations between these communities are unstable, there was evidence in this research to suggest that there might be grounds for optimism about the future of ethnic relations between them. I do not, of course, believe Tebbit's cricket test is valid. Advocates of such an essentialist discourse are, among other things, guilty of failing to acknowledge the complexities of sports fandom and the interplay between everyday practices of identity and spectacular ways of expressing them.[63] The ways we choose the teams we support are both political and whimsical. Being a sports fan and demonstrating allegiances can help define who a person is and says a great deal about them to other people. We should not forget that fandom is essentially a performance of identities and, with 14 June 2009 in mind, many British Asians utilized Lord's as an arena for expressing them.[64] The "cricket test" is more a reflection of the politics of "race" in Britain than an indication of British Asians' subjective sense of their own "Britishness."[65]

Cultural Spaces and British Citizenship

Sport fan communities are frequently defined on the basis of group demographics and represent discursively constructed and distinctively racialized symbolic spaces, which provide sites for practical and symbolic resistance to white sporting hegemonies.[66] In England there are ever-increasing numbers of minority ethnic communities who have to negotiate between their desire to belong, while also maintaining an imaginary attachment to their ancestral "home."[67] In the case of British Asians supporting teams from their respective countries of ancestry over England, for instance, the cricket ground is one place where British Asians can express the love for their home country, while sharing the experience with other British Asians. As the *Indian Express* says, "Among the close knit Indian community here, there's a sub-community of those who run into each other at cricket grounds."[68] Indeed, it is under these circumstances that Holmes and Storey argue how sports events "transform total strangers into a unified collectivity struggling against a common adversary."[69]

People are artistically creative and, equally, people attach great aesthetic value to their creative projects; whether that is through the clothes they wear, the television programs they watch, or the way they invest meaning in and support their team. On 14 June 2009 British Asians consciously transformed the Lord's cricket ground into a racialized space that was more indicative of them. Madan confirmed these motives in his discussion of Indian cricket supporters in Australia where he argues they mark their territory through common signifiers of culture (flags, drums, language, and dress), thereby using sport as a space to activate political identities and nationalist sentiments.[70]

By accepting and drawing on their common signifiers of culture, supporters are not only contesting the game and their patriotism, but reinforcing their unity as British Asians and creating a "local" reality in a "nonlocal" place—a kind of "resistance through ritual."[71] Spectatorship transforms the sports ground from an institutionally defined space into a space where agents can practice their politics of identity and allegiance —what Appadurai referred to as a "simulacrum of warfare."[72] Burdsey argues how spectatorship of the international game has facilitated greater opportunities for British Asians to recreate "traditional" forms of South Asian fandom.[73] And while he (among others) cites the increasingly stringent stewarding procedures at sporting venues as having a potentially damaging affect on these formations, he appreciates the agency of British Asians to celebrate the game on their terms. This is similar to Brah's conceptualization of the "diaspora space" highlighted earlier.[74] The role of sports stadia in the creation of diaspora spaces was expressed by Aylesworth's Zahar, who believed that the local signifiers of diasporic identities have greater impact when displayed outside one's home locality, in the cultural/racial spaces belonging to someone else:

> It's how you get noticed isn't it? No one's gonna notice you unless you stand out . . . where better to do this than somewhere like a cricket ground? . . . White people don't expect to see us (British Asians) there do they? So, if I'm decorated like a Pakistani flag, they're gonna notice me aren't they?[75]

While many British Asians prefer to support a team from the Indian subcontinent, most of the British Asian respondents in this research added how their sporting allegiances should be treated as a separate issue to their identification as British citizens, and they believed they should have the freedom to embrace both their British citizenship as well as their South Asian heritage if they wish to do so.[76] Jimmy said:

> I do support Pakistan, but that's not because I hate England. I've read people saying, "look at them Asians, living here, but hating England" and all this. That has nothing to do with it . . . Of course I want England to do well because most of my friends are English. When England is playing other nations, I want them to win; just not when they're playing Pakistan . . . I'm proud of where I've come from and I'd expect everyone to have these same values.[77]

Although this type of response was commonplace, many were unable to justify why they supported a team from the Indian subcontinent. The majority attributed their allegiance to how they had been socialized. Others simply believed it was natural.

In contrast, Aylesworth's Hamza Ilyas believed the tendency for British Asians to support a team from the Indian subcontinent to be more cultural than many of the white respondents anticipated and, as a result, this pattern will continue throughout future generations. Regardless of their level of integration within British society, British Asians will always take a great deal of comfort from supporting the team of their ancestral home:

> I see England, first and foremost, as my home. And you could turn around and say, "well, that's the case when England is playing against Pakistan," yeah? Maybe when I was growing up some of the things from my parents did wear off on me. If Pakistan

> was playing England and my dad's there supporting Pakistan, I'm
> going to support Pakistan. Now, because I'm supporting Pakistan,
> I think my little boy will do the same. This has nothing to do with
> whether we're British or not.[78]

In most cases, the allegiance of the British Asian respondents had never
been questioned like this. Instead, it was taken for granted, natural, and
believed to be instinctive. However, many like Jimmy above were also
quick to defend their choice of allegiance, which suggests that many
British Asians experience dissonance over their dual ethnicities and thus,
over whom they are and/or who they *feel they should be*. Both Jimmy
and Hamza Ilyas show an awareness that with British citizenship come
certain expectations inherent to ethnic minorities claiming British citizenship is the political philosophy of assimilation.[79]

Experiences of diaspora vary and therefore, the context of settlement (what Brah refers to as the "journey") will significantly influence
future behaviors and actions.[80] For Brah the question of diaspora is not
who travels but *when, how, and under what circumstances*?[81] She argues how
there is distinction between "feeling at home" and declaring a place as
home and, as a result, this "situatedness" is central to their level of identification with their host country/culture and their country (or countries) of ancestry.[82] Many South Asians for instance, did not choose to
leave the Indian subcontinent and were instead, forced to leave as a
result of persecution and expulsion.

Aylesworth's Addy, for instance, suggests that many British Asians
actively reject notions of "Englishness" (embodied through the England
team) because of historical antagonisms between white English people
and South Asian communities:

> Growing up, there's been a lot of hatred between the Asians and
> the whites—especially in cricket. Like when Pakistan are playing
> England, all the British Asians will be supporting Pakistan. Why
> don't they support England? They don't because many of us are
> still quite angry with English people for treating our ancestors so
> badly.[83]

Addy's testimony suggests how cricket's synonymy with "Englishness,"
Empire, and white racial supremacy could, in part, explain why so many
British Asians are reluctant to identify with the England team. The
debate does not end here. Juxtaposed with this is the question of why

British Asians support a team from the Indian subcontinent, despite having little personal association with it. The answer may be that, for many British Asians, supporting a South Asian nation facilitates the construction of an imagined community, which forges a symbolic link with the Indian subcontinent, enabling for the celebration of their traditions and feelings of belonging with the nation from which their forbears migrated.[84] As Chaudhary writes:

> I was born in England, but supporting India is for me, as for thousands of others, a reaffirmation of my cultural heritage. We are proud to be British, but we are also proud of our ancestry.[85]

In addition to this, sports fandom has a highly versatile element of resistance attached to it. Werbner argues that it is within the context of resistance that British Asians are able to articulate an "oppositional post-colonial sensibility," whereby the primary function of disavowing their association with the England team is to emphasize (where relevant) their sense of alienation from, and disaffection with, certain aspects of British society.[86]

"Is It Really That Bad Supporting Pakistan?": Interpretations of "Englishness" and "Britishness"

Historically, both "Englishness" and "Britishness" have been interpreted as being exclusive ethnicities. Gilroy specifically argues that "Englishness" and "Britishness" are reserved for white people and that Black (in this case South Asian) people are incompatible with either conceptualization.[87] If minority ethnic communities interpret either ethnicity in this way, it is understandable why they might be reluctant to identify with them. For many British Asians, the label "English" is the very antithesis to their inclusion. Many lament the term's right-wing connotations and prefer to endorse the more liberal politics of "Britishness." This perspective was supported by Aylesworth's Ali:

> I think that every person seeks his/her own identity that he/she feels confident with. I am happy to classify myself as British . . . which is an all encompassing identity . . . but I can't get on with the label, English. To be English I think I need more long standing historical roots.[88]

Ali's differentiation between being English and British is important because England and Britain are frequently "(con)fused."[89] For many minority ethnic communities, these notions have very different connotations in relation to concepts of citizenship and ethnicity. As Aylesworth's Rio commented:

> It seems to me that one of those labels is racist. To me "British" represents who I am. British is for people of all colours: white, Black, brown, yellow, pink, whatever. I would never say I was an "English-Asian" because to me, to be English you have to be white. I can't pretend to be white.[90]

The ongoing fragmentation of the British Empire, coupled with rapid globalization have made the distinction between Britain and England—particularly in ethnic terms—far more palatable. Maguire argues how globalization, as well as prompting a number of global integrative tendencies, has placed modern national identities in a state of flux and "ironic dislocation."[91] This means that national identity is no longer the sole defining marker of one's nationalism. Aylesworth's Taz, for instance, warned of the importance of upbringing and identification with one's local communities as significant markers in defining one's national identity and suggested that overt performances of support and fandom toward English teams might be unreliable indicators of loyalty and citizenship:

> You can pretend all you want. You can sit there and say "I support England," but how do you support a team that you don't really support? When your dad's been supporting Pakistan and the whole house supports Pakistan, naturally you are going to support them. So no, I don't think that's the ultimate test. I don't think it shows whether you're fully mingled in. I can understand it though. We live in this country, we've been brought up here, so why don't we support England? I'll tell you why . . . because we're still Pakistani. Yes, we're British, and yes there are British Asians playing for England, but we're still Pakistani . . . so is it really that bad supporting Pakistan?[92]

First and foremost, Taz considered himself to be Pakistani, but he emphasized his British "Asianness" when that worked more in his favor. For Taz, possessing dual ethnicity was a convenient vehicle for optimizing his level of integration, on the basis that, whether he is with white people or people of South Asian descent, Taz believed he could move effectively between his "Britishness" and "Asianness." He displayed what Ballard refers to as "biculturalism."[93] For Ballard, diasporic communities should be conceived of as being "cultural navigators," competent in and therefore able to switch between several cultural "codes" without experiencing disorientation.[94] At the very least he could acknowledge his affinity with "Britishness" without compromising other (more important) aspects of his identity; that is, his "Asianness." Clifford refers to this as "selective accommodation" and explains this as the desire to stay and be different.[95] Burdsey argues that joining together two political discourses in this way earmarks the potential for subverting any dominant association; albeit ephemerally.[96] Certainly, being British and Asian are not mutually exclusive, but the extent to which British Asians embrace both is contestable. When it comes to the type of fandom expressed by Taz above, it is clear that multiculturalism has brought about a newfound flexibility of English national identities.

"Anyone but England?": British Asians and Hybridity

There continues to be solidarities among some of Britain's minority ethnic communities in their supporting of *anyone* but England. However, this chapter argues that this should not be interpreted as a rejection of "Englishness" or "Britishness" and/or English or British people. The simplistic notion of being "for us" or "against us" neglects the complexity of social relations that shape the lived realities of young British Asians.[97] Taking a disliking to, or refusing to identify with, the England cricket team does not make anyone less English or less a full and equal member of the community, than anyone else.[98] These sentiments were well reflected by Aylesworth's Adeel:

> I think when Pakistan come over to play England it's one of the few opportunities we've got to get our Pakistan flags out and go out and express how good and Pakistani we are. I don't think supporting Pakistan is meant to cause offence. My dad put a banner out and he's as English as Asians get.[99]

Appadurai argues that cricket is of political significance in diasporas through the indigenization of cricket in the former British colonies.[100] He believes this is particularly the case in India, Pakistan, and the West

Indies, as the aesthetics of cricket have become an essential part of postcolonial self-image and national pride. Indeed, Fagerlid, like Adeel above, argues that cricket matches may be the only occasions when British Asians regard themselves as "Indian" or "Pakistani."[101]

Clearly, the relationship of the first generation to the place migration is different from that of subsequent generations. Brah argues how each generation's experiences are mediated by "memories of what was recently left behind, and by the experiences of disruption and displacement as one tries to re-orientate to form new social networks, and learns to negotiate new economic, political and cultural realities."[102] There is growing suggestion within sociology that British Asians are becoming more "Anglicized." In her study of female MP's and civil servants, Puwar explains this in terms of minority ethnic communities being exposed to "white civilizing spaces," such as education and the workplace.[103] Sport may also be viewed as a contemporary "white civilizing space." Many of the white respondents believed younger British Asians possess similar values to other white English people and, therefore, they were most likely to support England rather than a team from the Indian subcontinent.

Many of Britain's minority ethnic communities want to be reminded of their heritage and attachment to their ancestors—most notably their parents. Many of the younger generations have witnessed a growing separation from their elders as their cultural hybridity and dual ethnicities forcibly come between them. As Werbner argues, "living in the diaspora is a matter of continually negotiating the parameters of minority citizenship."[104] This was certainly the case for Adeel, who expressed his concern that he and other members of his family had divided loyalties because of their different upbringings:

> I support England. My dad supports Pakistan because obviously, that's where he's been brought up . . . I think for my dad, Pakistan is his home . . . it's hard to explain . . . he lives in England, but his home is Pakistan . . . When I went to Pakistan I was asked who I supported. When I said England, they were like, "why are you supporting England, you're a Pakistani, you should be supporting Pakistan" and I was like, "I'm not Pakistani, my dad's Pakistani, I'm English."[105]

It is crucial to stress that not all British Asians prefer to identify with teams from the Indian subcontinent. Many like Adeel have made England/ Britain their home and identify themselves as primarily English/British and thus, in a crude sense, would not have failed Tebbit's "cricket test." Individuals like Adeel are not averse to seeing themselves as English, but they are against constructions of "Englishness" that do not allow for their inclusion and/or demonize their cultural heritage.[106] While for many on the right, cultural hybridity seems to be a precursor to the successful integration of Britain's minority ethnic communities, for many people from minority ethnic backgrounds, the discourse of hybridity is nothing less than a denial of identity. Pieterse notes that the majority of arguments previously acknowledging hybridity have often done so with a "note of regret and loss—loss of purity, wholeness, authenticity."[107] Adeel, for instance, believed his hybridity, specifically in relation to English being his first language, had made it difficult for him to fully identify with a single culture, and he felt like this questioned his "Asianness":

> sometimes family will come over [from Pakistan] and me and my brothers and sisters will be there whilst everyone's speaking in Punjabi and we're all like "what are they talking about?" And you'll hear your name and then you're wondering "what are they saying about me?" And it's weird not being able to understand it when the rest of the family does it as part of their life. I sometimes think that it makes me less a part of the family, you know. I'm less Asian than them.[108]

Such a position is espoused well by Homi Bhabha, who refers to the migrant as the voice that speaks from two places at once and inhabits neither. This is the space of liminality, of "no place," or the "third Space" where the migrant lacks a central cultural narrative.[109] Nevertheless, many of the British Asian respondents in this research celebrated the flexibility and hybridity of their identities. British Asians arguably occupy a more privileged position than many white Britons because they are not defined by any singular ethnicity. They are free to explore their ethnic identities and, rather than this being interpreted as a denial of their "Britishness" or "Asianness," we should view hybrid identities as forming what Modood and colleagues refer to as "complex Britishness."[110]

Conclusion

Sport continues to be one of the primary means through which notions of "Englishness" and "Britishness" are constructed, contested, and resisted. For most, ethnic identity is taken for granted, part of the quotidian and iconography of everyday life.[111] However, those on the margins, in national or ethnic terms, provide us with greater appreciation and understanding that ethnic identities are complex and negotiable. The flags we fly, the shirts we wear, and the teams we cheer for are part of our interpretation, as individuals, communities, and cultures, of the connections that unite and divide us. When it comes to sport, British Asians face the dilemma of where to place their loyalties: their ancestral home or their adopted home. The fluidity, changeability, and hybridity of their identities are essential features of the British Asian experience.[112] Much has been made recently of the virtues of hybridity; that one can be British, while also being Asian and Muslim and so on. This chapter has shown that British Asians can be quite comfortable with more than one sense of ethnic identity and that, central to this, is the way they negotiate between their places of birth and places of ancestry. One should not, however, take these negotiations for granted or try to simplify what is a very complex process of identity negotiation. The alignment of British Asians to teams from the Indian subcontinent should not automatically be interpreted in dichotomous terms as either a statement of defiance or as a reflection of their insularity. Instead, national loyalties in sport should be conceptualized in terms of hybridity, as contributing toward a wider narrative of the diaspora condition and integration into British society. As Werbner argues, the fact that British Asians are confident enough to show dissent through expressing their ethnic identities actually demonstrates their rootedness rather than separation.[113]

CHAPTER 17

Usain Bolt, Celebration at Ninety: A Spatial Analysis of the Beijing 2008 Men's 100-Meter Final

James A. McBean Jr.,
Michael Friedman, and Callie Batts

The mark of apprehension resting upon the brows of the runners betrays the festive air surrounding the men's 100-meter Olympic final. Having set the world record at 9.72 seconds at the beginning of the 2008 running season and by turning in the fastest times in the quarter- and semi-finals, Jamaican sprinter Usain Bolt is considered the favorite for gold, but his relaxed mannerisms set him apart from his competitors. During prerace introductions, Bolt brushes his hands over his head grooming his hair and releases an imaginary arrow into the Beijing crowd reminiscent of Greek mythological god Artemis. As other runners nervously fidget their bodies as they focus on the impending race and come to rest into their starting positions, Bolt is expressive— speaking and singing to himself, rocking to a beat that only he can hear, and making various gestures, clearly at ease.

This relaxed calm seemingly absconds in the moments before the starting gun sounds. Bolt is relatively slow out of the blocks, but by 30 meters he is at the lead and at 50 meters has reached his top speed. By 60 meters, he is pulling away from the other competitors, including fellow Jamaican Asafa Powell, the previous holder of the world's record. At 90 meters, with Powell and all others out of contention and victory certain, with shoelaces undone Bolt decelerates, glances over his shoulder, arms outstretched, and in typical Jamaican fashion beats his chest all before crossing the finish line, creating a new world record in the process. In addition to his well-documented prerace expression on the track, after his victory the then twenty-one-year-old further expressed his joy running a victory lap with arms outstretched like that of a bird in flight and blew kisses to the crowd. With his shoes off and Jamaican flag draped over his glistening body, he danced.

He performs the "Gully Creepah" and "Nuh Lingah" in which he convulses his face, sways his arms and legs as he shuffled his feet, elevates and lowers his body, and undulates his back as if no spine held it aloft 9.69 seconds prior. Bolt later remains exuberant as he collects his gold medal and, from the medal stand, shoots yet another arrow into the crowd.

However, rather than being praised for his victories and feats, Bolt's expressive display was criticized by the International Olympic Committee (IOC) president Jacques Rogge, who stated, "you can't do that. That's not the way we perceive being a champion."[1] NBC Olympic host anchor Bob Costas reacted by stating, "[Bolt was] disrespectful to his competitors, to the Olympic Games and to the fans."[2] NBC track and field commentator Ato Bolden, a retired track champion from Trinidad who was known for his flamboyance, added to the criticism by saying, "it was a display that should not have been there . . . you kids at home, this is not how you behave as an Olympic Champion."[3] This opprobrium cast upon Bolt was indicative of the tone of media commentary regarding his premature and expressive victory celebration.

Although this race lasted just 9.69 seconds and occupied just 100 meters of a track in Beijing, the moment and its space are laden with complex and contradictory meanings. To begin to understand these deeper meanings of Bolt's celebration at 90 meters and reactions by Rogge and the press, we examine the event through the spatial theories of Henri Lefebvre as the 2008 Beijing Olympics men's 100-meter final is a space in which a multitude of power relations were produced, challenged, and reinscribed. In examining the actions of Bolt, the reaction of Rogge, and various media discourses, we deconstruct the various relationships between the physical elements of a space, the meanings ascribed to that space, and the ways in which people use and live within space. To do so, we have analyzed the moment through examining the discourses produced by the IOC and US media outlets and found that the case against Bolt was made by privileging the neocolonialist voices and subordinating the peripheral, postcolonial, creolized "voice" expressed through Bolt's actions. We suggest that Bolt's symbolic *reappropriation* of space is a form of cultural resistance, which interrupted the neocolonial, capitalist incursion into contemporary sport culture that has historically exploited the peripheral sporting body.[4] Moreover, Bolt's resistance also could be seen as challenging power relations by returning control of the peripheral athletic body back to the black athlete. As such, the cultural impact of Bolt's momentary resistance, and, in some ways, continuous reappropriation of social space, suggests grounds for optimism against the assault on the neocolonialist late capitalist machinery now dominating and consuming subaltern bodies on a global scale. While Bolt's Jamaican, Creole subjectivity has been commodified to some extent, Bolt's acts of resistance are not entirely "disarmed and reabsorbed" by late capitalism's cultural economy.[5]

The Multiple Spaces of Bolt's Celebration

In examining power relations within space, Lefebvre argued that social space is not static, neutral, nor a preexisting given. Instead, he recognized that space produces and is produced by an ever-changing set of social relations, stating that "social space is not a thing among other things, nor a product among other products: rather, it subsumes things produced and encompasses their interrelationships in their coexistence and simultaneity—their (relative) order and/or (relative) disorder."[6] Moreover, space is not a singular entity, but is multifaceted with multiple layers of meanings. This understanding that space is the medium, stake, and outcome of power-based social relations is essential for a Lefebvrean understanding of space. Power is contextualized, and like all social relations, made real in the (social) production of (social) space.[7] Essentially, Lefebvre argues that power relations are created in and expressed through space and that analyzing these spaces provides an important tool for understanding exploitative power relations, and, thereby enabling progressive interventions.

Toward understanding these complex relations of power. Lefebvre suggested a framework for spatial analysis that focuses upon the physical elements of the built environment (also known as *spatial practice* or *perceived space*), the intended meanings and understandings that developers attempt to incorporate into a space's design (*representations of space* or *conceived space*), and the ways in which the meanings and understandings of a space have been challenged, reinforced, and changed through its use (*spaces of representation* or *lived space*).[8] These categories are neither mutually exclusive nor determinative as all three moments of space help to constitute one another.[9] Spatial practice/perceived space can be described as the built environment and the everyday practices and routines that occur within it, such that it helps to regulate life by organizing and structuring social relations. Stuart Elden suggests that perceived space is "concrete, material, and physical,"[10] as spatial practices help to identify what places are accessible or forbidden, the boundaries that define and separate spaces from one another, and the types of interactions that occur within a space, as well as structuring the flows of people in and through space. The concrete materiality of spatial forms and physical interactions occurring within them allows spatial practice to be easily observed and empirically mapped. Perceived space includes such specific sites as a track, gymnasium, or basketball court, or could even encompass an entire region.

Lefebvre identified representations of space/conceived space as being imagined and constructed through discourse by elite groups, who shape understandings and meanings of space through the intersection of knowledge and power. As such, conceived space is "abstract, mental and geometric,"[11] and identifiable through examining the processes through which a space is physically designed and defined by those creating and managing it. These representations of space include countless specialized knowledges, tacit signs and codes that are condensed into transmissible representations.

Although dominant groups attempt to define the meanings as they create and manage space, their efforts are not necessarily determinative, as within spaces of representation/lived space, people express themselves and could potentially use spaces in ways different from the intentions of designers. As such, people living in space have the potential to transform that space, its meanings and uses through resistant actions or could reinforce power relations through conforming to dominant expectations.[12] In many ways, lived space is where people simultaneously negotiate the abstract meanings of conceived space and the physical realities of perceived space, and, in so doing, can be disruptive to both.

Usain Bolt in Space: Three Moments

The spatial triad provides an incisive way to examine the controversy surrounding Usain Bolt's performance in the 100-meter final at the Beijing Olympics. In this case, spatial practice refers to the performance spaces within the Olympic stadium from the time that Bolt entered the track area for the race through the medal ceremony. While not to discount the importance of either Bolt's prerace activities or his postrace celebration, the track and the race itself are the most significant physical spaces toward illuminating the power relations being instantiated into space by producers and challenged by Bolt. These representations of space are numerous as the various producers, such as the Olympic movement (both contemporary and historical), the media, transnational corporations, and national athletic federations, attempt to define the meanings of the space, expected and prohibited practices, and what behaviors are termed appropriate or inappropriate. As we discuss, Bolt challenged several different representations of the Olympic space: first, through his presence in that space as Bolt trained exclusively in Jamaica rather than becoming an athletic migrant; second, by his decelerating at 90 meters, which undermined the ethos of competition; and, third, through the exuberance of his postrace celebration in which his performances of Nuh Linga and Gully Creepah brought to the surface some of the deeper tensions within Jamaican culture.

Each of these three contestations are firmly based within a different form of colonialism, which can be defined as the historic and continuing social, cultural, political, and economic domination and exploitation of peoples living in geographically peripheral areas. Enshrined within the controversy surrounding Bolt's ephemeral moment of victory are traditional colonialism, the neocolonialism of transnational corporations, and postcolonial[13] struggles to define the nation—all of which besiege the track space for dominance of the black body. Bolt's performance challenged the colonial domination inherent within the Olympic movement and expressed through Rogge's outrage[14] and the logics of neocolonialism that promote the primacy of central states and naturalize their claim to exploit the physical talent of peripheral states. Finally, Bolt's victory celebration can be read as the promotion of a creolized postcolonial subjectivity on the world stage, a subjectivity that contrasts that of teammate Asafa Powell, who maintains a subdued protestant-like comportment on and off the track. Though the race lasted just 9.69 seconds and Bolt's display seems to be a spontaneous and exuberant (rather than political) act, these moments collide at 90 meters as Bolt decelerated and began his celebration before crossing the finish line.

HOW TO BE A CHAMPION: CHALLENGES IN COLONIAL SPACE

While the era of the great European colonial empires is over, both an imperialist and "colonial" spirit lives on and is evidenced in select moments of the 2008 Beijing Olympic Games. While not delving too deeply into the role of sport in colonialism,[15] the Olympic Games were created at the end of the nineteenth century as Western powers such as Great Britain, France, the United States, and Germany were subjugating people throughout the globe. Although a Frenchman, Baron Pierre de Coubertin, founded the Olympics, they were steeped in the ethos of the elite British boarding schools, which de Coubertin believed were at the foundation of the British Empire's global domination.[16] In *Beyond a Boundary*, C. L. R. James examined the role of sport in Britain's colonial domination as he critiqued his adolescent experiences playing cricket. James recognized that sport was an essential part of the way Great Britain was positioned in relation to his native Trinidad as he explained, "our school masters, our curriculum, our code of morals, everything began from the basis that Britain was the source of all light and leading, and our business was to admire, wonder, imitate, learn."[17]

James recognized this same form of domination within the Olympic Games, which claimed derivation from the ancient Greek games held at Olympia in worship to Zeus, whose temple was located there. Similarly, de Coubertin fashioned the modern Olympics Games after British cultural norms to have analogous "sacred" functions as nations could demonstrate their dominance in the international arena and athletes could use their spirit, mind, and body and endeavor to achieve maximum performance. This expectation is enshrined in the Olympic Motto *"Citius, Altius, Fortius"* (meaning "Swifter, Higher, Stronger") as the Olympic success proves which men (and nations) possess physical superiority.

While de Coubertin's ideas may seem anachronistic, they linger within contemporary understandings of the Olympic space that Rogge, as head of the International Olympic Committee, is bound to enforce. Within this perspective, the Olympics remain a sacred space with all participants expected to follow a specific code of conduct in which they take an oath to respect and follow the rules of their sports and to compete "in the true spirit of sportsmanship, for the glory of sport and the honor of our team."[18] These ideals, which were for a long time incorporated into the Olympics' code of amateurism and resistance to commodification, have lost much of their effective meaning, but remain as residuals meanings of the Olympics.

Bolt's actions, however, do not demonstrate strict compliance with these ideals. Instead of the personal restraint expected in sportsmanship, Bolt expresses his postcolonial body in all its flamboyance and splendor, unmoved despite being under the continuous gaze of the colonial moment. Rather than competing for the full "glory of sport," Bolt decelerates *and* celebrates at 90 meters, but still sets world and Olympic records. This victory, however, does not fit into the Olympic ethos because it is not his "swiftest." Bolt failed to give his full effort for the full measure of the race. In so doing, Bolt deprived the Olympics *its* glory—a reprehensible action in the eyes of Rogge and the IOC.

THE YAM-EATING FELLOW FROM TRELAWNY: CHALLENGES IN NEOCOLONIAL SPACE

Not only is Bolt a threat to the residual British ethos perpetuated by Rogge, Bolt threatens the new codes of the transnational corporate monoculturalism, which permeates the contemporary Olympics. The sporting globalization is a second moment of tension, which is defined by the imperialism of transnational corporations (TNC) based in the United States and Western Europe. This form of imperialism or neocolonialism has become globally dominant due to the collapse of the British Empire and the emergence of late capitalism. In many ways, it is a direct consequence of European colonial rule, which continues to exploit their former dominions as talented migrants from the Caribbean and other peripheral states transfer their skills to core states on the terms and conditions set by core states.

Within sport, this deskilling of peripheral areas occurs as the most talented athletes migrate to core countries for education, training, and professional opportunities, with track and field, baseball, and soccer as the most notable examples.[19] Inevitably, these athletic migrants are exploited by TNCs, often for the mass consumption of spectators from center states, or by the states themselves, which provide athletes with citizenship in exchange for their participation in international events.[20]

Jamaica has been repeatedly exploited in this manner as, despite being known for producing world-class sprinters, the country has seldom been able to hold on to them. Jamaican-born Ben Johnson, Donovan Bailey, and Linford Christie, all of whom emigrated from Jamaica as youths, won the 100-meter race in the Olympics in 1988, 1992, and 1996 while competing for Canada (Johnson and Bailey)[21] and Great Britain (Christie). Promising runners traditionally decamp for US universities as soon as scouts observe their talent. Jamaica's current women's 200m Olympic champion and 100-meter world champion, Veronica Campbell, graduated from the University of Arkansas. Campbell's partners in the medal-winning relay partners were also educated, trained, disciplined, and *culturalized* in the United States. Merlene Ottey, who won eight Olympic medals at five separate Games between 1980 and 1996 for Jamaica, attended the University of Nebraska for college and then, in 2002, took Slovenian citizenship and began to compete for her adopted nation.

Bolt's ongoing residence in Jamaica distinguishes him from many of the Jamaicans who have found success training and competing in or for other nations. Bolt is consistently hailed as the yam-eating fellow from a quintessential Jamaican village in Sherwood Content, a small town in the parish of Trelawny. Bolt trained with a little-known, underfunded, and meagerly resourced athletics club in unpleasant, poverty- and crime-laden Kingston. These facilities are a far cry from the superb, often corporate- sponsored, track and field centers in Europe and North America, two regions ever growing closer in ideology in this late capitalist space. By not pursuing higher education in the United States and rejecting that value system by staying put and training in Jamaica, consuming indigenous Jamaican foods, Bolt serves as a reminder to the world of the greatness that can be produced from a peripheral state.

While the *substance* of Rogge's response may have been related to the residual ideals of the Olympic Games, its intensity and amplification by US-dominated media outlets perhaps could be a response to the threat that Bolt represents to the dominance that TNCs exert over the peripheral athletic body. Bolt's celebration at ninety meters was more of a *casus belli* that provided the powers that be of sport an excuse to criticize Bolt and return him back to his "place." Though Bolt has not wholly rejected this structure (indeed, by accepting sponsorship and even competing, he does buy into it to some extent), he partakes of it on his own terms rather than those on the terms set by the core state, in which he would have been expected to attend a US college or that he would become an athletic migrant.[22] Indeed, Bolt's resistance to neocolonialism and his success in their space may actually be more dangerous, as his resistance and subsequent victories suggest a viable alternative to the structure that places the West and its dominance over the peripheral athlete at the center.

BAREFOOT AND EXUBERANT: CHALLENGES IN POSTCOLONIAL SPACE

> Yet rapidly we learned to obey . . . without question. We learned to play with the team, which meant subordinating your personal inclinations, and even interests, to the good of the whole . . . we were generous to opponents and congratulated them on victories, even when we knew they did not deserve it . . . on the playing field we did what ought to be done.[23]

While these ideals still permeate the Olympics, the space of the track, and the meanings associated with those spaces, many Jamaicans maintain and promote the colonial-based puritanical codes described by James. So while Bolt is respectful and revered by opponents and spectators alike, his refusal to adhere to these codes is highly controversial and raises the ire of the IOC and these Jamaicans. Instead of following these codes, Bolt expresses a creolized identity that challenges "Western European colonial systems of categorization and their emphasis on order, absoluteness, singular national narratives, and fixed identity."[24] By dancing the Gully Creepah and Nuh Linga as part of his Olympic celebration, Bolt displays a particular Jamaican cultural identity on the global stage that many Jamaicans would rather hide.

This tension is particularly evident within the reaction Bolt's teammate Asafa Powell received from his parents, the Reverend

William and Cislyn Powell, after his public performance of the two
dances in 2008. Citing her disapproval for his display of dancehall culture, Cislyn Powell stated, "God gave [Asafa] those feet to bring joy to
the world, but not in that form of dancing. We don't want Nuh Linga,
we just want Jesus."[25] Within this comment, Cislyn Powell exhibits the
Christian ethos imparted by European colonizers in the manner that
pious, conservative colonial subjects would. To her, Asafa demonstrated
a momentary lapse in judgment by expressing himself in this way, and
positioned this form of creolized Jamaican culture in opposition to the
virtues represented by religion. In this way, the Nuh Linga and Gully
Creepah are both unwholesome and nearly sacrilegious, and it is not
difficult to imagine that, as Bolt danced in celebration of his victory,
Cislyn Powell's reaction to this behavior may have been no less vehement than Rogge's.

In some ways, Reverend William and Cislyn Powell embody a postcolonial Jamaica that is distinct from that expressed by Bolt. Rather
than conforming to the British ethos of corporeal comportment, Bolt is
an explosive antithesis to that conception of the postcolonial Jamaican
body. Through these dance performances, Bolt not only salutes his
country, but he identifies himself with the specific classes from which
the dances emanate. Incidentally, these are the same classes which nurtured Bob Marley, who was similarly repudiated by the more pious elements of Jamaican society until approval came in the form of British
consumption of Marley's ghetto-based music. Bolt's expressive behavior
within the track space has helped to elevate him, in much the same
way as Marley, into an indisputable marker of Jamaican difference and
nationalism—a localized, indigenized reinscription of the received and
understood cultural codes of a formally dominant (sport) culture.

It is here that Bolt's body as text becomes an enlightening site for
interrogating the resistance of and challenge posed by postcolonial bodies to colonial and neocolonial dictates and expectations. In general,
the body is a discursive site in which power relations existing between
the colonizer-colonized and/or between the core-periphery can be perpetuated or resisted. In recognizing the body as a trope that contributed
to the manufacture of binary difference between the West and the non-
West, Said argues that cultural constructions of the body were significant in the ideological formulation of Western superiority that helped

to legitimize colonialism.[26] Mills and Sen support this position as they stated that the body was "at the center of justification for colonialism, of the objectives of colonialism and of the processes associated with colonialism."[27]

As an embodied activity, sport and physical activity were deeply implicated in the assertion and maintenance of colonial power relations with the Jamaican body as an important site for the mediation of politics and culture during colonialism. Given this colonial domination of the body, it should be little surprise that the bodies of athletes, such as Bolt and Powell, can now represent multiple, distinct, and differing postcolonial subjectivities. As we discuss below, during the 2008 Olympics, Bolt reclaimed and reinterpreted the postcolonial Jamaican body as one that rejects colonial legacy, resists late capitalist co-optation, and unabashedly celebrates a localized identity.

Celebrating at 90 Meters: A Lefebvrean Understanding

Although *The Production of Space* and the spatial triad from which it emerged have been frequently interpreted as being about space, for Lefebvre, space is only the entry point into a deeper examination of societal power relations that can be created, reproduced, and expressed through the body.[28] While Bolt's actions on the track may have challenged various structures involved in the construction of meanings regarding the Olympics, the relationship between core and peripheral countries and Jamaican identity, the effective responses of these structures reveal much more about the operation of power in this late capitalist moment.

HOW TO BE A CHAMPION: REINSCRIBING THE OLYMPIC IDEAL

In addition to his admonishment of Bolt's victory celebration, Rogge offered Bolt advice about the proper deportment of a champion, that Bolt should "show more respect for his competitors and shake hands, give a tap on the shoulder to the other ones immediately after the finish and not make gestures like the one he made in the 100 meters."[29] Whether such celebrations actually still occur is highly questionable, but Rogge's vehement reaction and advice speak to a much earlier model of athletic competition when the ideals, such as amateurism, sportsmanship, and the glory of sport, which the Olympic movement was created to promote, actually had much greater social meaning and effective power.

In many respects, de Coubertin created the Olympics as a space that would reproduce the dominance of upper-class, white Europeans. When their ideals were challenged, the IOC and other elite sporting organizations had the power to revoke medals (as per Jim Thorpe), bar athletes from the most important competition through revoking their amateur status (as per Jesse Owens), or remove them from the games (as per Tommie Smith and John Carlos). However, as sport has become increasingly controlled by TNCs, the Olympics have become increasingly commodified and the culture has shifted such that celebrations similar to Bolt's are considered the norm and Rogge's advice is considered quaint. The vehemence of Rogge's reaction, however, is not so much to the exuberance of the celebration, but to the location where it began: at 90 meters.

In his postrace comments, NBC analyst Ato Bolden suggested that Bolt "threw away a 9.58," which would have shattered Bolt's own world record of 9.72 seconds rather than just lowering it by 0.03 seconds. Although this was still a world record performance, it certainly was not the best of which Bolt was capable, as evidenced by the 9.58 that he indeed ran in the 2009 World Championships. For Bolt, his inevitable victory was sufficient cause for beginning his celebration during the final moments of the competition. For Rogge, the Olympic ideal demanded that Bolt run for the glory of sport—Olympic sport in particular. Lowering the world record by 0.14 seconds is an "Olympian" feat in much the same way that Bob Beamon's long jump in the 1968 Mexico City Olympics exceeded the previous record by more than two feet and stood for twenty-two years. Lowering the record by 0.03 seconds is not.

Bolt's injection of a Creole subjectivity into the conceived Olympic space challenges the dominance that, as IOC president Rogge sought to maintain and attempted to reinscribe through his criticism. By celebrating at 90 meters, Bolt reappropriated his power from those attempting to control him as he demonstrated that the agency that each athlete inherently possesses and that power is not bestowed upon athletes by the sporting powers that be. Ultimately, as demonstrated by the ceremonial wailing and gnashing of teeth by Rogge and the international press, the powers that be are impotent. The Olympic movement no longer has any real power to sanction Bolt. For his desecration of the Olympic space with his premature celebration, the IOC cannot take away his medals, expunge his name from the record books, suspend him from competition, or terminate his corporate sponsorships. As Bolt went on to be one of the few athletes featured by the international media at the 2012 London Games, Bolt possesses the true power in this relationship. The most that Rogge could do was to admonish Bolt and hope for "better" behavior in London.

UN-AMERICANIZABLE:
BOLT'S INTERRUPTION OF TRANSNATIONAL CORPORATE MACHINERY

By the logic of the globalized sports system under neocolonialism, Bolt should not even have been present at the Olympic Games, given his refusal of the "advanced" preparation and "superior" infrastructure "only" available to him in North America or Europe. Within this logic, there is the expectation that top athletes must perform in the core states for them to receive notoriety, legitimacy, or economic rewards.[30] This expectation has provided a five-decade-long flow of talent for the corporate machinery running sport to exploit and resulted in the deskilling of peripheral countries.[31] However, rather than attending American schools and participating in this circuit on terms defined by global capital, Bolt rejects the hegemony of the system by remaining in Jamaica.

Bolt's resistance is certainly not unique as many athletes choose to remain outside the system, but his success is. Given the totalizing conception of the system, Bolt should not have made it beyond the preliminary heats of the Olympic competition, nor should he have made it to the finals given the choices he made. If by happenstance he wins, he should not be able to set a world record. Moreover, if he decelerates at 90 meters, a postcolonial, undisciplined body like Bolt's most certainly cannot claim a world record or Olympic victory. Yet, Bolt did all of these as he beat all of those who availed themselves of the "advantages" promised by the system. He not only won Olympic gold and set the world record, but his time was *only* 9.69 because he *decelerated* doing so! Although Bolt challenges the core-periphery relationship within the structure of globalized sport, he does not reject the system as a whole. Indeed, he has allowed his very expression of ecstasy to be commoditized as a product, and has become the highest-paid track athlete in history with sponsorships from Puma, Gatorade, Jamaican telecom company Digicel, and Swiss luxury watchmaker Hublot.[32] Despite accepting these rewards, Bolt remains dangerous to the system as he presents a profound alternative to the structure of the dominant model of sport development that argues that it is the only path to success. Bolt's world record and his economic success are demonstrable proof to the contrary. While commoditization may be inevitable within the system, athletic migration and the deskilling of peripheral sports programs to the benefit of the former colonial overlords are not.

INTERRUPTING THE COLONIAL DISCOURSES OVER JAMAICAN IDENTITY

Perhaps if Bolt had become an athletic migrant and went to college in the United States, he would have learned, by way of acculturation, to suppress his Creole subjectivity and how to be a champion in Rogge's terms. Perhaps, with the "proper" instruction, his corporeal comportment and disciplinary regime would be similar to Asafa Powell's, whose parents expected him to choose Jesus over dancing Nuh Linga. Without these "advantages," Bolt lacked the discipline to repress his ecstatic and exuberant celebration that began at 90 meters. Instead, Bolt expressed himself naturally and authentically, in a way that demonstrates a new Jamaican identity that has emerged since Great Britain granted Jamaica its independence in August 1962 after roughly three hundred years as a colony. Nearly fifty years later, the island still grapples with defining its identity from among the range of possibilities ranging from the gentle, noble West Indian with English proclivities to that miserable child of poverty cosmically linked to debauchery, crime, and wickedness.

Bolt's lack of English proclivities freed him to incorporate the popular Jamaican dances of Nuh Linga and the Gully Creepah into his celebration on the global stage. As demonstrated by Cislyn Powell's reaction to her son's dancing, dancehall culture in Jamaica is notorious and controversial. The Gully Creepah created by the late David Alexander Smith (aka "Ice"), was named after the Gully, a word synonymous with "ditch," "ravine," "rut," "furrow," and "gorge." The name speaks to the dance's origin in a micro ghetto called "Cuba," which is within the heart of Kingston's Cassava Piece community that is oftentimes known for its culture of poverty and violence. Smith was a longtime member of the infamous Black Roses crew, which had been led by William "Willie" Haggart and Gerald "Bogle" Levy, who were two other incredibly talented dancers. Haggart and Levy also met very violent and untimely deaths in separate incidents that have further stigmatized Jamaica's dancehall culture. Yet, through his performance of the Gully Creepah at the Olympics (which is also featured in Puma's on-line advertisements), Bolt has helped to elevate this highly controversial dance from a localized expression of ghetto culture into a global representation of Jamaican culture.

Conclusion: There Is an Alternative

As Bolt embodies creolization and postcolonial sensibilities, and refuses to strictly conform his actions to the expectations of those creating the Olympic space, his celebration at 90 meters challenges the various colonial, neocolonial, and postcolonial forces that attempt to control his behavior and exploit his talent. By not giving his full effort for 100 meters, Bolt denied the Olympics its transcendent moment of ultimate sporting glory. By refusing to become an athletic migrant, Bolt denied the core states the ability to fully exploit his talent and provides the possibility that there is an alternative to the totalizing system of globalized sport. By elevating the Gully Creepah and Nuh Linga to the global stage, Bolt offers an image of Jamaican culture that Cislyn Powell and many in Jamaica who continue to subscribe to the residual ideals of their British imperial masters would rather not exist. Bolt's exuberant expression destabilized each of these spaces, which required that he be punished in order to restore the dominant social order.

Ultimately, the structure and culture of track and field are far more relevant than the results achieved by the athletes or the roles played by spectators.[33] Bolt's creolized, postcolonial performance resists and challenges this structure, and is, therefore, a threat to the colonial and capitalist hegemonies on which global sport is based. Bolt, who had only run the 100-meter race in four previous competitions, used the track space in ways that clashed with the expectations of the IOC and other domineering forces. Indeed, although the space conceived by the IOC may reinforce sociopolitical domination through expected sporting practices, the IOC's control is far from total. As Bolt's actions suggest, there is room, albeit limited, for people who are socially, politically, and geographically outside of the hegemonic power structure to manipulate those sporting practices toward contesting the dominant culture.

Herein this creolized display of exuberance lays Bolt's threat that required Rogge's acerbic response. Bolt's display is an affront to both the imperial conquests the Olympics are supposed to honor and the colonial ethos and discipline that sport is supposed to instill into "natives." As Bolt celebrated his victory in his own way, he destabilized the very absolutes that sport and the Olympics sought to convey and that were supposed to make him into a "good" colonial subject. However, his celebration was neither tasteless nor offensive, and, in its criticism of Bolt, the media also documented the adoration thousands of spectators showered upon Bolt for his expressive display. To the IOC overlords, athletic talent scouts, and even facets of the Jamaican community, however, Bolt's self-expression and unabashed sovereignty over his body encroaches upon the spaces and body they seek to control, which, inevitably and to their ire, they cannot. In this regard, Bolt can be read as representative of the black proletariat, a class that has rejected the hegemony of former colonizers and their dominance over peripheral, subaltern bodies. Bolt's overwhelming victory counters the fallacious notion that peripheral bodies cannot achieve dominance without the support or approval from those in the "developed" world who produce the spaces of global competition, enforce its rules, and define success.

Athletics may be emerging as a potential counterbalance to the debilitating effect of broken governance, weakened economies, and social unrest that have historically plagued peripheral countries. As the embodiment of the Jamaican athlete, Bolt pulls Jamaica back to a place of self-worth, self-reliance, and hope. Bolt's association with the proletariat through the way he celebrates, where he trains, and in his diet of the yams and tubers, which were the staple foods in Caribbean slave diets, all validate the black body. The hegemonic forces that exploited and still seeks to control that body now casts their gaze upon its dominance.

Bolt's performance does more than reposition the black body

against those that seek to exploit it, as his victory demonstrates that a person can achieve success without conforming to the Western mode of commercialized sport development. While Bolt does not propose an alternative system, his actions destabilize an existing system that attempts to deny the existence of other possibilities. Given this claim, any viable alternative is potentially threatening to the neocolonialist capitalist machinery that has all too often co-opted the body. For the present system dominating the sporting domain to maintain its power, people must believe there is no alternative and that the result of nonconformance and nonacceptance is failure and to be left behind—a position in which Bolt's rivals on and off the track all too often find themselves.

NOTES

CHAPTER 1

1. C. L. R. James, *Beyond a Boundary* (London: Hutchinson, 1963).

2. Michael Manley, *A History of West Indies Cricket* (London: Andre Deutsch, 1988).

3. Hilary McD. Beckles and Brian Stoddart, eds., *Liberation Cricket: West Indies Cricket Culture* (Manchester: Manchester University Press, 1995); Hilary McD. Beckles, *The Development of West Indies Cricket*, 2 vols. (London: Pluto, 1999).

4. Learie N. Constantine, *Cricket and I* (London: P. Allen, 1933); James, *Beyond a Boundary*; Vivian Richards, *Hitting across the Line* (London: Headline Books, 1991).

5. On the movement to independence of countries in the former British West Indies, see Gordon K. Lewis, *The Growth of the Modern West Indies* (Kingston, Jamaica: Ian Randle Press, 2004).

6. Beckles, *The Development of West Indies Cricket, Volume 1, The Age of Nationalism*, ch. 3; Hilary McD. Beckles, *Nation Imagined: The First West Indies Test Team: The 1928 Tour* (Kingston, Jamaica: Ian Randle Publishers, 2003).

7. Beckles, *The Development of West Indies Cricket, Volume 1, The Age of Nationalism*, ch. 4.

8. In the latest International Cricket Council ranking (December 2011) of test-playing nations, the West Indies is listed as seventh out of nine. However, in nine out of the past ten years the team has ranked eighth out of eight among the traditional test-playing nations: http://icc-cricket.yahoo.net/match_zone/historical_ranking.php (accessed 12 December 2011). The only other test teams ranked consistently below them in the last decade have been from the emerging cricket nations of Zimbabwe and Bangladesh. Compare this to the 1980s, when the West Indies was ranked as the number-one test team in the world for eighty-eight consecutive months.

9. Tim Hector, "On Lara and the Captaincy," *Trinidad Express* (Port-of-Spain), 10 December 1997; "Why Lara is a Loser," *Sydney Morning Herald*, 6 November 1998; Peter Roebuck, "How our man in Washington made Lara a Winner Again," *Electronic Telegraph* 4 April 1999.

10. Beckles, *The Development of West Indies Cricket, Volume 2: The Age of Globalisation*, esp. ch. 3.

11. See the report by West Indies team coach Otis Gibson to the WICB in July 2010, in which he listed the reasons for the poor performance of the team under the captaincy of Gayle, and the changes he believed were necessary. The latter included "Make representing the West Indies special again" and "Minutes of the West Indies Cricket Board Inc, Bay Gardens Hotel, St Lucia, July 17 and 18 2010." http://wicbexpose.files.wordpress.com/2011/04/gibsontourreport.pdf (accessed 12 December 2011).

12. Brian Lara, *Beating the Field: My Own Story* (London: Corgi, 1996).

13. For one view of the confrontation between Gayle and the board, see Lawrence Romeo, "Understanding the Gayle vs WICB Issue—A view from the inside," posted on http://*Caribbean Cricket.com*, 6 July 2011.

14. Beckles, *The Development of West Indies Cricket, Volume 2*, chs. 4 and 5.

15. Donna P. Hope, *Inna Di Dancehall: Popular Culture and the Politics of Identity in Jamaica* (Kingston, Jamaica: University of the West Indies Press, 2006); Carolyn Cooper, *Sound Clash: Jamaican Dance Hall Culture at Large* (London: Palgrave MacMillan, 2004).

16. Tony Becca, "South African Boss pledges full support to Tour," *Jamaica Gleaner*, 5 November 1998; *Sydney Morning Herald*, "Why Lara is a Loser," 6 November 1998; Christopher Martin-Jenkins, "'West Indies Dispute' case to dismiss in haste and repent at Leisure," *Electronic Telegraph*, 7 November 1998.

17. Beckles, *The Development of West Indies Cricket, Vol. 2*, 160–68; Peter May, *The Rebel Tours: Cricket's Crisis of Conscience* (Cheltenham: Sportsbooks, 2009); Richards, *Hitting across the Line*, 187.

18. Michelle MacDonald, "Bravo weighs in on WIPA/WICB dispute," http://Caribbeancricket.com, posted 30 March 2009.

19. James, *Beyond a Boundary*, 217.

20. Ibid.

CHAPTER 2

1. James C. Scott, *Dominance and the Arts of Resistance: Hidden Transcripts* (New Haven, CT: Yale University Press, 1990), frontispiece.

2. John Bale and Joe Sang, *Kenyan Running: Movement Culture, Geography and Global Change* (London: Frank Cass, 1996); John Bale, *Imagined Olympians: Body Culture and Colonial Representation in Rwanda* (Minneapolis: University of Minnesota Press, 2002).

3. John Eddy and Deryck Schreuder, "Introduction: Colonies into 'New Nations,'" in *The Rise of Colonial Nationalism: Australia, New Zealand, Canada and South Africa First Assert Their Nationalities, 1880–1914*, ed. John Eddy and Deryck Schreuder (Sydney: Allen and Unwin, 1988), 7.

4. Grant Farred, "'Theatre of Dreams': Mimicry and Difference in Cape Flats Township," in *Sport and Postcolonialism*, ed. John Bale and Mike Cronin (Oxford: Berg, 2003), 123–45.

5. Michael Taussig, *Mimesis and Alterity: A Particular History of the Senses* (London: Routledge, 1993).

6. For instance, the colonial subaltern is for the most part inactive in texts such as J. A. Mangan, *The Games Ethic and Imperialism: Aspects of the Diffusion of Ideal* (London: Frank Cass, 1998).

7. David Tomas, *Transcultural Space and Transcultural Beings* (Boulder, CO: Westview Press, 1996), 1.

8. Matthew Potolsky, *Mimesis* (London: Routledge, 2006), 1.

9. Bale and Cronin, *Sport and Postcolonialism*; Paul Dimeo, "Football and Politics in Bengal: Colonialism, Nationalism, Communalism," in *Soccer in South Asia: Empire, Nation, Diaspora*, ed. James Mills and Paul Dimeo (London: Frank Cass, 2001), 57–76; James Mills and Paul Dimeo, "'When Gold is Fired it Shines': Sport, the Imagination

and the Body in Colonial and Postcolonial India," in *Sport and Postcolonialism*, ed. Bale and Cronin, 107–22.

10. Wojciech Skalmowski, "Literary Deconstruction as a 'Newspeak,'" in *The Postmodern Challenge: Perspectives East and West*, ed. Bo Stråth and Nina Witoszek (Amsterdam: Editions Rodopi, 1999), 85–95.

11. On the archive, see Douglas Booth, "Sites of Truth or Metaphors of Power? Refiguring the Archive," *Sport in History* 26 (2006): 91–109; Martin Johnes, "Archives, Truths and the Historian at Work: A Reply to Douglas Booth's 'Refiguring the Archive,'" *Sport in History* 27 (2007): 127–35; on the challenge to history's theoretical deployments, see Douglas Booth, *The Field: Truth and Fiction in Sports History* (London: Routledge, 2005); Jeffrey Hill, *Sport and the Literary Imagination* (Bern, Switz.: Peter Lang, 2006); John Bale, *Anti-Sport Sentiments in Literature: Batting for the Opposition* (London: Routledge, 2008).

12. C. L. R. James, *Beyond a Boundary* (London: Stanley Paul & Co., 1963; reprint ed., London: Serpents' Tail, 1994); Homi K. Bhabha, *The Location of Culture* (London: Routledge, 2004).

13. This point is shown repeatedly in various contributions to P. J. Marshall, ed., *The Eighteenth Century*, vol. 2 of *Oxford History of the British Empire*, ed. William Roger Louis (Oxford: Oxford University Press, 1998); Andrew Porter, ed., *The Nineteenth Century*, vol. 3 of *Oxford History of the British Empire*, ed. William Roger Louis (Oxford: Oxford University Press, 1999); Judith Brown and William Roger Louis, eds., *The Twentieth Century*, vol. 4 of *Oxford History of the British Empire*, ed. William Roger Louis (Oxford: Oxford University Press, 1999); Philip D. Morgan and Sean Hawkins, eds., *Black Experience and the Empire*, Oxford History of the British Empire Companion Series (Oxford: Oxford University Press, 2004).

14. Claire Colebrook, *Irony* (London: Routledge, 2004), 1, 119, 123–25, 129.

15. Hayden White, *Metahistory: The Historical Imagination in Nineteenth-Century Europe* (Baltimore: Johns Hopkins University Press, 1973), 375.

16. David Lowenthal, *The Past Is a Foreign Country* (Cambridge: Cambridge University Press, 1985).

17. Ibid., xvi.

18. Clem Seecharan, *Muscular Learning: Cricket and Education in the Making of the British West Indies at the End of the 19th Century* (Kingston, Jamaica: Ian Randle, 2005), 230–64.

19. Clifford Geertz, "'From the Native's Point of View': On the Nature of Anthropological Understanding," in *Symbolic Anthropology: A Reader in the Study of Symbols and Meanings*, ed. Janet L Doglin, David S. Kemnitzer, and David M. Schneider (New York: Columbia University Press, 1977), 480–92.

20. Nicholas Thomas, *Out of Time: History and Evolution in Anthropological Discourse*, 2nd ed. (Ann Arbor: University of Michigan Press, 1996); Jean-Loup Amselle, *Mestizo Logics: Anthropology of Identity in Africa and Elsewhere* (Stanford, CA: Stanford University Press, 1998), especially 5–57; E. P. Thompson, *The Making of the English Working Class* (London: Pelican, 1980), 12.

21. Vinayek Chaturvedi, "Introduction," in *Mapping Subaltern Studies and the Postcolonial*, ed. Vinayek Chaturvedi (London: Verso, 2000), 1.

22. Ranajit Guha, *Dominance without Hegemony: History and Power in Colonial India* (Cambridge, MA: Harvard University Press, 1997).

23. Michele Wallace, "Modernism, Postmodernism and the Problem of Afro-American Visual Culture," in *Out There: Marginalization and Contemporary Culture*, ed. Russell Ferguson et al. (New York: New Museum of Contemporary Art/Cambridge, MA: MIT Press, 1990), 43, 39–50; Henry Louis Gates Jr., *Figures in Black: Words, Signs and the "Racial" Self* (New York: Oxford University Press, 1987).

24. Gates, *Figures in Black*, 247. Emphasis added by Gates.

25. Henry Louis Gates Jr., *The Signifying Monkey: A Theory of African-American Literary Criticism* (New York: Oxford University Press, 1988), 107.

26. Manning Clark, *History of Australia*, abridged by Michael Cathcart (Melbourne: Melbourne University Press, 1993), 551.

27. Peter Childs and Patrick Williams, *An Introduction to Post-Colonial Theory* (London: Prentice Hall/Harvester Wheatsheaf, 1997), 125.

28. Bhabha, *Location of Culture*, 122, 128, 125.

29. Ibid., 121–31.

30. *Lagaan: Once Upon a Time in India*, dir. Ashutosh Gowariker, Aamir Khan Productions Ltd, 2001, 224 min.

31. Gayatri Chakravorty Spivak, "Can the Subaltern Speak," in *Marxism and the Interpretation of Culture*, ed. Cary Nelson and Lawrence Grossberg (Urbana: University of Illinois Press, 1988), 271–313.

32. Colebrook, *Irony*, 1–46.

33. Edward Said, "C. L. R. James: The Artist as Revolutionary," *New Left Review* 175 (1989): 127.

34. Paul Buhle, *C. L. R. James: The Artist as Revolutionary* (London: Verso, 1988), 2.

35. Ibid., 2; James, *Beyond a Boundary*, 111.

36. Buhle, *C. L. R. James;* James, *Beyond a Boundary*, 25.

37. Ibid., 112.

38. Grant Farred, "The Maple Man: How Cricket Made a Postcolonial Intellectual," in *Rethinking C. L. R. James*, ed. Grant Farred (Cambridge, MA: Blackwell, 1996), 165–86.

39. Kenneth Surin, "'The Future Anterior': C. L. R. James and Going *Beyond a Boundary*," in *Rethinking C. L. R. James*, ed. Farred, 187–204; idem, "C. L. R. James' Material Aesthetic of Cricket," in *Liberation Cricket: West Indies Cricket Culture*, ed. Hilary McD. Beckles and Brian Stoddart (Manchester, UK: Manchester University Press, 1995), 313–41.

40. Neil Lazarus, "Cricket and National Culture in the Writings of C. L. R. James," in *Liberation Cricket*, ed. Beckles and Stoddart, 342–55; Michael Arthur and Jennifer Scanlon, "Reading and Rereading the Game: Reflections on West Indies Cricket," in *In the Game: Race, Identity, and Sports in the Twentieth Century*, ed. Amy Bass (New York: Palgrave Macmillan, 2005), 117–35.

41. Christopher Gair, "Beyond Boundaries: Cricket, Herman Melville, and C. L. R. James's Cold War," in *Beyond Boundaries: C. L. R. James and Postnational Studies*, ed. Christopher Gair (London: Pluto Press, 2006), 89–107; Stephen Howe, "C. L. R. James: Visions of History, Visions of Britain," in *West Indian Intellectuals in Britain*, ed. Bill Schwartz (Manchester, UK: Manchester University Press, 2003), 153–74.

42. Mark Kingwall, "Keeping a Straight Bat: Cricket, Civility, and

Postcolonialism," in *C. L. R. James: His Intellectual Legacies*, ed. Selwyn R. Cudjoe and William E. Cain (Amherst: University of Massachusetts Press, 1995), 359–87.

43. Kingwall. "Keeping a Straight Bat," 379–83.

44. Rudyard Kipling, "And what should they know of England who only England know?" "The English Flag," line 2, *Barrack Room Ballads*, 1892, http://www.btinternet.com/~brentours/ENGP22.htm (accessed 21 December 2006).

45. James, *Beyond a Boundary*, 219.

46. Ibid., 3–4.

47. Gordon Rohlehr, "C. L. R. James and the Legacy of *Beyond a Boundary*," in *A Spirit of Dominance: Cricket and Nationalism in the West Indies*, ed. Hilary McD. Beckles (Cave Hill, Barbados: Canoe Press, University of the West Indies, 1998), 140.

48. James, *Beyond a Boundary*, 4.

49. Ibid.

50. Ibid., 67.

51. Ibid.

52. Ibid.

53. Gates, *Signifying Monkey*, 107.

54. James, *Beyond a Boundary*, 67.

55. I am particularly grateful to one *Journal of Sport History* reviewer at this point for insisting that I revisit this case to consider the roles of both Telemarque and James in this sense of slyness. My analysis is less clear-cut than the reviewer's and points to a more ambivalent James and the need to read both text and evidence through Bhabha's lens.

56. Ibid., 68–69.

57. Ibid., 25.

58. Ibid.

59. Ibid., 69.

60. Ibid., 70.

61. Ibid.

62. Bhabha, *Location of Culture*, 122.

63. James, *Beyond a Boundary*, 25.

64. Ibid., 24–25.

65. Ibid., 25.

66. C. L. R. James, *The Black Jacobins: Toussaint L'Ouverture and the San Domingo Revolution* (London: Secker and Warburg, 1938; new ed., London: Penguin, 2001); idem, *The Case for West-Indian Self Government* (London: Hogarth Press, 1933); idem, *A History of the Pan-African Revolt* (orig. *A History of the Negro Revolt*, London: Fact Ltd., 1938; London: Race Today, 1986).

67. As useful as they are as analyses of anticolonial political struggles, John Newsinger, *The Blood Never Dried: A People's History of the British Empire* (London: Bookmarks, 2006), and Baruch Hirson, *Year of Fire, Year of Ash: The Soweto Revolt: Roots of a Revolution?* (London: Zed Press, 1979), are telling examples of texts that focus on confrontation—in Gramscian terms, wars of movement—rather than the everyday negotiations of resistance and cultural praxis—Gramsci's wars of position—as seen in more subtle and culturally sensitive works such as Vijay Prasad, *The Darker Nations: A People's History of the Third World* (New York: New Press, 2007).

CHAPTER 3

Epigraph. Bryan Turner, "Theoretical Developments in the Sociology of the Body," *Australian Cultural History* 13 (1994): 14.

1. For a recent elaboration on these perspectives, see Jennifer Hargreaves and Patricia Vertinsky, eds., *Physical Culture, Power and the Body* (London: Routledge, 2007).

2. Albert Grundlingh, "Playing for Power? Rugby, Afrikaner Nationalism and Masculinity in South Africa, c. 1900–c. 1970," in *Making Men: Rugby and Masculine Identity,* ed. John Nauright and Timothy Chandler (London: Frank Cass, 1996), 198–99. One cannot avoid racial terminology when discussing South Africa. The apartheid regime classified South Africans into four principal racial groups: African, "colored," Asian or Indian, and white. Black, the preferred term of the antiapartheid movement, denotes those groups collectively referred to by the former National Party government as nonwhite or non-European.

3. For a historiographical critique of this issue and, indeed, this incident, see Douglas Booth, "Beyond History: Racial Emancipation and Ethics in Apartheid Sport," *Rethinking History* 14 (2010): 461–81.

4. Robert Archer and Antoine Bouillon, *The South African Game: Sport and Racism* (London: Zed Press, 1982), 302.

5. See, for example, David Black and John Nauright, *Rugby and the South African Nation* (Manchester: Manchester University Press, 1998), and Douglas Booth, *The Race Game: Sport and Politics in South Africa* (London: Frank Cass, 1998).

6. Bryan Turner, *The Body and Society* (Oxford: Basil Blackwell, 1984).

7. Turner, "Theoretical Developments," in *The Body and Society,* 21–22 and 23. The reference to affects and emotions also highlights the biological foundations of bodies that historians and sociologists have been reluctant to embrace. This is now changing, especially in cultural studies. For an overview, see Constantina Papoulias and Felicity Callard, "Biology's Gift: Interrogating the Turn to Affect," *Body and Society* 16 (2010): 29–56.

8. Republic of South Africa, *Official Year Book of the Republic of South Africa* (Pretoria: Government Printer, 1974), 881. The editors deleted the reference to faction fighting as a sport in the following edition; in 1982 they deleted the reference to hunting and dancing.

9. This article develops ideas initially proposed by John Nauright in his *Sport, Cultures and Identities in South Africa* (London: Leicester University Press, 1997). Readers should note that this article focuses on male bodies: black sportswomen still remain largely absent from the literature on South African sport. For two recent contributions, see the chapters by André Odendaal (women's cricket) and Mari Haugaa Engh (women's soccer) in Scarlett Cornelissen ed., *Sport Past and Present in South Africa: (Trans)forming the Nation,* special issue of the *International Journal of the History of Sport* 28 (2011).

10. Hildi Hendrickson, *Clothing and Difference: Embodied Identities in Colonial and Post-Colonial Africa* (Durham, NC: Duke University Press, 1996), 15. Indeed, the face-to-face encounter with the Other and the choices these evoke lie at the heart of the work of the moral philosopher Emmanuel Lévinas that is increasingly being taken up by historians. See, for example, Robert Eaglestone, "The 'Fine Risk' of History: Post-structuralism, the Past and the Work of Emmanuel Levinas," *Rethinking History* 2 (1998): 313–20, and Booth, "Beyond History."

11. It must be stressed that the social constructionist approaches highlighted here conceptualize embodiment as "determined by sources . . . located outside of the body which are out of reach of the individuals subject to them." While Goffman views the body as significant for individuals, its true significance derives from the evaluations, judgments, and classifications made by others. Foucault believes that the meaning of the body is inscribed by discourses (see below), and Bourdieu maintains that embodiment corresponds to preassigned class bases. In Bourdieu's terminology, social location, habitus, and taste assign individuals their corporeal trajectories. For further discussion, see Chris Shilling, *The Body and Social Theory* (London: Sage, 1993), 88, 146.

12. Erving Goffman, *Interaction Ritual* (New York: Anchor Books, 1967), 77. See also, Erving Goffman, *Behavior in Public Places: Notes on the Social Organization of Gatherings* (New York: Free Press, 1963); Erving Goffman, *Stigma: Notes on the Management of Spoiled Identity* (Harmondsworth: Penguin, 1968); Erving Goffman, *The Presentation of Self in Everyday Life* (Harmondsworth: Penguin, 1981). Dunbar Moodie applies a Goffmanian approach to mining as a masculine occupational culture in South Africa. One particular focus of his work is how black mine migrants maintained personal and social integrity while moving between two worlds, peasant proprietorship and industrial exploitation. T. Dunbar Moodie with Vivienne Ndatshe, *Going for Gold: Men, Mines, and Migration* (Berkeley: University of California Press, 1994).

13. Andre Odendaal, "South Africa's Black Victorians: Sport and Society in South Africa in the Nineteenth Century," in *Pleasure, Profit, Proselytism: British Culture and Sport at Home and Abroad 1700–1914,* ed. J. A. Mangan (London: Frank Cass, 1988), 199–200.

14. Brian Willan, "An African in Kimberley: Sol T. Plaatje, 1894–1898," in *Industrialization and Social Change in South Africa: African Class Formation, Culture, and Consciousness, 1870–1930,* ed. Shula Marks and Richard Rathbone (London: Longman, 1982), 252.

15. Shilling, *The Body and Social Theory,* 151.

16. Odendaal, "Black Victorians," 200.

17. Pierre Bourdieu, *Distinction: A Social Critique of the Judgement of Taste* (London: Routledge, 1984), 218.

18. Odendaal, "Black Victorians," 201.

19. Bourdieu defines habitus in several different ways, none of which readily translate into English. John Loy defines it as a system of lasting unconscious dispositions and acquired schemes of thought and action, perception and appreciation, based on individuals' integrated social experiences under specific sets of objective social conditions (e.g., socialization into a given class) of the respective classes and in their inherent body schemes. Douglas Booth and John Loy, "Sport, Status, and Style," *Sport History Review* 30 (1999): 5. For a more detailed discussion of traditional working-class sporting practices, see Douglas Reid, "Beasts and Brutes: Popular Blood Sports c. 1780–1860," in *Sport and the Working Class in Modern Britain,* ed. Richard Holt (Manchester: Manchester University Press, 1990), 14; and John Hargreaves, *Sport, Power and Culture* (Cambridge: Polity, 1986), 67.

20. Rajab Benjamin, interview with John Nauright, 20 December 1994.

21. Bernard Magubane, "Sports and Politics in an Urban African Community:

A Case Study of African Voluntary Organizations" (Honor's dissertation, University of Natal, 1963), 12.

22. See, for example, Michel Foucault, *Discipline and Punish: The Birth of the Prison* (Harmondsworth: Penguin, 1979); Michel Foucault, "Body/Power," in *Michel Foucault: Power/Knowledge*, ed. Colin Gordon (Brighton: Harvester, 1980), 57–58. Michel Foucault, *The History of Sexuality: An Introduction* (Harmondsworth: Penguin, 1981).

23. William Pollock, *Talking about Cricket* (London: Victor Gollancz, 1941), 116, 152.

24. Louis Duffus, *Cricketers of the Veld* (London: Swinfern, 1947), 5–6, 11.

25. Archer and Bouillon, *The South African Game*, 121–22.

26. Davidson Jabavu, "Bantu Grievances," in *Western Civilization and the Natives of South Africa*, ed. Isaac Schapera (London: George Routledge and Sons, 1934), 298.

27. Jabavu, "Bantu Grievances," 293.

28. Odendaal, "Black Victorians," 204.

29. Ibid., 203–4. See also, Bruce Murray and Christopher Merrett, *Caught Behind: Race and Politics in Springbok Cricket* (Johannesburg: Wits University Press, 2004).

30. Isabel Hofmeyr, Neil Lazarus, Irwin Manoim, and Carola Steinberg, "Hamlet Through a Haze of Halchohol: Entertainment in White English Johannesburg, 1910–13" (Honor's dissertation, University of the Witwatersrand, 1977), 68.

31. Ibid., 74.

32. Ibid., 76.

33. Shilling, *The Body and Social Theory*, 76.

34. Alan Cobley, "A Political History of Playing Fields: The Provision of Sporting Facilities for Africans in the Johannesburg Area to 1948," *International Journal of the History of Sport* 11 (1994): 226.

35. Ibid., 229 n. 64.

36. Ibid., 218.

37. Achille Mbembe, "Passages to Freedom: The Politics of Racial Reconciliation in South Africa," *Public Culture* 20 (2008): 12.

38. White liberals initiated the Councils in the early 1920s as forums for inter-racial discussion.

39. Thomas Karis and Gail Gerhart, *From Protest to Challenge: A Documentary History of African Politics in South Africa*, Volume 5, 1964–79 (Bloomington: Indiana University Press, 1997), 368.

40. Colin Tatz, "Sport in South Africa: The Myth of Integration," *Australian Quarterly* 55 (1983): 416.

41. Richard Lapchick, *The Politics of Race and International Sport* (Westport, CT: Greenwood Press, 1975), 92.

42. Mr. Bauser, Kings Park Archery Club, interview with Douglas Booth, 22 March 1988.

43. Ali Mazrui, *The Africans: A Triple Heritage* (London: BBC Publications, 1986), 116.

44. John Lawrence, "Countering Apartheid Propaganda" (Paper presented at Commonwealth Secretariat, Media Workshop, London, 20–22 May 1985), 9.

45. Lapchick, *The Politics of Race*, 133.

46. "On the fairways of Soweto," *Sunday Star*, 24 January 1988.

47. Mono Badela, "vat hom Fikile!," *Leadership*, July 1993, 117.

48. World Health Organisation, *Apartheid and Health* (Geneva: WHO, 1983), 141, 145–47; Francis Wilson and Mamphela Ramphele, *Uprooting Poverty: The South African Challenge* (Cape Town: David Philip, 1989), 101; G. C. Jinabhai, H. M. Coovadia, and S. S. Abdool-Karim, "Socio-medical Indicators for Monitoring Progress Towards Health for All in Southern Africa," Carnegie Conference Paper No. 165, Second Carnegie Inquiry into Poverty and Development in Southern Africa (1984), 160.

49. Gassan Emeran, interview with John Nauright, 30 January 1995.

50. Don Pinnock, *The Brotherhoods: Street Gangs and State Control in Cape Town* (Cape Town: David Philip, 1984), 26.

51. Rajab Benjamin, interview with John Nauright, 20 December 1994.

52. Archer and Bouillon, *The South African Game*, 43.

53. Paul Hamann, *Black Men Bite* (South African Broadcasting Corporation, 1993), television documentary. Of course, white players are equally brutal. During a test match in 1994, Springbok Johan Le Roux bit an ear off New Zealand all-black captain Sean Fitzpatrick. While most commentators condemned Le Roux's actions, Springbok captain Francois Pienaar insisted that "things like that happen, . . . and we are feeling very, very sorry for Johan!" Former Springbok Colin Greenwood also defended Le Roux, blaming the controversy on television and pointing out that "similar and other serious offences" occurred in most tests. "Ear-bite Le Roux faces NZ probe," *Citizen*, 25 July 1994; "Le Roux won't play again—Luyt," *Citizen*, 26 July 1994.

54. Hamann, *Black Men Bite*.

55. Bourdieu, *Distinction*; Booth and Loy, "Sport, Status, and Style."

56. Grundlingh, "Playing for Power?," 196.

57. Charles Fortune, *Cricket Overthrown* (London: Bailey and Swinfern, 1960), 2.

58. Chris Greyvenstein, *Great Springbok Rugby Tests: 100 Years of Headlines* (Cape Town: Don Nelson, 1995), 168.

59. Grundlingh, "Playing for Power?," 196.

60. Lapchick, *The Politics of Race*, 150.

61. South African Institute of Race Relations (henceforth SAIRR), *A Survey of Race Relations in South Africa, 1975* (Johannesburg: SAIRR, 1976), 279.

62. Christopher Merrett, "Comrades of a Particular Type: An Alternative History of the Marathon, 1921–1983," *Natalia* 25 (1995): 73.

63. Archer and Bouillon, *The South African Game*, 280.

64. SAIRR, *A Survey of Race Relations in South Africa, 1976* (Johannesburg: SAIRR, 1977), 394.

65. SAIRR, *A Survey of Race Relations in South Africa, 1977* (Johannesburg: SAIRR, 1978), 560; SAIRR, *A Survey of Race Relations in South Africa, 1978* (Johannesburg: SAIRR, 1979), 491.

66. SAIRR, *A Survey of Race Relations in South Africa, 1977*, 564.

67. SAIRR, *A Survey of Race Relations in South Africa, 1980* (Johannesburg, SAIRR, 1981), 595.

68. Mark Mathabane, *Kaffir Boy: Growing Out of Apartheid* (London: Pan Books, 1987), 321–23.

69. Rob Louw, *For the Love of Rugby* (Johannesburg: Hans Strydom, 1987), 148. It is highly probable that Claassen, a member of the Broederbond, wanted to weaken Tobias's impact on the Springbok team. Tobias suffered no illusions about

his inclusion in the nation. He says that it wasn't until 27 April 1994—the date of South Africa's first universal suffrage election—that he felt like a real South African. "The future of sport in post-apartheid South Africa," *Time*, 29 May 1995.

70. Finlay Macdonald, *The Game of Our Lives* (Auckland: Viking, 1996), 93.

71. "CP vows to keep Springbok emblem," *Citizen*, 31 July 1994.

72. "Endangered species," *Sunday Times*, 10 February 1991.

73. "Trane oor vlag en volksleid," *Rapport*, 16 August 1992. For full details and analysis, see John Nauright, "A Besieged Tribe: Nostalgia, White Cultural Identity and the Role of Rugby in a Changing South Africa," *International Review for the Sociology of Sport* 31 (1996): 63–77.

74. Sharon Chetty, "Rugby . . . the last white outpost," *Sowetan*, 20 April 1995.

75. Recounted by Tim Noakes, University of Natal, Pietermaritzburg, public lecture, 25 October 1995.

76. Turner coins this approach "managerial athleticism." Turner, *Body and Society*, 111–12. Managerial athleticism is an example of the new disciplinary regimes identified by Foucault where individuals, in this case professional sportspeople, adopt certain behaviors to achieve their desires. For a fuller discussion, see John Hargreaves, "The Body, Sport and Power Relations," in *Sport, Leisure and Social Relations*, ed. John Horne, David Jary, and Alan Tomlinson (London: Routledge & Kegan Paul, 1987), 151–52.

77. "Mandela: I am proud of Boks," *Citizen*, 25 May 1995.

78. Ibid.

79. Emphasis added, "Boks back Masakhane," *Citizen*, 20 June 1995.

80. "On top of the world," *Sowetan*, 26 June 1995.

81. Mohamed Adhikari, *Not White Enough, Not Black Enough: Racial Identity in the South Africa Coloured Community* (Cape Town: Double Storey Books, 2005).

82. Jeremy Seekings, "The Continuing Salience of Race: Discrimination and Diversity in South Africa," *Journal of Contemporary African Studies* 26 (2008): 1–25.

83. Ashwin Desai, *We Are the Poors: Community Struggles in Post-apartheid South Africa* (New York: Monthly Review Press, 2000).

84. See, for example, the documentaries, *Injury Time*, Dir. Mark Fredericks, Prod. Underdogg, 2011 (URL = http://www.youtube.com/watch?v=7KtJdUxXQhc); *Tin Town*, Dirs. Nora Connor, Clementine Wallace, and Colton Margus, Prod. Barefoot Workshops, 2010 (URL = http://antieviction.org.za/2010/02/06/tin-town-a-short-documentary-on-the-symphony-way-anti-eviction-campaign/).

85. Neil Manthrop, "Zulu Warrior," *SA Sports Illustrated*, 20 January 1997.

86. Some excellent work on this framing of Zulu as warriors is being done by Benedict Carton and Robert Morrell; also see their chapter in this collection.

87. Aggrey Klaaste, "Strange things are happening to a closet racist," *Sowetan*, 9 January 1995.

88. "Debate over Springbok emblem ignited," *Business Day*, 27 June 1995.

89. James Mitchener provides a particularly graphic account of racial classification in *The Covenant* (London: Corgi Books, 1981), 921–39.

90. Jan Pieterse, *White on Black: Images of Africa and Blacks in Western Popular Culture* (New Haven, CT : Yale University Press, 1992), 149–50; R. W. Connell, *Masculinities* (Cambridge: Polity Press, 1995), 80.

CHAPTER 4

1. William McGregor, ed., *Encountering Aboriginal Languages: Studies in the History of Australian Linguistics* (Canberra: Pacific Linguistics, 2008).

2. Geoffrey Blainey, *Triumph of the Nomads: A History of Ancient Australia* (South Melbourne: Sun Books, 1976).

3. Henry Reynolds, *With the White People* (Ringwood, Vic: Penguin, 1990); Henry Reynolds, *The Other Side of the Frontier: Aboriginal Resistance to the European Invasion of Australia* (Kensington: University of New South Wales Press, 2006).

4. Charles Rowley, *The Destruction of Aboriginal Society* (Canberra: Australian National University Press, 1970); Henry Reynolds, *Nowhere People* (Camberwell, Vic: Penguin, 2008).

5. Katherine Ellinghaus, "Absorbing the 'Aboriginal Problem': Controlling Interracial Marriage in Australia in the Late 19th and Early 20th Centuries," *Aboriginal History* 27 (2003): 183–207; Colin Tatz, "The Destruction of Aboriginal Society in Australia," in *Genocide of Indigenous Peoples: A Critical Bibliographic Review*, vol. 8, ed. Samuel Totten and Robert Hitchcock (New Brunswick, NJ: Transaction Publisher, 2011), 87–116.

6. Rowley, *The Destruction of Aboriginal Society*; Russel McGregor, *Imagined Destinies: Aboriginal Australians and the Doomed Race Theory, 1880–1939* (Carlton, Vic: Melbourne University Press, 1997); Reynolds, *Nowhere People*.

7. Phillip Knightley, *Australia: A Biography of a Nation* (London: Jonathon Cape, 2000), 213.

8. Alexander Yarwood, *Asian Migration to Australia: The Background to Exclusion, 1896–1923* (Melbourne: Melbourne University Press, 1964).

9. John Horner and Marcia Langton, "The Day of Mourning," in *Australians: 1938*, ed. Bill Gammage and Peter Spearritt (Sydney: Fairfax, Syme and Weldon Associates, 1987), 29–35.

10. Ann Curthoys, *Freedom Ride: A Freedom Rider Remembers* (Sydney: Allen and Unwin, 2002), 117–18.

11. Noeline Briggs-Smith, *Moree Mob: Volume Two, Burrul Wallaay (Big Camp)* (Moree: Northern Regional Library and Information Service, 2003), 12–13.

12. Larissa Behrendt, "The Doctrine of Discovery in Australia," in *Discovering Indigenous Lands: The Doctrine of Discovery in the English Colonies*, Vol. 1, ed. Robert Miller, Jacinta Ruru, Larissa Behrendt, and Tracey Lindberg (Oxford: Oxford University Press, 2010), 171–87.

13. Kalervo Gulson and Robert Parkes, "From the Barrel of the Gun: Policy Incursions, Land, and Aboriginal Peoples in Australia," *Environment and Planning A* 42 (2010): 300–313.

14. Jon Altman and Melinda Hinkson, eds., *Coercive Reconciliation: Stabilise, Normalise, Exit Aboriginal Australia* (North Carlton, Vic: Arena Publications, 2007).

15. Australian Human Rights Commission, "A Statistical Overview of Aboriginal and Torres Strait Islander Peoples in Australia," 2008, http://www.hreoc.gov.au/social_justice/statistics/index.html#Heading34 (accessed 10 July 2010); Australian Bureau of Statistics, 1301.0—*Year Book Australia*. Canberra: Australian Bureau of Statistics, 2002, http://www.abs.gov.au/ausstats/abs@.nsf/94713ad445ff142 5ca2568200019 2af2/ bc28642d31c215cca256b350010b3f4!OpenDocument (accessed 10 July 2010).

16. Australian Bureau of Statistics figures for 2005–7 indicate that life expectancy of indigenous men is 11.5 years lower than for nonindigenous men, while life expectancy of indigenous women is 9.7 years lower than for nonindigenous women. Larine Statham, "Aborigines Have 'Worst' Life Expectancy," *Sydney Morning Herald*, 15 January 2010.

17. In 2001 the unemployment rate for indigenous Australians was 20.0 percent, compared to 7.2 percent for nonindigenous Australians. Australian Bureau of Statistics, 1301.0—*Year Book Australia*. Canberra: Australian Bureau of Statistics, 2004, http://www.abs.gov.au/Ausstats/abs@.nsf/0/bc6a7187473c6fb6ca256dea00053a29 (accessed 31 March 2010).

18. For example, 39 percent of indigenous students stayed on to year twelve at high school, compared with 75 percent for the total Australian population. Australian Bureau of Statistics, 1370.0—*Measures of Australia's* Progress. Canberra: Australian Bureau of Statistics, 2004, http://www.abs.gov.au/Ausstats/abs@.nsf/0/A03CAD 8F1C3F8 13BCA256E7D00002641 (accessed 31 March 2010). Both high unemployment and low levels of education have impacted on the economic circumstances of indigenous people. In 2002, the average household income for indigenous Australian adults was 60 percent of the nonindigenous average. Australian Bureau of Statistics, 1301.0—*Year Book Australia*. Canberra: Australian Bureau of Statistics, 2005, http://www.abs.gov.au /ausstats/abs@.nsf/0000000000000000000000000000000000/294322b c5648ead8ca256f7200833040!OpenDocument (accessed 31 March 2010).

19. Australian Bureau of Statistics figures for 2004 indicate that "Indigenous persons were eleven times more likely to be in prison compared with non-Indigenous persons," and that in 2003 some 20 percent of prisoners self-identified as indigenous. Australian Bureau of Statistics, 1301.0—*Year Book Australia*. Canberra: Australian Bureau of Statistics, 2005, http://www.abs.gov.au/ausstats/abs@.nsf/000000000 000000 00000000000000000/294322bc5648ead8ca256f7200833040!OpenDocument (accessed 31 March 2010).

20. Ronald Wilson, the Human Rights and Equal Opportunity Commission, and the National Inquiry into the Separation of Aboriginal and Torres Strait Islander Children from their Families (Australia), *Bringing Them Home: Report of the National Inquiry into the Separation of Aboriginal and Torres Strait Islander Children from their Families [Commissioner: Ronald Wilson]* (Sydney: Human Rights and Equal Opportunity Commission, 1997).

21. David Mellor, Di Bretherton, and Lucy Firth, "Aboriginal and Non-Aboriginal Australia: The Dilemma of Apologies, Forgiveness, and Reconciliation," *Peace and Conflict* 13 (2007): 11–36.

22. Altman and Hinkson, *Coercive Reconciliation*.

23. Gary Johns, "The Northern Territory Intervention in Aboriginal Affairs: Wicked Problem or Wicked Policy?" *Agenda: A Journal of Policy Analysis and Reform* 15 (2008): 65–86; Sarah Maddison, "What's Wrong with the Australian Government's 'Intervention' in Aboriginal Communities?" *Australian Journal of Human Rights* 14 (2008): 41–61.

24. Kevin Rudd, "Motion of Apology to Australia's Indigenous Peoples," *Australian Indigenous Law Review*, Special ed., 12 (2008): 1–5.

25. Colin Tatz, "Race, Politics and Sport," *Sporting Traditions* 1 (1984): 2–36; Colin Tatz, *Aborigines in Sport*, ASSH Studies no. 3 (Bedford Park, SA: Australian Society for

Sports History, 1987); Colin Tatz, *Obstacle Race: Aborigines in Sport* (Kensington: University of New South Wales Press, 1995); Colin Tatz, "Coming to Terms: '"Race,' Ethnicity, Identity and Aboriginality in Sport," *Australian Aboriginal Studies* 2 (2009): 15–31; Colin Tatz, "Sport, Racism and Aboriginality: The Australian Experience," in *Sport, Race and Ethnicity: Narratives of Difference and Diversity*, ed. Daryl Adair (Morgantown, WV: Fitness Information Technology Press, 2011), 95–114; Colin Tatz, "Race Matters in Australian Sport," in *Sport and Challenges to Racism*, ed. Jonathon Long and Karl Spracklen (Basingstoke, Hampshire: Palgrave, 2011), 100–116.

26. Tatz, "Race Matters in Australian Sport," 109.

27. Matthew Stephen, "Contact Zones: Sport and Race in the Northern Territory, 1869–1953" (Unpublished PhD thesis, Charles Darwin University, 2009), 121.

28. Matthew Stephen, "Football, 'Race' and Resistance: The Darwin Football League, 1926–29," *Australian Aboriginal Studies* 2 (2009): 61–77; Matthew Stephen, *Contact Zones: Sport and Race in the Northern Territory, 1869–1953* (Darwin: Charles Darwin University Press, 2010).

29. Lionel Rose and Rod Humphries, *Lionel Rose, Australian: The Life Story of a Champion* (Sydney: Angus and Robertson, 1969).

30. Tatz, "Race Matters in Australian Sport."

31. Kathy Lothian, "Moving Blackwards: Black Power and the Aboriginal Tent Embassy," in *Transgressions: Critical Australian Indigenous Histories*, ed. Ingereth Macfarlane and Mark Hannah (Canberra: ANU E-Press and Aboriginal History, 2007), 19–34.

32. Australian Football League, "AFL Indigenous Round: Round Nine," 22 May 2007, http://www.afl.com.au/Season2007/News/NewsArticle/tabid/208/Default. aspx?newsId=43746 (accessed 31 March 2010); Roy Masters, "League's Polynesian Powerplay Muscles in on Indigenous Numbers," *Sydney Morning Herald*, 24 April 2009.

33. Matthew Klugman and Gary Osmond, "That Picture: Nicky Winmar and the History of an Image," *Australian Aboriginal Studies* 2 (2009): 78–89.

34. Daryl Adair and Wray Vamplew, *Sport in Australian History* (Melbourne: Oxford University Press, 1997), 68.

35. Adair and Vamplew, *Sport in Australian History*, 68.

36. Greg Gardiner, "Racial Abuse and Football: The Australian Football League's Racial Vilification Rule in Review," *Sporting Traditions* 14 (1997): 3–26; Ian Warren and Spiros Tsousis, "Racism and the Law in Australian Rules Football: A Critical Analysis," *Sporting Traditions* 14 (1997): 27–54.

37. Tatz, "Race Matters in Australian Sport," 105.

38. Stella Coram, "Performative Pedagogy and the Creation of Desire: The Indigenous Athlete/Role Model and Implications for Learning," *Australian Journal of Indigenous Education* 36 (2007): 46–54.

39. Tatz, "Race Matters in Australian Sport," 112.

40. Toni Bruce and Chris Hallinan, "Cathy Freeman: The Quest for Australian Identity," in *Sports Stars: The Cultural Politics of Sporting Celebrity*, ed. David Andrews and Steve Jackson (London: Routledge, 2001), 257–70.

41. Toni Bruce and Emma Wensing, "'She's Not One of Us': Cathy Freeman and the Place of Aboriginal People in Australian National Culture," *Australian Aboriginal Studies* 2 (2009): 90–100.

42. Chris Hallinan and Barry Judd, "Race Relations, Indigenous Australia and the

Social Impact of Professional Australian Football," *International Journal of the History of Sport* 26 (2009): 2358–75.

43. Chris Hallinan, Toni Bruce, and Jason Bennie, "Freak Goals and Magical Moments: Commonsense Understandings About Indigenous Footballers," *TASA 2004 Conference Proceedings*, ed. Katy Richmond (Melbourne: Australian Sociological Association, 2004, CD ROM, ISBN: 0–9598460–4-2).

44. Andrew Ramsey, "The Fostering of Aboriginal Talent in South Australia," in *AFL's Black Stars*, ed. Colin Tatz (Melbourne: Lothian, 1998), 87.

45. Hallinan, Bruce, and Bennie, "Freak Goals and Magical Moments"; Chris Hallinan, Toni Bruce, and Michael Burke, "Fresh Prince of Colonial Dome: Indigenous Logic in the AFL," *Football Studies* 8 (2005): 68–78; Stella Coram, "Race Formations (Evolutionary Hegemony) and the 'Aping' of the Australian Indigenous Athlete," *International Review for the Sociology of Sport* 42 (2007): 391–409; Tatz, "Coming to Terms."

46. Chris Munro, "Marngrook Debate Flares Again," *National Indigenous Times*, 29 May 2008.

47. Hallinan and Judd, "Race Relations, Indigenous Australia."

48. Darren Godwell, "Aboriginality and Rugby League in Australia: An Exploratory Study of Identity Construction and Professional Sport" (Unpublished master's thesis, Department of Kinesiology, University of Windsor, Ontario, 1997).

49. John Hoberman, *Darwin's Athletes: How Sport Has Damaged Black America and Preserved the Myth of Race* (New York: Houghton Mifflin, 1997).

50. Darren Godwell, "Playing the Game: Is Sport as Good for Race Relations as We'd Like to Think?," *Australian Aboriginal Studies* 1 (2000): 13.

51. Ibid.

52. Ibid., 19.

53. Ibid., 17.

54. Ibid., 16.

55. Megan Stronach, "Sport Career Transition and Retirement: Stories of Elite Indigenous Australian Sportsmen" (Unpublished PhD thesis, School of Leisure, Sport and Tourism, University of Technology, Sydney, 2011).

56. Megan Stronach, "Sport Career Transition," ch. 4.

57. Ibid.

58. John Sugden, *Boxing and Society: An International Analysis* (Manchester: Manchester University Press, 1996).

59. Sean Gorman, *Brotherboys: The Story of Jim and Phillip Krakouer* (Crows Nest, NSW: Allen and Unwin, 2005).

60. Gorman, quoted in Che Cockatoo-Collins, Sean Gorman, John Harms, and David Headon, "Force for Good: How Indigenous Australians Have Enriched Football," Audio on Demand, National Museum of Australia, Canberra, 15 September 2009, http://nma.gov.au/audio/detail/force-for-good-how-indigenous-australians-have-enriched-football (accessed 31 March 2010).

61. Cockatoo-Collins et al., "Force for Good."

62. Glenn McFarlane, "Junior Boy," *Sydney Morning Herald*, 2 August 2009.

63. ABC Television, *7.30 Report*, "From the Northern Territory to New York Marathon for 6 black native Australian First Nation runners," 14 January 2010, ABC Television (Australia), accessed via YouTube, http://www.youtube.com/watch?v=qkDGUhw TuPo (31 March 2010).

64. Daryl Adair, "'We Might Find a Real [Black] Gem': White Dreaming and Indigenous Australian Marathon Runners" (Paper presented to the 18th Sporting Traditions Conference. Tweed Coast, NSW, 5–8 July 2011).

65. Godwell, "Playing the Game," 18.

66. Ibid.

67. Geoff Slattery and the Australian Football League, eds., *The Australian Game of Football: Since 1858* (Docklands, Vic: Geoff Slattery Publishing for the Australian Football League, 2008).

68. Munro, "Marngrook Debate."

69. Tim Morrisey, "Adam Goodes Called a Racist—Swans star in the middle of a spiteful debate over Australian football's indigenous origins," *Daily Telegraph*, 15 May 2008.

70. Munro, "Marngrook Debate."

71. Ibid.

72. See *Spike: Meanjin's Blog*, 11 May 2009, http://meanjin.com.au/spike-the-meanjin-blog/post/football-s-history-wars/ (accessed 31 March 2010).

73. Brett St. Louis, "Brilliant Bodies, Fragile Minds: Race, Sport and the Mind/Body Split," in *Making Race Matter: Bodies, Space and Identity*, ed. Claire Alexander and Caroline Knowles (New York: Palgrave Macmillan, 2005), 113–31.

74. John Hoberman, "The Price of 'Black Dominance,'" *Society* 37 (2000): 49–56.

75. Godwell, "Playing the Game," 16.

76. Simon Santow, "Prominent Australians Get Behind Indigenous Job Training," *World Today*, ABC Radio, 19 March 2010, http://www.abc.net.au/worldtoday/content/2010/s2850612.htm?site=midnorthcoast (accessed 15 April 2010).

77. Daryl Adair, "Shooting the Messenger: Australian History's Warmongers," *Sporting Traditions* 22 (2006): 49–69.

CHAPTER 5

1. David Rowe, "The Televised Sport 'Monkey Trial': Race and the Politics of Post-Colonial Cricket," in *Sport: Race, Ethnicity and Identity: Building Global Understanding,* ed. Daryl Adair (London, Routledge, 2008), 56.

2. Ibid.

3. See, for instance, James W. Keating, "Sportsmanship as a Moral Category," and Randolph M. Feezell, "Sportsmanship," in *Ethics in Sport*, ed. William J. Morgan (Champaign, IL: Human Kinetics, 2007).

4. FA Regulatory Commission 2011, *The Football Association and Luis Suarez—Reasons of the Regulatory Commission*, 26: http://www.thefa.com/TheFA/Disciplinary/NewsAndFeatures/2011/~/media/Files/PDF/TheFA/Disciplinary/Written%20reasons/FA%20v%20Suarez%20Written%20Reasons%20of%20Regulatory%20Commission.ashx (accessed 27 July 2012).

5. Ibid., 47.

6. Ibid., 27.

7. Ibid.

8. Ibid.

9. Ibid., 28.

10. Ibid.

11. Ibid.

12. Ibid., 18.

13. Ibid.

14. Ibid., 57.

15. Ibid., 87.

16. Ibid., 110.

17. Ibid., 107.

18. Ibid., 107f.

19. Ibid., 28.

20. Ibid., 108.

21. Ibid.

22. Rodney Hinds, "Luis Suarez's ban for racism has helped football regain credibility," *Guardian,* 21 December 2011.

23. FA Regulatory Commission 2011: The Football Association and Luis Suarez—Reasons of the Regulatory Commission, 115.

24. Ibid., 48.

25. Les Murray: "Why Suarez is a racist," *World Game,* 25 December 2011: http://theworldgame.sbs.com.au/les-murray/blog/1086893/Why-Suarez-is-a-racist?# (accessed 20 August 2012).

26. Ibid.

27. Dan Hodges, "We either adopt zero tolerence towards racism in football or we don't. It's as simple as that," *Telegraph,* 30 September 2011: http://blogs.telegraph.co.uk/news/danhodges/100125657/we-either-adopt-zero-tolerance-towards-racism-in-football-or-we-dont-its-as-simple-as-that/ (accessed 20 August 2012).

28. Tim Vickery, "Luis Suarez ban for racist abuse of Patrice Evra leaves Uruguay bemused," *BBC Sport,* 20 December 2011, http://www.bbc.co.uk/sport/0/football/16262537 (accessed 21 August 2012).

29. See, for instance, Alan Bairner, "Sportive Nationalism and Nationalist Politics: A Comparative Analysis of Scotland, The Republic of Ireland, and Sweden," *Journal of Sport and Social Issues* 23 (1996): 314–34.

30. Ibid.

31. Ibid.

32. Ibid.

33. TV2: "Jurister: Okay at råbe perker på banen" ("Lawyers: Okay to shout Paki at somebody on the pitch," *TV2–News,* 3 April 2012, http://nyhederne.tv2.dk/article.php/id-49395730:jurister-okay-at-r%C3%A5be-perker-p%C3%A5-boldbanen.html (accessed 27 September 2012).

34. Ibid.

35. Raymond Boyle and Richard Haynes, *Power Play: Sport, the Media and Popular Culture* (Edinburgh: Edinburgh University Press, 2009), 110.

36. Steven Pinker, *The Stuff of Thought—Language as a Window into Human Nature* (London: Penguin, 2008), 124.

37. *Guardian,* "Liverpool fan banned for racist abuse of Patrice Evra," *Guardian* 22 June 2012, http://www.guardian.co.uk/football/2012/jun/22/liverpool-fan-banned-racist-abuse-evra (accessed 1 September 2012).

38. FA Regulatory Commission 2011, *The Football Association and Luis Suarez—Reasons of the Regulatory Commission,* 28.

CHAPTER 6

1. A. B. (Banjo) Paterson, "The Cycloon, Paddy Cahill and the G R," in *North of the Ten Commandments: A Collection of Northern Territory Literature*, ed. David Headon (Sydney: Hodder and Stoughton, 1991), 213.

2. D. J. Mulvaney, *Encounters in Place: Outsiders and Aboriginal Australians 1606–1985* (Brisbane: University of Queensland Press, 1989), 109.

3. During the construction of the Northern Territory Railway between 1886 and 1888, the Chinese population grew to 6,122, outnumbering whites 6 to 1. See P. F. Donovan, *A Land Full of Possibilities: A History of South Australia's Northern Territory* (Brisbane: University of Queensland Press, 1981), 173. In 1914, the Northern Territory population was estimated at 3,720 made up of Europeans, 2,452; Chinese, 1,033; Japanese, 77; Malays, Philipinos, 89; Half-castes, 72. *Northern Territory of Australia, Report of the Administrator for the Year 1914–15*, CPP 240/1915, Melbourne, November 1915, 89. The Aboriginal population was not counted during the colonial period.

4. Benedict Anderson, *Imagined Communities: Reflections on the Origin and Spread of Nationalism* (London: Verso, 1983).

5. Ibid., 4.

6. Stuart Hall, "The Spectacle of the 'Other,'" in *Representation: Cultural Representations and Signifying Practices*, ed. Stuart Hall (London: Sage, 1997), 258.

7. Terence Ranger, "The Invention of Tradition in Colonial Africa," in *The Invention of Tradition,* ed. Eric Hobsbawm and Terence Ranger (London: Cambridge University Press, 1983), 211.

8. Peta Stephenson, *The Outsiders Within: Telling Australia's Indigenous-Asian Story* (Sydney: University of New South Wales Press, 2007), 60.

9. Susan Sickert, *Beyond the Lattice: Broome's Early Years* (Fremantle: Fremantle Arts Centre Press, 2003), 53.

10. Robert Young, *Colonial Desire: Hybridity in Theory, Culture and Race* (London: Routledge, 1995), 5.

11. E. J. Hobsbawm, *The Age of Empire 1875–1914* (London: Weidenfeld and Nicolson, 1987).

12. Greg Ryan, *The Making of New Zealand Cricket* (London: Frank Cass, 2004), 7.

13. Marilyn Lake and Henry Reynolds, *Drawing the Global Colour Line: White Men's Countries and the Question of Racial Equality* (Melbourne: Melbourne University Press, 2008), 4.

14. Claire Lowry, "In Service of Empire: Domestic Service and Colonial Mastery in Singapore and Darwin, 1890s–1930s" (PhD thesis, University of Wollongong, 2009), 47.

15. Authors to apply Anderson's imagined communities to sport include Mike Cronin and David Mayall, "Introductory Remarks," in *Sporting Nationalism: Identity, Ethnicity, Immigration and Assimilation*, ed. Mike Cronin and David Mayall (London: Frank Cass, 1998), 1; Karl Spracklen, "Black Pearl, Black Diamonds: Exploring Racial Identities in Rugby League," in *"Race," Sport and British Society*, ed. Ben Carrington and Ian McDonald (London: Routledge, 2001), 76.

16. *Moonta Herald and Northern Territory Gazette*, 2 January 1869.

17. Ibid.

18. Matthew Stephen, "Northern Territory Sport and Leisure Database." From 1869 to 1911, twenty-six minstrel shows were performed in Palmerston. Sixteen occurred between 1883 and 1898. The first blackface entertainment in Australia was reported in Sydney in 1838. See Richard Waterhouse, "Minstrel Show and Vaudeville House: The Australian Popular Stage, 1838–1914," *Australian Historical Studies* 93 (October 1989): 366. Professional minstrel troupes, including black American troupes, were very popular in Australian in the latter half of the nineteenth century, and many toured the capital cities and regional centers on the Eastern seaboard. See Waterhouse, "Minstrel Show and Vaudeville House," 374.

19. The first attempts at British colonization in North Australia were the colonial outposts of Fort Dundas (1824–1827), Raffles Bay (1827–1829), and Port Essington (1838–1849) and South Australia's first attempt at settlement at Escape Cliffs (1864–1866).

20. William Webster Hoare, "1869 Adventures Port Darwin. My Diary W. W. Hoare," 24 May 1869, Mortlock Library, SLSA, Adelaide, 4 August 1869.

21. Edward Napoleon Buonaparte Catchlove, "Dairies of Edward Napoleon Buonaparte Catchlove, Volume 2 1870." 1870. Northern Territory Collection, NTL, Darwin, 9.

22. Ibid.

23. David Neufeld, "Public Memory and Public Holidays: Discovery Day and the Establishment of a Klondike Society," *Public History Review* 8 (2000): 74. See also Ryan, *The Making of New Zealand Cricket*, 20.

24. *South Australian Register*, 23 June 1872.

25. *South Australian Advertiser*, 3 June 1872. See also Catchlove, Diaries, Volume 2, 48.

26. David K. Wiggins, *Glory Bound: Black Athletes in a White America* (New York: Syracuse University Press, 1997), 1–19.

27. Colin Tatz, *Obstacle Race: Aborigines in Sport* (Sydney: University of New South Wales Press, 1995), 43.

28. Wray Vamplew and Brian Stoddart, eds., *Sport in Australia: A Social History* (Melbourne: Cambridge University Press, 1994), 68. See also Richard Cashman, *Paradise of Sport: The Rise of Organised Sport in Australia* (Melbourne: Oxford University Press, 1995), 132.

29. Tatz, *Obstacle Race*, 88.

30. Vamplew and Stoddart, *Sport in Australia*, 17.

31. Ibid., 262. In a rowing race on Moreton Bay 1848, Aboriginal rowers were given clothes instead of the prize of money on offer.

32. The British Australian Telegraph Company was merged into the Eastern Extension and China Cable Company in 1873 but the staff was referred to as BAT until well into the twentieth century.

33. Jan Morris, *Pax Britannica: The Climax of an Empire* (Harmondsworth: Penguin Books, 1979), 62.

34. Anderson, *Imagined Communities*, 151.

35. Ernestine Hill, *The Territory* (Australia: Angus & Robertson, 1995), 126.

36. Alan Powell, *Far Country: A Short History of the Northern Territory* (Melbourne: Melbourne University Press, 1982), 115.

37. *Northern Territory Times and Gazette* (1873–1932). The *North Australian* (1883–1889) was incorporated into the *Northern Territory Times* when it closed in 1889.

38. Anderson, *Imagined Communities,* 63.

39. An "at home" was a social event held in the home of a prominent citizen. Most often, they required a formal invitation and were advertised in the local paper. They tended to be smaller than social occasions organized by sporting or social clubs and societies. For a full account of sport in Northern Territory, see Mathew Stephen, "Contact Zone: Sport and Race in the Northern Territory, 1869–1953" (PhD thesis, Charles Darwin University, 2009).

40. Ranger, "The Invention of Tradition in Colonial Africa," 238–39.

41. Genevieve Clare Blades, "Australian Aborigines, Cricket and Pedestrianism: Culture and Conflict, 1880–1910" (Honor's thesis, University of Queensland, 1985). See also Bernard Whimpress, *Passport to Nowhere: Aborigines in Australian Cricket 1850–1939* (Petersham: Walla Walla Press, 1999); Tatz, *Obstacle Race,* chs. 4–5; D. J. Mulvaney and Rex Harcourt, *Cricket Walkabout: The Australian Aborigines in England* (South Melbourne: Macmillan in association with the Department of Aboriginal Affairs, 1988).

42. Morris, *Pax Britannica,* 283.

43. Eric Hobsbawm, "Mass-Producing Traditions: Europe, 1870–1914," in *The Invention of Tradition,* ed. Eric Hobsbawm and Terence Ranger (London: Cambridge University Press, 1983), 299. See also Mangan, *The Games Ethic and Imperialism* (Harmondsworth: Viking, 1985).

44. J. A. Mangan, ed., *The Cultural Bond: Sport, Empire, Society* (London: Frank Cass, 1992), 1.

45. John Lowerson, *Sport and the English Middle Classes 1870–1914* (Manchester: Manchester University Press, 1993), 24.

46. Anthony Kirk-Greene, "Badge of Office: Sport and His Excellency in the British Empire," in Mangan, *The Cultural Bond,* 192.

47. Matthew Stephen, "Northern Territory Sport and Leisure Database." During the period 1869 to 1911, of the 132 recorded minstrel performers 57 percent were also known cricketers.

48. *Northern Territory Times,* 3 October 1874.

49. In its classic form minstrel performers sat in a semicircle with the interlocutor (the master of ceremonies and straightman), in the center, the tambo and bones (the comedians) as end men, and the singers in between. Performances often included a stump speech in which one of the performers harangued the audience on some local political issue of the day such as education, temperance, or women's rights. Christy Minstrels, named after E. P. Christy, further refined the program into a three-part form, the first part, olio, and the "Ethiopian Opera." See Richard Waterhouse, "Minstrel Show and Vaudeville House: The Australian Popular Stage, 1838–1914," *Australian Historical Studies* 93 (October 1989): 368.

50. The traditions of cricket were so strong that remarkably, Palmerston cricketers insisted in playing cricket during Christmas holidays and the "Wet." Although summer was traditionally the cricket season in other Australian colonies, December to March was the worst possible time to play in Palmerston because of the extreme heat and humidity. Change was very slow in coming but the Port Darwin Cricket Club resolved the issue with a Solomon-like decision. The 1898 cricket season would finish on the thirty-first of December, and thereafter the cricket season would be 1 January to 31 December.

51. Ranger, "The Invention of Tradition in Colonial Africa," 215.

52. *Northern Territory Times*, 7 November 1874.

53. Ibid., 7.

54. Lowerson, *Sport and the English Middle Classes*, 9.

55. John Tosh, *Manliness and Masculinities,* 200, in Lowry, "In Service of Empire," 131.

56. Lowry, "In Service of Empire," 19.

57. A. Grenfell Price, *The History and Problems of the Northern Territory, Australia with Maps: The John Murtagh Macrossan Lectures* (Adelaide: University of Queensland, A. E. Acott, 1930), 2.

58. Ian Mackintosh Hillock, *Broken Dreams and Broken Promises: The Cane Conspiracy: Plantation Agriculture in the Northern Territory 1878–1889* (Darwin: Northern Territory University Press, 2000), 34.

59. Anderson, *The Cultivation of Whiteness: Science, Health and Racial Destiny in Australia* (Melbourne: Melbourne University Press, 2002), 80.

60. Donovan, *A Land Full of Possibilities*, 106.

61. Lowry, "In Service of Empire," 129.

62. Ibid., 118.

63. Ibid., 131–33.

64. Kirwan, Uhr, and Pickford, "Memorial to the Government Resident Re: Chinese Poll Tax," 5 April 1886, GRIC, A8975, NTAS, Darwin.

65. In March 1888, a poll tax of £10 was imposed on all Chinese arriving in the Northern Territory with further poll tax of £10 on those crossing an imaginary line two hundred miles south of Darwin. The South Australia government passed the Chinese Immigration Restriction Act 1888, which restricted landing of Chinese to one per 500 tons burden of vessels, the imposition of a permit. The Northern Territory Gold Mining Act 1895 effectively banned Chinese from the goldfields.

66. Powell, *Far Country,* 110.

67. Deborah Bird Rose, *Hidden Histories: Black Stories from Victoria River Downs, Humbert River and Wave Hill Stations* (Canberra: Aboriginal Studies Press, 1991), 20.

68. See Stephen, "Contact Zones," chapter 4, for a discussion of frontier race relations in the Northern Territory.

69. Ann McGrath, *Born in the Cattle: Aborigines in the Cattle Country* (Sydney: Allen and Unwin, 1987), 99.

70. *Select Committee of the Legislative Council on the Aborigines Bill, 1899, Minutes of Evidence and Appendices*, SAPP, 77/1899, Adelaide, 1899.

71. Ibid., 26.

72. Ibid., 112.

73. Ibid., 3, 113.

74. Ibid., 2.

75. Ibid., 110.

76. Dashwood's proposed bill, based on the Queensland Aboriginals Protection and Restriction of the Sale of Opium Act of 1897, was passed by the South Australian House of Assembly in July 1899, but when sent to the Legislative Council committee it lapsed due to a change of government. See Gordon Reid, *A Picnic with the Natives: Aboriginal-European Relations in the Northern Territory to 1910* (Melbourne: Melbourne University Press, 1990), 168.

77. Bill Wilson, "A Force Apart? A History of the Northern Territory Police

Force, 1870–1926" (PhD thesis, Northern Territory University, 2000), 327–28. See also C. D. Rowley, *The Destruction of Aboriginal Society* (Melbourne: Penguin, 1972), 205.

78. *Northern Territory Times*, 25 December 1880.

79. Daryl Adair and Wray Vamplew, *Sport in Australian History* (Melbourne: Oxford University Press, 1997), 134.

80. Arthur Hang Gong was born in 1867, the son of a prominent Darwin Chinese merchant, Lee Hang Gong, and Sarah Bowman, an Englishwoman best known as a midwife. Hang Gong participated in numerous sports alongside Europeans in the 1880s and 1890s including cricket, athletics, and horse racing. See Carment et al., *Northern Territory Dictionary of Biography*, Vol. 2, 80–84.

81. *Northern Territory Times*, 6 August 1881, 13 August 1881.

82. Alfred Searcy, *In Australian Tropics* (Adelaide: George Robertson & Co., 1909; Carlisle: reprint, Facsimile Edition, Hesperian Press, 1984), 349.

83. *Northern Territory Times*, 23 December 1882.

84. W. H. Bundey, *Manly Sports, Exercise, and Recreations and the Beneficial Effects of Their Practice within Reasonable and Proper Bounds* (Adelaide: Advertiser and Chronicle Printing Offices, 1880), 16.

85. *Northern Territory Times*, 5 April 1889; 10 August 1889.

86. Richard Waterhouse, "Antipodean Odessey: Charles B. Hicks and the New Georgia Minstrels in Australia, 1877–1880," *Journal of the Royal Australian Historical Society* 72 (1986): 33.

87. *Northern Territory Times*, 22 December 1877.

88. Harold Perkin, "Teaching Nations How to Play: Sport and Society in the British Empire and Commonwealth," in Mangan, *The Cultural Bond*, 213.

89. *Northern Territory Times*, 17 November 1888.

90. The town oval was first cleared in 1882. *Northern Territory Times*, 25 November 1882. The Palmerston Rifle Club constructed its first rifle range in July 1881. *Northern Territory Times*, 23 July 1881. A tennis court was noted at the BAT. See William J. Sowden, *The Northern Territory as It Is: A Narrative of the South Australian Parliamentary Party's Trip and Full Descriptions of the Northern Territory; Its Settlements and Industries* (Adelaide: W. K. Thomas & Co., 1882), 137.

91. *Northern Territory Times*, 1 June 1883.

92. *North Australian*, 3 January 1890.

93. Tatz, *Obstacle Race*, 91.

94. *North Australian*, 3 January 1890.

95. Ibid., 11 April 1890.

96. David K. Wiggins, *Glory Bound*, 213.

97. G. H. Lamond, *Tales of the Overland: Queensland to Kimberly in 1885* (Perth: Hesperian Press, 1986), 75, provides a contradictory account of this unusual episode. The account that claims the "Darwin Sports" brought in Floyd, an Aboriginal ring-in from Sydney, is unsubstantiated and could have been an invention by the "Darwin sports" to cover their embarrassment at being taken to the cleaners by an Aborigine.

98. *Northern Territory Times*, 4 January 1895.

99. Ibid., 2 October 1896.

100. Ibid., 17 February 1898.

101. John Hoberman, *Darwin's Athletes: How Sport Has Damaged Black America and Preserved the Myth of Race* (New York: Houghton Mifflin Company, 1997), 109.

102. *Northern Territory Times*, 7 April 1893.

103. Ibid., 26 October 1894. "Nim" is a name often given to Aborigines and thought to mean boy or young boy.

104. Ibid., 2 November 1894. Although the use of "(ab)" to identify Aborigines was common in other colonies, it was not in the Northern Territory.

105. Ibid., 2 November 1894.

106. Ibid., 16 November 1894.

107. Ibid., 4 and 11 November 1898. Allen played in both games and Antonio Spain in the second.

108. Ibid., 4, 11, and 15 November 1898.

109. Ibid., 1 June 1900.

110. Ibid., 21 September, 19 October 1900.

111. Willie Allen, "Australian Military Forces, Australian Imperial Force, Attestation Paper of Person Enlisted for Service Abroad," National Archives of Australia, Canberra, 10 December 1917.

112. George Thompson, "List of Half Castes in the Northern Territory," 12 December 1899, GRIC, 10441, NTAS, Darwin. Larrakia are the traditional Aboriginal owners of the land where Darwin now stands.

113. Robert Young, *Colonial Desire: Hybridity in Theory, Culture and Race* (London: Routledge, 1995), 174.

114. Lyn Spain, e-mail to author, 20 December 2007. Massey was born in London in 1864 and in 1884 migrated alone to Australia arriving in Brisbane but later moved to Cairns where she was working as a domestic. The correspondence included genealogical information undertaken by Dr. A. Shnukal.

115. Stephen, "Northern Territory Sport and Leisure Data Base."

116. *Northern Territory Times*, 4 January 1901.

117. *Morning Post*, 28 May 1906; Lake and Reynolds, *Drawing the Global Colour Line*, 164.

118. *Northern Territory Times*, 4 January 1901.

119. Searcy, *In Australian Tropics*, 349.

120. *Northern Territory Times*, 20 January 1905, 27 January 1905, 12 January 1909, 12 March 1909.

121. Ibid., 19 March 1909. On the 26 December 1908, Tommy Burns the white champion was defeated by black American Jack Johnson in a world heavyweight title fight at Rushcutters Bay, Sydney. Johnson's victory caused considerable moral outrage. See Richard Broome, "The Australian Reaction to Jack Johnson, Black Pugilist, 1907–9," in *Sport in History: The Making of Modern Sporting History*, ed. Richard Cashman and Michael McKernan (St. Lucia: University of Queensland Press, 1979), 343–63.

122. Fred Blakely, *Hard Liberty* (Sydney: George G. Harrap & Company, 1938), 265.

123. Ibid., 268.

124. Ibid., 269.

125. *Northern Territory Times*, 2 April 1909.

126. *Northern Territory. Report Government Resident for the Year 1910,* Melbourne, 1911, 42.

127. F. H. Bauer, *Historical Geography of White Settlement in Part of Northern*

Australia: Part 2, The Katherine—Darwin Region (Canberra: Commonwealth Scientific and Industrial Research Organization, 1964), 194.

128. *Northern Territory Times*, 30 June 1911.

129. P. F. Donovan, *At the Other End of Australia: The Commonwealth and the Northern Territory 1911–1978* (Brisbane: University of Queensland Press, 1984), 4. Palmerston was officially renamed Darwin in 1911.

130. Ibid., 94.

131. Herbert Basedow, Department of Aboriginal Affairs, Office of the Chief Protector and Chief Medical Inspector, Letter to Willie Allen, 11 August 1911. This was Allen's first marriage to Lilly Helliman. Helliman died in 1911. *Northern Territory Times*, 29 September 1911.

132. *Northern Territory Times*, 26 May 1911.

133. Ibid., 12 August 1911.

134. Ibid., 6 October 1911.

135. Ibid., 20 October 1911.

136. Ibid., 20 November 1911.

137. Ibid. Performers in concerts are identified but not all guests.

138. There had been no minstrel shows in Palmerston since 1906. After 1911 there are records of only four minstrel performances. See Stephen, *NT Sport and Leisure Database*. The last was a plantation song, "Melon Time," *Northern Territory Times*, 3 November 1922.

139. *Northern Territory Times*, 5 January 1912.

140. Hoberman, *Darwin's Athletes*, xxiv.

141. Patricia Vertinsky and Gwendolyn Captain, "More Myth than History: American Culture and Representations of the Black Female's Athletic Ability," *Journal of Sport History* 25, no. 3 (1988): 537.

CHAPTER 7

1. Author interviews: R. Nxumalo, 19 November 1992; Makhabeleni, Natal, South Africa; S. Ntuli, 20 February 1993, Nkandla, KwaZulu, South Africa; M. Cele, 24 December 1997, Makhabeleni, KwaZulu-Natal (KZN), South Africa.

2. Peter Alegi, *Laduma! Soccer, Politics and Society in South Africa* (Pietermaritzburg: University of KwaZulu-Natal Press, 2004), 9–10; Mxolisi Mchunu, "A Modern Coming of Age: Zulu Manhood, Domestic Work, and the 'Kitchen Suit,'" in *Zulu Identities: Being Zulu Past and Present*, ed. Benedict Carton, John Laband, and Jabulani Sithole (New York: Columbia University Press, 2009), 573–82.

3. Testimony of Mkando, 20 August 1902, in C. De B. Webb and J. Wright, eds., *The James Stuart Archive of Recorded Oral Evidence Relating to the History of the Zulu and Neighbouring Peoples*, vol. 3 (Pietermaritzburg: University of Natal Press, 1986), 184–85. This volume is part of *The James Stuart Archive of Recorded Oral Evidence Relating to the History of the Zulu and Neighbouring Peoples* (Pietermaritzburg: University of Natal Press, 1976–2001; 5 vols.), hereafter referred to as *James Stuart Archive*. Author interviews: F. Nzama, 15 March 1993, Makhabeleni; M. Cele, 24 December 1997, Makhabeleni.

4. R. W. Connell, *Which Way is Up? Essays on Class, Sex and Culture* (Sydney: Allen and Unwin, 1983); R. W. Connell, *Gender and Power: Society, the Person and Sexual*

Politics (Palo Alto: Stanford University Press, 1987); R. W. Connell, *Masculinities*, 2nd ed. (Berkeley: University of California Press, 2005).

5. Rob Gilbert and Pam Gilbert, *Masculinity Goes to School* (London: Routledge, 1998), 70; Michael Messner and Donald Sabo, eds., *Sport, Men and the Gender Order: Critical Feminist Perspectives* (Champaign, IL: Human Kinetics Publishers, 1990); J. Hearn, *The Violences of Men* (Thousand Oaks, CA: Sage, 1998); Jim McKay, Michael A. Messner, and Don Sabo, eds., *Masculinities, Gender Relations, and Sport* (Thousand Oaks, CA: Sage, 2000).

6. Anne Mager, "Youth Organisations and the Construction of Masculine Identities in the Ciskei and Transkei, 1945–1960," *Journal of Southern African Studies* 24 (1998): 653–67; Robert Morrell, "Of Boys and Men: Masculinity and Gender in Southern African Studies," *Journal of Southern African Studies* 24 (1998): 605–30.

7. Phyllis Martin, *Leisure and Society in Colonial Brazzaville* (Cambridge: Cambridge University Press, 1995); Emmanuel Akyeampong, *Drink, Power, and Cultural Change: A Social History of Alcohol in Ghana* (Portsmouth, NH: Heinemann, 1996); Cecile Badenhorst and Charles Mather, "Tribal Recreation and Recreating Tribalism: Culture, Leisure and Social Control on South Africa's Gold Mines, 1940–1950," *Journal of Southern African Studies* 23 (1997): 473–89; Laura Fair, *Pastimes and Politics: Culture, Community, and Identity in Post-Abolition Urban Zanzibar, 1890–1945* (Athens: Ohio University Press, 2001); Robert Morrell, ed., *Changing Men in Southern Africa* (London: Palgrave, 2001); John Nauright, *Long Run to Freedom: Sport, Cultures and Identities in South Africa* (Morgantown: Fitness Information Technology Press, 2010).

8. Emmanuel Akyeampong and Charles Ambler, "Leisure in African History: An Introduction," *International Journal of African Historical Studies* 35 (2002): 1–16.

9. IsiZulu definitions of leisure and sport: C. Doke, D. Malcolm, J. Sikakana, and B. Vilakazi, *English-Zulu Dictionary* (Johannesburg: Witwatersrand University Press, 1958), 264, 462; C. Doke and B. Vilakazi, *Zulu-English Dictionary* (Johannesburg: Witwatersrand University Press, 1948), xxiv, 152, 315; C. Roberts, *The Zulu-Kafir Language,* 3rd ed. (London: Kegan Paul, Trench, Trubner & Co., 1909), 140, 160; P. La Hausse de la Louvie`re, "'The Cows of Nongoloza': Youth, Crime and Amalaita Gangs in Durban, 1900–1936," *Journal of Southern African Studies* 16 (1990): 86–87.

10. Age-set migrant labor and colonial *isibalo,* that is, compulsory public works: Shula Marks, *Reluctant Rebellion: The 1906–1908 Disturbances in Natal* (Oxford: Clarendon Press, 1970), 43–44.

11. Gavin Whitelaw, "A Brief Archaeology of Agriculturists in KwaZulu-Natal," *Zulu Identities,* ed. Carton et al., 47–61; Jeff Guy, "Analysing Pre-capitalist Societies in Southern Africa," *Journal of Southern African Studies* 14 (1987): 18–37.

12. Sifiso Ndlovu, "A Reassessment of Women's Power in the Zulu Kingdom," in *Zulu Identities,* ed. Carton et al., 112–13.

13. See, for example, R. C. Samuelson, *Long, Long Ago* (Durban: Knox, 1929); Rev. C. Callaway, *The Religious System of the Amazulu: Izinyanga Zokubula; or Divination, as Existing Among the Amazulu in Their Own Words* (Pietermaritzburg: Davis and Sons, 1870).

14. David Hedges, "Trade and Politics in Southern Mozambique and Zululand, c. 1750–1830" (DPhil thesis, University of London, 1978), 208–14; John Wright, "Pre-Shakan Age-Group Formation among the Northern Nguni," *Natalia* 8 (1978): 22–30; John Wright and Carolyn Hamilton, "Traditions and Transformations: The Phongolo-

Mzimkhulu Region in the Late Eighteenth and Early Nineteenth Centuries," in *Natal and Zululand: From Earliest Times to 1910*, ed. Andrew Duminy and Bill Guest (Pietermaritzburg: University of Natal Press, 1989), 49–82.

15. Samuelson, *Long, Long Ago*, 390–91.

16. Ibid., 354–55.

17. Peter Colenbrander, "The Zulu Kingdom, 1828–79," in Duminy and Guest, *Natal and Zululand*, 96–109.

18. Testimony of Mtshanyankomo, 11 January 1922, *James Stuart Archive*, vol. 4, 115; J. Stuart, *uHlangakula* (London: Longmans, Green, 1924), 105–19.

19. Zulu's King Zwelithini and President Jacob Zuma joined together at the 2009 *umkhosi wokweshwama*: http://www.news24.com/SouthAfrica/News/Ukweshwama-ritual-under-way-20091205 (accessed 12 November 2011). Zuma's traditional childhood in Nkandla: Benedict Carton, "Why is the '100% Zulu Boy' So Popular?" *Bulletin of Concerned African Scholars* 84 (2010).

20. J. Guy, *The Destruction of the Zulu Kingdom* (London: Longmans, 1979), 41–50; R. Cope, *Ploughshares of War: The Origins of the Anglo-Zulu War of 1879* (Pietermaritzburg: University of Natal Press, 1999), 236–41.

21. H. Bartle Frere, "On the Laws Affecting the Relations Between Civilized and Savage Life, as Bearing on the Dealings of Colonists with Aborigines," *Journal of the Anthropological Institute of Great Britain and Ireland* 11 (1882): 329, 332–37; Cope, *Ploughshares of War*, 236–41; Carl Griesbach, "On the Weapons and Implements Used by the Kaffir Tribes and Bushmen of South Africa," *Journal of the Anthropological Institute of Great Britain and Ireland* 1 (1872): cliv–clv. Griesbach traveled extensively in Natal and Portuguese East Africa in 1869 and 1870.

22. John Laband, *Kingdom in Crisis: The Zulu Response to the British Invasion of 1879* (Pietermaritzburg: University of Natal Press, 1992), 81–86; Guy, *Destruction of the Zulu*, 54–61.

23. Land shortage: Statement Resident Commissioner, 9 July 1896, Minutes Meeting of Chiefs, Eshowe, pp. 4–5, NKA309/95, Nkandla Minute (Min.) Papers, 3/2/1/1, 1/NKA, Pietermaritzburg Archives Repository (PAR); John Lambert, *Betrayed Trust: Africans and the State in Colonial Natal* (Pietermaritzburg: University of Natal Press, 1995), 71–85, 90–97, 105–6, 123.

24. Jeff Guy and Motlasi Thabane, "The Ma-Rashea: A Participant's Perspective," in *Class, Community and Conflict*, ed. Belinda Bozzoli (Johannesburg: Ravan Press, 1987), 455; P. Mayer and I. Mayer, "Self-Organization of the Red Xhosa," in *Socialization: The Approach from Social Anthropology*, ed. P. Mayer (London, Tavistock, 1970), 159–74; T. Dunbar Moodie and Vivienne Ndatshe, *Going for Gold: Men, Mines, and Migration* (Berkeley: University of California Press, 1994), 180–210.

25. E. Brookes and N. Hurwitz, *Natal Regional Survey: The Native Reserves of Natal*, vol. 7 (Cape Town: Oxford University Press, 1957); Aran MacKinnon, "The Persistence of the Cattle Economy in Zululand, South Africa, c. 1900–50," *Canadian Journal of African Studies* 33 (1999): 98–136; Charles Simkins, "Agricultural Production in the African Reserves of South Africa, 1918–1969," *Journal of Southern African Studies* 7 (1981): 256–83.

26. Testimony of Seme, 14 May 1925, *James Stuart Archive*, vol. 5, 273–76.

27. Struggles to control black urban "leisure" in Natal: Goolam Vahed, "Control of African Leisure Time in Durban in the 1930s," *Journal of Natal and Zulu History* 18 (1998): 67–123.

28. Veit Erlmann, "'Horses in the Race Course': The Domestication of Ingoma Dancing in South Africa, 1929–39," *Popular Music* 8 (1989): 259–73; Paul La Hausse de la Louvie`re, "'The Cows of Nongoloza': Youth Crime and Amalaita Gangs in Durban, 1900–1960," *Journal of Southern African Studies* 16 (1990): 79–111; Alegi, *Laduma!*, 9–11, 13–16, 24–38.

29. Testimony of Sisekelo, 13 April 1902, *James Stuart Archive*, vol. 5, 364; Helen Bradford, *A Taste of Freedom: The ICU in Rural South Africa, 1924–1930* (New Haven, CT: Yale University Press, 1987), 46–48; La Hausse de la Louvie`re, "Cows of Nongoloza," 87.

30. Author interviews: F. Nzama, 15 March 1993, Makhabeleni; M. Cele, 24 December 1997, Makhabeleni; Marie-Heleen Coetzee, "Zulu Stick Fighting: A Socio-Historical Overview," in *InYo: Journal of Alternative Perspectives* (2002), n.p. (http://ejmas.com/jalt/jaltart_Coetzee_0902.htm [first accessed June 2006]). As Anne Mager shows for the Transkei in the mid-1900s, vanquished Xhosa stick fighters could display "excessively aggressive behaviour towards girls." Future investigations ought to probe whether Zulu stick fighters, in Mager's words, aimed to "extract f eminine obedience literally through the wielding of sticks": Mager, "Youth Organisations," 663.

31. See, for example: Administrator of Native Law Criminal Record Book, 1898–1903, Mahlabathini Magistrate, 1/2/1/1, PAR; Rep. Secretary for Native Affairs (SNA), August 1900, p. 22, 1430/1900, Min. Papers SNA, 1/1/290, 1/SNA, PAR; Statement of Ziboni, 25 October 1905, p. 5, 985/1905, Min. SNA, Min. Papers SNA, 1/1/328, 1/SNA, PAR.

32. Margrethe Silberschmidt, "Disempowerment of men in rural and urban east Africa: Implications for male identity and sexual behavior," *World Development* 29 (2001): 657–71; Thokozani Xaba, "Masculinity and Its Malcontents: The Confrontation between 'Struggle Masculinity' and 'Post-Struggle Masculinity' (1990–1997)," in *Changing Men in Southern Africa*, ed. R. Morrell (Pietermaritzburg: University of Natal Press, 2001), 105–24; Thembisa Waetjen, *Workers and Warriors Masculinity and the Struggle for Nation in South Africa* (Champaign: University of Illinois Press, 2004).

33. This stark dichotomy between rightless black subjects and rights-bearing settler citizens is analyzed in an important study of late-colonialism in Natal and other territories of British-ruled Sub-Saharan Africa: Mahmood Mamdani, *Citizen and Subject: Contemporary Africa and the Legacy of Late Colonialism* (Princeton, NJ: Princeton University Press, 1996).

34. Jonathan Clegg, "*Ukubuyisa Isidumbu*—'Bringing Back the Body': An Examination into the Ideology of Vengeance in the Msinga and Mpofana Rural Locations, 1882–1944," in *Working Papers in Southern African Studies,* ed. P. Bonner, vol. 2 (Johannesburg: Ravan Press, 198), 168–69.

35. Men were allowed to carry only one stick. Stick-fighting regulations and prohibitions against *umkhosi* and similar rituals: Circular, Under Secretary for Native Affairs (USNA), 1907, SNA 738/1907, I183/1907, Impendhle (Polela) Min. Papers, 3/1/3, 1/IPD, PAR; Telegram, Civil Commissioner, Eshowe, to Colonial Secretary, 1 April 1898, 705/1898, 1/1/280, 1/SNA, PAR; Min. Mag. Umsinga, to USNA, 29 December 1896, 117/1897, Weenen Min. Papers, 3/2/2, 1/WEN, PAR; Testimony of Maziyana, 25 April 1905, *James Stuart Archive*, p. 292.

36. Annual Rep. Mag. Kranskop, 31 December 1898, KK1A/1899, Min. Papers Kranskop, 3/1/2, 1/KRK, PAR; *Mvinjwa and 17 others versus Rex*, 15 July 1903, SNA Min. Papers, 1/1/302, 1/SNA, PAR. Court Statement, Official Witness Nyandeni Mvalase; Statement Headman Lundayi, Umsinga; Umsinga, 28 November 1905, 3213/1905, SNA Min. Papers, 1/1/330, 1/SNA, PAR; Benedict Carton, *Blood from Your Children: The Colonial Origins of Generational Conflict* (Charlottesville: University Press of Virginia, 2000), 61–62, 92–93.

37. Clegg, *"Ukubuyisa Isidumbu*—'Bringing Back the Body.'"

38. It should be noted that our respondents also admired the advantages of other athletic bodies; namely, the lithe, lightning-quick competitor who could inflict damage as he lunged into the clench: Author interviews: S. Mchunu, 23 January 1993; R. Nxumalo, 19 November 1992; Makhabeleni; S. Ntuli, 20 February 1993, Nkandla; M. Cele, 24 December 1997, Makhabeleni; personal communication between Johnny Clegg and Benedict Carton, 6 January 2006, Makhabeleni; Daniel Mck. Malcolm, "Broadcasts Talks on the Bantu," 292(8), c. 1940s, Daniel Mck. Malcolm Papers, Killie Campbell Library (KCL), University of KwaZulu-Natal (UKZN), Durban. In the 1930s and 1940s, Malcolm visited rural Zulu communities as chief inspector of native education in Natal.

39. Testimony of Mangati, 15 December 1920, *James Stuart Archive*, vol. 2, 215, 222; see also Testimony of Maxibana, 31 December 1913, *James Stuart Archive*, vol. 2, 241–42; Colenbrander, "The Zulu Kingdom," 104; Author interview: M. Dube, 17 September 1992, Thukela River Mouth, Eshowe, Natal.

40. Samuelson, *Long, Long Ago*, 373–74.

41. J. Clegg, "The Social Construction of Zulu Masculinity—Stick-fighting, the Giya and the Dance," Department of Social Anthropology, University of the Witwatersrand (Johannesburg), 2004, Mimeo; E. Gunner and M. Gwala, *Musho! Zulu Popular Praises* (Lansing: Michigan State University Press, 1991), 230; Bonner and Ndima, "Roots of Violence and Zuluness"; Coetzee, "Zulu Stick Fighting"; Author interviews: S. Mchunu, 23 January 1993; F. Nzama, 15 March 1993; Makhabeleni.

42. For historical evidence of the "war captain" as *igoso*, see Bradford, *Taste of Freedom*, 46.

43. Samuelson, *Long, Long Ago*, 373; J. Clegg, "The Social Construction of Zulu Masculinity"; *Regina versus Mamfona and Others*, 27 October 1897, 1177/97, Stanger Min. Papers, 1/5/1/4, 1/SGR, Durban Archives Repository (DAR); Author interviews: R. Nxumalo, 19 November 1992; Makhabeleni; S. Ntuli, 20 February 1993, Nkandla; M. Cele, 24 December 1997, Makhabeleni; Mck. Malcolm, "Broadcasts Talks on the Bantu," 292.

44. Samuelson, *Long, Long Ago*, 373.

45. Personal communication, Dingani Mthethwa and Benedict Carton, 6 April 2006; 8 August 2006; Washington, DC; Gunner and Gwala, *Musho!*, 1–2; Erlmann, "Horses in the Race Course," 267; A. Vilakazi, *Zulu Transformations* (Pietermaritzburg: University of Natal Press, 1965), 80–85.

46. Samuelson, *Long, Long Ago*, 373–77; Coetzee, "Zulu Stick Fighting."

47. Personal communication, Dingani Mthethwa and Benedict Carton, 6 April 2006, Washington, DC; Benedict Carton interviews: S. Mchunu, 23 January 1993; R. Nxumalo, 19 November 1992; Makhabeleni, Natal; S. Ntuli, 20 February 1993, Nkandla, KwaZulu; Testimony of Mpatshana and Nsuze, 31 May 1912, *Stuart Archive*,

vol. 3, 325–26; Clegg, *"Ukubuyisa Isidumbu*—'Bringing Back the Body,'" 165–81; Jonathan Clegg, "Towards an Understanding of African Dance: The Zulu *Isishameni Style*," in *Papers Presented at the Second Symposium on Ethnomusicology,* ed. A. Tracey (Grahamstown, Rhodes University, 1982), 8; Alegi, *Laduma!* 10.

48. Clegg, *"Ukubuyisa Isidumbu*—'Bringing Back the Body'"; Benedict Carton, "Locusts Fall from the Sky: Manhood and Migrancy in KwaZulu," in Morrell, *Changing Men,* 136–38; Bradford, *Taste of Freedom,* 46; Vilakazi, *Zulu Transformations,* 80–85; Mck. Malcolm, "Broadcast Talks on the Bantu," 292; violent ("factional") conflicts over resources: Min. SNA to Mag. Kranskop, 29 January 1902; Statement Zikizwayo, Umvoti, 24 July 1902, 299/2902; SNA Min. Papers, 1/1/295, 1/SNA, PAR.

49. The word for *ingwadi/umgwadi*, namely umakoti, is a *hlonipha* term: Testimony of Mkando, 20 August 1902, *James Stuart Archive,* vol. 3, 184–85.

50. Testimony of Mpengula Mbande, in "Part IV. Abatakati; or, Medical Magic and Witchcraft," in Callaway, *The Religious System of the Amazulu: Izinyanga Zokubula,* 439–40; Author interviews: F. Nzama, 15 March 1993; M. Cele, 24 December 1997; Makhabeleni.

51. Shaka's "illegitimacy" and resulting development as a warrior: Testimony of Baleni, 14 May 1914; Testimony of Jantshi, 16 and 17 February 1903; *James Stuart Archive,* vol. 1, 32; 188–89, 199–200; Testimony of Mkebeni, 17 September 1921, *James Stuart Archive,* vol. 3, 198–200; Testimony of Ndhlovu, 9 November 1902, *James Stuart Archive,* vol. 4, 201–6;

52. Yandisa Sikweyiya and Rachel Jewkes, "Force and Temptation: South African Men's Accounts of Coercion into Sex by Men and Women," *Culture, Health & Sexuality,* 11 (2009): 529–41.

53. Testimony of Mpengula Mbande, in "Part IV. Abatakati; or, Medical Magic and Witchcraft," in Callaway, *The Religious System of the Amazulu: Izinyanga Zokubula,* 439–40.

54. *Long, Long Ago,* 399.

55. Testimony of Seme, 14 May 1925, *James Stuart Archive,* vol. 5, 273; R. Rive and T. Couzens, *Seme: The Founder of the ANC* (Johannesburg: Skotaville, 1991), 75–81.

56. Testimony of Seme, 18 May 1925, *James Stuart Archive,* vol. 5, 275–76.

57. Ibid., 271–72.

58. Mark Hunter, "Fathers without *Amandla*: Zulu-Speaking Men and Fatherhood," in *Baba: Men and Fatherhood in South Africa,* ed. Linda Richter and Robert Morrell (Pretoria: HSRC Press, 2006), 99–107; Paul Maylam, "The Changing Political Economy of the Region," in *Political Economy and Identities in KwaZulu-Natal: Historical Perspectives,* ed. Robert Morrell (Durban: Indicator Press, 1996), 98–101; Testimony of Mbokodo, 6 November 1913, *James Stuart Archive,* vol. 3, 11; personal communication between Johnny Clegg and Benedict Carton, 6 January, 7 January 2006; Author interview: M. Cele, 24 December 1997, Makhabeleni.

59. *Ngoma* spinoffs include isishameni: Clegg, "Towards an Understanding of African Dance," 8–14; H. Tracey, *Lalela Zulu: 100 Zulu Lyrics* (Johannesburg: African Music Society, 1948), 12, 92; La Hausse, "Cows of Nongoloza," 88.

60. Erlmann, "Horses in the Race Course," 268.

61. *Third Annual Natal Native Dancing Championships* (Durban: A. Fishwick & Co., 1941), Washington, DC: Edgar-Carton Collection.

62. Correspondence, Chief Constable to Town Clerk, Durban, 11 October 1934, Durban Town Clerk, File 6, 467, DAR; Erlmann, "Horses in the Race Course."

63. Erlmann, "Horses in the Race Course," 265, 267; La Hausse, "Cows of Nongoloza," 95, 97.

64. La Hausse, "Cows of Nongoloza," 88.

65. Ibid., 89–91, 98.

66. Benedict Carton, "Remaking Zulu Identity in the Era of Globalization," *Global Studies Review* 1 (2005), 8; see also Gerhard Schutte, "Tourists and Tribes in the 'New' South Africa," *Ethnohistory* 50 (2003): 473–87.

CHAPTER 8

1. Peggy Pascoe, "Miscegenation Law, Court Cases, and Ideologies of 'Race' in Twentieth-Century America," *Journal of American History* 83 (1996): 44–69.

2. Chuck Wills, *Destination America: The People and Cultures That Created a Nation* (New York: DK Publishing, 2005), 164. Half of that number traveled between 1900 to 1910.

3. Richard D. Alba, ed., *Ethnicity and Race in the USA: Toward the Twenty-First Century* (New York: Routledge, 1989), 139; Pascoe, "Miscegenation Law"; Matthew Frye Jacobson, *Whiteness of a Different Color: European Immigrants and the Alchemy of Race* (Cambridge, MA: Harvard University Press, 1998), 56–57; Regina Barreca, ed., *Don't Tell Mama* (New York: Penguin Books, 2002), 217; Thomas Guglielmo, "No Color Barrier: Italians, Race, and Power in the United States," in Guglielmo and Salerno, eds., *Are Italians White?*, 29–43 (quote, 36).

4. Frances M. Malpezzi and William A. Clements, *Italian-American Folklore* (Little Rock: August House, 1992); Raymond A. Belliotti, *Seeking Identity: Individualism versus Community in an Ethnic Context* (Lawrence: University of Kansas Press, 1995), 162–63; Gay Talese, *Unto the Sons* (New York: Alfred A. Knopf, 1992), 227; John Graf and Steve Skorpad, *Chicago Monuments, Markers, and Memorials* (Chicago: Arcadia, 2002), 43; Orm Overland, *Immigrant Minds: American Identities: Making the United States Home, 1870–1930* (Urbana: University of Illinois Press, 2000), 9, 69–75.

5. Dickerson's ethnic identity is still a matter of some contention. Baseball Hall of Fame Archives, Bodie files. Brian Mc Kenna, "Professional Baseball and Football: A Close Relationship," *Coffin Corner* 29, no. 6 (2007): 12–16; *Chicago Tribune*, 8 March 1911, 21; 8 February 1912, C2; 15 May 1911, 12; 26 May 1911, 11; 29 May 1911, 11; 16 July 1911, B2; 24 August 1911, 10; 7 August 1912, 16; 15 March 1914, B2; 4 June 1913, 15; 16 October 1913, 13; 18 April 1914, 15; 4 May 1914, 15.

6. Lazzeri cited in the *Sporting News*, 11 December 1930, in Lawrence Baldassaro, "Go East Paesani: Early Italian Major Leaguers from the West Coast," in *Italian Immigrants Go West: The Impact of Locale on Ethnicity*, ed. Janet E. Worrall, Carol Bonomo Albright, and Elvira G. Di Fabio (Cambridge, MA: Italian American Historical Association, 2003), 100–108 (quote 106).

7. Stephen Fox, *Big Leagues: Professional Baseball, Football, and Basketball in National Memory* (New York: William Morrow & Co., 1994), 106–7; Baldassaro, "Go East Paesani," 106.

8. For examples, see *Manitowoc (WI) Herald News*, 22 June 1927, 9; *San Antonio Light*, 28 July 1927, 14; *Burlington (NC) Daily Times*, 1 September 1927, 4; *Port Arthur (TX) News*, 12 March 1928, 18; *Newcastle (PA) News*, 2 July 1928, 18; *Bismarck (ND) Tribune*, 13 September 1928, 12; *Ogden (UT) Standard Examiner*, 8 February 1931; *Lima (OH) News*, 11 June 1931, 6; *Frederick (MD) News-Post*, 10 March 1932, 3; *Jefferson City (MO) Post Tribune*, 22 June 1929, 8; *Altoona (PA) Mirror*, 29 April 1937, 13; *Arizona Independent Republic*, 9 October 1939, 8; *Lowell (MA) Sun*, 10 June 1947, 1; *Racine (WI) Journal Times*, 13 July 1948, 17.

9. *Outing* 30 (June 1897): 306; *Outing* 33 (October 1898): 92; *Outing* 34 (June 1899): 316; *La Notizia*, 13 October 1933, 6; *Boston Daily Globe*, 31 July 1916, 7; "Brignolia Recalls His Many Sports Feats," *Portland Press Herald*, 20 July 1950, 17. Accounts variously spell the surname as Brignoli, Brignola, and Brignolia.

10. Matthew Llewellyn, "'Viva Italia! Viva Italia!' Dorando Pietri and the North American Professional Marathon Craze," *International Journal of the History of Sport* 25 (2008), 710–36; *New York Times*, 18 November 1908, 7; 23 November 1908, 9; 26 November 1908, 1; 28 November 1908, 6; 4 December 1908, 9; 7 December 1908, 7; 16 December 1908, 1; 12 January 1909, 7; 16 March 1909, 7; 3 April 1909, 7; 9 May 1909, S1; *Chicago Tribune*, 26 November 1908, 14; 14 January 1909, 10; 17 January 1909, B1; 20 January 1909, 10; 26 February 1909, 10; 16 March 1909, 8; 4 April 1909, C1; 22 November 1911, 8. My own analysis of named spectators in the *Chicago City Directory, 1909* (Chicago: Chicago Directory Co., 1909) provided insight into the social class of participants.

11. http://www.ddavid.com/formula1/depalma.htm; http://motorsportshall offame.com/main/03_halloffame.htm.

12. http://www.exploratorium.edu/baseball/nelson.html; http://www.barbara gregorich.com/clem.htm; Sarah Bair, "American Sports, 1910–1919," in *Encyclopedia of Sports in America: A History from Foot Races to Extreme Sports*, ed. Murry Nelson (Westport, CT: Greenwood Press, 2009), 160–61.

13. Gail Ingham Berlage, "From Bloomer Girls' Baseball to Women's Softball: A Cultural Journey resulting in Women's Exclusion from Baseball," in *The Cooperstown Symposium on Baseball and American Culture, 1999*, ed. Peter M. Rutkoff (Jefferson, NC: McFarland & Co., 2000), 245–60; "Margaret Gisolo," photocopy adopted from Barbara Gregorich, *Women at Play*, 30–31, in Italian American Renaissance Foundation Library, miscellaneous folder; http://www.niashf.org/index2.cfm?ContentID=58& InducteeID=100 (accessed 6 June 2009); Angela Teja and Marco Impiglia, "Italy," in *European Cultures in Sport: Examining the Nations and Regions*, ed. James Riordan and Arnd Kruger (Bristol, UK: Intellect Books, 2003), 139–59 (quote, 145–46).

14. http://www.niashf.org/index2.cfm?ContentID=40&InducteeID=96 (accessed 6 June 2009); http://www.ishof.org/honorees/92/92egsaville.html (accessed 6 August 2009); http://www.hickoksports.com/history/usgymchamps. shtml (accessed 2 August 2010); http://www.sports-reference.com/olympics/ athletes/ca/connie-caruccio-lenz-1.html (accessed 2 August 2010). Thanks to Gertrud Pfister for alerting me to the gymnasts.

15. Thomas Hauser and Stephen Brunt, *Italian Stallions: Heroes of Boxing's Glory Days* (Toronto: Sports Media Publishing, 2003), 14–15; http://www.hickoksports. com/biography (accessed November 16, 2008).

16. "Frank Klaus Sees Firpo in Action, " *New York Times*, 2 September 1923, 18.

17. "Firpo Had the Title Within His Grasp," *New York Times*, 25 September 1923, 1.

18. Stephen Fox, *The Unknown Internment: An Oral History of the Relocation of Italian Americans during World War II* (Boston: Twayne Publishers, 1990), 15, 21–33, 69.

19. Gardaphe, *From Wise Guys to Wise Men*, 27, 34; Andrew F. Rolle, *The Italian Americans: Troubled Roots* (Norman: University of Oklahoma Press, 1980), 171–72; Ellexis Boyle, "Measuring Up to American Manhood: Racism and the Development of 'Race' in the History of Competitive Bodybuilding," *Stadion* 31 (2005): 71–85; J. F. Kasson, *Houdini, Tarzan, and the Perfect Man: The White Male Body and the Challenge of Modernity in America* (New York: Hill and Wang, 2001), 32; Charles Gaines, *Charles Atlas, Yours in Perfect Manhood* (New York: Simon and Schuster, 1982).

20. Rolle, *The Italian Americans*, 171–72.

21. http://en.wikipedia.org/wiki/Tony_Sansone (accessed 24 April 2009).

22. Patricia Boscia-Mule, *Authentic Ethnicities: The Interaction of Ideology, Gender Power, and Class in the Italian-American Experience* (Westport, CT: Greenwood Press, 1999); Richard W. Rees, *Shades of Difference: A History of Ethnicity in America* (Lanham, MD: Rowman and Littlefield, 2007), 5–31; 72–109.

23. Richard Gambino, *Blood of My Blood: The Dilemma of the Italian-Americans* (Garden City, NY: Anchor Books, 1975 [1974]), 128–33 (quote, 128); Richard Ben Cramer, *Joe Di Maggio: The Hero's Life* (New York: Simon and Schuster, 2000).

24. Willie Pep with Robert Sacchi, *Willie Pep remembers . . . Friday's Heroes* (New York: Friday's Heroes, 1973), 4–8, 5 (quote).

25. "Prisoners in Our Home"; Guglielmo, *White on Arrival*, 173; Mormino, *Immigrants on the Hill*, 219–20; Yogi Berra and Ed Fitzgerald, *Yogi: The Autobiography of a Professional Baseball Player* (Garden City, NY: Doubleday & Co., 1961), 67–78; Robert Elias, *The Empire Strikes Out: How Baseball Sold U.S. Foreign Policy and Promoted the American Way Abroad* (New York: New Press, 2010), 338; Larry Smith, *Iwo Jima: World War II Veterans Remember the Greatest Battle of the Pacific* (New York: W. W. Norton & Co., 2008), 96–97 (quote). Paola A. Sensi-Isolani, "Tradition and Transition in a California Paese," in Vecoli, *Italian Immigration in Rural and Small Town America*, 88–109; Mangione, *An Ethnic at Large*, 345; Gambino, *Blood of My Blood*, 313–16, 321, estimates as many as 1,500,000 Italian American men in US military services during the war. Official records are indeterminant.

26. Gallo, *Old Bread, New Wine*, 232; Jerre Mangione and Ben Morreale, *La Storia: Five Centuries of the Italian American Experience* (New York: HarperCollins, 1992), 341; Italian American Sports Hall of Fame, New Orleans; Pete Hamill, *Why Sinatra Matters* (Boston: Little, Brown & Co., 1998), 133, states thirteen Italian Americans were awarded the Medal of Honor. http://www.cimorelli.com/pie/heroes/basilone.htm (15 May 2009); Jim Proser with Jerry Cutter, *I'm Staying with My Boys: The Heroic Life of Sgt. John Basilone, USMC* (New York: St. Martin's Griffin, 2010); Luconi, "Forging an Ethnic Identity," 30.

27. John E. Dreifort, "Anything but Ordinary: POW Sports in a Barbed Wire World," *Journal of Sport History* 34 (2007): 415–37; Bryan Smith, "To hell and back," *Chicago Sun-Times*, 3 February 2002, 24A.

28. Smith, "To hell and back," 23A–26A.

29. Laura Hillenbrand, *Unbroken: A World War II Story of Survival, Resilience, and Redemption* (New York: Random House, 2010); http://www.usc.edu/dept/pubrel/trojan_family/summer03/F_Zamperini.html (accessed 4 June 2009).

30. Salvatore J. La Gumina, *Wop! A Documentary History of Anti-Italian Discrimination* (Toronto: Guernica, 1999 [1973]), 289–98; Gambino, *Blood of My Blood*, 245, on the education survey, 329–46 versus blacks; Michael Novak, *The Rise of the Unmeltable Ethnics: Politics and Culture in the Seventies* (New York: Macmillan Co., 1972 [1971]), 20–25; Gerald D. Suttles, *The Social Order of the Slum: Ethnicity and Territory in the Inner City* (Chicago: University of Chicago Press, 1968); Stefano Luconi, *From Paesani to White Ethnics: The Italian Experience in Philadelphia* (Albany: State University of New York Press, 2001), 125–39; Richard W. Rees, *Shades of Difference: A History of Ethnicity in America* (Lanham, MD: Littlefield, 2007), 5, 151; James R. Barrett and David Roediger, "In Between Peoples: Race, Nationality, and the 'New Immigrant' Working Class," *Journal of American Ethnic History* 16 (Spring 1997): 3–44; Gallo, *Old Bread, New Wine*, 277–89 (quote, 286); A. V. Margavi and Jerome J. Salomone, *Bread and Respect: The Italians of Louisiana* (Gretna, LA: Pelican Pub., 2002), 189–90, 197. Among the studies on ethnic social mobility, see David L. Featherman, "The Socioeconomic Achievement of White Religio-Ethnic Subgroups: Social and Psychological Explanations," *American Sociological Review* 36 (1971): 207–22.

31. Maria Laurino, *Were You Always an Italian? Ancestors and Other Icons of Italian America* (New York: W. W. Norton & Co., 2000), 122–31, 150–58; Leonard Maltin, "Pacino De Niro Together," *USA Weekend*, 5–7 September 2008, 6–8.

32. Anderson Cooper, "60 Minutes: Lady Gaga," 5 June 2011.

33. Jon Pareles, "Lady Gaga's roaring retort," *International Herald Tribune*, 21–22 May 2011, 21.

34. Belliotti, *Seeking Identity*, 166–89; Tuisani quote in Maria Perrino, ed., *Italian American Autobiographies* (St. Paul: University of Minnesota Immigration History Research Center, 1993), vi.

CHAPTER 9

1. *Chicago Defender*, 31 July 1948, 11.

2. See John Hoberman, *Darwin's Athletes: How Sport Has Damaged Black America and Preserved the Myth of Race* (Boston: Houghton Mifflin Company, 1997), xxi.

3. Scholarly work on the subject of race and sport, particularly the African American experience, has exploded in the last ten to fifteen years. Recent influential studies on some of the key issues involved in the subject are Hoberman, *Darwin's Athletes*, and David K. Wiggins, *Glory Bound: Black Athletes in a White America* (Syracuse, NY: Syracuse University Press, 1997). There are also excellent biographies on Jackie Robinson and Jesse Owens that provide valuable historical context and take up issues of athleticism and the cultural construction of race, such as Jules Tygiel, *Baseball's Great Experiment: Jackie Robinson and His Legacy*, expanded ed. (New York: Oxford University Press, 1997), and William J. Baker, *Jesse Owens: An American Life* (New York: Free Press, 1986). John Carroll has covered similar territory for football with a lesser-known twentieth-century athlete in *Fritz Pollard: Pioneer in Racial Advancement* (Urbana: University of Illinois Press, 1998). Two valuable historiographical essays exist on the subject. Jeffrey T. Sammons, "'Race' and Sport: A Critical Historical Examination," *Journal of Sport History* 21 (Fall 1994): 203–78, although at this juncture somewhat dated, provides an important assessment of the scholarship, especially his summary on gender on pages 266–69. For a recent, extensive bibliography, see

David K. Wiggins, "The African American Athletic Experience," in *The African American Experience: An Historiographical and Bibliographical Guide,* ed. Arvarh E. Strickland and Robert E. Weems Jr. (Westport, CT: Greenwood Press, 2001), 255–77. While the field of African American women in sports has lagged somewhat behind that of men, the 1990s has witnessed substantial growth in this area as well. Some of the best include "'Cinderellas' of Sport: Black Women in Track and Field," in Susan K. Cahn, *Coming on Strong: Gender and Sexuality in Twentieth-Century Women's Sport* (New York: Free Press, 1994), 110–39; "Members Only: Class, Race, and Amateur Tennis for Women in the 1950s," in Mary Jo Festle, *Playing Nice: Politics and Apologies in Women's Sports* (New York: Columbia University Press, 1996), 53–71; Gwendolyn Captain, "Enter Ladies and Gentlemen of Color: Gender, Sport, and the Ideal of African American Manhood and Womanhood During the Late Nineteenth and Early Twentieth Centuries," *Journal of Sport History* 18 (Spring 1991): 81–102; Patricia Vertinsky and Gwendolyn Captain, "More Myth than History: American Culture and Representations of the Black Female's Athletic Ability, " *Journal of Sport History* 25 (Fall 1998): 532–61; Cindy Himes Gissendanner, "African-American Women in Competitive Sport, 1920–1960," in *Women, Sport, and Culture,* ed. Susan Birrell and Cheryl L. Cole (Champaign, IL: Human Kinetics, 1994); Gissendanner, "African American Women Olympians: The Impact of Race, Gender, and Class Ideologies, 1932–1968," *Research Quarterly for Exercise and Sport* 67 (June 1996): 172–82; and Linda D. Williams, "Sportswomen in Black and White: Sports History From an Afro-American Perspective," in *Women, Media and Sport: Challenging Gender Values,* ed. Pamela J. Creedon (Thousand Oaks, CA: Sage, 1994), 45–66. One interesting phenomenon that exists in the study of black women athletes is the absence of historical biographies of these women. While biographies of Jackie Robinson, Jesse Owens, Muhammad Ali, and other male black athletes abound, the stories of even better-known women athletes such as Althea Gibson and Wilma Rudolph have been relegated to children's books. Indeed, the question of why the stories of black women athletes are appropriate for children's books but not adult literature deserves further study. In addition to Gibson and Rudolph, Alice Coachman and her quest for the gold has also been created in juvenile literature. Furthermore, the trend continues into the present. Both Jackie Joyner-Kersee and Marion Jones, two recent African American female Olympic gold medal winners, have had their stories limited to this genre.

4. Cahn, *Coming on Strong,* 114–17.

5. Ibid., 117–18. For more on the influence of work on the identity of African American women, see Jacqueline Jones, *Labor of Love, Labor of Sorrow: Black Women, Work, and the Family from Slavery to the Present* (New York: Basic Books, 1985).

6. Cahn, Coming on Strong, 121, 125–28.

7. Festle, *Playing Nice,* 55, 58. Dr. Reginald Weir was the first African American to play in a USLTA tournament, the National Indoor Championships, also in New York. This is not to be confused with the famed Forest Hills tournament, which was the National Outdoor Championships, where Althea Gibson eventually broke the color barrier in 1950. Althea Gibson, *I Always Wanted to Be Somebody* (New York: Harper and Brothers, 1958), 55.

8. Gibson, *I Always Wanted to Be Somebody,* 46.

9. Michael D. Davis, *Black American Women in Olympic Track and Field* (Jefferson, NC: McFarland & Company, 1992), 40; Ed Decker, "Alice Coachman," in *Contemporary*

Black Biography: Profiles from the International Black Community, 32 vols., ed. Shirelle Phelps (Detroit: Gale Research, 1992), 18: 29.

10. My references to the "white press" are inclusive of the following newspapers —*New York Times, Chicago Tribune, Boston Globe, Atlanta Constitution*—and *Time* and *Life* magazines. "Black press" references include the following black weeklies: *New York Age, New York Amsterdam News, Chicago Defender, Baltimore Afro-American*, and *Pittsburgh Courier* as well as *Ebony* magazine. Research into these publications' reporting of Alice Coachman's career covers 1939 through 1948, and 1950 through 1958 for Althea Gibson's. Although Gibson was featured regularly in the black press in the ate 1940s as a dominant force in the black American Tennis Association, she did not emerge in the white press until 1950. In the white press, the New York and Atlanta papers were chosen in particular because they represent the closest to a "home town" paper available for Gibson and Coachman. The black weeklies were selected in general because of their prominence in the black community as well as the influence of sportswriters such as Sam Lacy (*Baltimore Afro-American*) and Wendell Smith (*Pittsburgh Courier*) in the black sporting world.

11. The extent to which the white press highlighted gender in their news accounts is further illustrated when the neglect of women's track and field is compared with the extensive treatment accorded American female swimmers during the Olympics. Women swimmers received considerably more coverage than women track athletes, including spreads in several newspapers complete with photographs. The difference is largely attributable to the fact that swimming was an acceptable sport for women. Swimming was not thought to be injurious to women's bodies, nor did it detract from their femininity. Historian Susan Cahn argues that the acceptability of swimming over track also speaks to race and class distinctions since most swimmers were white, middle-class women. See Cahn, *Coming on Strong*, 130.

12. The *New York Times* did feature a picture of the women's track and field team marching in the opening ceremonies, although the caption did not identify them. However, no members of the U.S. women's track and field team were photographed participating in their sport. See *New York Times*, 1 August 1948, sec. 5, 3.

13. Audrey Patterson became the first African American woman to medal in the Olympic Games, taking a bronze in the 200-meter sprint.

14. "American Athletes Sweep the Olympics," *Life*, 23 August 1948, 28; *New York Times*, 15 August 1948, sec. 5, 1.

15. *Chicago Tribune*, 5 July 1942, sec. 2, 2; *Boston Globe*, 1 July 1945, sec. 2, 4; *New York Times*, 11 January 1946, 24.

16. *Chicago Tribune*, 1 July 1945, sec. 2, 4; *New York Times*, 9 July 1944, sec. 3, 1; *New York Times*, 5 August 1946, 27.

17. *New York Times*, 15 August 1948, sec. 5, 1.

18. *New York Times*, 1 July 1945, sec. 3, 3; *New York Times*, 5 August 1946, 27.

19. *Atlanta Constitution*, 8 August 1948, sec. B, 11. The *Chicago Tribune* subordinated both gender and race in their Olympic coverage but not to highlight Coachman as an athlete. Rather, it portrayed her as a victorious American. The *Tribune* dramatized the high-jump competition, describing how darkness and drizzling rain descended upon the stadium, with Coachman in the end victorious. "Thus the track meet ended as begun eight days ago, with victory for an American and the Star Spangled Banner of the United States providing the closing music" (*Chicago Tribune*,

8 August 1948, sec. 2, 1). By the 1950s, the victory would be not only for an American but also for America, as the United States and the Soviets discovered the world of international sports as another arena in which to wage their cold war. As a result, women's track and field would gain acceptability in the United States as part of the arsenal to assert American superiority over the Soviet system. For more on the Cold War status of the sport, see Cahn, *Coming on Strong,* 130–33.

20. *Pittsburgh Courier,* 9 July 1941, 16; *Baltimore Afro-American,* 11 July 1942, 23.

21. *Baltimore Afro-American,* 13 July 1940, 19. The *Chicago Defender's* Fay Young also discusses women's track and field in his weekly column, pointing to the white press's biased coverage of the 1941 AAU Indoor Nationals. See the *Chicago Defender,* 19 April 1941, 24.

22. *Chicago Defender,* 21 August 1943, 19; *Baltimore Afro-American,* 15 August 1944, 18; *Pittsburgh Courier,* 7 July 1945, 18.

23. *Baltimore Afro-American,* 7 July 1945, 18; *Baltimore Afro-American,* 15 July 1944, 18.

24. *Baltimore Afro-American,* 12 July 1941, 19. This effort to imbue Coachman with feminine qualities resurfaced during the Olympics. Although discussing in some detail that she was favored to win the high jump, the *Pittsburgh Courier* suggested that the two-year course in tailoring she completed at Tuskegee made her popular with her teammates when they needed help mending their uniforms. See the *Pittsburgh Courier,* 7 August 1948, 26.

25. *Baltimore Afro-American,* 13 July 1940, 19.

26. Coverage of the later war years and 1948 Olympic Games likewise reflects Coachman's ambiguous status within the black press community. When newspapers began to scale back their press in support of the war effort, photographic coverage of the women all but disappeared while pictures of male track and field athletes continued. Even Coachman's Olympic coverage, although expansive compared to white papers, does not compare favorably with the extensive press she received in the early years of her career.

27. Biographical information for Althea Gibson is extracted from her autobiography, Gibson, *I Always Wanted to Be Somebody* and a bio-piece written for the *New York Post,* reprinted in the magazine section of the *Pittsburgh Courier* in installments, 21, 28 September and 5, 12, 19, and 26 October 1957.

28. Festle, *Playing Nice,* 60.

29. Festle has likewise explored the theme of women tennis players being criticized for playing too masculine a game. See Festle, *Playing Nice,* 67.

30. *New York Times,* 9 September 1957, 33; "That Gibson Girl," *Time,* 26 August 1957, 44; *Chicago Tribune,* 31 August 1950, sec. 4, 2; *Boston Globe,* 9 September 1957, 11.

31. *New York Times,* 24 June 1956, sec. 5, 3; "A Cowpuncher and Negro Make Tennis History," *Life,* 23 September 1957, 56.

32. Festle, *Playing Nice,* 67.

33. *New York Times,* 7 July 1957, sec. 5, 4; *Atlanta Constitution,* 5 July 1958, 10; "Cowpuncher and Negro," 56.

34. Also at issue for Gibson that had not been a concern for Coachman was the standard of propriety and class demanded by the tennis elite. When such standards were breached, the white press could be brutal. During the 1957 Wimbledon contest, the *Boston Globe* reported that, after receiving their trophies from Queen Elizabeth II,

"Althea backed away in the prescribed fashion but the irrepressible Miss Hard turned
her back and blithely skipped toward the dressing room." As a result, Gibson's opponent became referred to as "California's chunky Darlene Hard" and the "chirpy
blonde waitress." See the *Boston Globe*, 7 July 1957, 57; "The Power Game," *Time*,
15 July 1957, 61; *Chicago Tribune*, 7 July 1957, sec. 2, 1.

35. This is not to say that race was absent from the *Times* coverage of Gibson.
Kenneth Love likened her to a "panther on an Arizona mesa" when he described how
at home she was on the tennis court. "As she waits, half crouching for a serve," he
wrote, "the comparison comes naturally to mind" (*New York Times*, 24 June 1956, sec.
5, 3). Even in describing her play at the 1957 Wimbledon win, another *Times* journalist could not resist the animal comparison: "Behind her serves and her severe ground
shots, Althea moved tigerishly to the net to cut away her volleys" (*New York Times*,
7 July 1957, sec. 5, 1).

36. For example, see *New York Times*, September 1956, sec. 2, 34; 8 July 1957, 20;
10 September 1957, 32; and 9 September 1958, 34. The reference to "our own Althea
Gibson" is from 8 July 1957, 22.

37. C. Vann Woodward, *The Strange Career of Jim Crow*, 3rd rev. ed. (New York:
Oxford University Press, 1974), 130–31.

38. For an excellent study of the integration of major league baseball, see Tygiel,
Baseball's Great Experiment. For football, see Thomas G. Smith, "Outside the Pale: The
Exclusion of Blacks from the National Football League, 1934–1946," *Journal of Sport
History* 15 (Winter 1988): 277.

39. For a good overview of the importance of the Cold War to the African
American civil rights movement, see especially the introduction in Mary L. Dudziak,
Cold War, Civil Rights: Race and the Image of American Democracy (Princeton, NJ:
Princeton University Press, 2000), 3–17.

40. Festle, *Playing Nice*, 62.

41. Gibson, *I Always Wanted to Be Somebody*, 101. Emmett Till was a fourteen-
year-old African American teenager from Chicago who was beaten and lynched for
"flirting" with a white woman in 1955. Gibson was mistaken about the location, however. The crime occurred in Mississippi, while Till was visiting his uncle. The two
men arrested for the crime were acquitted by an all-white jury in September of the
same year. Bruce Adelson, *Brushing Back Jim Crow: The Integration of Minor-League
Baseball in the American South* (Charlottesville: University Press of Virginia, 1999),
160–61.

42. Dudziak, *Cold War*, 115–18.

43. *Pittsburgh Courier*, 12 August 1950, 23; *New York Amsterdam News*, 9 September
1950, 27.

44. In particular, see sports sections in the *Baltimore Afro-American*, the *Pittsburgh
Courier*, and the *Chicago Defender* for the period 1952–1955, which all featured Gibson
and her victories in the black ATA tournaments but stayed conspicuously silent as she
struggled to regain her foothold in the white USLTA tournaments.

45. Vertinsky and Captain, "More Myth than History," 545.

46. *Chicago Defender*, 21 July 1956, 17; *Baltimore Afro-American*, 22 June 1957, 16;
Baltimore Afro-American, 30 June 1956, 14; *Baltimore Afro-American*, 21 July 1956, 7.

47. Cahn, *Coming on Strong*, 117–18.

48. *Pittsburgh Courier*, 2 September 1950, 1; *Pittsburgh Courier*, 13 July 1957, 24;
"Tennis Queen From Harlem," *Ebony*, October 1957, 91.

49. *Chicago Defender*, 7 July 1956, 17; *Chicago Defender*, 14 July 1956, 17.

50. *Chicago Defender*, 27 July 1957, 1; *Chicago Defender*, 2 July 1957, 24; *Pittsburgh Courier*, 27 July 1957, 24.

51. *Chicago Defender*, 12 July 1958, 1; *Pittsburgh Courier*, 3 August 1957, 27.

52. *Chicago Defender*, 14 July 1956, 17; *Chicago Defender*, 7 July 1956, 17; *Baltimore Afro-American*, 29 June 1957, magazine section, 2, 6.

53. *Baltimore Afro-American*, 13 July 1957, 14. For Lacy's contribution to the Jackie Robinson crusade, see Tygiel, *Baseball's Great Experiment*, 42–43, 63–64.

54. *Chicago Defender*, 7 July 1956, 17; *Pittsburgh Courier*, 27 July 1957, 24.

55. *Baltimore Afro-American*, 20 September 1958, 13; *Pittsburgh Courier*, 10 August 1957, 24.

56. *Pittsburgh Courier*, 21 September 1957, 24; *Pittsburgh Courier*, 26 October 1957, magazine section, 3; "That Gibson Girl," *Time*, 26 August 1957, 48.

57. Gibson, *I Always Wanted to Be Somebody*, 158–59.

58. See conclusion of note 3.

59. *New York Times*, 24 June 1956, sec. 5, 3.

CHAPTER 10

1. Ben Carrington, David Andrews, Steven J. Jackson, and Zbigniew Mazur, "The Global Jordanscape," in *Michael Jordan, Inc.: Corporate Sport, Media Culture, and Late Modern America*, ed. David Andrews (Albany: SUNY Press, 2001), 177–216.

2. Jean Lave and Etienne Wegner, *Situated Learning: Legitimate Peripheral Participation* (New York: Cambridge University Press, 1991).

3. W. Warner Wood, *Made in Mexico: Zapotec Weavers and the Ethnic Art Market* (Bloomington: Indiana University Press, 2008), 16.

4. Matthew Atencio and Canan Koca, "Gendered Communities of Practice and the Construction of Masculinities in Turkish Physical Education," *Gender and Education* 23 (2011): 59–72.

5. According to Mexico's Comisión Nacional Para El Desarrollo de Los Pueblos Indígenas (CDI), the Zapotec population of Mexico is approximately 777,000 and the Mixtec population is 726,000, with the majority of each residing in the state of Oaxaca.

6. See Jan Nederveen Pieterse, *Globalization and Culture: Global Mélange* (Lantham, MD: Rowman and Littlefield, 2004).

7. John Comaroff and Jean Comaroff, *Ethnicity, Inc.* (Chicago: University of Chicago Press, 2009).

8. Benjamin Feinberg, *The Devil's Book of Culture: History, Mushrooms, and Caves in Southern Mexico* (Austin: University of Texas Press, 2003), 104.

9. Lynn Stephen, *Transbordered Lives: Indigenous Oaxacans in Mexico, California, and Oregon* (Durhman, NC: Duke University Press, 2007), 315.

10. Carole Nagengast and Michael Kearney, "Mixtec Ethnicity: Social Identity, Political Consciousness and Political Activism," *Latin American Research Review* 25 (1989): 69.

11. Lynn Stephen, *Transbordered Lives: Indigenous Oaxacans in Mexico, California, and Oregon* (Durhman, NC: Duke University Press, 2007), 211; Douglas Massey, "Racial Formation and Practice: The Case of Mexicans in the United States," *Race and Social Problems* 1 (2009): 12–26.

12. Sam Quinones, *True Tales From Another Mexico: The Lynch Mob, the Popsicle Kings, Chalino, and the Bronx* (Albuquerque: University of New Mexico Press, 2001).

13. Fieldnote, 10 May 2010.

14. Personal communication, 2005.

15. Norman K. Denzin, "Symbolic Interactionism, Poststructuralism, and the Racial Subject," *Symbolic Interaction* 24 (2001): 243–49.

CHAPTER 11

1. I use the term "migrants" for individuals and groups who have migrated to and live in a different country from their country of origin. If possible and necessary, I refer to the different generations because individuals born in the host country live in a different situation from that of their parents. However, information is often lacking, and some information refers to first-generation migrants as well as their descendants.

2. Pierre Bourdieu, *Distinction: A Social Critique of the Judgment of Taste* (Cambridge, MA: Harvard University Press, 1984).

3. Thomas Faist, "Transnationalization in International Migration: Implications for the Study of Citizenship and Culture," *Ethnic and Racial Studies* 23 (2000): 189–222.

4. Steffen Mau, *Social Transnationalism: Lifeworlds beyond the Nation State* (London: Routledge, 2010).

5. Yvonne Mørck, *Bindestregsdanskere: Fortællinger om køn, generationer og etnicitet* (Rosenørns: Forlaget Sociologi, 1998); Charles Stewart, "Creolization, Ethnography, Theory," in *Creolization: History, Ethnography, Theory*, ed. Charles Stewart (Walnut Creek, CA: Left Coast Press, 2007), 1–26.

6. Peggy Levitt and B. Nadya Jaworsky, "Transnational Migration Studies: Past Developments and Future Trends," *Annual Review of Sociology* 33 (2007): 129–56.

7. Anthony Giddens, *The Consequences of Modernity* (Stanford, CA: Stanford University Press, 1990).

8. Ilknur Hacisoftaoglu and Gertrud Pfister, "Transitions: Life Stories and Physical Activities of Turkish Migrants in Denmark," *Sport in Society* 15 (2012): 385–98.

9. Anika Liversage and Vibeke Jakobsen, "Sharing Space-Gendered Patterns of Extended Household Living among Young Turkish Marriage Migrants in Denmark," *Journal of Comparative Family Studies* 41 (2010): 693–715.

10. Patricia R. Pessar and Sarah J. Mahler, "Transnational Migration: Bringing Gender In," *International Migration Review* 37 (2003): 812–46.

11. Canan Koca and Ilknur Hacisoftaoglu, "Struggling for Empowerment: Sport Participation of Women and Girls in Turkey," in *Muslim Women and Sport*, ed. Tansin Benn, Gertrud Pfister, and Haifaa Jawad (London: Routledge, 2010), 154–65.

12. Claudia Diehl, Matthias Koenig, and Kerstin Ruckdeschel, "Religiosity and Gender Equality: Comparing Natives and Muslim Migrants in Germany," *Ethnic and Racial Studies* 32 (2009): 278–301.

13. A. Toprak, *Das schwache Geschlecht—die türkischen Männer. Zwangsheirat, häusliche Gewalt, Doppelmoral der Ehre* (Freiburg im Breisgau: Lambertus Verlag, 2005).

14. Judith Lorber, *Breaking the Bowls: Degendering and Feminist Change* (New York: W. W. Norton, 2005), 6.

15. Lana F. Rakow, "Rethinking Gender Research in Communication," *Journal of Communication* 36 (1986): 11–26.

16. Candace West and Don Zimmermann, "Doing Gender," in *The Social Construction of Gender,* ed. Judith Lorber and Susan A. Farrell (Newbury Park, CA: Sage Publications, 1991), 137.

17. Anne Flintoff, Hayley Fitzgerald, and Sheila Scraton, "The Challenges of Intersectionality: Researching Difference in Physical Education," *International Studies in Sociology of Education* 18 (2008): 73–85; Gabriele Winker and Nina Degele, *Intersektionalität: Zur Analyse sozialer Ungleichheiten* (Bielefeld: Transcript, 2009).

18. Joan Acker, "Hierarchies, Jobs, Bodies: A Theory of Gendered Organisations," *Gender and Society* 4 (1990): 139–58; Sheila Scraton, Jayne Caudwell, and Samantha Holland, "Bend It Like Patel," *International Review for the Sociology of Sport* 40 (2005): 71–88; Jennifer C. Nash, "Re-thinking Intersectionality," *Feminist Review* 89 (2008): 1–15.

19. P. Bourdieu, "Program for a Sociology of Sport," *Sociology of Sport Journal,* 5 (1988): 153–61.

20. Ibid., 158.

21. Klaus Heinemann, *Einführung in die Soziologie des Sports* (Schorndorf: Hofmann, 2007).

22. Raewyn W. Connell, *Gender* (Cambridge, UK: Polity, 2002). See also John Horne, Alan Tomlinson, and Garry Whannel, *Understanding Sport: An Introduction to the Sociological and Cultural Analysis of Sport* (London: Routledge, 1999), 129–59.

23. Gert Allan Nielsen, Stine Birk Nissen, and Lene Winther Ringgaard, *Unges livsstil og dagligdag 2004* (København: Kræftens Bekæmpelse, 2005); Gert Allan Nielsen and Lene Winther Ringgaard, *Fysisk aktivitet i dagligdagen blandt 16–20årige i Danmark* (Copenhagen: Kræftens Bekæmpelse, 2004).

24. Gertrud Pfister, "Muslim Women and Sport in Diasporas," in *Muslim Women and Sport,* ed. Tansin Benn, Gertrud Pfister, and Haifaa Jawad (London: Routledge, 2010), 41–76.

25. Tansin Benn, Gertrud Pfister, and Haifaa Jawad, ed., *Muslim Women and Sport* (London: Routledge, 2010).

26. In this article I use the term *sport* in a broad sense including sport for all.

27. Paul de Knop et al., "Implications of Islam on Muslim Girls' Sport Participation in Western Europe: Literature Review and Policy Recommendations for Sport Promotion," *Sport, Education and Society* 1 (1996): 147–64.

28. http://www.dji.de/cgi-bin/projekte/output.php?projekt=66.

29. Nancy Fussan and Tina Nobis, "Zur Partizipation von Jugendlichen mit. Migrationshintergrund in Sportvereinen," in *Soziale Integration jugendlicher Vereinsmitglieder,* ed. Tina Nobis and Jürgen Baur (Köln: Sportverlag Strauß, 2007), 277–97.

30. http://www.sportunterricht.de/news/sprintkommentare.html; see Sebastian Braun and Tina Nobis, *Migration, Integration und Sport: Zivilgesellschaft vor Ort* (Wiesbaden: VS, 2011).

31. Michael Mutz, "Sportbegeisterte Jungen, sportabstinente Mädchen? Eine quantitative Analyse der Sportvereinszugehörigkeit von Jungen und Mädchen mit ausländischer Herkunft," *Sport und Gesellschaft* 6 (2009): 95–121.

32. Ursula Boos-Nünning and Yasemin Karakaşoğlu-Aydın, *Viele Welten leben: Zur Lebenssituation von Mädchen und jungen Frauen mit Migrationshintergrund* (Münster: Waxmann, 2005). Christa Kleindienst-Cachay, *Mädchen und Frauen mit Migrationshintergrund im organisierten Sport: Ergebnisse zur Sportsozialisation: Analyse ausgewählter Maßnahmen zur Integration in den Sport* (Baltmannsweiler: Schneider Verlag Hohengehren, 2007); Mutz, *Sportbegeisterte Jungen, sportabstinente Mädchen.*

33. Mutz, *Sportbegeisterte Jungen, sportabstinente Mädchen,* 99.

34. Ibid.

35. Ibid., 109.

36. Michael Mutz and Ulrike Burrmann, "Sportengagement jugendlicher Migranten," in *Migration, Integration und Sport: Zivilgesellschaft vor Ort,* ed. Braun and Nobis, 98–105, 109.

37. Mutz, *Sportbegeisterte Jungen, sportabstinente Mädchen,* 110.

38. Mutz and Burrmann, *Sportengagement jugendlicher Migranten.*

39. Kleindienst-Cachay, *Mädchen und Frauen mit Migrationshintergrund,* 27 ff. Christa Kleindienst-Cachay, "Balancing between the Cultures: Sport and Physical Activities of Muslim Girls and Women in Germany," in *Muslim Women and Sport,* ed. Tansin Benn, Gertrud Pfister, and Haifaa Jawad (London: Routledge, 2010), 92–109.

40. Sine Agergaard, *Unges idrætsdeltagelse og integration i idrætsforeninger i Århus Vest* (Århus: Institut for Idræt, Århus Universitet, 2008).

41. Pfister, *Muslim Women and Sport in Diasporas.*

42. Bjarne Ibsen, *Børns idrætsdeltagelse i Københavns Kommune* (Odense: Syddansk Universitet, Institut for Idræt og Biomekanik, 2007); Agergaard, *Unges idrætsdeltagelse.* A survey of sports participation among children and adolescents (eleven to sixteen years of age) in four Danish municipalities.

43. Flemming Mikkelsen, *Indvandrere og civilsamfund. En forskningsoversigt vedrørende etniske minoriteters deltagelse i civilsamfundet samt kulturmøder mellem minoriteter og danskere på arbejdspladsen, i boligområder og i foreninger* (Ålborg: AMID, Ålborg Universitet, 2002), 18.

44. Martin Gregersen, *Vi har ikke indvandrere, men fodboldspillere. En rapport om fodbold som social integration i Øresundsområdet* (Copenhagen: IfI, 2011).

45. Diethelm Blecking, *Polen, Türken, Sozialisten: Sport und soziale Bewegungen in Deutschland* (Münster: Lit, 2001); Silvester Stahl, "Ethnische Sportvereine zwischen Diaspora-Nationalismus und Transnationalität," in *Jenseits von 'Identität oder Integration': Grenzen überspannende Migrantenorganisationen,* ed. Ludger Pries and Zeynep Sezgin (Wiesbaden: VS Verlag für Sozialwissenschaften, 2010), 87–114.

46. In 2004, Türkiyemspor founded a girls' section, starting with youth team. In the next years, teams were established in the next higher age groups in order to ensure development. In 2009, Türkiyemspor is represented in all age classes of girls' and women's football.

47. http://www.morgenpost.de/printarchiv/berlin/article1268944/Huelya-ein-Fussballstar-aus-Kreuzberg.html.

48. See the overview in Pfister, *Muslim Women and Sport in Diasporas.*

49. Read more at http://www.newyorker.com/reporting/2011/03/07/110307 fa_fact_batuman#ixzz1T28FzGrt.

50. Matthew Atencio and Canan Koca, "Gendered Communities of Practice and the Construction of Masculinities in Turkish Physical Education," *Gender and Education* 23 (2011): 59–72.

51. Atencio and Koca, "Gendered Communities of Practice," 64.

52. Cengiz Demir, "Impacts of Demographic Variables on the Preference of Sport Activities Carried Out by Undergraduate Students: An Implication from Turkey," *Journal of Sport & Tourism* 8 (2003): 302–12.

53. http://www.turkishpress.com/news.asp?id=358952.

54. Debbie Epstein et al., "Boys and Girls Come Out to Play: Making Masculinities and Femininities in School Playgrounds," *Men and Masculinities* 4 (2001): 159.

55. Gregersen, *Vi har ikke indvandrere, men fodboldspillere.*

56. http://cmsv049.rrzn.uni-hannover.de/fileadmin/sport/pdf/online publikationen/pil_eth.pdf.

57. Canan Koca, F. Hülya Asci, and Sadettin Kirazci, "Gender Role Orientation of Athletes and Nonathletes in a Patriarchal Society: A Study of Turkey," *Sex Roles* 52 (2005): 217–25.

58. Y. Dilek, *Parents' Role in Pre-School Children's Gender Role Socialisation* (Unpublished master's thesis, Middle East Technical University, Ankara, Turkey, 1997).

59. Deniz Kandiyoti, "Women and the Turkish State: Political Actors or Symbolic Pawns?," in *Women-Nation-State,* ed. Floya Anthias and Nira Yuval-Davis (London: Macmillan, 1989); Deniz Kandiyoti, "Ataerkil örüntüler: Türk toplumunda erkek egemenliğinin çözümlenmesine yönelik notlar [Patriarchal Patterns: Notes about the Solution of Man Hegemony in Turkish Society]," in *1980'ler Türkiye'sinde kadın bakış açısından kadınlar* [Women from the Perspective of Women in 1980s' Turkey], ed. Şirin Tekeli (Istanbul: Iletişim Yayınları, 1995), 367–82; Koca, Ascii, and Kirazci, *Gender Role Orientation;* Canan Koca et al., "Constraints on Leisure-Time Physical Activity and Negotiation Strategies in Turkish Women," *Journal of Leisure Research* 41 (2009): 225–52.

60. M. Muftuler-Bac, "Turkish Women's Predicament—A Short History," *Women's Studies International Forum* 22 (1999): 304.

61. Muftuler-Bac, *Turkish Women's Predicament.*

62. Koca and Hacısoftaoğlu, *Struggling for Empowerment.*

63. http://en.wikipedia.org/wiki/Women%27s_football_in_Turkey. The website of the Turkish Football Federation does not contain in-depth information about women's football.

64. Koca, Ascii, and Kirazci, *Gender Role Orientation.*

65. İlknur Hacısoftaoğlu and Nefise Bulgu, *Constructing Gender Identity in a Male Dominated Sport: Women and Wrestling in Turkey* (Stellenbosch, S. Africa: 16th IAPESGW World Congress, 16–19 July, 2009), 131.

66. Demir, *Impacts of Demographic Variables,* 307.

67. Ali Tekin, "The Influence of Religious and Socio-Cultural Variables on the Participation of Female University Studies in Leisure Activities," *Middle East Journal of Scientific Research* 8 (2011): 77–84.

68. Hacısoftaoğlu and Pfister, *Transitions.*

69. Koca et al., *Constraints on Leisure-Time Physical Activity.*

70. Cengiz Demir, "Perceived Significance of Factors Influencing Leisure Participation by Gender: Implications from Turkey," *Leisure: Journal of the Canadian Association for Leisure Studies = Loisir: Revue De L'Association Canadienne D'études En Loisir* 29 (2005): 121.

71. Koca et al., *Constraints on Leisure-Time Physical Activity.*

72. http://www.berlinonline.de/berliner-zeitung/spezial/dossiers/menschen bilder/115678/index.php about Hülya Kaya, who was appointed to play on the Turkish national team.

73. E-mail from Ilknur Hacısoftaoğlu, 30 August 2011.

74. Interview with Berlingske Tidende, 5 July 2011.

75. Epstein et al., *Boys and Girls Come Out to Play.*

CHAPTER 12

1. See, for example, Inger-Lise Lien, "The Concept of Honour, Conflict and Violent Behaviour among Youths in Oslo," in *The Eurogang Paradox*, ed. Malcolm W. Klein et al. (Dordrecht: Kluwer Academic Publishers, 2001), 165–74; Unni Wikan, *Generous Betrayal: Politics of Culture in the New Europe* (Chicago: University of Chicago Press, 2002).

2. See, for example, Willy Pedersen and Viggo Vestel, "Tvetydige Maskuliniteter, Appelerende Seksualitet," *Tidsskrift for samfunnsforskning* 46 (2005): 3–34; Annick Prieur, "Respekt og Samhold: Unge Innvandrermenn, Kriminalitet og Maskulinitet," in *Oppvekst i Barnets Århundre: Historier om Tvetydighet*, ed. An-Magritt Jensen et al. (Oslo: Ad Notam Gyldendal, 1999), 251–97; Sveinung Sandberg, "Stereotypiens Dilemma: Iscenesettelser av Etnisitet på 'Gata'," *Tidsskrift for ungdoms-forskning* 5 (2005): 27–46; Anita Sundnes, "Sparrer Kontra Fighter: Mannlighetsidealer i Ungdoms Fornærmelsespraksis," *Tidsskrift for ungdomsforskning* 4 (2004): 3–19.

3. Accounts of this are found for example in the United Kingdom; see Claire E. Alexander, *The Asian Gang: Ethnicity, Identity, Masculinity* (Oxford: Berg, 2000); Katherine Germany and Ewing Pratt, *Stolen Honor: Stigmatizing Muslim Men in Berlin* (Palo Alto, CA: Stanford University Press, 2008).

4. Alan Petersen, *Unmasking the Masculine: "Men" and "Identity" in a Sceptical Age* (London: Sage, 1998), 127.

5. Tim Carrigan, R. W. Connell, and John Lee, "Toward a New Sociology of Masculinity," *Theory and Society* 14 (1985): 551–604; R. W. Connell, *Masculinities* (Cambridge: Polity Press, 1995).

6. Connell warns against oversimplification when recognizing multiple mascu-linities: "It is easy in this framework to think that there is a black masculinity or a working-class masculinity," Connell, *Masculinities*, 76. There is, however, in Connell's framework a constant emphasis on the marginalization of black or working-class masculinities, relative to the dominant form.

7. Stephen M. Whitehead, *Men and Masculinities: Key Themes and New Directions* (Cambridge: Polity Press, 2002), 92.

8. Richard Cashman, "The Subcontinent," in *The Imperial Game: Cricket, Culture and Society*, ed. Brian Stoddart and Keith A. P. Sandiford (Manchester: Manchester University Press, 1998), 116.

9. As of January 2012, 13.1 percent of the population in Norway have either immigrated themselves, or are born in Norway of two immigrant parents. Out of these 665,170 persons, 32,737 persons (4.9 percent) are descendants from Pakistan. While the Norwegian Pakistani population has been growing at a slower rate in later years, other migrant groups have grown considerably; for example, people from Poland, Sweden, Lithuania, Somalia, and Iraq surpassing or almost equaling the

Pakistani migrant population in numbers. See Statistics Norway, "Persons with Immigrant Background by Immigration Category, Country Background and Gender," 1 January 2012.

10. Ben Carrington, "Sport, Masculinity, and Black Cultural Resistance," *Journal of Sport and Social Issues* 22 (1998): 285.

11. Ibid.

12. Edwin Ardener, "The Problem Revisited," in *Perceiving Women*, ed. Shirley Ardener (London: Dent, 1975), 19–27.

13. Jack Williams, "South Asians and Cricket in Bolton," *Sports Historian* 14 (1994): 56–65.

14. *Orientalism* was introduced as an analytic concept in the seminal work by Edward Said; Edward W. Said, *Orientalism* (London: Penguin, 1995). While not formally being a colonizing state, Norway's cultural proximity to other European imperial states, as well as the legacy of the Danish-Norwegian throne, makes it relevant to include Norway in an analysis of colonial and postcolonial thinking.

15. Pernilla Ouis, "Från Njutningsmänniska till Frustrerad Puritan: Muslimsk Sexualitet i ett Historisk Perspektiv," *Tidsskrift for kjønnsforskning* 3 (2005): 51–66.

16. Ibid.: 52., my translation from Swedish.

17. Ardener, "The Problem Revisited," 22.

18. Henrietta L. Moore, *Feminism and Anthropology* (Cambridge: Polity Press, 1988), 4.

19. Ibid., 3.

20. Walle, *A Passion for Cricket*.

21. The names of players and clubs are pseudonyms, as is common in much social anthropological research. To some extent, this counters the players' wish for recognition and visibility, but it has been important in my work to prevent any unfortunate consequences of my choice of analytic topics and juxtapositions.

22. Merete Lindstad and Øivind Fjeldstad, *Av Utenlandsk Opprinnelse. Nye Nordmenn i Avisspaltene* (Kristiansand: IJ-forlaget, 2005). In a survey of some of the major newspapers in Norway, the authors find that most of the articles on Norwegian Pakistanis deal with their particular position as "immigrants" (although many of the younger ones have never migrated), the overall majority of articles are on men, and the focus is on gang-related crime and other modes of asocial conduct.

23. Omar Noman, *Pride and Passion: An Exhilarating Half Century of Cricket in Pakistan* (Karachi: Oxford University Press, 1998), 16–34, 347.

24. Ulla Haslund, "Kriminalitet—Straffede Innvandrere," in *Innvandrere i Norge—Hvem er de, og Hvordan går det med dem? Del II Levekår*, ed. Lars Østby, *Notater* (Oslo: Statistisk Sentralbyrå, 2004), 114–31, Tormod Øia, "Innvandrerungdom—Kultur, Identitet og Marginalisering," in *NOVA Rapport* (Oslo: Norsk institutt for forskning om oppvekst, velferd og aldring, 2003).

25. First Division matches in Norway are limited to forty overs during regular league play.

26. While most of the Norwegian Pakistani cricketers were fluent in Norwegian, Punjabi and Urdu would regularly be the language of choice when they were talking among themselves.

27. Postcolonial theory is a wide theoretic field, but is often ascribed to the works of Gayatri Spivak and Edward Said. See, for example, Said, *Orientalism*; Gayatri

Chakravorty Spivak, "Can the Subaltern Speak?," in *Marxism and the Interpretation of Culture*, ed. Cary Nelson and Lawrence Grossberg (London: Macmillan, 1988), 271–313.

28. Amel Adib and Yvonne Guerrier, "The Interlocking of Gender with Nationality, Race, Ethnicity and Class: The Narratives of Women in Hotel Work," *Gender, Work and Organization* 10 (2003): 413–32.

29. As mentioned above, this is elaborated in Ouis, "Från Njutningsmänniska."

30. See, for example, Dominic Malcolm, "Stacking in Cricket: A Figurational Sociological Reappraisal of Centrality," *Sociology of Sport Journal* 14 (1997): 263–82.

31. Connell, *Masculinities*.

32. See, for example, Joseph S. Alter, "*Kabaddi*, a National Sport of India: The Internationalism of Nationalism and the Foreignness of Indianness," in *Games, Sports and Cultures*, ed. Noel Dyck (Oxford: Berg, 2000), 83–115; Arjun Appadurai, "Playing with Modernity: The Decolonization of Indian Cricket," in *Consuming Modernity: Public Culture in a South Asian World*, ed. Carol A. Breckenridge (Minneapolis: University of Minnesota Press, 1995), 23–48; Ashis Nandy, *The Tao of Cricket: On Games of Destiny and the Destiny of Games* (New Delhi: Oxford University Press, 2000); Noman, *Pride and Passion*; Peter Parkes, "Indigenous Polo and the Politics of Regional Identity in Northern Pakistan," in *Sport, Identity and Ethnicity*, ed. Jeremy MacClancy (Oxford: Berg, 1996), 43–67.

33. Appadurai, "Playing with Modernity," 25–26.

34. Malcolm Tozer, "Imperial Manliness: E. W. Hornung and 'the Game of Life,'" in *Sport, Culture, Society: International, Historical and Sociological Perspectives. Proceedings of the Viii Commonwealth and International Conference*, ed. J. A. Mangan and R. B. Small (Glasgow: Jordanhill College of Education, 1986). Also see Daryl Adair, Murray Phillips, and John Nauright, "Sporting Manhood in Australia: Test Cricket, Rugby Football, and the Imperial Connection, 1878–1918," *Sport History Review* 28 (1997): 46–60; Appadurai, "Playing with Modernity," Aviston D. Downes, "From Boys to Men: Colonial Education, Cricket and Masculinity in the Caribbean, 1870–c. 1920," *International Journal of the History of Sport* 22 (2005): 3–21; Timothy Lockley, "'The Manly Game': Cricket and Masculinity in Savannah, Georgia in 1859," *International Journal of the History of Sport* 20 (2003): 77–98.

35. Manu Madan, "'It's Not Just Cricket!' World Series Cricket: Race, Nation, and Diasporic Indian Identity," *Journal of Sports and Social Issues* 24 (2000): 24–35; Garry Whannel, *Media Sport Stars: Masculinities and Moralities* (London: Routledge, 2002).

36. Connell, *Masculinities*, 54.

37. Ibid.

38. Whannel, *Media Sport Stars*.

39. Ibid. Also see Appadurai, "Playing with Modernity," for a discussion on consequences of the commoditization of cricket in India.

40. Madan, "Not Just Cricket," 24. After fieldwork, the introduction at Twenty20 cricket, with a maximum of twenty overs per innings, has increased this gap even further.

41. See, for example, J. A. Mangan, *Athleticism in the Victorian and Edwardian Public School* (London: Frank Cass, 1986).

42. Madan, "Not Just Cricket."

43. An analysis of the dualities of Pakistani masculinities is presented in Thomas Michael Walle, *"Så God som en Mann kan bli!" Maskuline Idealer og Mannlig Praksis i Lahore, Pakistan*, Institutt og Museum for Antropologi (Oslo: Universitetet i Oslo, 1999). Also see Thomas Michael Walle, "Virginity vs. Decency: Continuity and Change in Pakistani Men's Perception of Sexuality and Women," in *South Asian Masculinities: Context of Change, Sites of Continuity*, ed. Radhika Chopra, Caroline Osella, and Filippo Osella (New Delhi: Kali/Women Unlimited, 2004).

44. Shahid Afridi would later climb to the position as both Twenty20 and ODI captain. It is beyond the scope of this article to assess if this decision was related to changes, real or anticipated, in Afridi's private life.

45. An analysis of the controversies around Shahid Afridi's personality and playing style leading up to and during the Indian-Pakistani tournament in Pakistan in 2004 is found in Walle, *A Passion for Cricket*.

46. Pnina Werbner, "'The Lion of Lahore': Anthropology, Cultural Performance and Imran Khan," in *Anthropology and Cultural Studies*, ed. Stephen Nugent and Cris Shore (London: Pluto Press, 1997), 47.

47. Madan, "Not Just Cricket."

48. Walle, "Virginity vs. Decency."

49. Viggo Vestel, *A Community of Differences—Hybridization, Popular Culture and the Making of Social Relations among Multicultural Youngsters in "Rudenga," East Side Oslo* (Oslo: Norsk institutt for forskning om oppvekst, velferd og aldring, 2004).

50. Ibid.

51. For an elaboration of this point, see Walle, *A Passion for Cricket*.

52. Such arguments can be seen, for example, in Inger-Lise Lien, "Ære, Vold og Kulturell Endring i Oslo Indre By," *Nytt Norsk Tidsskrift* 19, no. 1 (2002): 27–41, Yvonne Mørck, "Hyphenated Danes: Contested Fields of Gender, Generation and Ethnicity," *Young* 8, no. 3 (2000): 2–16, Annick Prieur, *Balansekunstnere: Betydningen av Innvandrerbakgrunn i Norge* (Oslo: Pax, 2004), Sissel Østberg, *Muslim i Norge: Religion og Hverdagsliv blant Unge Norsk-Pakistanere* (Oslo: Universitetsforlaget, 2003).

53. Thomas Michael Walle, "Making Places of Intimacy—Ethnicity, Friendship, and Masculinities in Oslo," *NORA: Nordic Journal of Women's Studies* 15 (2007): 144–57.

54. Whitehead, *Men and Masculinities*.

55. Connell, *Masculinities*, 80.

56. Ibid., 81.

57. Carrington, "Black Cultural Resistance."

CHAPTER 13

1. Hilary McD. Beckles, *The First West Indies Cricket Tour: Canada and the US in 1886* (Kingston, Jamaica: Canoe Press, 2006); Hilary McD. Beckles, *The Development of West Indies Cricket: Volume 2, The Age of Globalization* (Kingston: University of the West Indies Press, 1999); Brian Stoddart, *Sport, Culture and History* (New York: Routledge, 2008); Michael Manley, *A History of West Indies Cricket* (London: Andre Deutsch, 1995); CLR James, *Beyond a Boundary*, (London: Hutchinson, 1963).

2. Hubert Devonish, "African and Indian Consciousness at Play: A Study in West Indies Cricket and Nationalism," in *Liberation Cricket: West Indies Cricket Culture*, ed. Hilary McD. Beckles and Brian Stoddart (Manchester: Manchester University

Press, 1995), 179–91; Kevin Yelvington, "Ethnicity 'Not Out,' The Indian Cricket Tour of the West Indies and the 1976 Elections in Trinidad and Tobago," *Liberation Cricket*, ed. Beckles and Stoddart, 205–21.

3. James, *Beyond a Boundary.*

4. Stoddart, *Sport, Culture and History*, 227.

5. Pierre Bourdieu, "Sport and Social Class," *Social Science Information* 17 (1978): 819–40; Pierre Bourdieu, "Program for a Sociology of Sport," *Sociology of Sport Journal* 5 (1988): 153–60.

6. Bourdieu, "Program for a Sociology of Sport."

7. Alan Tomlinson, "Pierre Bourdieu and the Sociological Study of Sport," in *Sport and Modern Social Theorists*, ed. Richard Giulianotti (New York: Palgrave Macmillan, 2004), 161–72.

8. Ibid.

9. Philip White and Brian Wilson, "Distinction in the Stands: An Investigation of Bourdieu's 'Habitus,' Socioeconomic Status and Sport Spectatorship in Canada," *International Review for the Sociology of Sport* 34 (1999): 254–64.

10. Bourdieu, "Sport and Social Class."

11. White and Wilson, "Distinction in the Stands."

12. Bridget Brereton, *A History of Modern Trinidad 1783–1962* (Oxford: Heinemann, 1981).

13. CARICOM Capacity Development Programme, 2000 Round of Population and Housing Census Data Analysis sub-budget. National Census Report, Trinidad and Tobago, 3.

14. Brereton, *A History of Modern Trinidad*, 103.

15. Kevin Yelvington, *Trinidad Ethnicity* (Hong Kong: Macmillian Press, 1993), 12.

16. Brereton, *A History of Modern Trinidad*; Yelvington, *Trinidad Ethnicity.*

17. Yelvington, *Trinidad Ethnicity.*

18. Selwyn Ryan, *The Jhandi and the Cross: The Clash of Cultures in Post-Creole Trinidad and Tobago* (St. Augustine: Sir Arthur Lewis Institute of Social and Economic Studies, the University of the West Indies, 1999); Selwyn Ryan, ed., *Social and Occupational Stratification in Contemporary Trinidad and Tobago* (St. Augustine: Sir Arthur Lewis Institute of Social and Economic Studies, The University of the West Indies, 1991); Selwyn Ryan (ed.), *Trinidad and Tobago: The Independence Experience 1962–1988* (St. Augustine: Sir Arthur Lewis Institute of Social and Economic Studies, University of the West Indies, 1988); Yelvington, "Ethnicity 'Not Out';" Yelvington, *Trinidad Ethnicity.*

19. Yelvington, "Ethnicity 'Not Out.'"

20. Ibid.

21. Beckles, *The Development of West Indies Cricket: Volume 2*; Richard Burton, "Cricket, Carnival and Street Culture in the Caribbean," in *Liberation Cricket*, ed. Beckles and Stoddart, 89–106; Maurice St. Pierre, "West Indian Cricket, Part II: An Aspect of Creolization," Ibid., 125–40.

22. Orlando Patterson, "The Ritual of Cricket," Ibid., 141–47.

23. Gordon Rohler, "Music, Literature, and West Indies Cricket Values," in *An Area of Conquest: Popular Democracy and West Indies Cricket Supremacy*, ed. Hilary McD. Beckles (Kingston: Ian Randle Publishers, 1994), 109.

24. Rohler, "Music, Literature, and West Indies Cricket Values," in *An Area of Conquest*, ed. Beckles, 55–102.

25. Ibid.

26. Beckles, *The Development of West Indies Cricket: Volume 2*; Rohler, "Music, Literature, and West Indies Cricket Values."

27. Beckles, *The Development of West Indies Cricket: Volume 2*.

28. James, *Beyond a Boundary*; Yelvington, "Ethnicity 'Not Out.'"

29. James, *Beyond a Boundary*.

30. Frank Birbalsingh, *Indo-West Indian Cricket* (London: Hansib Publishing, 1988).

31. Devonish, "African and Indian consciousness at play"; Yelvington, "Ethnicity 'Not Out.'"

32. West Indies Cricket Annual 1990, "How the Media Dominated the Controversy," 33.

33. Ramesh Deosaran, "The 'Caribbean Man': A Study in the Psychology of Perception and the Media," *Caribbean Quarterly* 27 (1981): 60–95.

34. In April 1990, Norman Tebbit proposed the "Cricket test," which was to be used to test ethnic minorities support for the English cricket team as opposed to the teams of their ancestry such as India, Pakistan, Bangladesh, Sri Lanka, and the West Indies. For more on this, see chapter 16 in this volume.

35. Beckles, *The Development of West Indies Cricket: Volume 2*.

36. Tebbit, 1990.

CHAPTER 14

1. M. Atkinson and K. Young, *Tribal Play: Subcultural Journeys through Sport* (Bingley, UK: Elsevier, 2008).

2. R. Stebbins, *Serious Leisure: A Perspective for Our Time* (New Brunswick, NJ: Transaction, 2006).

3. T. Allen, *The Invention of the White Race* (London: Verso, 1994).

4. M. Berger, *White Lies: Race and the Myths of Whiteness* (New York: Farrar, Straus & Giroux, 1999).

5. A. Bonnett, *White Identities: Historical and International Perspectives* (Harlow: Prentice-Hall, 2000).

6. R. Dyer, *White* (New York: Routledge, 1997).

7. M. Hill, *After Whiteness: Unmaking an American Majority* (New York: New York University Press, 2004).

8. R. Jensen, *The Heart of Whiteness: Confronting Race, Racism and White Privilege* (New York: City Lights Publishers, 2005).

9. G. Lipsitz, *The Possessive Investment in Whiteness: How White People Profit from Identity Politics* (Philadelphia: Temple University Press, 2006).

10. D. Roediger, *The Wages of Whiteness: Race and the Making of the American Working Class* (New York: Verso, 1991).

11. R. Young, *White Mythologies: Writing History and the West* (London: Routledge, 1990).

12. T. Wise, *White Like Me: Reflections on Race from a Privileged Son* (New York: Soft Skull Press, 2007).

13. For similar studies, see J. Landsman, *Growing Up White* (Minneapolis: Rowman and Littlefield, 2008); K. McKinney, *Being White: Stories of Race and Racism* (London: Routledge, 2004); P. Rivel, *Uprooting Racism: How White People Can Work for Racial Justice* (Gabriola Island: New Society Publishers, 2002).

14. M. Atkinson, *Deconstructing Men and Masculinities* (Toronto: Oxford University Press, 2010).

15. A. Clare, *On Men: Masculinity in Crisis* (London: Chatto and Windus, 2000).

16. b. hooks, *We Real Cool: Black Men and Masculinity* (New York: Routledge, 2003).

17. A. Neal, *New Black Man* (New York: Routledge, 2005).

18. T. Wise, *White Like Me: Reflections on Race from a Privileged Son* (New York: Soft Skull Press, 2007).

19. See R. Rinehart and S. Sydnor, *To the Extreme: Alternative Sports, Inside and Out* (Albany: SUNY, 2003); B. Wheaton, *Understanding Lifestyle Sport: Consumption, Identity and Difference* (London: Routledge, 2004).

20. D. LeBreton, "Playing Symbolically with Death in Extreme Sports," *Body and Society* 6 (2000): 1–11.

21. B. Erickson, "Style Matters: Explorations of Bodies, Whiteness and Identity in Rock Climbing," *Sociology of Sport Journal* 22 (2005): 373–96.

22. S. Ray, "Risking Bodies in the Wild," *Journal of Sport and Social Issues* 33 (2009): 257–84.

23. R. Nash, *Wilderness and the American Mind* (New Haven, CT: Yale University Press, 1967).

24. S. Lyng, "Risk-taking in Sport: Edgework and Reflexive Community," in *Tribal Play: Subcultural Journeys Through Sport*, ed. M. Atkinson and K. Young (Bingley, UK: Elsevier, 2008), 83–109.

25. S. Faludi, *Stiffed: The Betrayal of the American Man* (New York: William Morrow & Co, 1999).

26. S. Goldberg, *The Inevitability of Patriarchy* (New York: Maurice Temple Smith, 1977).

27. R. Horrocks, *Masculinity in Crisis: Myths, Fantasies and Realities* (Basingstoke, UK: St. Martin's Press, 1994).

28. A. Petersen, *Unmasking the Masculine: "Men" and "Identity" in a Sceptical Age* (Thousand Oaks, CA: Sage, 1998).

29. M. Kimmel and M. Messner, *Men's Lives* (New York: Macmillan, 1998).

30. M. Males, *The Scapegoat Generation: America's War on Adolescents* (Monroe: Common Courage Press, 1996).

31. L. Tiger, *The Decline of Males: The First Look at an Unexpected New World for Men and Women* (New York: Griffin Trade Paperback, 2000).

32. W. Farrell, *Does Feminism Discriminate Against Men?* (New York: Oxford University Press, 2007).

33. S. Whitehead, *Men and Masculinities: Key Themes and New Directions* (Cambridge: Polity Press, 2002).

34. Faludi, *Stiffed: The Betrayal of the American Man.*

35. S. Brayton, "'Black-Lash': Revisiting the White Negro through Skateboarding," *Sociology of Sport Journal* 22 (2005): 356–77; R. Hewitt, *White Backlash and the Politics of Multiculturalism* (New York: Cambridge University Press, 2005); K. Hylton, *Race and Sport: Critical Race Theory* (London: Routledge, 2008); T. Wise, *White Like Me: Reflections on Race from a Privileged Son* (New York: Soft Skull Press, 2007).

36. Stebbins, *Serious Leisure.*

37. P. Gilroy, "Post-Colonialism and Multiculturalism," in *The Oxford Handbook of*

Political Theory, ed. J. Dryzek, B. Honig and A. Phillips (Oxford: Oxford University Press, 2006), 656–76.

38. E. Said, *Orientalism* (New York: Vintage, 1978).

39. G. Spivak, "Can the Subaltern Speak?," in *Colonial Discourse and Post-Colonial Theory: A Reader*, ed. P. Williams and L. Chrisman (New York: Harvester Wheatsheaf, 1994), 66–111.

40. Brayton, "'Black-Lash': Revisiting the White Negro through Skateboarding"; Hill, *After Whiteness*.

41. B. Anderson, *Imagined Communities* (London: Verso, 1991).

42. R. Hewitt, *White Backlash and the Politics of Multiculturalism*.

43. J-M. Delaplace, *George Hébert: Sculpter du Corps* (Paris: Vuibert, 2005).

44. BBC, *Jump London*. Originally aired 9 September 2003.

45. Ibid.

46. B. Pronger, *Body Fascism: Salvation in the Technology of Physical Fitness* (Toronto: University of Toronto Press, 2004).

47. D. LeBreton, "Playing Symbolically with Death in Extreme Sports."

48. S. Lyng, "Risk-taking in Sport: Edgework and Reflexive Community."

49. R. Callois, *Les Jeux et le Hommes* (Paris: Gallimard, 1967).

50. Ibid., 23.

51. G. Bataille, *Inner Experience* (Albany: SUNY Press, 1988).

52. M. Foucault, *Madness and Civilisation: A History of Insanity in the Age of Reason.* (New York: Random House, 1961).

53. J. Baudrillard, *America* (Paris: Grasset, 1998).

54. LeBreton, "Playing Symbolically with Death in Extreme Sports."

55. M. Csikszentmihalyi, *Beyond Boredom and Anxiety* (San Francisco: Jossey Bass, 1975).

56. J-F. Lyotard, "Scapeland," in *The Lyotard Reader*, ed. A. Benjamin (Oxford: Basil Blackwell, 1987), 212–19.

57. M. Heidegger, "On the Question Concerning Technology," in *Martin Heidegger: Basic Writings*, ed. D. Krell (New York: Harper and Row, 1977[1954]), 283–317.

58. J. Derrida, *Of Grammatology* (Baltimore: John Hopkins University Press, 1967).

59. M. Heidegger, "On the Question Concerning Technology."

60. Ibid.

61. Ibid.

62. Ibid.

63. Ibid.

64. D. Suzuki, *The Sacred Balance: Rediscovering Our Place in Nature* (Vancouver: Greystone Books, 2000).

65. M. Heidegger, *Being and Time* (London: SCM Press, 1927).

66. Ibid.

67. Ibid.

68. B. Wheaton, *Understanding Lifestyle Sport: Consumption, Identity and Difference* (London: Routledge, 2004).

69. M. Atkinson and K. Young, *Tribal Play: Subcultural Journeys through Sport* (Bingley, UK: Elsevier, 2008).

CHAPTER 15

1. Robbie McVeigh, "'There's no Racism Because There's no Black People Here': Racism and Anti-racism in Northern Ireland," in *Divided Society*, ed. Paul Hainsworth (London: Pluto Press, 1998), 11–32.

2. Ibid.

3. Stuart Garner, *Racism in the Irish Experience* (London: Pluto, 2004).

4. Paul Hainsworth, "Politics, Racism and Ethnicity in Northern Ireland," In *Divided Society*, ed. Hainsworth, 33–51.

5. David Hassan, "A People Apart: Soccer, Identity and Irish Nationalists in Northern Ireland," *Soccer and Society* 3 (2002): 65–83.

6. McVeigh, "There's no Racism."

7. Kathryn Bell, Neil Jarman, and Thomas Lefebvre, *Migrant Workers in Northern Ireland* (Belfast: Institute for Conflict Research, 2004).

8. Gareth Fulton, "Northern Catholic Fans of the Republic of Ireland Soccer Team," in *Sport and the Irish*, ed. Alan Bairner (Dublin: University College of Dublin Press, 2005), 140–56.

9. Paul Connolly, *"Race" and Racism in Northern Ireland: A Review of the Research Evidence* (Belfast: OFDFM, 2002).

10. Liz Fawcett, "Fitting In: Ethnic Minorities and the News Media," in *Divided Society*, ed. Hainsworth, 104–26.

11. The Race Relations (Northern Ireland) Order (1997) No. 869 (N.I. 6) Northern Ireland, 19 March 1997, 34.

12. Paul McGill and Quintin Oliver, *A Wake-Up Call on Race: Implications of the Macpherson Report for Institutional Racism in Northern Ireland: A Report for the Equality Commission for Northern Ireland* (Belfast: Equality Commission for Northern Ireland, 2002).

13. Robbie McVeigh, *The Next Stephen Lawrence? Racist Violence and Criminal Justice in Northern Ireland* (Belfast: NI Council for Ethnic Minorities, 2006).

14. Institute of Conflict Research, *Responding to the UEFA Ten Point Plan Sectarianism, Racism and Football in Northern Ireland* (Belfast: IFA, 2007).

15. *A Racial Equality Strategy for Northern Ireland 2005–2010* (Belfast: OFDFM: N. Ireland, 2005), 12.

16. Bell et al., *Migrant Workers in Northern Ireland*.

17. McVeigh, "There's no Racism."

18. Hainsworth, "Politics, Racism and Ethnicity in Northern Ireland."

19. Robbie McVeigh, "There's no Racism."

20. H. McDonald, *Observer*, 12 October 2006.

21. John Sugden and Alan Bairner, *Sport, Sectarianism and Society in a Divided Ireland* (Leicester: Leicester University Press, 1993).

22. Institute of Conflict Research, *Responding to the UEFA Ten Point Plan*.

23. Committee for the Administration of Justice, *Racism in Northern Ireland: The Need for Legislation to Combat Racial Discrimination in Northern Ireland*. The report of a C.A.J. conference held on 30 November 1991 in Dukes Hotel, Belfast (Belfast: Committee on the Administration of Justice, 1992).

24. Robbie McVeigh and Bill Rolston, "From Good Friday to Good Relations: Sectarianism, Racism and the Northern Ireland State," *Race and Class* 48 (2007): 1–23.

25. Ibid., 5.

26. Ibid., 7.

27. Thomas Carter, Hastings Donnan, Shaun Ogle, and H. Wardle, *Global Migrants: The Impact of Migrants Working in Sport in Northern Ireland* (Belfast: SCNI, 2003).

28. Thomas Carter, "The Migration of Sporting Labour into Ireland," in *Sport and the Irish*, ed. Bairner, 191–205.

29. Peter Shirlow and Brendan Murtagh, *Belfast: Segregation, Violence and the City* (London: Pluto Press, 2006).

30. *Irish News*, 12 May 2006.

31. McVeigh and Rolston, "From Good Friday to Good Relations."

32. Ibid.

33. Bell et al., *Migrant Workers in Northern Ireland*.

CHAPTER 16

1. "British Asian" is a very broad category and subsumes a tremendous "plurality of identities" (see Y. Hussain and P. Bagguley, "Citizenship, Ethnicity and Identity: British Pakistanis after the 2001 'Riots,'" *Sociology* 39, no. 3: 407–25). Though it is often the case in practice, the internal diversity of British Asian communities cannot be reduced to the labels of "Indian," "Pakistani," "sri Lankan," and "Bangladeshi"; rather it requires an appreciation of what Brah refers to as "axes of differentiation," see A. Brah, *Cartographies of Diaspora: Contesting Identities* (London: Routledge, 1996). For Brah, "race" and ethnicity are not unitary; they are multidimensional, processual, and require meticulous appreciation of power and differentiation. In spite of this, and the fact that there are very distinct cultural and religious differences between and within groups, the term *British Asian* is often used to categorize / essentialize members of the Indian, Pakistani, Sri Lankan, and Bangladeshi communities who have settled in Britain. Crucially, while no categorization is wholly accurate when attempting to generalize what are diverse phenomena, the term British Asian is generally known and understood within the academy to delineate individuals of South Asian descent who were either born in Britain or who have migrated to Britain and claimed British citizenship.

2. *The Indian Express,* "Home or Away?: Lords Turns Out Lighter Shade of Blue," 15 June 2009, http://www.lexisnexis.com/uk/frame.do?toenkey=rsh-20.380 823.9100344787 (accessed 16 June 2009).

3. A. Ratna, "Who are ya?" Supporter Identities amongst British Asian Football Fans, forthcoming, *Sociological Review*.

4. M. Halstead, "In Defence of Multiculturalism," in *Philosophy of Education in the Era of Globalization*, ed. Y. Raley and G. Preyer (London: Routledge, 2010).

5. D. Malcolm, "Clean Bowled? Cricket, Racism and Equal Opportunities," *Journal of Ethnic and Migration Studies* 28 (2001): 307–25.

6. K. Sandiford, "Cricket and the Victorian Society," *Journal of Social History* 17 (1983): 303–17; T. Fletcher, "The Making of English Cricket Cultures: Empire, Globalisation and Colonialism," *Sport in Society* 14 (2011): 17–36.

7. C. L. R. James, *Beyond a Boundary* (London: Hutchinson, 1963).

8. F. Anthias, "Evaluating 'Diaspora': Beyond Ethnicity?" *Sociology* 32 (1998): 557–80; F. Anthias, "New Hybridities, Old Concepts: The Limits of 'Culture,'" *Ethnic and Racial Studies* 24 (2001): 619–41; Brah, *Cartographies of Diaspora*.

9. P. Lewis, *Young, British and Muslim* (London: Continuum, 2008).

10. A. Saeed, "Northern Racism: A Pilot Study of Racism in Sunderland," in *Thinking Northern: Textures of Identity in the North of England*, ed. C. Ehland (Amsterdam: Kodopi, 2007), 163–92.

11. Parekh, *Rethinking Multiculturalism: Cultural Diversity and Political Theory*, 2nd ed. (Basingstoke: Palgrave Macmillan, 2006).

12. T. Fletcher, "'Aye, but it Were Wasted on Thee': 'Yorkshireness,' Cricket, Ethnic Identities, and the 'Magical Recovery of Community,'" *Sociological Research Online* 16 (2012): http://www.socresonline.org.uk/16/4/5.html; T. Fletcher, "All Yorkshiremen are from Yorkshire, but some are more Yorkshire than Others," *Sport in Society* 15 (2012): 227–45.

13. D. Day, *Community and Everyday Life* (London: Routledge, 2006).

14. Parekh, *Rethinking Multiculturalism.*

15. T. Fletcher, "All Yorkshiremen are from Yorkshire."

16. The loyalty rhetoric expressed through Tebbit's cricket test has became more formalized in the requirements under Labour government of Tony Blair and Gordon Brown, where allegiance to the nation was an essential part of the citizenship process. The Home Office, *Earning the Right to Stay: A New Points Test for Citizenship* (London: HMSO, 2009).

17. Interview, 23 March 2009.

18. D. Burdsey, "'If I Ever Play Football, Dad, Can I Play for England or India?': British Asians, Sport and Diasporic National Identities," *Sociology* 40 (2006): 11–28; P. Wilby, "Not-Cricket Cricket." http://83.137.212.42/siteArchive/catalystmagazine (accessed 4 August 2009).

19. V. S. Kalra, R. Kaur, and J. Hutnyk, *Diaspora and Hybridity* (London: Sage, 2005), 36.

20. See Anthias, "Evaluating 'Diaspora'"; Anthias, "New Hybridities, Old Concepts."

21. The etymology of the word *diaspora* goes back to Ancient Greece, as a term used "to describe their spreading all over the then known-world. For the Ancient Greeks, diaspora signified migration and colonialism." See M. Georgiou, "Thinking Diaspora: Why Diaspora is a Key Concept for Understanding Multicultural Europe," *Multicultural Skyscraper Newsletter* 1 (2001): 1.

22. Anthias, "Evaluating 'Diaspora.'"

23. Kalra et al., *Diaspora and Hybridity;* also see P. Gilroy, *The Black Atlantic: Modernity and Double Consciousness* (London: Verso, 1993).

24. See the chapter by Walle in this volume.

25. Ratna, "Who are ya?"

26. Brah, *Cartographies of Diaspora.*

27. Anthias, "New Hybridities, Old Concepts," 632.

28. Hall, "Cultural Identity and Diaspora," 235.

29. Kalra et al., *Diaspora and Hybridity.*

30. Ibid., 29, author's emphasis.

31. Parekh, "National Identity in a Multicultural Society," 205.

32. Anthias, "Evaluating 'Diaspora.'"

33. Madan, "'It's not Just Cricket,'" 27.

34. Brah, *Cartographies of Diaspora.*

35. Vertovec, *The Hindu Diaspora.*

36. Sayyid, "BrAsians: Postcolonial People, Ironic Citizens," in *A Postcolonial People: South Asians in Britain*, ed. N. Ali, V. S. Kalra, and S. Sayyid (London: Hurst), 1–10; Fletcher, "All Yorkshiremen are from Yorkshire."

37. Brah, *Cartographies of Diaspora;* Anthias, "Evaluating 'Diaspora.'"

38. Clifford, "Diasporas."

39. Anthias, "New Hybridities, Old Concepts."

40. Brah, *Cartographies of Diaspora.*

41. Ibid., 209.

42. Kalra et al., *Diaspora and Hybridity.*

43. Hall, "Old and New Identities."

44. Bale, *Sport, Space and the City.*

45. Moore, "Sports Heritage and the Re-imagined City." There are a number of cricket grounds around the world that have been invested with great cultural and symbolic significance. Above all, however, Lord's has remained the prime example of a cricket ground that has taken on a far more symbolic social role. For over two hundred years Lord's has commanded pilgrimage aspirations for players, spectators, and administrators alike, which, perhaps, no other sports venue could. See Stoddart, "At the End of the Day's Play."

46. *Indian Express*, "Home or Away?"

47. England and Wales Cricket Board, "England Lifted by Boo Boys."

48. Campbell, "Hussain Lashes British Asians as Unpatriotic."

49. Interview, 19 January 2009.

50. Crabbe, "The Public Gets What the Public Wants."

51. K. Granstrom, "Cheering as an Indicator of Social Identity and Self-regulation in Swedish Ice Hockey Supporter Groups," *International Review for the Sociology of Sport* 47 (2012): 133–48.

52. Campbell, "Hussain Lashes British Asians as Unpatriotic."

53. Chaudhary, "A Question of Support."

54. Ibid.

55. Brah, *Cartographies of Diaspora*, 191.

56. Kaushal, "The Tebbit test is just not cricket."

57. Burdsey, *British Asians and Football.*

58. Hall, "There's a Time to Act English and a Time to Act Indian."

59. Interview, 20 June 2009.

60. Fletcher, "Being Inside and Outside the Field."

61. Geaves, "Negotiating British Citizenship and Muslim Identity."

62. Modood, "Remaking multiculturalism after 7/7"; Modood, "A Defence of Multiculturalism"; Halstead, "In Defence of Multiculturalism."

63. Crawford, *Consuming Sport.*

64. Hills, *Fan Cultures.*

65. Anthias, "Evaluating 'Diaspora.'"

66. Bradbury, "From Racial Exclusions to New Inclusions."

67. Anderson, *Imagined Communities.*

68. *Indian Express*, "Home or Away?"

69. Holmes and Storey, "Transferring National Allegiance," 253.

70. Madan, "It's Not Just Cricket."

71. Hall and Jefferson, *Resistance through Rituals.*

72. Appadurai, *Modernity at Large,* 110.

73. Burdsey, *British Asians and Football.*

74. Brah, *Cartographies of Diaspora.*

75. Interview, 22 January 2009.

76. Ratna, "Who are ya?"

77. Interview, 9 March 2009.

78. Interview, 3 December 2008.

79. Day, *Community and Everyday Life.*

80. Brah, *Cartographies of Diaspora.*

81. Ibid., 182.

82. Ibid., 183.

83. Interview, 2 March 2009.

84. Anderson, *Imagined Communities.*

85. Chaudhary, "A Question of Support."

86. Werbner, *Imagined Diasporas amongst Manchester Muslims,* 468.

87. Gilroy, *The Black Atlantic,* 27–28.

88. Interview 13 March 2009.

89. McCrone, "Who Do You Say You Are?"

90. Interview, 16 March 2009.

91. Joseph Maguire, "Globalisation, Sport and National Identities: The Empire Strikes Back," *Leisure/Loisir* 16 (1993): 293–322.

92. Interview 12 December 2008.

93. Ballard, *Desh Pardesh.*

94. Ibid., 30–33.

95. Clifford, "Diasporas."

96. Burdsey, "Half of Some and Half of the Other."

97. Ratna, "Flying the Flag for England," 118.

98. Marqusee, *Anyone but England.*

99. Interview, 13 February 2009.

100. Appadurai, *Modernity at Large.*

101. Fagerlid, cited in Walle, *A Passion for Cricket,* 206.

102. Brah, *Cartographies of Diaspora,* 194.

103. Puwar, *Space Invaders.*

104. Werbner, *Imagined Diasporas amongst Manchester Muslims,* 471.

105. Interview, 13 February 2009.

106. In a report on national identity published by the Office for National Statistics 75 percent of Indians, Pakistanis, and Bangladeshis in the UK identified themselves as British. This contrasted with data showing that the groups "least likely to identify themselves as British were those recording themselves as 'other white,' including Europeans and Americans. Less than 40% of this group said they were British, English, Scottish, Welsh or Irish." Add to this the figures of those who saw themselves as predominantly Scottish (73 percent in Scotland) and Welsh (62 percent in Wales) and we can ascertain that British Asians are identifying with Britain more openly than other groups. Engel, "The White Rose Meets its Match."

107. Pieterse, "Globalisation as Hybridisation," 54–55.

108. Interview, 13 February 2009.

109. Bhabha, *The Location of Culture*, 38.

110. Modood et al., *Ethnic Minorities in Britain*, 10.

111. McCrone, "Who do you say you are?"

112. Anthias, "Evaluating 'Diaspora,'" "New Hybridities, Old Concepts."

113. Werbner, *Imagined Diasporas among Manchester Muslims*.

CHAPTER 17

1. Jo Ling Kent, "IOC President Tells Jamaican 'Showbolt' to Simmer Down, Carl Lewis Says He's Just Young," *ABC World News Daily Blog*, 21 August 2008, http://blogs.abcnews.com/theworldnewser/2008/08/ioc-president-t.html (accessed 18 January 2011).

2. Jared McCallister, "Coverage of Usain Bolt raises controversy in community," *New York Daily News*, 22 August 2008, http://www.nydailynews.com/new-york/brooklyn/coverage-usain-bolt-raises-controversy-community-article-1.314101 (accessed 19 January 2011).

3. McCallister, "Coverage of Usain Bolt."

4. See David Andrews, "Sport, Culture and Late Capitalism," in *Marxism, Cultural Studies and Sport*, ed. Ben Carrington and Ian McDonald (London: Routledge, 2009), 378; see also John Bale and Joseph Maguire, "Labour Migration in the Global Arena," in *The Global Sports Arena: Athletic Talent Migration in an Interdependent World*, ed. John Bale and Joseph Maguire (London: Frank Cass, 1994), 1–21.

5. Frederick Jameson, *Postmodernism: Or, the Cultural Logic of Late Capitalism* (Durham, NC: Duke University Press, 1991), 49. See also Andrews, "Sport, Culture and Late Capitalism."

6. Henri Lefebvre, *The Production of Space*, trans. Donald Nicholson-Smith (Malden, MA: Blackwell, 1999), 73.

7. Cathy Van Ingen, "Geographies of Gender, Sexuality and Race," *International Review for the Sociology of Sport* 38 (2003): 201–16.

8. Lefebvre, *Production of Space*, 37–39. See also Michael Friedman and Cathy van Ingen, "Bodies in Space: Spatializing Physical Cultural Studies," *Sociology of Sport Journal* 28 (2011): 85–105.

9. Andrew Merrifield, *Henri Lefebvre: A Critical Introduction* (New York: Routledge. 2006).

10. Stuart Elden, *Understanding Henri Lefebvre: Theory and the Possible* (London: Continuum, 2004).

11. Elden, *Understanding Henri Lefebvre*, 189.

12. Iain Borden, *Skateboarding, Space and the City: Architecture and the Body* (Oxford: Berg, 2001). See also Friedman and van Ingen, "Bodies in Space," and van Ingen "Geographies of Gender."

13. An important consideration to note here is the usage of the term *postcolonial* —as opposed to the hyphenated version post-colonial—suggests a constant interplay between conditions under colonialism and their continual legacies after independence, at both a local and global level. Rather than simply marking a temporal condition of "after" colonialism and signaling its demise, we use postcolonial to refer to a plurality of approaches that criticize the "material and discursive legacies of colonialism that are still apparent in the world today"; see Cheryl McEwan, *Postcolonialism and Development* (New York: Routledge, 2009), 18.

14. McCallister, "Coverage of Usain Bolt."

15. C. L. R. James, *Beyond a Boundary* (Kingston, Jamaica: Sangster's, 1963).

16. Sigmond Loland, "Pierre de Coubertin's Ideology of Olympism from the Perspective of the History of Ideas," *Olympika: The International Journal of Olympic Studies* 4 (1995), 49–78.

17. James, *Beyond a Boundary,* 38.

18. United States Olympic Committee, "Olympic Oath." Last Modified 23 June 2008. http://www.teamusa.org/resources/olympic-facts-figures/olympic-history.

19. Joseph Maguire, Grant Jarvie, Louise Mansfield, and Joe Bradley, *Sport Worlds: A Sociological Perspective* (Champaign, IL: Human Kinetics, 2004).

20. Andrews, "Sport, Culture and Late Capitalism." See also Maguire et al., *Sport Worlds.*

21. At the 1988 Olympics, Johnson was disqualified due to doping. After Johnson's disqualification, Christie received the silver medal.

22. Maguire et al., *Sport Worlds.*

23. James, *Beyond a Boundary,* 34.

24. Nicole King, *CLR James and Creolization: Circles of Influence* (Jackson: University Press of Mississippi, 2001), 10.

25. Winston Still, "I Don't Want Asafa Dancing—Athlete's parents not pleased," *Jamaica Star,* 7 October 2008, http://www.jamaica-star.com (accessed 1 July 2010).

26. Edward Said, *Orientalism* (New York: Random House, 1978).

27. James Mills and Satadru Sen, *Confronting the Body* (London: Anthem Press, 2004), 2.

28. Kristen Simonsen, "Bodies, Sensations, Space and Time: The Contribution from Henri Lefebvre," *Human Geography* 87 (2005): 1–14. See also Friedman and van Ingen, "Bodies in Space."

29. Kent, "IOC President."

30. Bale and Maguire, "Labour Migration."

31. Maguire et al., *Sport Worlds.*

32. Frances Perraudin, "Usain Bolt Now World's Best Paid—and Quickest—Athletic Star," *Time.com.* 25 August 2010, http://newsfeed.time.com/2010/08/25/usain-bolt-now-worlds-best-paid-and-quickest-athletic-star/#ixzz1BdCZzSNA (accessed 18 January 2011).

33. See James, *Beyond a Boundary.*

CONTRIBUTORS

DARYL ADAIR is Associate Professor of Sport Management at University Technology, Sydney, in Australia. Daryl is on the editorial board of the academic journals *Sporting Traditions, Sport in Society, Performance Enhancement and Health*, and the *Journal of Sport History*. He is the author and editor of several books dealing with sport, race, and ethnicity and also coauthor of a history of St. Patrick's Day.

MICHAEL ATKINSON is Associate Professor in the Faculty of Kinesiology and Physical Education at the University of Toronto. Michael's central areas of teaching and research interest pertain to non-mainstream physical cultures, suffering, body modification, bio-pedagogical practices in physical cultures, and bioethics. Michael is editor of the *Sociology of Sport Journal,* and author/coauthor of seven books including *Battleground: Sports* (2008); *Deviance and Social Control in Sport* (with Kevin Young, 2008); and *Boys' Bodies: Speaking the Unspoken* (with Michael Kehler, 2010).

CALLIE BATTS earned a PhD in Kinesiology from the University of Maryland in 2012 with a specialization in Physical Cultural Studies. She spent two years conducting ethnographic research in India for her dissertation, exploring the ongoing relationship between the West and India as represented, experienced, and contested in the realms of sport, recreation, and physical culture. She has published previous work on political protests during the 2003 Cricket World Cup, the mobilization of the disabled soldier/athlete within the Paralympic movement, and the power of collective sporting memory. At the time of publication Callie was living in north India, where she is pursuing independent research on the performative embodiment of yoga.

SIR HILARY MCD. BECKLES is Pro-Vice Chancellor and Principal of the University of the West Indies, Cave Hill, in Barbados. He is the author and editor of numerous books in Caribbean history with particular interest in the history of cricket. He has published a two-volume history of cricket in the Caribbean, a national history of Barbados, and edited *Liberation Cricket* with Brian Stoddart.

DOUGLAS BOOTH is Professor of Sport Studies and Dean of the School of Physical Education at the University of Otago, New Zealand. He is the author of *The Race Game* (1998), *Australian Beach Cultures* (2001), and *The Field* (2005), among numerous other books and articles in sports studies. Douglas serves on the editorial boards of *Rethinking History, Journal of Sport History,* and *Sport History Review* and is an executive member of the Australian Society for Sport History.

BENEDICT CARTON is Associate Professor of History and Africa Coordinator of African & African American Studies at George Mason University. Over the last twenty-five years, he has lived and worked for extended periods in South Africa, mostly in Zululand. Carton is the author of *Blood from Your Children: Colonial Origins of Generational Conflict in South Africa* (2000) and coauthor and coeditor of *Zulu Identities: Being Zulu, Past and Present* (2008). His articles have appeared in the *Journal of Southern African Studies, Journal of Social History, International Journal of African Historical Studies,* among other journals. His next book, with Robert Vinson, is titled *Shaka's Progeny, A Transnational History: Zulu Peoples and African Americans in the Arc of Racial Justice, 1820–2000*.

ALAN G. COBLEY is Pro Vice-Chancellor, Undergraduate Studies for the University of the West Indies and Professor of History at the University of the West Indies, Cave Hill, in Barbados. Born in the UK, Cobley studied at the Universities of Manchester and York before completing his doctorate in African History at the School of Oriental and African Studies in London. He has served the UWI in a wide variety of capacities, including terms as acting head of the Centre for Gender and Development Studies, head of the Department of History and director of the School of Education. He served seven years as Deputy Dean, and five as Dean of the Faculty of Humanities and Education. He has also been Campus Coordinator for Graduate Studies and Research at Cave Hill. He is a member of the board of directors of the Cave Hill School of Business and the Board of Codrington College. He has published extensively on aspects of South African and Caribbean History.

THOMAS FLETCHER is a Senior Lecturer in Carnegie Faculty at Leeds Metropolitan University, UK. His current research interests are broadly related to the sociology of sport and leisure and include "race"/ethnicity, social identities, heritage, and equity and diversity. He is currently guest editing a special issue of the journal *Identities*, co-guest editing a special issue of the journal *Sport in Society*, and coediting a book entitled *Sports Events, Society and Culture*, to be published by Routledge early 2014. Thomas is currently working on a number of research projects in the areas of sport and fatherhood, media portrayal of class at the London 2012 Olympics, disability cricket, and sports heritage.

MICHAEL FRIEDMAN is a Research Assistant Professor in the Physical Cultural Studies program at the University of Maryland, College Park. His research focuses on the relationship between sport and governance in the postindustrial city with a perspective informed by cultural studies and cultural geography. His research has been published in the *Sociology of Sport Journal, International Review for the Sociology of Sport, Journal of Sport History, Journal of Urban Affairs*, and *Economic Development Quarterly*.

GERALD R. GEMS is Professor in the Health and Physical Education Department at North Central College in Naperville, Illinois. He is a Fulbright Scholar, the past president of the North American Society for Sport History, and author of numerous books and articles on race and ethnicity in sport, including *Sport and the Shaping of Italian American Identity* (2013) and *Boxing: A Social History of the Sweet Science* (forthcoming).

DAVID HASSAN is Professor of Sports Studies at the University of Ulster in Northern Ireland. He has published seven books and over sixty academic articles/book chapters, including many dealing with identity politics and various forms of discrimination in and through sport. He is Deputy Executive Academic Editor of *Sport in Society*, the international, peer-reviewed journal published by Taylor and Francis.

JENNIFER H. LANSBURY formerly served as Assistant Professor of History and Director of the sport and American culture minor at George Mason University. She has focused her research and writings on the history of African American women in sport. Her recent book, *A Spectacular Leap: Black Women Athletes in Twentieth-Century America* (April 2013), is the first full-length scholarly monograph on the subject.

MALCOLM MACLEAN studied anthropology and history, and is Associate Dean, Quality & Standards, at the University of Gloucestershire where he teaches in the Faculty of Applied Science. He has previously taught history in New Zealand, and worked in the New Zealand Ministry of Justice. His primary research interests are cultural politics, sport as a form of body and movement culture, and the political economy of knowledge production in contemporary higher education. He has a particular interest in colonial and postcolonial settings. His publications deal with sports-related antiapartheid protests, as well as in the cultural politics of settlement colonies and associated discourses of indigeneity associated with sport, body, and movement cultures. He is editor (with Emily Ryall and Wendy Russell) of *The Philosophy of Play*. Malcolm is actively involved in international sports studies networks and was chair of the British Society of Sports History.

JAMES A. MCBEAN JR. is a doctoral student in the Physical Cultural Studies program at the University of Maryland, College Park. He is a Jamaican native and holds a master's of Public Policy from Johns Hopkins University as well as bachelors in Economics and Spanish Language & Literature from Brandeis University. His research centers on understanding the dialectical relationship between physical cultures of the subaltern black body, and the spaces in which they exist. His long-term goals include creating effective, normative ways to create and to develop culturally based social intervention programs in which marginalized demographics can achieve sustained personhood. McBean is the founder and recently elected president of the Kingston-based Jamaican Fencing Federation (JFF). He currently lives outside of Mexico City, Mexico.

KEN MCHUE is a Cultural Planner in the International Department of Sport Against Racism Ireland where he is director of the program Sport Aid from Africa to Ireland. He is visiting lecturer in Sport and Social Responsibility at De Montfort University, UK, and the International

Centre for Sports Studies, Switzerland. He is a member of Industrial Workers of the World.

VERNER MØLLER is Professor of Sport and Body Culture at Aarhus University, Denmark and Visiting Professor at George Mason University, Virginia, in the Center for the Study of Sport and Leisure in Society. He also directs the International Humanistic Doping Research Network. He has authored and edited a number of books in sports studies including *Doping and Anti-Doping Policy in Sport: Ethical, Legal and Social Perspectives*; *The Scapegoat*; *The Ethics of Doping and Anti Doping*; *Elite Sport, Doping, and Public Health*; and *The Essence of Sport* (with John Nauright).

ROBERT MORRELL works in the Research Office at the University of Cape Town in South Africa. He has been studying issues of masculinity in Africa and particularly in southern Africa since the early 1990s. He is author of *From Boys to Gentlemen: Settler Masculinity in Colonial Natal, 1880–1920* (2001) and has edited *Changing Men in Southern Africa* (2001), *African Masculinities* (with Lahoucine Ouzgane, 2005), and *Baba: Men and Fatherhood in South Africa* (with Linda Richter, 2006). His most recent (edited) book is *Books and Babies: Pregnancy and Young Parents in Schools* (with Deevia Bhana and Tamara Shefer, 2012).

JOHN NAURIGHT is Professor of Sport and Leisure Cultures, Director of the Centre for Sport, Tourism and Leisure Studies, and Assistant Head of School (Research) in the School of Sport and Service Management at the University of Brighton in Eastbourne, England. He is also Visiting Professor of Sports Studies at Aarhus University in Denmark. He holds a PhD in African history from Queen's University in Canada and has held academic positions in Canada, New Zealand, Australia, Denmark, England, Scotland, Barbados, and the United States. He is the author or editor of seventeen books, including *Sport Around the World: History, Culture, Practice*; *The Routledge Companion to Sports History*; *Long Run to Freedom: Sport, Cultures and Identities in South Africa*; *Making Men: Rugby and Masculine Identity*; and *The Essence of Sport* (with Verner Møller). He has also authored over one hundred articles and book chapters dealing primarily with sport, leisure, and tourism in society.

GERTRUD PFISTER looks back to a long academic career starting with a PhD in history (1976, University of Regensburg), followed by another PhD in sociology (Department of Sociology of the Ruhr-University Bochum, 1980). From 1980 to 2000, she was employed as professor at the University Berlin and was appointed to a professor position at the University of Copenhagen in 2001. Gertrud Pfister was guest professor at several foreign universities, among others, of the University of Jyväskylä and the Gama Filho University in Rio de Janeiro. In Germany and in Denmark, Pfister conducted several large national and international research projects, among others funded by the IOC, the German Ministry of Women and Youth or the Danish Agency of Science, Technology and Innovation. She has published more than two hundred articles and twenty books. She is past president of the International Society for the History of Physical Education and Sport of the International Sport Sociology Association. In addition, she supports women and sport associations (IAPESGW and WSI), among other things, by providing advice or organizing networks.

ANAND RAMPERSAD is completing his PhD at the University of the West Indies, St. Augustine in Trinidad and Tobago, where he also lectures courses in cultural anthropology, introductory sociology, and classical and modern social theory. His research interests are sport and gender, sport and youth development, culture and globalization, and lifestyles and sexuality.

CHARLES FRUEHLING SPRINGWOOD, Professor of Anthropology at Illinois Wesleyan Illinois University, examines race, gender, sport, performance, and social theory in his teaching and writing. His books include *Cooperstown to Dyersville: A Geography of Baseball Nostalgia; Team Spirits: The Native American Mascots Controversy;* and *Beyond the Cheers: Race as Spectacle in College Sport.* His newest research focuses on guns and embodiment.

MATTHEW STEPHEN has been the manager of the Northern Territory Archives Service Oral History Unit in Darwin, Australia, since 2007. He holds a PhD from Charles Darwin University. He is a historian with deep and abiding interest in sport and the role it plays in understanding society. He is the author of *Contact Zones: Sport and Race in the Northern Territory, 1869–1953*.

THOMAS MICHAEL WALLE holds a PhD in Social Anthropology and is Senior Curator at Norsk Folkemuseum—Norwegian Museum of Cultural History, in Oslo, Norway. He has been writing and lecturing on the topic of gender, masculinities, and ethnicity for several years, and was appointed member of the Norwegian Gender Equality Commission 2010–2012. Among his publications are *A Passion for Cricket—Masculinity, Ethnicity, and Diasporic Spaces in Oslo* (2010); "Virginity vs. Decency: Continuity and Change in Pakistani Men's Perception of Sexuality and Women," in *South Asian Masculinities: Context of Change, Sites of Continuity*, ed. Chopra, Osella, and Osella (2004); and contributions to *NORA—Nordic Journal of Women's Studies* and *South Asian Popular Culture*. His current field of research is migration, material culture, and representation at museums.

DAVID K. WIGGINS is Professor and Codirector of the Center for the Study of Sport and Leisure in Society at George Mason University. Academically prepared at San Diego State University and the University of Maryland, he has a particular interest in the history of American sport, particularly the study of the interconnection among race, sport, and American culture. Among his many publications are *Glory Bound: Black Athletes in a White America* (1997); *Sport and the Color Line: Black Athletes and Race Relations in Twentieth-Century America* (2004); *The Unlevel Playing Field: A Documentary History of the African American Experience in Sport* (2003); *Out of the Shadows: A Biographical History of African American Athletes* (2006); and *Rivals: Legendary Matchups that Made Sport History* (2010). He is a member of the National Academy of Kinesiology and a three-time recipient of the research writing award from the *Research Quarterly for Exercise and Sport*.

KEVIN YOUNG is Professor of Sociology at the University of Calgary. His research interests bridge criminology and the sociology of sport, and his most recent books include *Sport, Violence and Society* (2012*)* and *Qualitative Research on Sport and Physical Culture* (2012, with Michael Atkinson).

INDEX

Abbott, Cleve, 159
Aboriginals Ordinance 191, 120
Aborigines, 63–76, 99–123
Aborigines Bill 1899, 111
A.C. Milan, 192
Adair, Daryl, xi, 4
African Americans, in track and field, 159–69; in tennis, 169–78
African National Congress (ANC), 132,134,140
Afridi, Shahid, 231–32
After Whiteness: Unmaking An American Majority (Hill), 261
A History of Negro Revolt (James), 38
Akhtar, Shoaib, 231–32
Akram, Wasim, 231
Ali, Muhammad, xi
Allen, Willie, 117–18, 121–22
Amateur Athletic Union (AAU), 163–67
Ameche, Alan, 155
American Tennis Association (ATA), 169, 173
Anderson, Benedict, 100
apartheid, 41, 43, 50–62
Ardener, Edwin, 213
Armstrong, Gary, 257–58
Atkinson, Michael, 255–56
Atlas, Charles (Angelo Siciliano), 150–51
Australian Game of Football: Since 1858 (Hibbins), 74
Australian Institute of Sport, 73

Badela, Mono
Bailey, Donovan, 320
Bale, John, 17, 19
Barath, Adrian, 252
Basilone, John, 153
basketball, among the Zapotecs, 185–94
Bataille, Georges, 269
Batts, Callie, 257
Beamon, Bob, 324

Beckles, Sir Henry, xi, 3
Beijang, 257, 313–14, 317
Being and Time (Heidegger), 276
Belle, David, 267–68, 270
Bellino, Joe, 155
Berra, Yogi, 153
Bertelli, Angelo, 153
Beyond a Boundary (James), xi, 3, 15, 20, 30, 181–82; and a reinterpretation, 17–39, 240, 255, 257, 318
Bhabha, Homi K., 20–21, 26–28, 31, 34, 36, 39, 265, 311
biological determinism, 71–75
Black Jacobians (James), 38
Blankers-Koen, Fanny, 164–65
Blatter, Sepp, 88
Bolden, Ato, 314, 324
Bolt, Usain, 75, 257, 313–29
Bondman, Matthew, 32–34, 36, 39
Booth, Douglas, 4, 19
Borac, Arthur, 289
Boston Bloomer Girls, 148
Bourdieu, Pierre, 44–45, 241–42
Braemar, Scotland, 271
Bravo, Dwayne, 13
Brignoli, Lawrence, 147
Bringing Them Home Report, 66
British Asians, 256, 293–312
British Youth Hostel Association, 272
Brown v. Board of Education, 172
Bueno, Maria, 170

Caillois, Roger, 269
Campbell, Veronica, 320
Caputo, Jennie, 149
Carlos, John, 324
Carnera, Primo, 149–50, 153
Caribbean Cricket Club, 213
Carrington, Ben, xi, 213
Carton, Benedict, 96
Caruccio, Consetta, 149

Cashman, Richard, 213
Centre For Contemporary Studies, 259
Chanderpaul, Shivnarine, 252
Chinese, 110–12, 114, 116, 119, 242
Christie, Linford, 320
Clegg, Jonathan, 134–36
Cliftonville FC, 286
Coachman, Alice, 97, 159–71, 178
Cohen, Jeff, 187–88
Colangelo, Jerry, 156
Collingwood, Paul, 293, 300
Colonial Desire (Young), 101
Connell, Raewyn, 212, 224, 227, 237
Constantine, Learie, 8, 181
Costas, Bob, 314
Craven, Danie, 53
cricket, 7–17, 29–39; in Australia's
    Colonial Far North, 99–123; among
    Pakistini immigrants, 212–38, 300,
    308–12; in Trinidad and Tobago,
    239–52, 293–312
Cricket World Cup, 251
Cronin, Mike, 19
Crosetti, Frank, 146
Crusaders FC, 286–87
Cumiskey, Lunardoni, 149

Danish, 196–97, 202–5, 207, 209–10
Darwin Cricket Club, 121
Darwin Nigger Minstrels, 122
Decastella, Robert, 73–74
Decline of Males (Tiger), 264
deCoubertin, Baron Pierre, 257, 318
Dempsey, Jack, 149
DePalma, Ralph, 147
Derry City, 287
Dhanraj, Ranjidra, 246
Dhoni, Mahendra Singh, 300
diaspora, 296–99
Didrickson, Babe, 161
Dimaggio, Joe, 150, 152
Dimeo, Paul, 19
discrimination, 102, 177, 222–23, 280–92
Donatelli, Augie, 154
Dundee, Johnny (Giuseppe Carrora),
    147
Dungannon Swifts, 287

Eccentrics Cricket Club, 45
Elden, Stuart, 316
English Premier League, 4, 77
European Union (EU), 281–82
European Union Racial Equality
    Directive, 282
Evra, Patrice, and controversy with
    Luis Suarez, 77–92

fandom, 296–303
Farred, Grant, 18
Feinberg, Ben, 186–87
Fell Running, 255, 260, 264, 271–77
Fell Runners Association, 272
femininity, 161–62, 166–68, 170–71, 174
Fifa World Cup, 61
Firpo, Luis Angel, 149
Fletcher, Thomas, 182, 256–57
football, 77–92, 202–6, 279–92
Foucan, Sebastien, 267–68, 270
Foucault, Michel, 44, 269
Freeman, Cathy, 70
Friedman, Michael, 257

Gaelic Athletic Association (GAA), 280
Ganga, Darren, 252
Garagiola, Joe, 153
Garcia, Zeus, 190–91, 194
Gates, Henry Louis, 25, 27–28
Gayle, Christopher, 10–13, 251
Geertz, Clifford, 24
Gems, Gerald, 96–97
George Mason University, xii
German, 195–205, 209–10
German DJI-Youth Survey, 200–1
Giamatti, Bart, 156
Gibson, Althea, 97, 160–63, 169–78
Gisolo, Margaret, 148
Glentoran FC, 286
Glory Bound (Wiggins), 104
Godwell, Darren, 71–72, 74–75
Goffmann, Erving, 44
Goldsmith, Jemima, 232
Goolagong, Evonne, 68
Grasso, Mickey, 154
Graziano, Rocky, 152
Greaney, Paul, 82

Haiti: The Case for West Indian Self Government (James), 38
Hallinan, Chris, 70–71
Hall, Stuart, 100–101
Hard, Darlene, 174
Hassan, David, 256
Haugenstua Cricket Club, 227–30
Heart of Whiteness: Confronting Race, Racism, and White Privilege (Jensen), 261
Hebert, George, 266–67
Heinemann, Klaus, 198–99
Hendricks, Krom, 48
Henning, Harold, 51
Herman, Pete (Peter Gulotta), 147
Hibbins, Gillian, 74–75
Hill, Jeff, 19
Hind, Rodney, 86
History of West Indies Football (Manley), 7
Hoberman, John, 71
Hodges, Dan, 87
Holding, Michael, 13
Hooper, Carl, 13
Hussain, Nasser, 301

identity formation, and Zapotecs basketball, 183–94
immigrants, 110–11, 183–84, 188–91, 193–210, 295–99
Immigration Restriction Act 1901, 118
Indian Professional League, 13
Indians, 242–43, 245–50
Institute FC, 286–87
International Cricket Council (ICC) World Twenty 20 Cup, 293
International Journal of African Historical Studies, 127
International Olympic Committee (IOC), 314, 319, 328
Invention of the White Race (Allen), 260
Invisible Man (Ellison), 25
Irish Football Association (IFA), 283
Irish Rugby Football Union (IRFU), 280
Italian Americans, and baseball, 146, 152–52; and track and field, 147; and boxing, 147, 149–50, 152; and auto racing, 147; and women athletes, 148–49; and body building, 150–51; and masculinity, 150–51; and military service, 153–55; and social mobility, 155–56

Jamaica, 257
James, C. L. R., xi–xii, 3, 5, 7–9, 15, 29–38, 95, 97, 181–82, 240, 255, 257, 294, 318
Johnson, Ben, 320
Judd, Barry, 70–71
Jump London (Documentary), 268

Khan, Imran, 231–33
Khosi, Humphrey, 51
King William's Town African Cricket Team, 45
Klaaste, Aggrey, 61
Kuyt, Dirk, 81

Lacy, Sam, 167–76
LaMotta, Jake, 152
Landis, Kenesaw Mountain, 148
Lansbury, Jennifer H., 97
Lara, Brian, 9–13, 231, 251
Larne FC, 287
Lazzeri, Tony, 146–47
Leon, Casper (Gaspare Leoni), 147
Linfield FC, 286
Lisbon Distillery, 287
Little Children Are Sacred (Report), 66
Liverpool FC, 77, 79, 90
Lloyd, Clive, 13
Location of Culture (Bhabha), 20
Lombardi, Vince, 155
Los Angeles, and Zapotec basketball, 188–94
Los Lobos, 186
Love, Kenneth, 178
Lowenthal, David, 21

Maclean, Malcolm, 4
Manchester United, 77, 79, 91
Mandela, Nelson, 13, 59–60
Manley, Michael, 7
manliness, 109
Marble, Alice, 169–70

Marciano, Rocky, 155
Marley, Bob, 322
Masculinities (Petersen), 212
masculinity, 109, 132, 136, 146, 150–51,
    161–62, 167–69, 211–30, 263–65
Mathabane, Mark, 57
Mazrui, Ali, 51
McBean, James A. 257
McDonald, Michael, 91
Migrapolis (Documentary), 220
Miller, Patrick, 96
minstrels, 113–14, 122–23
Mohammad, Dave, 252
Mohammed, Timur, 246
Moller, Verner, 4
Moore, Henrietta, 217
Moosai, Prakash, 246
Morrell, Robert, 96
Murray, C.A., 115–16
Murray, Les, 86
Muslims, 200
Muslim Western Province Coloured
    Rugby Union, 53
Myth of Male Power (Ferrell), 264

Nanan, Rangy, 246
Natural Method, 266–67
Nauright, John, 4
Nelson, Maud (Clementine Brida), 148
New Black Militancy (Neal), 261
North Australia Cycling Club, 118
North Australian Cycling and Athletics
    Association Sports, 121
Northern Ireland, 256, 279–92
Northern Territory Aborigines Act 1910
Northern Territory Football League
    (NTFL), 68
Northern Territory Times (Newspaper),
    106, 108, 114, 117–19
Norwegian National Cricket Team, 220
N.T. Royal Troupe of Gymnastics, 108

Oaxacan, 181, 183–94
Olympic Games, 257, 313–14, 317–21,
    323–25, 327–28
Orientalism (Said), 265
Ottey, Marlene, 320

Ouis, Rebecca, 216
Owens, Jesse, 324

Palmerston New Year Athletic Sports,
    115–16
Palmerston Rifle Club, 121
Parkour, 255, 260, 264, 266–71, 275
Parks, Rosa, 172
Parodi, Josephine, 148
Patensie Rugby Football Club, 54
Patterson, A.B., 99
Patterson, Audrey, 164
Pep, Willie, 152
Pereira, Maxi, 88
Perkins, Charlie, 65
Pessano, Lewis (aka Buttercup
    Dickerson , 146)
Peterson, Alan, 211–12
Pfister, Gertrud, 181
Phillips, Trevor, 294
Pietri, Dorando, 147
Pizzola, Francisco (Ping Bodie), 146
Popham, Glen, 62
Port Darwin Cricket Club, 115
*Possessive Investment in Whiteness: How
    White People Profit From Identity
    Politics* (Lipsitz), 261
postcolonialism, 17–23, 26, 322, 325, 327
Powell, Asafa, 313, 318, 321–22, 326
Price, Grenfell, 109

Queensland Amateur Athletics
    Association, 67
Queens Park Cricket Club, 34, 345, 247
Queens Park Oval, 249
Quinones, Sam, 188, 190–91

Race Relations Order, 282
Racial Equality Strategy, 284
Rafi Memorial Cricket Festival, 220
Rajah ,Aneil, 246
Ramadhin, Sonny, 246
Ramdin, Denesh, 252
Ramnarine, Dinadanth, 246
Rampaul, Ravi, 252
Rampersad, Anand, 182
Raza, Unida, 191

Richard, Vivian, 8, 11, 13, 246
Rioli, Cyril, 73
Robinson, Jackie, 161, 172, 176–77
Rogge, Jacques, 314, 319–20, 323–25
Rohler, Gordon, 244–45
Rose, Lionel, 68
Rowe, David, 78
rugby, in South Africa, 58–60
Rugby World Cup, 60

Sacred Balance (Suzuki), 274
Seereram, Rabindranath, 246
Samuelson, R. C., 129–30
Sansone, Tony, 151
Sarwan, Ramnaresh, 252
Saville-Garatti, Eleanor, 148–49
Schifano, Helen, 149
Seecharan, Clem, 22
Sickert, Susan, 101
Singh, Harbhajian, 78
Smith, Tommie, 324
Sobers, Sir Gary, 4, 11
Social Darwinism, 64, 101
South Africa, and race and body
     culture, 41–62
South African Cricket Union, 51
South African National Olympic
     Committee, 50
Spain, Antonio, 117–18
Spivak, Gayatri, 265
Sport Against Racism Ireland
     (SARI), 280
Sport Northern Ireland (Sport NI),
     288, 291
Springboks, 59–60
Springwood, Charles Freuhling,
     xi, 181
SPRINT study, 200–1
State Department tours, of Althea
     Gibson, 172–73, 177
Stearns, Peter N., xii
Stephen, Matthew, 68, 96
Stephens, Helen, 161
Stiffed: The Betrayal of the American Man
     (Faludi), 263
Strode, Woody, 172
Stronach, Megan, 71–72

Suarez, Luis, and controversy with
     Patrice Evra, 77–92
Subcommander Marcos, 192
Symonds, Andrew, 78

Tagliabue, Paul, 156
Tatz, Colin, 67, 69, 104
Taussig, Michael, 18
Tebbit, Norman, 252, 294–95
Tendulkar, Sachin, 231
tennis, and Althea Gibson, 160–63, 169–
     78; and the black press, 173–78
Third International Conference on Race
     and Ethnicity in Sport, xi
Thorpe, Jim, 324
Tomas, David, 19
Tonelli, Mario "Motts", 154
Torres Strait Islander (ATSI), 63, 66, 69
track and field, and Alice Coachman,
     159–71, 178; and the black press,
     166–69, 178
Tranvaal Rugby Union, 58
Trinidad and Tobago Cricket Board
     (TTCB), 248
Trinidad and Tobago Cricket Board of
     Control (TTCBC), 248
Turkish, 195–97, 199, 201, 203–10
Tuskegee Institute, 159, 163–68

Umkhosi Wokweshwama, 131
United States Lawn Tennis Association
     (USLTA), 162, 169, 173, 175
University of Hull, 7
University of the West Indies, Cave
     Hill, xi

van der Walt, Ronnie, 62
Vickery, Tim, 87–88

*Wages of Whiteness: Race and the Making
     of the Working Class* (Roediger), 261
Walsh, Stella, 161,163, 165–67
Wanderers Cricket Club, 48, 247
Washington, Kenny, 172
We Real Cool (hooks), 261
Western Province Coloured Rugby
     Union, 53

West Indies, and cricket, 7–15, 29–39
West Indies Cricket Board (WICB), 11, 13–14
Whannel, Gary, 229
White (Dyer), 260
White Backlash: The Politics of Multiculturalism (Hewitt), 266
White, Hayden, 21
Whitehead, Stephen, 212
White Identities: Historical and International Perspectives (Bonnett), 260
White Lies: Race and the Myths of Whiteness (Berger), 260
White Like Me (Wise), 261
White Mythologies: Written History and the West (Young), 261
Wiggins, David K. 104
Williams, Bryan, 57–58
Williams, Jack, 215

Winmar, Nicky, 69
Works Project Administration, (WPA), 152
World Game, 86
World Series Cricket, 230
Worrell, Sir Frank, xi, 3, 15

Young, Kevin, 255–56
Young, Robert, 101

Zamperini, Lou, 154–55
Zapista National Liberation Army (EZLN), 192
Zapotecs, and basketball, 185–94
Zen Buddhist, 268
Zulu stick fighting, and women, 128; and military combat, 129–32; as symbol of black resistance, 132–36, 139–43; and marriage ceremonies, 136–38